ROOM AT
THE INN

JILL ADAM

BOOKS

Editor: Jill Adam

Cover design: Rob Howells
Cover illustration: Steve Caplin
Illustrations: Geoff Roberts
Maps: Perrott Cartographics
Managing Editor: Mark Webb

Printed by WSOY, Finland

ISBN 1-85249-150-7

Published by CAMRA Books, Campaign for
Real Ale Ltd, 230 Hatfield Road,
St Albans AL1 4LW

© CAMRA Books 1999

Conditions of sale:
This book shall not, by way of trade or otherwise, be lent, resold, hired out or otherwise
circulated without the publisher's prior consent
in any form of binding or cover other than in
which it is published and without similar
conditions being imposed on the subsequent
purchaser. All rights reserved. No parts of this
publication may be reproduced, stored in
retrieval systems, or transmitted in any form or
by any means, electronic, mechanical,
photocopying or otherwise, without the prior
permission of CAMRA Books.

CONTENTS

DEDICATION

This book is dedicated to my Dad, Gordon Harvey (1924-1998) who was always more than willing to conduct research for me on CAMRA guides. He'd go anywhere for a pint of good ale and a steak and kidney pie.

INTRODUCTION

The establishments listed in this guide cover a wide range of styles and tastes, to suit all budgets – and age groups! There are four-star hotels with the service and amenities to match the prices and there are homely little pubs with maybe just two or three rooms where you have to share a bathroom – but don't dismiss these too easily, the accommodation is often very good value, and the homeliness extends to good traditional English cooking. There are many ancient inns whose histories stretch back over centuries with many a tale to tell and ghosts that roam, and there are modern establishments with up to the minute facilities. There are pubs to suit business people, close to city centres and there are rural retreats, ideal for a romantic weekend which, once found, can be very hard to leave. There are many which offer that little bit extra, such as activity or themed breaks for golfers, anglers and other sports enthusiasts. Whatever you require in the way of accommodation you should find something here to fit the bill. Of course, at the end of your search you will be rewarded with a good pint of real ale – without that a pub cannot be included in a CAMRA guide however charming, historic or idyllic it may be.

AIMS IN COMMON

The Campaign for Real Ale (CAMRA) was set up more than 25 years ago to promote cask ale, and many of its aims are shared by the The British Institute of Innkeeping, the fastest growing professional members organisation in UK hospitality. This is the first CAMRA guide to highlight pubs whose licensees are members of the Institute by including their logo at the end of the pub entry.

All lovers of good pubs should keep an eye out for outlets bearing the British Institute of Innkeeping logo and membership plaques, as its aims are to promote high standards of professionalism in licensed retailing and to provide the skills, training and nationally recognised qualifications to help members run some of the best pubs in the country. Licensees and their staff can't flick a switch marked 'Atmosphere', but they can go a long way to guaranteeing contented customers by availing themselves of information and advice offered by the Institute whose membership has rocketed to 17,000 – a 50% increase within the last three years.

There are strict conditions for membership; every individual applicant is personally assessed – entry is not automatic. In 1998 the Institute awarded 50,000 qualifications to licensees and staff; bearing in mind that there are 60,000 pubs in the UK, that's making a real difference. The success of the British Institute of Innkeeping is reflected in a raising of standards in many thousands of pubs across the UK. This is good for Britain's pubs, and something that CAMRA fully supports, but of course, the ultimate beneficiary is the pub-goer.

BRITISH INSTITUTE *of* INNKEEPING
MEMBER
SETTING *professional* STANDARDS

I would like to thank Brigitte Rushmore at the Institute for her help with this second edition of Room at the Inn. Mainly, however, I would like to thank the dedicated CAMRA members all around the country without whom this book would never have been produced. It is always difficult to single out individuals, but I would like to say a particular thank you to Jon Addinall in Scotland and to all my colleagues at CAMRA HQ, especially the ever-patient Cressida Feiler and Abi Maddock.

LEISURE GENERATION

During the production of this guide, I found my mind frequently drifting to thoughts of retirement – it wasn't that the work was that onerous – it was more the feeling that it is the senior citizens today who seem to have most of the fun! According to reports I have seen in the press it is the 'younger, active retired' members of our community who have the most disposable income and the leisure to spend it. This was brought home to me by the number of photographs sent in to my office from pubs where a good proportion of the customers were grey-haired. What's more I frequently hear complaints from my contemporaries that their own (retired) parents are too busy going off on holidays and trips to take their grandchildminding duties seriously!

Personally, I am indebted to my Mum and late father for their help during the production of this guide – always willing to research pubs and never shirking their responsibilities towards their grandsons! I recently came across an old clipping that Dad had taken from a newspaper some years ago. It was from the time when acronyms – YUPPIES, DINKY, etc. were all the rage and an insurance company was trying to come up with a more appealing epithet for Old Age Pensioner – which really doesn't describe many of the people that now officially fall into this category. The one that tickled us was ELDERADOS – Elder Retired Ageless Doyen of Society. Well for all the Elderados who may use this guide, I wish you many happy years of travelling.

I am honestly not trying to wish my life away, looking forward to my retirement. There are plenty of pubs in this guide that I would be pleased to visit at any time. The majority of them cater for families – some obviously have more facilities than others – and most offer favourable rates for young children. Quite a few pubs will accommodate pets too, so even they do not have to be left behind.

HOW TO USE THIS GUIDE

The entries in this guide are presented in a fairly straightforward way. The listings are by county, but some counties have been combined, for instance Durham and Tyne & Wear, Leicestershire, Rutland and Northamptonshire, and Warwickshire and West Midlands. The maps at the back of the book will help readers locate pubs, but are no substitute for a decent road map. Where pubs are difficult to find, we have included directions in the descriptions. Rooms are listed as single, double, twin-bedded or family rooms. In many cases pubs do not have single rooms and most, unfortunately, charge a supplement for single occupancy of a double room. A family room is usually a room with at least three single beds, or a double room where an extra bed can be added for family use. Cots are sometimes available (check when booking).

Since our last edition, quite a number of pubs have been updated to offer en-suite accommodation as demanded by today's guests. This is, of course, not always possible given the layout of some old buildings and planning regulations. Unless it is absolutely essential for you to have a private bathroom, do consider those with shared amenities, or you could be missing a 'gem'.

SPECIAL NEEDS

Very few pubs have rooms adapted for wheelchair users. This is mainly because of the inaccessibility of first-floor bedrooms, particularly in old buildings, where it is impractical to install a lift. Many old pubs cannot even admit the wheelchair-bound into their bars. However, I do find it disappointing that, even when new accommodation is added, not enough consideration is given to the needs of less able guests. Some pubs state that their accommodation is suitable for guests with disabilities, but in fact this often only implies that there is a ground-floor room, which although accessible, might not be specially adapted. For this reason, we have usually said rooms may be suitable for guests with disabilities, and we would recommend that you check the facilities are what you require when booking.

BREAKFAST AND OTHER MEALS

Most of the pubs listed include breakfast in the room price. This is usually a full (cooked) English breakfast, but may be a simpler continental style, or a choice of either. In my view, one of the joys of staying in a pub is the traditional fry-up – and not having to cook it myself – but best of all are the pubs that offer that little extra, such as locally-made sausages or home-made jams and marmalade. Some pubs charge for the room only, as they believe customers should have the option of paying for breakfast only if they require it; while others offer a complete breakfast menu and you pay for what you choose. The majority of inns featured here offer meals other than breakfast. Some pubs have restaurants with excellent reputations, often under the command of a top chef. Many are humbler establishments offering simple pub fare of pies, pasties and ploughman's lunches. In a few cases it is necessary to book lunch or dinner in advance. A few of the pubs listed also feature in CAMRA's *Good Pub Food* so they make ideal culinary destinations – see the back of this book for details of where to get the latest editions of all CAMRA's specially researched guides.

PRICES

Pubs often charge per room, rather than per person, but for the purposes of this book we have given price bands which refer to charges per person, per night for bed and breakfast (usually a cooked meal) as follows. If the rate given is for room only, we say so on the individual entry.

£	=	under £25 per person (sometimes as low as £15)
££	=	£25-35 per person
£££	=	£35-45 per person
££££	=	over £45 per person

Children are generally charged at half price or less. In some cases no charge is made at all for young children. Some pubs quote on the spot, according to the number and ages of the children. As mentioned previously, surcharges are often imposed on single people occupying a double room. Some pubs accept pet dogs and may charge for their accommodation – always let the landlord/lady know in advance if you wish to bring your faithful friend.

OPENING HOURS

All day opening (11am-11pm; noon-10.30pm on Sunday) is now well established, but many pubs do still close at least for a while during the afternoons. Opening hours may be seasonal, too; those in tourist areas may be open for the maximum permitted time during the holiday period, but revert to the old afternoon closure in winter. Pubs with residential licences can serve food and drink at any time (provided they have the staff available). Children can stay in pubs with guest rooms, but under 18s cannot be served in bars, and children under 16 cannot be served alcohol in pub dining rooms. Children can be admitted to designated areas in the pub if it holds a children's certificate, but these certificates often impose a time limit on entry to those areas – for example, no children after 8pm. Children's certificates are more common in Scotland, where the scheme was started earlier than in the rest of the UK. Some pubs do not have a certificate but may have a separate family room.

REAL ALE

Real ale, also described as cask-conditioned or traditional draught beer, is defined as a British beer style in the Oxford English Dictionary. It is a top-fermented beer that undergoes a natural secondary fermentation in the cask and is served without gas pressure. Some pubs do keep their beers under a blanket of carbon dioxide, but this practice is frowned upon by CAMRA. Most pubs in the country serve their real ales by means of a simple handpump on the bar which draws the beer from the cask in the cellar. Less commonly, the beer might be served direct from the cask (gravity dispense) or by electric pump; in Scotland, beer is still occasionally drawn by air pressure (look for tall founts on the bar). CAMRA was launched in the early 1970s to promote real ale, which was then fast being replaced in our pubs by keg. Over 25 years later, the Campaign is still going strong, fighting for the rights of beer-lovers and pub-goers everywhere. As this is a CAMRA guide, we do not feature any establishment that does not serve at least one real ale, and many of course offer a good range. The beers themselves are as declared by the pub itself but note that the beer range may change at any time; where we know it changes regularly we have said so. Guest beers feature in many pubs, and may be changed weekly, monthly or sometimes more or less frequently. Full details of the various breweries and their products are provided in CAMRA's invaluable *Good Beer Guide*, published annually in October.

RECOMMENDATIONS

The facilities offered by the pubs listed here were checked as late as possible in the production process, but unfortunately, landlords and even breweries change. We appreciate any feedback from readers about the pubs in this guide, and any recommendations you would like to make for future editions will be well received. A form for this purpose is printed at the back of the book.

Jill Adam

KEY

Each entry in *Room at the Inn* contains a reference section. The first example given below describes what each icon (pictogram) represents and what kind of information you will find. The second, bottom, example is a real entry from the book to give you and idea of what to expect.

    The number of rooms and type of accommodation available
£   The price guide (see Introduction text)
    A list of beers which are regularly available, and occasional guests
|●| The type of food available and what time of day it is served
CC Whether credit cards are accepted or not

    Ten double, seven twin-bedded and two family rooms
£   £ (££ en-suite)
    Adnams Bitter; Crouch Vale Best Bitter; Tolly Cobbold Bitter
|●| Snacks and meals daily, lunchtime and evening
CC accepted

Member of the British Institute of Innkeeping

ENGLAND

BEDFORDSHIRE

—— ASTWICK ——

Tudor Oaks Lodge
Taylors Road, Astwick, Hitchin SG5 4AZ
☎/FAX *(01462) 834133*
Directions: on the A1, midway between Letchworth and Biggleswade

Do not be fooled by the postal address, this pub is in Bedfordshire, and a splendid old place it is too. Dating in part back to the 16th century, the Tudor Oaks is an ensemble of buildings, grouped around a central courtyard with ample parking. The whole complex comprises a pub, restaurant and a lodge which houses the guest bedrooms. This characterful establishment boasts no less than five original fireplaces and a Jacobean staircase. The bar offers seven real ales, mostly from small, independent breweries, including Nethergate, Crouch Vale, Mauldons and Ash Vine, as well as a traditional cider. The guest rooms are on the ground floor and all offer en-suite facilities. Within range are the Imperial War Museum's aerodrome at Duxford, the stately homes at Knebworth, Hatfield and Woburn, where the Safari park is a big attraction. Children are welcome and pets can be accommodated.

- Six single, six double and one twin-bedded room
- £ (single £££)
- Beer range varies
- Snacks and meals daily, lunchtime and evening
- **CC** accepted

—— BEDFORD ——

De Parys Hotel
41-45 De Parys Avenue, Bedford MK40 2UA
☎ *(01234) 352121;* FAX *(01234) 353889*
Directions: De Parys Avenue runs between the A428 Cambridge-Northampton road and the A6172

Robert De Parys founded a religious order in Bedford and the tree-lined De Parys Avenue was built in the 1880s on the site of the sanctuary he established there. This red-brick hotel is built in typical late Victorian style, and is just ten minutes' walk from Bedford town centre. Hidden from view behind the hotel is a delightful garden, popular in the summer with families who can enjoy the occasional barbecue when weather permits. If it rains, you can retreat into the conservatory. The 24 rooms have en-suite bathrooms, TV, tea/coffee making equipment and direct dial telephone. There are reduced rates for weekend stays of two nights. This family-run hotel has a friendly bar, with a children's certificate and a restaurant with a wide-ranging menu including Tex-Mex specialities. The river Ouse offers plenty of opportunities to stretch your legs along its banks, as does Bedford Park, just a short walk from the hotel. The county museum is well worth a visit. Next door is the Cecil Higgins Art Gallery.

- Eight single, eight double, five twin-bedded, three family rooms
- £ £ (single room ££££)
- Wells Eagle; Guest beers
- Snacks and meals daily, lunchtime and evening Mon-Sat; noon till 10pm Sun
- **CC** accepted

—— LEIGHTON BUZZARD ——

Hunt Hotel

19 Church Road, Linslade, Leighton Buzzard LU7 7LR
☎ *(01525) 374692;* FAX *(01525) 382782*
Directions: near railway station

The Hunt is a modest hotel, convenient for rail travellers, in a quiet position near the station, with its own car park. Leighton Buzzard is an old market town, surrounded by open countryside, with the NT's Ascott House and Waddesdon Manor both within easy reach. The pub has two bars where meals are served, plus a restaurant. The overnight accommodation has been updated so that all 15 rooms have private facilities. Pets can be accommodated.

⊨ Three singles, nine doubles, two twin-bedded and one family room
£ ££
🍺 Draught Bass; Fuller's London Pride; Tetley Bitter
🍽 Snacks and meals daily, lunchtime and evening
CC accepted

—— SALFORD ——

Red Lion Hotel

Wavendon Road, Salford, near Milton Keynes MK17 8AZ
☎ *(01908) 583117*
Directions: between junctions 13 and 14 of the M1

Salford is one of the attractive villages that lie on the outskirts of Milton Keynes, just six miles from the centre, but far enough away to maintain its own character. The restaurant draws business people as well as families, with its extensive menu, and children are welcome to stay at the pub (although there is no designated family room). Woburn Abbey, with its famous collection of Canalettos, Safari Park, Antiques Centre and extensive grounds is just four miles away. Three of the guest rooms, decorated in cottage style, are in the main pub building, the rest are in a more modern, chalet-style building in the pub grounds. All but two of the rooms have en-suite amenities, and some feature four-poster beds. TV, telephones and tea/coffee making facilities are available in all the rooms.

⊨ Six double, two twin-bedded rooms
£ £ (££ single occupancy)
🍺 Wells Eagle, Bombardier
🍽 Snacks and meals daily, lunchtime and evening
CC accepted

—— TURVEY ——

Three Cranes
High Street, Turvey MK43 8EP
☎/FAX *(01234) 881305*
Directions: on A428, midway between Bedford and Northampton

A warm welcome awaits at this attractive, stone-built, 17th-century former coaching inn which stands in the conservation area of Turvey village, next to the Saxon church. Good for rural pursuits such as walking in Harrold Country Park and fishing on the River Ouse, it is also convenient for Santa Pod Raceway, Silverstone and Woburn Abbey and Safari Park. The en-suite rooms are furnished in cottage-style and have tea and coffee making facilities and colour TV. The price includes continental breakfast; full English breakfast is available for a supplement. Excellent home-cooking is provided in the bar and restaurant. There is no family room as such but children can be accommodated.

🛏   One single, one double and two twin-bedded rooms
£   £ (££ single room)
🍺   Courage Best Bitter, Directors; Fuller's London Pride; Hook Norton Best Bitter; guest beers
🍴   Snacks and meals daily, lunchtime and evening
CC   accepted

BERKSHIRE

—— ASTON ——

Flower Pot Hotel
Ferry Lane, Aston, near Henley-on-Thames RG9 3DG
☎ *(01491) 574721*
Directions: down Aston Lane, off A423 Maidenhead–Henley road

This solid Victorian hotel stands right by the Thames and has its own landing stage, half a mile from Hambleden Lock, so is ideal for 'boaters' looking for a bed on dry land. The Flower Pot, tucked away in a peaceful setting down a winding rural lane on the Remenham side of the river, has a basic, but homely bar, with a wood floor and a collection of stuffed fish. It serves the full range of the local Brakspear ales. The smarter, comfortable lounge is warmed by an open fire. The guest rooms also put comfort as a high priority; two of them have en-suite bathrooms, plus all the usual amenities. Children are welcome and there is a large garden for them to enjoy.

- Two double and two twin-bedde
- £ (£££ single occupancy)
- Brakspear Mild, Bitter, Old Ale, Special, Bee Sting (summer)
- Snacks and meals daily, lunchtime and evening (except Sunday evening)
- CC accepted

—— COMPTON ——

Swan Hotel at Compton
High Street, Compton, near Newbury RG20 6NQ
☎ *(01635) 578269;* FAX *(01635) 578765*
Directions: Off A34, six miles north of M4 jct 13; turn off to East Ilsley; Compton is two miles further on

Hosts Liz and Garry Mitchell are determined to make your stay at their family-run hostelry as enjoyable and as healthy as possible. Regular winners of Healthy Eating awards, their menus use as much freshly prepared food as possible, often featuring fish. One of the bathrooms has a sauna and there is plenty of scope for exercise as the pub is close to the long distance Ridgeway Path, with opportunities for golf and watersports locally. Set in a downland village, seven miles from Newbury race course, the Swan featured in the TV series *Trainer*. This well renovated Morland house is popular with business people (there are conference facilities for up to 60 guests) and for weekend breaks. The gardens are pleasant, and the pub also has a games room. The five guest rooms all have showers and TV; the family room has bunkbeds for children. Pets are welcome.

- One double, three twin-bedded and one family room
- £
- Greene King Abbot; Morland Bitter, Old Speckled Hen (winter); Ruddles Best Bitter; guest beers
- Snacks and meals daily, at all times
- CC accepted

—— GORING ON THAMES ——

Catherine Wheel

Station Road, Goring On Thames, Reading RG8 9HB
☎ *(01491) 872379*

The accommodation provided by the Catherine Wheel is not in the pub itself but in a nearby Victorian cottage, where the three rooms share bathroom facilities. Children are welcome to stay. 'Proper' inns being a bit thin on the ground in Berkshire, we did not want to pass this lovely old oak-beamed pub by. Oxford and Reading are easily accessible by road, rail or even river. Ten minutes' drive takes you to the NT's Basildon Park, a classical 18th-century house set in formal gardens and woodlands. Meals can be enjoyed either in the pub's bar or restaurant. The room price includes a full English breakfast.

- ⛶ Two double, one twin-bedded room
- £ £ (££ single occupancy)
- 🍺 Brakspear Mild, Bitter, Old Ale, Special, seasonal beers
- 🍽 Snacks and meals daily, lunchtime and evening (except Sunday evening)
- CC accepted

—— LITTLEWICK GREEN ——

Cricketers

Coronation Road, Littlewick Green SL6 3RA
☎/FAX *(01628) 822888*
Directions: off the A4

Popular with locals and ramblers, the Cricketers is also a haven for weary travellers who shun the 'delights' of airport hotels. Littlewick Green is just 30 minutes from Heathrow via the M4, and would have much appeal for foreign visitors enjoying their first night in England, since it is a very traditional inn, in a traditional setting overlooking the village green and (of course) cricket pitch. The main bar, where meals are served, is dominated by an open fire and a railway clock. Among the many local attractions is a Shire Horse Centre. The three guest rooms all have en-suite facilities, and children can be accommodated.

- ⛶ Two double, one twin-bedded room
- £ £
- 🍺 Brakspear Bitter, Fuller's London Pride, guest beers
- 🍽 Snacks and meals available daily, lunchtime and evening
- CC accepted

—— WARGRAVE ——

Bull

High Street, Wargrave RG10 8DD
☎ *(0118) 9403120*
Directions: on the A321 by the central traffic lights

Since our last edition, this Brakspear's tied house has had a new tenant, but I am pleased to say is still recommended by CAMRA members for inclusion. This 15th-century former coaching inn boasts a wealth of exposed oak beams and two inglenooks. Traditionally furnished, with an abundance of brasses, the Bull attracts customers from far and wide for its meals which are served in the bar or the more intimate restaurant. Only one of the bedrooms has en-suite facilities, but each has a handbasin, plus colour TV and tea and coffee making facilities. An extra bed can be put in one of the double rooms for a child. Residents can enjoy the secluded, vine-clad patio and walled garden to the rear. Wargrave is a pleasant Thamesside village to the east of Reading, within easy reach of Henley (three miles), Windsor (ten miles) and other local beauty spots. The Bull boasts a large garden, but has no car park.

- Two single, two double and two twin-bedded rooms
- £ (££ single room)
- Brakspear Bitter, Special, seasonal beers
- Snacks and meals daily, lunchtime and evening
- CC accepted

—— WOODSPEEN ——

Five Bells

Lambourn Road, Woodspeen, Newbury RG20 8BN
☎ *(01635) 48763*
Directions: near M4 jct 13, on Lambourn Valley road, two miles north-west of Newbury; OS451688

This small, Victorian Morland pub, nestling in a hamlet at the bottom end of the Lambourn valley, has been extended, so that its main feature is the 50-seater lounge/restaurant. It also has a large, well-equipped garden and the small, roadside terrace at the front catches the sun beautifully on summer evenings. The bedrooms are comfortable and have washbasins, TV and tea/coffee making facilities. The bathroom is shared. A full English breakfast is provided. Pets can be accommodated. Attractions nearby include the famous Watermill Theatre, Donnington Castle and Newbury's racecourse.

- One single, one twin-bedded room
- £
- Draught Bass; Flowers Original; Ruddles Best Bitter; Wells Bombardier; guest beer
- Snacks and meals daily, lunchtime and evening
- CC accepted

BRISTOL: SEE GLOUCESTERSHIRE & BRISTOL

BUCKINGHAMSHIRE

—— AYLESBURY ——

Aristocrat

1-3 Wendover Road, Aylesbury HP21 7SZ
☎ *(01296) 415366*

BRITISH INSTITUTE *of* INNKEEPING
🎖 MEMBER
SETTING *professional* STANDARDS

Directions: on the gyratory system at the end of Walton Street, A413

A Fuller's pub within walking distance of the town centre, the Aristocrat has a good atmosphere which makes it popular with all ages. There is a lot of social activity here: regular pub games, discos, karaoke and live music. It is also a frequent stop for commercial travellers, who enjoy the hearty, traditional breakfasts and other meals which are very good value and include vegetarian options. A full English breakfast is provided. For tourists, it is convenient for the NT's splendid Waddesdon Manor and the Chiltern Brewery at Terrick (both 15 minutes' drive). The latter has a small museum and shop selling its own beer-related products. The comfortable bedrooms have tea/coffee making facilities and TV and share two bathrooms. Children can be accommodated. There is a public car park behind the pub.

🛏 Two twin-bedded rooms
£ £ (££ single occupancy)
🍺 Fuller's London Pride, ESB, seasonal beers
🍴 Snacks and meals daily, lunchtime and Monday-Thursday evening
CC accepted

—— IBSTONE ——

Fox

Ibstone, near High Wycombe HP14 3GG
☎ *(01491) 638289; FAX (01491) 638873*
Directions: one and a half miles from the M40, jct 5

The Fox is a smart country hotel, offering a high standard of accommodation in delightful wooded surroundings. Privately owned, and dating back to the 17th-century, the inn offers modern amenities. All the nine bedrooms have en-suite shower, direct dial telephone, TV, radio, hospitality tray and trouser press. Popular with business users during the week, the hotel offers special breaks at weekends – contact them for details. Meals are of a similarly high quality, and may be enjoyed either in the restaurant or the bar, which retains the feel of a country inn and is warmed in winter by an open fire. There is a large garden for summer days. A good range of real ales is served, supplemented by regular guest beers, plus a traditional cider. Pets can be accommodated. The inn stands opposite Ibstone Common in a designated area of natural beauty. For walkers, the Rideway path is close by and NT members will find plenty of places to visit in the area including Waddesdon Manor, the home of the Rothschilds, Cliveden, the former home of Lady Astor and Hughenden Park, bought in 1847 by Benjamin Disraeli.

- ⇄ Six double, three twin-bedded rooms
- £ ££ (single occupancy ££££)
- 🍺 Brakspear Bitter; Fuller's London Pride; Old Luxters Barn Ale; Wadworth 6X; guest beers
- 🍽 Snacks and meals daily, lunchtime and evening
- CC accepted

—— NEWPORT PAGNELL ——

Bull

33 Tickford Street, Newport Pagnell MK16 9AE
☎ *(01908) 610325*
Directions: Between the Iron Bridge and the Aston Martin works

Popular with anglers, the Bull often caters for fishing parties, in particular those taking part in the National Coarse Fishing championships held locally. For business visitors, it is just four miles from central Milton Keynes, whilst for tourists, an unusual local attraction is the Aston Martin Lagonda factory which offers tours of the works. The 1999 *Good Beer Guide* describes the Bull as a 'permanent beer festival' – it usually has eight beers on tap, which are changed regularly. The house beer, Life's a Bitch is brewed by Morrells. A traditional cider is also available in summer. Wonderfully unmodernised, the pub, which is a free house, can get very crowded. Neither the bar nor the lounge (which is unusually decorated with original newspapers headlining notable events) is particularly large and the pool room is even smaller. A good value varied menu is served in the bar. The four bedrooms share bathroom facilities and are not suitable for children. A full English breakfast is provided.

- ⇄ Four double rooms
- £ £
- 🍺 Beer range varies
- 🍽 Snacks and meals daily, lunchtime and evening
- CC not accepted

—— STONY STRATFORD ——

Bull Hotel
64 High Street, Stony Stratford, Milton Keynes MK11 1AQ
☎ *(01908) 563104;* FAX *(01908) 563765*
Directions: off A5

The brochure from the Bull likens its position on the edge of Milton Keynes to that of Hampstead to London: an historic and individual town wholly convenient for all the commerce and amenities of Britain's most dynamic new city. Stony Stratford, now bypassed by the A5 has not always been a sleepy backwater; in former times it stood, like its neighbour, The Cock, on the coaching route to London. The many lurid tales from those times are said to have inspired the saying 'cock and bull story'. Now the coaching stables at the Bull have become a popular wine bar, whilst its Vaults bar plays host to popular folk and blues sessions. The restaurant specialises in Mexican and Spanish dishes. The hotel's 14 rooms all offer en-suite facilities and special rates are available for weekend guests. Children are welcome and pets can be accommodated.

- ⊨ Five single, four double and five twin-bedded rooms
- £ ££
- 🍺 Draught Bass; Eldridge Pope Royal Oak; Fuller's London Pride; Marston's Pedigree; Tetley Bitter; Wadworth 6X; Worthington Bitter; guest beers
- 🍽 Snacks and meals daily, lunchtime and evening
- CC accepted

—— WEST WYCOMBE ——

George & Dragon
West Wycombe HP14 3AB
☎ *(01494) 464414;* FAX *(01494) 462432*
Directions: In the village centre

The substantial brick-built George and Dragon is owned by the National Trust – as is the whole village! Overlooking the village is West Wycombe Park (also NT), a Palladian house, set in landscaped gardens, designed in the 18th century for Sir Francis Dashwood. Another nearby attraction (not NT) are the West Wycombe caves. Also within easy reach are Marlow (five miles), Henley (12 miles) and Bekonscot Model Village (a favourite with children, six miles). The former coaching inn mainly dates from the 18th century, but some parts of the building are nearly 600 years old, so it is not surprising that it is said to be haunted. This doesn't deter most visitors who consider it just adds to the charm of an already characterful hotel. Each of its eight en-suite rooms is furnished differently, and two have four-poster beds; all rooms have tea/coffee making facilities and colour TV. Special weekend rates apply. Pets can be accommodated. The food is recommended.

- ⊨ One single, five doubles, one twin-bedded, one family room
- £ ££ (single ££££)
- 🍺 Courage Best Bitter; guest beer
- 🍽 Snacks and meals daily, lunchtime and evening
- CC accepted

CAMBRIDGESHIRE

——— HILTON ———

Prince of Wales
Potton Road, Hilton, Huntingdon PE18 9NG
☎/FAX *(01480) 830257*
Directions: on the B1040, between St Ives and Biggleswade

The Prince of Wales comes recommended not only by CAMRA members – it has put in regular appearances in the *Good Beer Guide* – but also by the English Tourist Board. It is set in the picturesque village of Hilton which boasts a large green (thought to have been laid out by 'Capability' Brown) with a turf maze at one end commemorating the restoration of Charles II. Convenient for Cambridge (15 minutes' drive) and Peterborough, this friendly, comfortable inn offers modern amenities in traditional surroundings. The guest rooms all have en-suite shower and WC, with TV, radio, direct dial telephone and hospitality tray. The pub retains two bars – pool and darts are played in the public, while the cosy lounge is warmed by a log fire in winter. Weekenders staying two or three consecutive nights are offered a free two-course dinner on one night. Children over five are welcome (in their own room) and pets can be accommodated by prior arrangement.

- 🛏 Two single, one double, one twin-bedded room
- £ **££ (£££** single)
- 🍺 Adnams Bitter; Elgood's Black Dog Mild; guest beers (occasionally)
- 🍴 Snacks lunchtime, meals lunchtime and evening, daily
- CC accepted

——— HORSEHEATH ———

Old Red Lion
Linton Road, Horseheath CB1 6QF
☎ *(01223) 892909;* FAX *(01223) 894217*
Directions: on A1307, three miles west of Haverhill

The Red Lion's owners are the Old English Pub Company who, in keeping with the image that their name suggests, take pains to restore their tied houses sympathetically. Consequently, this lovely 17th-century inn boasts flagstone floors, open fires and a wealth of timber beams. It is very pleasing to note too, that when the company refurbished the bedrooms they adapted two of them to suit the needs of guests with disabilities. Two of the rooms feature four-poster beds. All 12 rooms have en-suite bath or shower, TV, tea/coffee making facilities, and other amenities. A good range of snack meals, such as jacket potatoes or filled hot baguettes, is available in the bar, while main meals are served in the restaurant where children (who can also be accommodated overnight) are welcome. A small room is available for meetings. Horseheath is a pretty little village, convenient for Cambridge, Newmarket, the M11 and Stansted Airport.

- 🛏 12 double rooms
- £ Room rate **££** (single occupancy **£££**)
- 🍺 Marston's Pedigree; John Smith's Bitter; Wadworth 6X; guest beer
- 🍴 Snacks and meals daily, lunchtime and evening (except Sunday evening)
- CC accepted

—— HUNTINGDON ——

Old Bridge Hotel
1 High Street, Huntingdon PE18 6TQ
☎ *(01480) 452681;* FAX *(01480) 411017*
Directions: Huntingdon lies between the A1 and A14; the hotel is off the inner ring road after the exit to Godmanchester and Cambridge

This fine old building, formerly a private bank is now an upmarket hotel, with prices to match. The hotel has been refurbished in keeping with its 18th-century origins, and the 26 guest bedrooms are all individually styled to give each its own character. As one would expect in an establishment of this standard, all the rooms have en-suite, modern facilities. The hotel is equipped for business conferences and private parties. Huntingdon, the birthplace of Oliver Cromwell, lies on the Great Ouse and boating trips can be arranged from the hotel's private jetty. Other water sports can be enjoyed at nearby Graffham Water, and Cambridge can be reached in 15 minutes by car. Children and pets can be accommodated, but disappointingly, none of the rooms has been adapted to suit the needs of guests with disabilities.

- ⊨ Six single, ten double and three twin-bedded rooms
- £ ££££
- ▧ Adnams Best Bitter; City of Cambridge Hobson's Choice
- ❑ Snacks and meals daily, lunchtime and evening
- CC accepted

—— ST IVES ——

Old Ferryboat Inn
Holywell, St Ives PE17 3TG

BRITISH INSTITUTE *of* INNKEEPING
◆ MEMBER
SETTING *professional* STANDARDS

☎ *(01480) 463227;* FAX *(01480) 494885*
Directions: Holywell is signposted from the A1123 between St Ives and Earith

A sad tale lies (literally) buried beneath the Old Ferryboat Inn. More than a thousand years ago a village girl committed suicide because of unrequited love, and being denied burial in the local churchyard was laid to rest on the site of the inn. She is said to walk on the anniversary of her death each year. This is just one of the ancient stories surrounding this lovely old thatched inn that once claimed Hereward the Wake as a customer! Today's travellers will revel in the old atmosphere of the inn, while enjoying the up-to-date amenities in its seven en-suite bedrooms. Conveniently situated for visiting the historic cities of Cambridge and Ely, the inn offers a hearty breakfast to set you up for a day's sightseeing.

- ⊨ Seven double rooms
- £ ££ – £££
- ▧ Greene King Abbot; Marston's Bitter, Pedigree; Fuller's London Pride; Taylor Landlord; guest beers (occasionally)
- ❑ Snacks and meals daily, lunchtime and evening
- CC accepted

—— STILTON ——

Bell Inn
Great North Road, Stilton, Peterborough PE7 3RA
☎ *(01733) 241066; FAX (01733) 245173*
Directions: on old North Road (now bypassed), six miles south of Peterborough

The Bell Inn is a famous pub, not least because of its claim to be the first pub to have sold Stilton cheese – to travellers on the Great North Road as far back as the 1720s. The Great North Road was naturally very busy with coach traffic, and, so it follows, with highwaymen. Dick Turpin is said to have hidden at the pub for nine weeks to escape capture for his wrongdoings. The inn has been beautifully restored to feature its bare stone walls and open beams. The 20 en-suite guest rooms are all decorated and equipped to a very high standard, with the deluxe-rated rooms offering four-poster beds and whirlpool baths. Meals are available in the cosy village bar or the award-winning restaurant, while the Marlborough Suite is a popular venue for conferences and social functions.

- ⊨ Two singles, 15 doubles, one twin-bedded and one family room
- £ **£££** (single room **££££**)
- ⌷ Marston's Pedigree; Oakham JHB; Tetley Bitter; guest beers
- ⦿ Snacks and meals daily, lunchtime and evening
- **CC** accepted

—— STRETHAM ——

Red Lion
47 High Street, Stretham, Ely CB6 3JQ
☎ *(01353) 648132; FAX (01353) 648327*
Directions: near the junction of the A10 and the A1123

This attractive 17th-century hostelry has been extremely well renovated and extended to include a conservatory restaurant, which is popular for candlelit meals. There is waiter service here, or meals can be taken in either of the comfortable bars. The food is good – vegetarian are well catered for, with salads being a speciality. The public bar is popular with locals for games and sports. The comfortable rooms all have modern en-suite facilities, with TV and tea/coffee making equipment. Some maybe suitable for guests with disabilities and children are welcome to stay (charged at £12.50 per head bed and breakfast). Pets can be catered for by arrangement. The inn enjoys a commanding position at the centre of a conservation village. Ely, with its fine cathedral is just four miles away and Cambridge 12 miles.

- ⊨ Two singles, five double, two twin-bedded and three family rooms
- £ **£** (single **££**)
- ⌷ Ansells Mild; Greene King IPA; Tetley Bitter; guest beers
- ⦿ Snacks and meals daily, lunchtime and evening
- **CC** accepted

CHANNEL ISLANDS: SEE OFFSHORE BRITAIN

CHESHIRE

—— ALTRINCHAM ——

Old Packet House

Navigation Road, Broadheath, near Altrincham WA14 1LW
☎/FAX *(0161) 929 1331*
Directions: on the A56, between Altrincham and Sale

Manager, John Mansfield is a keen CAMRA supporter, but offering good beer is only part of the attraction of this charming black and white pub. Pleasing to the eye as soon as you approach it, with its hanging baskets and pretty garden, the Old Packet House is also very smart inside, which is why it appeals to the business community as well as travellers. It does not forget however, its role as a pub for the community as it supports the local football team. The guest bedrooms are nicely decorated and all have en-suite facilities and the usual amenities. If you do not want to have a full meal, the pub offers a large range of sandwiches; and there is a no-smoking area for diners. A choice of either full English or continental breakfast is included in the room price, and although there are no special facilities, children can be accommodated.

- ⋈ One single, two double and one twin-bedded room
- £ ££ (£££ single room)
- ⬛ Boddingtons Bitter; Courage Directors; Webster's Yorkshire Bitter; Wilson's Original; guest beers
- ⦿ Snacks and meals daily, lunchtime and evening (Sunday evening by arrangement only)
- CC accepted

—— ASTBURY ——

Egerton Arms Hotel,

Astbury Village, near Congleton CW12 4RQ
☎ *(01260) 273946;* FAX *(01260) 277273*
Directions: on the A34, one and a half miles south of Congleton

This friendly, family-run inn, dating back to the 15th century, lies at the heart of the Cheshire countryside, but within easy reach of Congleton. It stands next to the Norman church of St Mary's and near other sites of tourist interest, such as Jodrell Bank and the NT's Little Morton Hall, a fine moated timber-framed manor house, noted for its long wainscoted gallery and knot garden. An extensive home-made menu, with a good vegetarian selection, is served in the restaurant or the bar; children are catered for both for meals and accommodation and they will enjoy the garden which has a safely fenced play area. A spacious, comfortable pub, warmed in winter by log fires, it offers six guest rooms with shared facilities.

- ⋈ Two single, two double and two twin-bedded rooms
- £ £
- ⬛ Robinson's Best Bitter, Frederics
- ⦿ Snacks and meals daily, lunchtime and evening
- CC accepted

—— BOLLINGTON ——

Church House Inn
Chapel Street, Bollington SK10 5PY
☎ *(01625) 574014*
Directions: off the A523, three miles north of Macclesfield

If real ale is your tipple, and golf your sport, you couldn't spend a better weekend than at the Church House, at the heart of the North-West's prime golfing area. The annual fixture list includes the Norman Wisdom Classic at Shrigley Hall and the Howard Keel Classic at Mere. The proximity of Chatsworth House, Tatton Hall and the Peak District National Park might entice you to spend longer than a weekend. The comforts of the inn are certainly hard to leave, with its excellent menu of home-cooked food (booking is advisable), and pleasant en-suite bedrooms which all have colour TV and tea/coffee making facilities. An added attraction for tourists, rather than business visitors, is the reduced rates at weekends. If you do have to work, there are meeting rooms available with fax facilities, and Manchester airport is just 30 minutes' drive away. Children are welcome.

🛏 Three singles, one double, one twin-bedded room
£ ££
🍺 Flowers IPA; S&N Theakston Best Bitter; Wadworth 6X
🍴 Snacks and meals daily, lunchtime and evening
CC accepted

—— BURWARDSLEY ——

Pheasant Inn
Higher Burwardsley, Tattenhall CH3 9PF
☎ *(01829) 770434;* FAX *(01829) 771097*
Directions: eight miles from Chester, via the A41

Like most of our selections for Cheshire, this pub also enjoys an excellent reputation for its food, With a menu that is changed regularly due to its emphasis on seasonal produce. It would be hard to find a pub in a more pleasant setting either, standing as it does in its own grounds atop the Peckforton Hills with views over the Cheshire Plain to Wales. It lies halfway along the Sandstone Trail, a waymarked walk from Whitchurch to Frodsham, so the pub is ideal for ramblers. This 300-year old inn has been well restored in sympathy with its farmhouse origins. The lounge bar has a vast open hearth, while the restaurant was the original kitchen. The ten en-suite guest rooms are in a converted barn and equipped to a very high standard with hospitality tray, colour TV and direct dial telephone. Most of the rooms have panoramic views and, being away from the main public area, they offer a peaceful night's rest. Weekend guests who are able to stay over from Friday to Monday, are not charged for accommodation on the Sunday night. Children are charged at £10 per night bed and breakfast. Pets can be accommodated by arrangement. Visit the Cheshire Workshops nearby to see the craft of candlemaking.

🛏 Six double, two twin-bedded and two family rooms
£ ££ (££££ single occupancy)
🍺 Draught Bass; guest beer
🍴 Snacks and meals daily, lunchtime and evening
CC accepted

—— CHESTER ——

George & Dragon

Liverpool Road, Chester CH2 1AA
☎ *(01244) 380714;* FAX *(01244) 380782*
Directions: just outside the city wall, off St Oswald's Way, which lies parallel to the canal

Tony Chester is the appropriately named owner of this striking black and white hotel near the centre of Cheshire's principal town. Convenient for both bus and rail stations, the George and Dragon makes an ideal base for exploring this fascinating and historic place. The most complete walled city in Britain, Chester is famous for its 13th-century 'Rows', the streets of half-timbered galleried shops, and is well situated for trips into North Wales and the Wirral. The recently refurbished guest rooms all offer en-suite facilities and the usual amenities. A full English breakfast is included in the room rate. Meals can be taken in either the restaurant or the bar which boasts the widest selection of real ales in Chester. Perhaps its only drawback is that it doesn't accommodate children.

- ⊨ Seven double and seven twin-bedded rooms
- £ ££
- 🍺 Boddingtons Mild, Bitter; Flowers IPA, Original; Fuller's London Pride; Morland Old Speckled Hen; Taylor Landlord; Wadworth 6X; guest beers
- ⦿ Snacks and meals daily, lunchtime and evening
- CC accepted

Mill Hotel

Milton Street, Chester CH1 3NF
☎ *(01244) 350035;* FAX *(01244) 345635*
Directions: opposite the ring road

The CAMRA member that recommended the Mill says that it is not (heaven forfend) 'twee', nor even architecturally interesting, but that the licensee is committed to cask ale and as such won the local CAMRA *Pub of the Year* award in 1996. The lively, welcoming bar offers an ever-changing range of ales, mostly from independent breweries, including a house beer from Coach House. In summer, drinkers can spill out on to the small canalside patio. The hotel also offers a good range of reasonably-priced food – its restaurant is a converted barge moored on the canal, but if the thought of that makes you queasy, you can eat in the bar. Other attractions include a health club and swimming pool. Dinner dances are held every Friday and Saturday evening. In a city that is very popular with tourists, this hotel offers no less than 81 rooms. All are en-suite with modern facilities, and some are adapted to suit the needs of disabled guests. Seven of the rooms are classed as 'superior' with slightly higher rates. A full English breakfast is provided. The hotel is convenient for Chester's historic centre and for the railway station. If you feel lucky, take a trip to the race course – the oldest in England.

- ⊨ One single, 55 double, 21 twin-bedded and four family rooms
- £ ££ (££££ single)
- 🍺 Boddingtons Bitter; Mill Premium; Weetwood Best Bitter; many guest beers
- ⦿ Snacks and meals daily, lunchtime and evening
- CC accepted

——— OVER PEOVER ———

Dog Inn
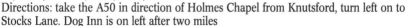

Well Bank Lane, Over Peover, Knutsford WA16 8UP
☎ *(01625) 861421;* FAX *(01625) 864800*
Directions: take the A50 in direction of Holmes Chapel from Knutsford, turn left on to Stocks Lane. Dog Inn is on left after two miles

Over the last few years a quarter of a million pounds has been spent upgrading the Dog Inn, including its six well-appointed en-suite guest rooms. Still maintaining an 'olde-worlde' feel, enhanced by the hanging baskets outside, it has a single bar serving the tap room (favoured by locals with its real fire, Sky TV and pub games) and three small snugs. Two large areas of the pub are given over to non-smokers. It is highly popular for its food, prepared by a chef who is a member of the *Salon Culinaire*. Meals can be taken in any part of the inn. There is a WC for wheelchair users in the pub itself, but unfortunately none of the guest rooms are adapted for visitors with special needs. Children, however, are welcome. Along with the more usual amenities, all rooms offer telephone access to the Internet. Fax and photocopying facilities are also available for business guests. The picturesque village of Over Peover lies three miles from Knutsford (worth a visit in its own right), and near the popular tourist haunts of Tatton Park, Jodrell Bank, Holmes Chapel and Styal Mill.

⊨ Four double, three twin-bedded rooms
£ £££ (single occupancy ££££)
🍺 Flowers IPA; Moorhouse's Black Cat Mild; Tetley Bitter
🍴 Snacks and meals daily, lunchtime and evening
CC accepted

——— TARPORLEY ———

Foresters Arms
92 High Street, Tarporley CW6 0AX
☎ *(01829) 733151;* FAX *(01829) 730020*
Directions: village is just off the A51, midway between Chester and Crewe

Tarporley is a picturesque village set in some of Cheshire's loveliest countryside. The village became established in the 17th century as a coaching stop on the London to Liverpool road (see the old milestone in the High Street) and the Foresters still caters for travellers as well as visitors to the area. There is plenty to see and do locally: Tarporley itself has some attractive shops, and among the places of tourist interest in the vicinity are Oulton Park motor racing circuit, Stapeley Water Gardens and several golf courses. Many make a bee-line for Beeston's popular market, while historic Chester is just 10 miles away. The Foresters is a cosy inn which prides itself on offering traditional hospitality, comfortable beds, good home-cooked food and cask ales. The double room is fully en-suite, whilst one of the twin rooms has a shower. A full English breakfast is provided. Children are welcome.

⊨ One double, two twin-bedded rooms
£ £ (££ single occupancy of en-suite room)
🍺 Greenalls Mild, Bitter; guest beer
🍴 Snacks and meals daily, lunchtime and evening (except Sunday evening)
CC accepted

TRY ALSO:

Railway Inn
153 Manchester Road, Broadheath, Altrincham WA6 5NT
☎ *(0151) 941 3383*

Recently saved by local campaigners from demolition to make way for a retail park, the Railway offers five en-suite rooms at reasonable prices. B&B £

Boot & Slipper
Long Lane, Wettenhall, Winsford CW7 4DN
☎ *(01270) 528238*
You'll find this handy pub just off the A51, midway between Nantwich and Winsford. B&B ££

CORNWALL

—— CRAFTHOLE ——

Liscawn Inn

Crafthole, near Torpoint PL11 3BD
☎ *(01503) 230863*
Directions: off the B3247, east of the village

The *Good Beer Guide* describes Crafthole as 'forgotten corner of Cornwall'. If you take the trouble to find this charming 14th-century hotel, you will have good reason to remember it. Set in eight acres of delightful countryside, just a short walk from the beach, this family-run establishment currently offers seven en-suite guest rooms with more planned for the near future in a converted barn. Apart from the obvious attractions of Dartmoor, right on the hotel's doorstep, there are also three golf courses within an eight-mile radius and it is convenient for the tourist sites of both Cornwall and Devon. The friendly owners welcome children and can accommodate pets. An extensive menu and occasional guest ale add to the appeal.

ᨑ Five double, one twin-bedded and one family room
£ £
◖ Draught Bass, Theakston Old Peculier; Wells Bombardier; guest beer (occasionally)
◗ Snacks and meals daily, lunchtime and evening
CC accepted

—— CRACKINGTON HAVEN ——

Coombe Barton Inn

Crackington Haven, near Bude EX23 0JG
☎ *(01840) 230345;* FAX *(01840) 230788*
Directions: turn off the A39 at Wainhouse Corner and follow the road down to the beach

Some of the bedrooms of this 200-year-old hotel overlook the beach in a beautiful Cornish cove, noted for its spectacular rock formations. If you want a dramatic backdrop to your wedding day, the pub is licensed to conduct the ceremony. Being set on the NT's South West Coastal Path makes the inn ideally situated for exploring the natural surroundings of cliff walks and wooded valleys. Children, who are welcome to stay at the inn, enjoy the beach with its rock pools and safe swimming and surfing. Other local leisure facilities include tennis, golf and fishing. Half of the bedrooms have private facilities, the other three share a bathroom. The menu includes charcoal grilled steaks, fresh fish and home-baked Cornish pasties. Pets can be accommodated.

ᨑ Four double, one twin-bedded and one family room
£ £ (££ en-suite)
◖ Dartmoor Best Bitter; St Austell Tinners, HSD; Sharp's Doom Bar Bitter; guest beers
◗ Snacks and meals daily, lunchtime and evening
CC accepted

—— GUNNISLAKE ——

Rising Sun
Calstock Road, Gunnislake PL18 9BX
☎ *(01822) 832001*
Directions: Gunnislake is on the A390; Calstock Road leads off the main square

This pretty, whitewashed inn is set in lovely gardens boasting views of the Tamar Valley, a designated area of outstanding natural beauty. Inside, the pub is crammed with a fascinating collection of china and bric-a-brac. Highly regarded locally for its freshly prepared food, including a good selection for vegetarians, and a five-course breakfast, the pub also offers a range of local beers and cider. There are many tourist attractions within a 20-minute drive, including the award-winning Morwellham Quay visitor centre, where a riverside village has been restored as a living museum. If you don't wish to drive, the scenic Tamar Valley branch railway line to Plymouth is a good alternative. The pub has just three guest rooms, with en-suite amenities, but unfortunately, no facilities for children.

🛏 Two double, two twin-bedded rooms
£ ££
🍺 Draught Bass; St Austell Tinners, HSD; Sharp's Cornish Coaster; guest beers
🍽 Snacks daily lunchtime; meals daily lunchtime and evening
CC accepted

—— GUNWALLOE ——

Halzephron
Gunwalloe, Helston TR12 7QB
☎ *(01326) 240406*
Directions: off the A3083, three miles south of Helston

A smugglers' haunt – what else would one expect of a 400-year-old inn on a Cornish clifftop? If you don't believe it, ask to see the shaft which still connects the pub via an underground tunnel to the beach. In an unspoilt setting, adjoining NT protected countryside on the west coast of the Lizard, the Halzephron enjoys spectacular views of Mount's Bay. Nearby are the South Cornwall footpath, Gunwalloe Fishing Cove and an 18-hole golf course. Owners, Angela and Harry Davy Thomas will help you get the most from your stay – being native to the county, they have a fund of local knowledge. This traditional country inn is a stranger to modern electronic intrusion, free from jukebox, fruit machines or piped music. However, both the en-suite rooms, furnished in comfortable cottage-style, do have modern appliances such as colour TV and tea/coffee making facilities. Meals, whether in the bar areas or the bistro-style restaurant, are based on local produce and highly recommended. The pub's unusual name, by the way, is a corruption of the old Cornish 'Als Yfferin', meaning cliffs of hell, alluding to the numerous wrecks along this stretch of the coast.

🛏 Two double rooms
£ ££
🍺 Dartmoor Best Bitter; Sharp's Doom Bar Bitter, Own
🍽 Snacks and meals daily, lunchtime and evening
CC accepted

—— LANLIVERY ——

Crown Inn

Lanlivery, near Bodmin PL30 5BT
☎ *(01208) 872707*
Directions: off the A390 Lostwithiel road, two miles west of St Austell

A remote, former long farmhouse building, the Crown is set in its own grounds offering views over rolling countryside and woodland. Close to the Saints' Way Walk and a mile from the Helman Tor beauty spot, this peaceful, welcoming inn is just seven miles from the bustling harbour town of Fowey. The guest rooms are not in the pub itself, but are designed as two individual, comfortable 'apartments' in a converted stone building in a secluded corner of grounds, with a private garden and patio. Each has twin brass beds which can be zipped together to form a king-sized double. A traditional Cornish breakfast is provided, and other meals can be taken in the bar or one of two restaurant areas.

🛏 Two twin-bedded rooms
£ ££
🍺 Draught Bass; Sharp's Own; guest beer
🍽 Snacks and meals daily, lunchtime and evening
CC accepted

—— LOSTWITHIEL ——

Royal Oak

Duke Street, Lostwithiel PL22 OAG.
☎ *(01208) 872552*
Directions: just off the A390 (Queen Street)

Lostwithiel is the old capital of Cornwall, dominated by the ruins of Restormel Castle. The Royal Oak dates back to the 13th century, and its cellar is reputedly connected to the castle by an underground tunnel which is likely to have been used for smuggling or even as an escape route. This pub offers a treat for real ale lovers, serving four regular beers and two guests which change weekly, often featuring local brews. There is also a good choice of bottled beers. The pub, whose stone-floored public bar contrasts with the comfortable lounge and restaurant, has been well restored and offers comfortable, airy guest rooms (five are en-suite) with TV and tea/coffee making facilities. The river Fowey, noted for its salmon fishing and good sailing amenities is close by and there is local golf course. Children are welcome, although there are no special facilities. Pets can be accommodated.

🛏 Five double, one twin-bedded room
£ ££
🍺 Draught Bass; Fuller's London Pride; Marston's Pedigree; Sharp's Own; guest beers
🍽 Snacks and meals daily, lunchtime and evening
CC accepted

MEVAGISSEY

Fountain
Cliff Street, Mevagissey PL26 6QH
☎ *(01726) 842320*
Directions: in St George's Square at the village centre

Mevagissey is one of those charming little Cornish fishing ports that swells to bursting during the summer season, which must be both a blessing and a curse to the local people. Despite the onslaught of holidaymakers and their demands, the Fountain has managed to remain as true to its origins as possible. The oldest in Mevagissey, this 15th-century inn retains two bars, the 'Smugglers' and the front bar, featuring slate floors, low beams and open fires, where jukeboxes and fruit machines are not allowed to ruin the olde-worlde charm. A small restaurant on the first floor is open from March to October and specialises in steaks and locally caught fish. Two of the three guest rooms have en-suite bathrooms, the third has a private, but separate bathroom. Pets can be accommodated.

🛏 Three double rooms
£ £
🍺 St Austell Tinners, HSD
🍽 Snacks and meals daily, lunchtime and evening
CC accepted

THE FALCON INN
ST MAWGAN
CORNWALL

—— POLPERRO ——

Old Mill House Hotel
Mill Hill, Polperro, near Looe PL13 20Z
☎/FAX *(01503) 272362*

The charming village of Polperro has long been a favourite with visitors to Cornwall and the accommodation provided by the Old Mill House, makes it possible to stay right at the heart of the village. A short walk through narrow streets takes the visitor to Polperro's famous fishing harbour, still a working port and much favoured by artists. The pub has an extensive bar where guest beers are usually sold at a special low price. The bistro offers superb home-cooking, including fish dishes from the 'Catch of the Day'. The hotel's eight pleasantly appointed rooms all have en-suite facilities. Guests with special needs can also be catered for. Out of season visitors can take advantage of special winter breaks. Dogs are allowed in the bar (Bonios provided) and pets can be accommodated by arrangement.

⊨ Four double, two twin-bedded and two family rooms
£ £
🍺 Draught Bass; Ind Coope Burton Ale; many guest beers
🍽 Snacks and meals daily, lunchtime and evening
CC accepted

—— ST AGNES ——

Driftwood Spars
Trevaunance Cove, St Agnes TR5 0RT
☎ *(01872) 552428;* FAX *(01872) 553701*
Directions: bear right down steep hill past church, turn sharp left at the bottom to the beach

St Agnes beach is very popular with surfers, but has a history of being treacherous for ships. Indeed the 'Spars' in the pub's name refer to the huge ships' timbers used in its building which were taken from wrecks. This area of Cornwall has many attractions for visitors, but recently Trevaunance Cove has built up a reputation for quality craftwork. Close to the beach a purpose-built centre showcasing the talents of local craftsmen and women is open all year. It also forms part of the St Agnes Craft Trail which takes in other galleries in the area. The Driftwood Spars is popular both with visitors and locals, particularly at the weekends when it becomes a venue for live music. All the guest rooms have en-suite facilities. Enormous Cornish breakfasts are provided, and the hotel is well regarded for its other food, particularly its famous Cornish pasties. Pets can be accommodated.

⊨ Seven double, one twin-bedded and one family room
£ ££
🍺 Draught Bass; Ind Coope Burton Ale; St Austell HSD; Sharp's Own; Skinner's Betty Stogs Bitter; Tetley Bitter; guest beers
🍽 Snacks and meals daily, lunchtime and evening (all day in August)
CC accepted

—— ST MAWGAN ——

Falcon Inn

St Mawgan, Newquay TR8 4EP
☎ *(01637) 860225;* FAX *(01637) 860884*
Directions: from the A30 follow signs to Newquay Airport, then St Mawgan village

The Falcon is set in that increasingly rare phenomenon, an unspoilt Cornish village. Situated in the beautiful Lanherne valley, it enjoys a good central location from which to explore all that the county has to offer. Helen and Andy Banks offer a high standard of accommodation; the rooms all have modern furnishings, colour TV, tea/coffee making facilities, although only two of the rooms have en-suite bathrooms. Another attraction of this characterful inn are its award-winning gardens. A full English breakfast is served; meals can be taken in either the bar or restaurant. Children can be accommodated, and so can pets, provided they bring their own bedding (pets that is). Parking can be a slight problem when the pub is very busy.

- ⇔ One single, two double, one twin-bedded room
- £ £ (££ en-suite)
- 🍺 St Austell Tinners, Trelawny's Pride, HSD
- 🍽 Snacks and meals daily, lunchtime and evening
- CC accepted

—— TREMATON ——

Crooked Inn

Stoketon Cross, Trematon, Saltash PL12 4RZ
☎ *(01752) 848177;* FAX *(01752) 843203*
Directions: from the Tamar Bridge, follow the A38 for two miles towards Liskeard; turn left at the second lane signed Trematon

A family-run pub, where families are made genuinely welcome. The overnight accommodation here is separate from the inn itself, understandable when you consider the pub was originally cottages, and the attractive bedrooms are in a converted stable block. Children enjoy the playground and pets corner, and all residents can make use of the outdoor heated swimming-pool in the extensive grounds. Although only half a mile from the main road to Penzance, the pub benefits from the peaceful rural surroundings of the unspoilt Lynher Valley and is within easy reach of beaches and the city of Plymouth (six miles). Excellent home-cooked meals, using as much local produce as possible, are served in the timber-beamed bar which is warmed by an open log fire. The bedrooms are very well appointed – all are en-suite with comfortable furnishings, colour TV, tea/coffee making facilities and hairdryers. Pets can be accommodated.

- ⇔ Eight double rooms
- £ ££ (single occupancy £££)
- 🍺 Draught Bass; St Austell HSD; Sharp's Doom Bar Bitter, Own; Skinner's Betty Stoggs Bitter, Cornish Knocker
- 🍽 Snacks and meals daily, lunchtime and evening
- CC accepted

—— VERYAN ——

New Inn
Veryan, Truro TR2 5QA
☎/FAX *(01872) 501362*
Directions: in the village centre, off A3078 between Tregony and St Mawes

The picturesque village of Veryan is set on the Roseland peninsula, about a mile from the popular sandy beaches of Carne and Pendower. Originally two cottages, built in the 16th century, this small granite pub, with its single bar, is still very much an unspoilt village local, but caters well for visitors with three guest rooms, and a residents' lounge upstairs. The rooms are spacious and comfortable, with shared facilities. Renowned locally for its good value food, a wide range of meals is served in the bar where the two beers are served direct from the cask. The Roseland peninsula, which benefits from a particularly mild climate, offers lots of opportunities for walkers amid some spectacular scenery, with safe, sandy beaches about a mile away. The towns of Truro and St Austell are both within 12 miles and visitors can take the King Harry ferry to visit the Trelissick Gardens and Falmouth. Pets can be accommodated, but there are no facilities for children.

🛏 One single, one double, one twin-bedded room
£ £
🍺 St Austell Tinners, HSD
🍴 Snacks and meals daily, lunchtime and evening (except Sunday evening)
CC accepted

—— ZELAH ——

Hawkins Arms
Zelah, near Truro TR4 9HU
☎ *(01872) 540339*
Directions: a quarter of a mile off the A30

The bypass to relieve the village was completed around 10 years ago, so Zelah reverted to being a peaceful spot, just a few minutes' drive from the bustling city of Truro, and the beaches of Perranporth and Newquay. The current owners, Jackie and Dave Eyre have also been at the pub 10 years and in that time have offered no less than 1,000 different guest ales. The bar boasts seven handpumps, of which three are dedicated to guests, which change almost daily; a traditional cider is stocked, too. Not surprisingly, the Hawkins Arms attracts a loyal local following, and fields three darts and two pool teams. It is also popular for its good, old-fashioned home-made food, such as steak and ale pie, liver and onions and cottage pie. The menu, served both in the homely, beamed bar and the non-smoking dining area, includes a daily fresh fish dish, and a children's menu. Children staying overnight are charged half price in the already budget-priced rooms. The low prices for the bad and breakfast reflect the fact that the rooms are fairly basic, with shared amenities, but they do all have TV and tea/coffee makers, and a full English breakfast is provided. The pub has a garden.

🛏 one double, two family rooms
£ £
🍺 Draught Bass; Dartmoor Best Bitter; Greene King Abbot; Tetley Bitter; three guest beers
🍴 Snacks and meals daily, lunchtime and evening
CC accepted

TRY ALSO:

Rising Sun
Altarnun, Launceston PL15 7SN
☎ *(01566) 86636*

A remote, 16th-century inn on the edge of a picturesque village on Bodmin moor. B&B £

Coachmakers Arms
Newport Square, Callington PL17 7AS
☎ *(01579) 382567*

Friendly inn serving good food. Four en-suite rooms. B&B £

Port Gaverne Hotel & Restaurant
Port Gaverne, Port Isaac PL29 3SQ
☎ *(01208) 880244*

Well run hotel in a tiny cove. Nineteen en-suite rooms. B&B ££££

CUMBRIA

—— ALLONBY ——

Ship Hotel
Main Street, Allonby, Maryport CA15 6PD
☎ *(01900) 881017*
Directions: on the B5300 Silloth–Maryport road

This former coaching inn is situated in a peaceful spot on the beautiful Solway coast, bene-fiting from marvellous views over the Firth, particularly at sunset. Horses and ponies roam freely on the green opposite the pub which is within easy reach of Carlisle and the Lake District. The Cumbrian Coastal Way passes the door and there are miles of safe beaches to enjoy. Other local pursuits included golf, horse-riding and sailing at Maryport's new mari-na. The hotel has eight comfortable, traditionally furnished bedrooms (three of which are en-suite). Yates Brewery's sole tied house, the Ship boasts a wealth of beams and cast iron fireplaces. There is a small dining room, and bar meals are also available. The inn is proud of its literary connections: Charles Dickens and Wilkie Collins stayed here in 1857 while they collaborated on the *Lazy Tour of Two Idle Apprentices*. A discount is available for CAMRA members; children and pets can be accommodated.

- ⇔ One single, five double, one twin-bedded and one family room
- £ £ - ££
- ◨ Yates Bitter, Premium; guest beer
- ⦿ Snacks and meals daily, lunchtime and evening
- **CC** accepted

—— ARMATHWAITE ——

Duke's Head Hotel
Armathwaite, near Carlisle CA4 9PB
☎ *(016974) 72226*
Directions: signed off the A6, between Penrith and Carlisle

Former *Good Beer Guide* editor, Neil Hanson once wrote a book about walking (and drink-ing!) in the Eden Valley* and ever since reading it I have wanted to explore this delightful, but rugged part of the country. The Duke's Head, at the heart of the valley, makes an ideal base for an outdoor holiday, not least because they have their own cycles for hire, and offer free fly fishing facilities in season. The area is also a haven for birdwatchers, while Hadrian's Wall is just a short drive away. The hotel offers all-inclusive breaks which means you could try the famous roast duck or 'fresh fish night' on Friday. Some visitors from Belgium wrote to tell me how impressed they were by the excellent food – praise indeed, as Belgian cuisine is among the best in Europe. Meals are served in a pretty restaurant, or the informal lounge where service is friendly and efficient. Three of the bedrooms are en-suite, children are wel-come. Guests bringing pets are requested to bring their own animal bedding. **Walking Through Eden* (Futura, 1991)

- ⇔ Five double, one twin-bedded room
- £ £ (££ single occupancy)
- ◨ Boddingtons Bitter; guest beers (occasionally)
- ⦿ Snacks and meals daily, lunchtime and evening
- **CC** accepted

—— BARNGATES ——

Drunken Duck Inn
Barngates, Ambleside LA22 0NG
☎ *(015394) 36347;* FAX *(015394) 36781*
Directions: take the Hawkshead turn off the B5285, after a mile turn right up Duck Hill

Despite its isolated position, this famous old inn is perennially popular, and now boasts a new attraction – its own brewery. One could be inclined to stay a long time here enjoying the mountain views, open fires and imaginative meals. An added bonus is the lack of juke box, TV and other electronic intrusions that so often spoil the atmosphere of our rural hostelries. The pub is in fact set in 60 acres of privately owned woodland and fell, yet is close to many popular tourist attractions such as Ambleside, Coniston and Langdale. The guest rooms are extremely attractively presented, and all different, featuring antique furniture and crisp white bed linen. All nine rooms have private bathrooms and the usual amenities. There is a choice of full English or continental breakfast. Children are welcome. Dogs can be accommodated (£5 per night).

⊨ Eight double and one twin-bedded room
£ £££
🍺 Barngates Cracker Ale, Chesters Strong & Ugly; Jennings Bitter; Theakston Old Peculier; Yates Bitter
🍽 Snacks and meals daily, lunchtime and evening
CC accepted

—— BOOT ——

Burnmoor Inn
Boot, Eskdale CA19 1TG
☎ *(019467) 23224;* FAX *(019467) 23337*
Directions: off the road between the Eskdale and Hardnott Passes

The Burnmoor's situation, in a fold in the hills at the foot of Scafell, with mountain tarns and waterfalls within easy walking distance, makes it a magnet for ramblers and tourists. The famous La'al Ratty steam railway terminus is also nearby, as is the Roman Fort on Hardnott Pass. Set in its own five acres with an attractive garden, the inn, parts of which are over 400 years old, has been well modernised. Very much a family business, it has a well-deserved reputation for its food, which includes Austrian specialities, prepared by proprietor Heidi Foster. Popular with locals as well as visitors, the Burnmoor offers comfortable rooms with tea and coffee making facilities, and of course, marvellous views. Six rooms are fully en-suite, two just have showers.

⊨ One single, three doubles, three twin-bedded, one family room
£ ££ (£ not en-suite)
🍺 Jennings Bitter, Cumberland Ale, Snecklifter, guest beers (occasionally)
🍽 Snacks and meals daily, lunchtime and evening
CC accepted

── BROUGHTON IN FURNESS ──

Manor Arms
The Square, Broughton in Furness LA20 6HY
☎ *(01229) 716286;* FAX *(01229) 716256*
Directions: on the A5092 in the town centre

Although it is smaller than many villages, Broughton, at the gateway to the Duddon Valley, is in fact a Charter Town – the Charter is read out in front of the Manor Arms Hotel each year to warn residents of what they can and can't do – overstep the mark and the stocks may be brought back into use. Convenient for the less visited western lakes of the Lake District, the Manor Arms, is a favourite haunt of *Watership Down* author Richard Adams. This traditionally run, family free house is also very popular with CAMRA members who delight in its range of perfectly-kept, mostly local, beers in a traditional bar, warmed by a blazing fire; indeed it has often been voted local CAMRA *Pub of the Year* and made it to the national finals in 1995. The hearty English breakfasts (or continental version for the faint-hearted) can be served in the guest rooms, which are comfortable and homely. All have en-suite facilities (including showers), colour TV and tea/coffee making facilities. Children are welcome to stay.

⇔ Two double, one twin-bedded room
£ £
🍺 Draught Bass; Butterknowle Banner Bitter; Coniston Bluebird; Yates Bitter; guest beers from small breweries
🍽 Hot snacks 12 noon-10pm; meals daily, lunchtime and evening
CC accepted

Old Kings Head Hotel
Church Street, Broughton in Furness LA20 6HJ
☎/FAX *(01229) 716293*

BRITISH INSTITUTE *of* INNKEEPING
🔷 **MEMBER**
SETTING *professional* STANDARDS

Directions: take Griffin Street off the main square, the hotel is at the corner with Church Street

This is a family-run hotel, where owners, Jackie and Gary McClure make a point of catering well for families. They offer a children's menu and if parents wish to have their children eat earlier than they themselves want to, then that can be arranged in the family dining room, which is separate from the main, cosy restaurant. Children sharing their parents' room are charged at lower rates and a cot is available. The garden features an activity play area and a pets corner. The McClures feel guests should be able to eat when it suits them, and to this end, they offer morning coffee and afternoon teas as well as a good range of bar snacks. The main lounge is comfortably furnished and served by a single long bar. There is a pool table, but this does not detract from the tranquil atmosphere. The breakfast menu offers more than just the usual 'full English' with options including fresh fruit and home-made yogurt. Four of the guest rooms are en-suite and all have tea/coffee making facilities and a TV. CAMRA members who visited the hotel recently praised the friendly owners' attitude toward their guests 'nothing is too much trouble'. Pets can be accommodated.

⇔ Four double, one twin-bedded and one family room
£ £
🍺 Boddingtons Bitter; Castle Eden Ale; Wadworth 6X; up to three guest beers
🍽 Snacks and meals daily, noon-9pm
CC accepted

——— CARTMEL ———

Cavendish Arms

Cartmel LA11 6QA
☎ *(0153 95) 36240;* FAX *(0153 95) 36620*
Directions: leave the M6 at jct 36, head to Newby Bridge along the A590, Cartmel is signed

The *Good Beer Guide* gives a no-nonsense description of the Cavendish Arms:'large old inn with central bar – diners one side, drinkers the other'. It tell us that its only disadvantage is its popularity – which means it sometimes gets smoky. This doesn't deter the local drinkers or diners, however who come for the varied menu which offers unusual specials and the Sunday roasts which are prepared on an open spit. Near Grange-over-Sands in southern Lakeland, and less crowded than the popular spots around Windermere, Cartmel is a charming village which has been described as a '14th-century cathedral city in miniature', the 'cathedral' being Cartmel Priory. The Cavendish is the only inn offering accommodation in the village. Some of the guest rooms are in the 16th-century part of the building, others are more modern, but all are well-appointed (one boasts a four-poster bed) and all have private bathroom, tea/coffee making facilities and TV. Children are welcome to stay.

- ⇔ Eight doubles, two twin-bedded rooms.
- £ ££
- ◀ Marston's Pedigree; Morland Old Speckled Hen; Robinson's Hartleys XB; Tetley Bitter; guest beers
- ◉ Snacks lunchtime; meals daily, lunchtime and evening
- **CC** accepted

——— CONISTON ———

Sun Hotel and Coaching Inn

Dixon Ground, Coniston LA21 8HQ
☎ *(0153 94) 41248;* FAX *(0153 94) 41219*
Directions: 200 yards up a steep hill off the A593

The Sun started life in the 16th century as a coaching inn and an hotel was built on to it in Victorian times to serve visitors to this popular resort. It is ten minutes' walk from Lake Coniston on whose shore stands the former home of the 19th-century writer and art historian John Ruskin. The lake found fame this century due to the water speed record attempts of Donald Campbell, who died during his last foray in 1967 and whose life and exploits are commemorated in the main bar of the Sun. Beams, horse brasses and a cheery open fire welcome climbers and ramblers here off the fells, where they can sup the local ales or dine (either in the bar or restaurant). All but two of the hotel's guest rooms have en-suite facilities, and the price includes a full English breakfast. Children are welcome (and are allowed in the bar until 9 pm). Pets can be catered for. The hotel has its own car park (an asset in a busy tourist town), gardens and a terrace for drinking in good weather.

- ⇔ One single, seven double and three twin-bedded rooms
- £ ££
- ◀ Coniston Bluebird; Jennings Cumberland Ale; Theakston Best Bitter, XB; guest beers (occasionally)
- ◉ Snacks lunchtime, meals daily, lunchtime and evening
- **CC** accepted

—— DALTON-IN-FURNESS ——

Black Dog Inn
Holmes Green, Broughton Road, Dalton-in-Furness LA15 8JP
☎/FAX *(01229) 462561*
Directions: between Dalton, Ireleth and Malton, half a mile north of South Lakes Wild
Animal Park

Originally a coaching inn on the old route to Carlisle, the Black Dog was later frequented by the Furness iron ore waggoners. Today it is popular with the farming community and CAMRA members, winning the local *Pub of the Year* award in 1998, and is a meeting place for geologists, ramblers and wildfowlers – the Duddon estuary is noted for its birdlife and fishing. The Dog offers budget priced bed and breakfast to visitors to the area, with a full English breakfast included in the very reasonable prices. The overnight accommodation has its own entrance from the car park; the bright rooms all have TV, and three doubles have en-suite showers. The cosy, friendly bar is a low-beamed room, warmed by open log fires and serving a good range of home-cooked dishes, including ham hock (whole hams are often hung from the beams in the bar), cockles from the Duddon estuary and local rabbit stew. Meal prices again represent great value. The beer range is excellent, too, with four hand-pumps offering a selection of often local guest beers, alongside two traditional ciders and two perries. Children can be accommodated (the pub has a children's certificate) and pets can be accommodated.

🛏 One single, five double rooms
£ £
🍺 Coniston Bluebird; Yates Bitter; guest beers
🍽 Snacks and meals daily, noon-9pm
CC not accepted

—— ELTERWATER ——

Britannia Inn
Elterwater, Ambleside LA22 9HP
☎ *(0153 94) 37210;* FAX *(015394) 37311*

The Britannia is a very popular village inn situated on the green amidst stunning scenery. Home-cooked food and local ales can be enjoyed in the cosy bars warmed by log fires; there is also a restaurant. To tempt winter visitors, there is a price reduction for a stay of three or more nights. At the heart of the Lake District National Park, there is plenty to attract visitors at any time of year, and it is probably advisable to try to see the more famous local sites such as Wordsworth's Dove Cottage and Beatrix Potter's house out of season. Nine of the inn's guest rooms have en-suite facilities, and whilst there is no family room as such, children are welcome to stay. Pets can also be accommodated.

🛏 One single, nine double and three twin-bedded rooms
£ £ (££ en-suite)
🍺 Coniston Bluebird; Dent Aviator; Jennings Bitter
🍽 Snacks and meals daily, lunchtime and evening
CC accepted

—— ENNERDALE BRIDGE ——

Shepherd's Arms Hotel
Ennerdale Bridge, Cleator CA23 3AR
☎/FAX *(01946) 861249*
Directions: one mile from the A5086, Cockermouth–Egremont road

This attractive free house stands on one of the most beautiful stretches of the Coast to Coast long distance footpath, and is very popular with walkers. The area also offers possibilities for many other outdoor pursuits, such as canoeing, pony trekking and birdwatching. This family-run village free house has a friendly, relaxed atmosphere and is open all day, throughout the year. The bar has become a popular venue for local musicians, with folk groups and jazz bands performing regularly in autumn and winter. The pub is highly regarded for the quality of its food, whether you choose the freshly cooked, but simple, selection in the bar, or the no-smoking restaurant where fresh fish and game are specialities on a daily-changed menu. Vegetarians are well catered for and a traditional cider is stocked. The comfortable guest rooms have recently been refurbished and all but two have en-suite facilities. One double rooms can be adapted to suit a family (children are charged £12 per night) and all have tea/coffee making facilities and a TV. Special three-day breaks are available, apart from the high season in summer. Pets can be accommodated.

- ⊨ One single, six doubles, one family room
- £ ££
- 🍺 Courage Directors; Theakston Best Bitter, XB; weekly guest beer
- 🍽 Snacks and meals daily, lunchtime and evening
- CC accepted

—— INGS ——

Watermill Inn
Ings, near Staveley, Kendal LA8 9PY
☎*(01539) 821309;* FAX *(01539) 822309*
Directions: off the A591 between Kendal and Windermere

This lovely old stone pub started life as a woodmill, powered by the River Gowan which flows through the grounds. When it was converted in 1990, care was taken to create a homely, yet characterful pub. The bar was created from old church pews, and the chimney was uncovered so a log burning fire could be installed. The inn is free from electronic games machines and juke boxes, so a peaceful atmosphere encourages conversation. Up to 15 real ales from all over the country are on tap at any one time, along with traditional cider, while the menu incorporates as much local fresh food as possible. The five guest rooms have en-suite showers, colour TV and tea/coffee making facilities; one room can accommodate a family. Just two miles from Windermere, the Watermill enjoys beautiful, peaceful surroundings, and is a regular local CAMRA award-winner. Well behaved dogs can be accommodated on request.

- ⊨ One single, four double rooms
- £ £-££
- 🍺 The beer range varies
- 🍽 Snacks and meals daily, lunchtime and evening
- CC accepted

—— KIRKBY LONSDALE ——

Snooty Fox Tavern

Main Street, Kirkby Lonsdale LA6 2AH
☎ *(0152 42) 71308;* FAX *(0152 42) 72642*

This charming Jacobean inn is at the centre of the old Westmorland market town of Kirkby Lonsdale in the southern lakes area. Within 20 minutes you can be in the Yorkshire Dales or the Bowland Forest. The pub has two bars, full of unusual memorabilia. The recommended meals are served in the dining area at the front, while the back bar has a partly flagstoned floor and a juke box. The attractive bedrooms all have en-suite bathrooms. Children sharing a room with parents are charged £10 per night. Pets can be accommodated.

🛏 Six double, two twin-bedded and one family room
£ ££ – £££
🍺 Robinson's Hartleys XB; Taylor Landlord; Theakston Best Bitter
🍴 Snacks and meals daily, lunchtime and evening
CC accepted

—— KIRKBY STEPHEN ——

Black Swan Hotel

Ravenstonedale, Kirkby Stephen CA17 4NE
☎ *(0153 96) 23204;* FAX *(0153 96) 23206*
Directions: leave the M6 at jct 38 and follow the A685 for six and a half miles

This stylish, grey stone Victorian hotel stands in its own wooded gardens, with a trout lake, leading down to the river Eden. Although easily accessible from the M6, the village (known locally as Rassendale) is a quiet backwater. For the active holidaymaker good fell walking and spectacular views can be had just nearby. For those who are not so mobile, but can nonetheless enjoy the spectacular scenery, the hotel is one of the few in this guide that offers ground floor guest rooms. All the rooms are attractively presented and all have private facilities. There is a residents' lounge, with plenty of reading matter provided and an open fire as well as a popular stone-walled public lounge. Children are welcome and pets can be accommodated.

🛏 Two single, ten double and four twin-bedded rooms
£ £££
🍺 Bateman Hill Billy; Black Sheep Best Bitter; Hesket Newmarket Doris's 90th Birthday Ale; Taylor Landlord
🍴 Snacks and meals, daily lunchtime and evening
CC accepted

—— OUTGATE ——

Outgate Inn

Outgate, near Hawkshead LA22 0NQ
☎ *(0153 94) 36413*
Directions: on the B5286, between Ambleside and Kendal

In the heart of Wordsworth country, this 18th-century inn lies between lakes Windermere and Coniston, close to the well-known beauty spot of Tarn Howes. This is a very traditional rural inn, where no juke boxes or electronic machines intrude, but which has built up a reputation for its Friday night live jazz (alternate weeks in winter). The inn holds two fishing permits, allowing guests to fish freely in the local tarns, lakes and rivers. The guest rooms have recently been refurbished and all have en-suite facilities. A full English breakfast is provided and main meals can be taken in the bar or restaurant. Pets can be accommodated, but unfortunately, not children.

⇌   Two double, one twin-bedded room
£   ££
🍺   Robinson's Hartleys XB, Best Bitter, Frederics (summer)
🍽   Snacks lunchtime; meals daily, lunchtime and evening
CC   not accepted

—— PENRITH ——

Queen's Head Inn

Tirril, near Penrith CA10 2JF
☎ *(01768) 863219;* FAX *(01768) 863243*
Directions: two and a half miles from M6 jct 40, via the A66, A6 and B5320 (direction of Ullswater)

The village of Tirril is on the edge of the Lake District National Park, just over two miles from Ullswater. Dating from 1719, the pub was owned in the 1830s by Wordsworth – the Wordsworth Debenture displayed in the bar, signed and sealed by the poet, is the proof. The inn was extended earlier this century into the adjoining cottages, currently used as a dining room. Now a privately owned free house, it boasts a wealth of beams and brasses and no less than four open fireplaces. An extensive, award-winning menu is served, where traditional English dishes are often complemented by the more exotic, such as kangaroo and ostrich. Four of the guest rooms have en-suite bathrooms; all have tea/coffee making facilities and colour TV.

⇌   Five double, two twin-bedded and one family room
£   £ (££ single occupancy)
🍺   Black Sheep Best Bitter; Boddingtons Bitter; Jennings Cumberland Ale; guest beers (usually local)
‰   Snacks and meals daily, lunchtime and evening
CC   accepted

—— THIRLSPOT ——

King's Head

Thirlspot, near Keswick CA12 4TN
☎ *(0176 87) 72393;* FAX *(0176 87) 72309*
Directions: on the A591, three and a half miles south of Keswick

The backdrop to the King's Head is impressive – it lies at the foot of Helvellyn at the heart of the Lake District and enjoys open views toward Blencathra and Skiddaw. This former coaching inn is now owned and run by the Sweeney family who offer a warm welcome. It has 17 well-appointed rooms, all individually decorated and all but one have private bathrooms. Most offer views of the fells. There is a residents' lounge and a games room and guests can take advantage during their stay of free membership of the nearby Low Wood health and leisure club which offers a swimming pool, sauna and gym. Mid-week winter breaks offer reduced prices, but there are also special packages for Christmas and New Year. Pets can be accommodated.

⇥ Four single, six double, four twin-bedded and three family rooms
£ ££
🍺 Black Sheep Best Bitter; Jennings Bitter; Theakston Best Bitter, Old Peculier
🍽 Snacks and meals served any time from 12 noon until 9.30 pm
CC accepted

TRY ALSO:

Albert Hotel
Queen's Square, Bowness on Windermere LA23 3BY
☎ *(0153 94) 43241*

Centrally situated Robinson's tied house, offering six double en-suite rooms, plus bunk rooms for backpackers. B&B ££ (£££ high season)

Bridge Hotel
Buttermere CA13 9UZ
☎/FAX *(0176 87) 70252*

Very well appointed hotel; also self-catering apartments available. Twenty-two rooms. B&B from ££.

Strickland Arms
Great Strickland, Penrith CA10 3DF
☎ *(01931) 712238*

A small inn with just two letting rooms, five miles from Penrith. B&B £

Stork Hotel
Rowrah, Frizington CA26 3XJ
☎/FAX *(01946) 861213*

Very basic, but cheap accommodation in five rooms. B&B £

Hare & Hounds
Talkin Village, near Brampton CA8 1LE
☎ *(0169 77) 3456;* FAX *(0153 94) 31938*

Charming old inn with simple accommodation. B&B £

Queen's Head Hotel
Town Head, Troutbeck, near Windermere LA23 1PW
☎ *(0153 94) 32176*

Eight en-suite rooms in a 17th-century former coaching inn. B&B ££ (£££ single occupancy)

DERBYSHIRE

—— BAKEWELL ——

Monsal Head Hotel
Monsal Head, near Bakewell DE45 1NL
☎ *(01629) 640250*
Directions: take the Ashford turn off the A6 between Buxton and Bakewell, turn left into Ashford village then right, one and a half miles to Monsal Head

At the centre of the Peak District National Park, this Victorian hotel overlooks the lovely Monsal Dale. There is a restaurant and bar in the hotel itself, while the adjoining pub, converted from stables, serves eight draught ales, including a house beer from the Derbyshire brewery, Lloyds, and traditional cider. Above the Stables is a craft gallery open to the public. The hotel is very close to Bakewell and just a few minutes from the magnificent Chatsworth House and Haddon Hall which recently had a starring role in the film *Elizabeth*. For walkers, there is the waymarked Monsal Trail. The guest rooms come in two varieties: the 'countryside' rooms have period furniture and Laura Ashley decor, while the 'Dale' rooms have heated balconies offering panoramic views of the dale. All but two of the rooms have en-suite bathrooms. Pets can be accommodated by arrangement.

🛏 Seven double, one family room
£ £ - ££
🍺 Black Sheep Best Bitter; Courage Directors; Marston's Pedigree; Theakston Best Bitter, Old Peculier; Whim Hartington Bitter; guest beers
🍴 Snacks and meals daily, lunchtime and evening
CC accepted

—— BASLOW ——

Robin Hood Inn
Chesterfield Road, Baslow, Bakewell DE45 1PQ
☎ *(01246) 583186;* FAX *(01246) 583032*

Directions: at the junction of the A619 and B6050, one and a half miles from Baslow towards Chesterfield

The Robin Hood has only a couple of rooms, but has been recommended by keen walkers who appreciated its low prices and the 'Hiker's Den' bar (where boots do not have to be left at the door). Well situated for walkers and climbers, the pub also boasts Chatsworth House as a neighbour. Good, wholesome bar food is offered on a fairly extensive yet reasonably priced menu. The pub has a children's certificate and families are welcome to stay. Although walkers' dogs are welcome in the Hiker's Den, there are no amenities for them to be accommodated overnight. The guest rooms are strictly for non-smokers. Both have TV and tea/coffee making facilities and share a bathroom.

🛏 One single, one twin-bedded room
£ £
🍺 Mansfield Riding Mild, Riding Bitter, Bitter, Old Baily
🍴 Snacks and meals daily, lunchtime and evening
CC accepted

—— BIRCH VALE ——

Waltzing Weasel

New Mills Road, Birch Vale SK22 5BT
☎/FAX *(01663) 743402*
Directions: on the A6015, between Hayfield and New Mills

The Weasel successfully combines the quality (and prices) of an upmarket hotel with the pleasurable atmosphere of a local pub. This stone-built inn, hard by Kinder Scout, has a quiet, traditional bar, replete with old settles, grandfather clock, prints and a log fire. Lunches served from the bar range from carvery salads through to lobster, whilst the small but stylish restaurant has won many plaudits for its imaginative menu and good wine list. The en-suite bedrooms really show a touch of landlady Lynda Atkinson's artistic flair, and they are well furnished with some nice antique pieces. They have all the usual amenities, including TV, telephone, hospitality tray, hair dryer and trouser press. Children are welcome to stay, and pets can be accommodated. Situated just 40 minutes from Manchester airport, the inn provides a good starting point for touring the Peak District.

ᛒ Five double, two twin-bedded rooms
£ £££ – ££££
🍺 Marston's Bitter, Pedigree; guest beers (occasionally)
🍽 Snacks and meals daily, lunchtime and evening
CC accepted

—— BUXWORTH ——

Navigation Inn

Buxworth, Stockport SK23 5NE
☎ *(01663) 732072*
Directions: one and a half miles the off A6, between Whaley Bridge and New Mills, towards Chinley

Buxworth is a small hamlet, seven miles from Buxton, but not marked on all maps. It was originally called 'Bugsworth' but local people objected to the insect connotations and the name was changed in the 1930s. The Navigation is a listed building situated right by the Buxworth Basin, itself a listed ancient monument, and the only remaining canal/rail interchange in the UK, currently the subject of a restoration programme. The pub (once owned by the late actress, Pat Phoenix of *Coronation Street* fame) makes the most of its situation with displays of canal memorabilia, traditional ware, pictures and souvenirs. There is a public bar, where snacks are served, a good restaurant, a coffee lounge, games room and a snug. All but one of the country-style bedrooms have en-suite bathrooms, one features a four poster. Children over three years old are charged at £9 per night. With the pub standing on the edge of the Peak District National Park, there are many places of tourist interest locally, including Lyme Park.

ᛒ Two singles, four doubles, one family room
£ £ (single room ££)
🍺 Marston's Pedigree; Taylor Landlord; Webster's Yorkshire Bitter; guest beers
🍽 Snacks and meals daily, served from midday through until 9.30 pm
CC accepted

—— CHINLEY ——

Squirrels Hotel

1 Green Lane, Chinley SK23 6AA
☎ *(01663) 751200;* FAX *(01663) 750210*
Directions: between Chapel-en-le-Frith and New Mills

Built at the turn of the century to service the railways, this rambling hotel fell into dilapidation, until Stuart and Sylvia Allison bought it as little more than a shell in 1993. Now completely restored and refurbished, it is probably the most imposing building in Chinley, a quiet village in the High Peak. The spacious, functional bar has a convivial atmosphere and the restaurant area serves an extensive, inventive and good value menu. Snooker can be played. Although no longer relying on the railway for its trade, the hotel is well located for visitors to both Manchester and Sheffield, as well as the Peak District. Efficient but friendly service is the keynote here, both in the pub and the six en-suite letting rooms. Pets can be accommodated.

- ⇥ Three single, one double, two family rooms
- £ £ (single room ££)
- 🍺 Greene King Abbot; Wards Best Bitter; guest beers
- 🍴 Snacks and meals daily, lunchtime and evening
- CC accepted

—— DERBY ——

Alexandra Hotel

230 Siddals Road, Derby DE1 2QE
☎/FAX *(01332) 293993*
Directions: four minutes' walk from Derby station

Mark Robins only started offering overnight accommodation for guests at the Alexandra in 1995. He had four rooms comfortably refurbished to provide en-suite facilities, TV and tea/coffee making equipment. This friendly, traditional pub is very convenient for Derby city centre (half a mile) and close to both the rail and bus stations, making it ideal for business visitors. Tourists can easily reach the Peak District (20 miles), Matlock Bath (14 miles) and Britain's brewing capital, Burton-on-Trent (12 miles). The brewing of real ale is a prime consideration in this traditional ale house where the simple furnishings and wood floors are complemented by much 'breweriana'. Alongside the two regular beers, Mark offers up to nine ever-changing guest beers, three draught continental beers and a large range of malt whiskies. The bar is, not surprisingly, very popular with CAMRA members who benefit from a 10% discount on the overnight accommodation. The food here is good too, with substantial breakfasts provided, and other snacks and meals available at all times, Monday-Saturday, as well as a traditional Sunday roast at lunchtime and in the evening. This two-roomed pub has a section for non-smokers and an outside drinking area.

- ⇥ Four double rooms
- £ £
- 🍺 Bateman XB; Marston's Pedigree; guest beers
- 🍴 Snacks and meals daily at all times (lunchtime and evening on Sunday)
- CC not accepted

—— GLOSSOP ——

George Hotel

Norfolk Street, Glossop SK13 9QU
☎ *(01457) 855449;* FAX *(01457) 857033*
Directions: in the town centre, opposite the station

The George is very conveniently situated, both for the centre of the market town of Glossop itself, and also for Manchester (accessible by train) and its airport. For business guests there are meeting and conference rooms, plus fax and photocopying services available. As Glossop is surrounded on three sides by the Peak District National Park, this friendly, family-run establishment is also a popular choice as a base for touring. Six of the nine guest rooms have a private bathroom, and they all have tea/coffee making facilities, TV and telephone. A solid stone building, occupying an extensive corner site, the hotel also has two lounge bars open to the public, sometimes frequented by coach parties, and a dining room.

🛏 Four singles, three doubles, one twin-bedded and one family room
£ £
🍺 Courage Directors; Theakston Best Bitter; guest beers
🍽 Snacks and meals daily, lunchtime and evening
CC accepted

—— HAYFIELD ——

Royal Hotel

Market Street, Hayfield SK22 2EP
☎ *(01663) 742721;* FAX *(01663) 742997*
Directions: in the village centre, just off the A624

The Royal has at various times in its history served as both a pub and a parsonage. Originally built as a home for the vicar of St Matthew's church, the Rev. Bradley, a particular friend of John Wesley who stayed and preached in Hayfield several times, it was subsequently used as both an inn and a vicarage until finally settling as the Royal Hotel in the 1860s. It has recently undergone a complete refurbishment, but has happily retained its oak-panelled walls and open fires. The Royal offers a relaxed atmosphere in its bars and bistro restaurant. All the guest rooms (where a no smoking rules applies) are en-suite and have TV and tea and coffee making facilities. The Honeymoon suite boasts a jacuzzi and four-poster bed. Short break packages are available and there are many opportunities locally for rural pursuits in this area of outstanding natural beauty; Kinder Scout, the Peak District's highest point, is right on the doorstep. Noted for its selection of real ales, the pub hosts a beer festival annually in October.

🛏 Three doubles, one twin-bedded and one family room
£ ££
🍺 Marston's Pedigree; John Smith's Bitter; Theakston Best Bitter; two ever-changing guest beers
🍽 Snacks and meals daily, lunchtime and evening
CC accepted

—— MATLOCK ——

Boat House Inn

110 Dale Road, Matlock DE4 3PP
☎ *(01629) 583776*
Directions: on the A6 in Matlock

An unpretentious inn near the centre of Matlock, the Boat House offers a homely welcome. Dating back 250 years, and warmed by log fires, this listed building offers an extensive menu of home-made bar food, including various local specialities. Beware, the Kimberley Mild is on misleading dispense. Matlock stands at the gateway to the Dales and the inn offers low-priced accommodation in guest rooms with shared facilities. The landlord says that well-behaved children and dogs are welcome. Visitors to this eastern side of Derbyshire may like to visit the Peak District Mining Museum, The Blue John Mines (source of the rare Blue John stone discovered by the Romans) and the NT's Hardwick Hall and country park.

⊨ One single, two double and two twin-bedded rooms
£ £
🍺 Hardys & Hansons Kimberley Best Bitter, Classic, seasonal beers
🍴 Snacks lunchtime, meals daily, lunchtime and evening
CC accepted

—— MELBOURNE ——

Railway Hotel

BRITISH INSTITUTE *of* INNKEEPING
MEMBER
SETTING *professional* STANDARDS

222 Station Road, Melbourne D73 1BQ
☎ *(01332) 862566;* FAX *(01332) 862591*
Directions: on the eastern edge of town

Situated on the main road into the village, in the south of the county, the Railway has been recently refurbished and features a light airy decor enhanced by wooden floors and tiling. A house beer is brewed for the pub by Townes, a small independent brewery based in Chesterfield. There is a small restaurant where the theme is based on the Donnington Race Track, which is just a mile away. Note, however, that meals are not always available (except, of course, for the full English breakfast which is included in the room price). The guest rooms themselves are situated behind the pub, and all have en-suite facilities. Some rooms are accessible to guests with special needs.

⊨ One single, two double, three twin-bedded and one family room
£ £ - ££
🍺 Courage Directors; Marston's Pedigree; guest beers
🍴 Snacks and meals available lunchtime Tuesday-Thursday, and all day Friday-Sunday from noon-9 pm
CC accepted

—— OVER HADDON ——

Lathkil Hotel

Over Haddon, Bakewell DE45 1JE
☎/FAX *(01629) 812501*
Directions: off the B5055, midway between Bakewell and Monyash

The setting of this hotel is not far short of idyllic, with panoramic views of Lathkil Dale, possibly one of the most picturesque in the whole Peak District. Surrounded by rolling fields and dales, this is certainly the place for a peaceful break, which is ensured in the pub itself by the absence of jukeboxes and gaming machines. The fine, old oak-panelled bar offers a wide range of meals from its buffet, or you may choose to eat in the restaurant which also has a reputation for excellent quality, and good, old-fashioned hospitality. Guests are even offered packed lunches to take with them while sightseeing: Bakewell (just two miles away), Buxton and Matlock Bath are all popular with tourists, as are Chatsworth and Haddon Hall nearby; less well known is Eyam, the 'Plague Village'. All four bedrooms offer good views, and are well appointed with bath or shower, colour TV, tea-making facilities and a personal bar/refrigerator. Hairdryers, irons, etc. are available on request. Children are welcome. Pets can be accommodated by prior arrangement.

- ⊨ Four double/twin-bedded rooms
- £ ££
- 🍺 Wards Mild, Best Bitter, Waggle Dance; Whim Hartington Bitter; guest beers
- 🍽 Snacks and meals daily, lunchtime and evening
- CC accepted

—— ROWARTH ——

Little Mill Inn

Rowarth SK22 1EB
☎ *(01663) 746305;* FAX *(01663) 742686*
Directions: signed off Siloh Road, off Mellor Road

A real must for rail buffs: the overnight accommodation at this pretty little pub is situated in the converted dining car of the old Brighton Belle! A long way from its first home, the carriage now contains five tastefully converted rooms, all en-suite, with colour TV, fridge and tea/coffee making facilities. Guests with disabilities can be accommodated and there are also self-catering cottages available. Children are welcome to stay, as are pets (by arrangement). The pub itself lies in the foothills of the Derbyshire Peak District, just outside Greater Manchester. A trout stream runs through the grounds, which also contain a small adventure playground. The pub has an interesting history: it used to be a mill where candlewick was produced for many years, and it boasts, at over 36 feet, probably the tallest waterwheel in the north of England. Not that it helped the landlord in 1929 who was drowned when the waterwheel was washed away during a cloudburst.

- ⊨ Five double rooms
- £ £ (single occupancy ££)
- 🍺 Banks's Mild, Bitter; Camerons Strongarm; Marston's Pedigree; Robinson's Frederic's; guest beers
- 🍽 Snacks and meals daily, at all times
- CC accepted

—— ROWSLEY ——

Grouse & Claret

Main Road, Rowsley, Matlock DE4 2EB
☎ *(01629) 733233;* FAX *(01629) 733010*
Directions: on the A6 between Bakewell and Matlock

This attractive old stone building is well situated on the main A6, alongside the River Derwent at the 'Gateway to the Peaks'. The village is noted for Caudwells Mill, one of the only working water-powered mills in the country – its craft workshops and gift shop are open to the public. Most of the Peak District's most popular sites are within easy reach, as are several villages where the ancient practice of 'well dressing' still continues. The pub has been refurbished with care to retain its original features which include a tap room (popular with hikers). A good variety of wholesome pub food is available at all times, and special food evenings are held on occasion. The bedrooms all have TV and tea/coffee making facilities; some are suitable for families. They have washbasins, but not en-suite bathrooms.

⊨ Two single, three double rooms
£ £
🍺 Mansfield Riding Bitter, Bitter, Old Baily, seasonal beers
🍽 Snacks and meals daily, noon-9.30 pm
CC accepted

TRY ALSO:

Devonshire Arms
Ashwood Dale, Bakewell Road, Buxton SK17 9TA
☎ *(01298) 26031*

Inexpensive accommodation at an inn on the River Wye. Three rooms. B&B £

Old Hall Inn
Whitehough, Chinley, Stockport SK12 6BR
☎ *(01663) 750529*

Traditional pub with weekly guest beers. Four rooms. B&B ££

Bulls Head Hotel
Fountain Square, Church Street, Youlgreave DE45 1UR
☎ *(01629) 636307*

Welcoming pub in a picturesque Peak District village. Accommodation includes two family rooms. B&B £

DEVON

BLACKAWTON

George Inn

Main Street, Blackawton, Totnes TQ9 7BG
☎ *(01803) 712342*
Directions: one mile off the A3122

This unspoilt whitewashed pub is not only very popular with local CAMRA members, it has been recommended by several other readers from as far afield as Scotland. It is much appreciated for its cottagey atmosphere and regularly changing beer list. It hosts mini beer festivals throughout the year and it also keeps a house beer from the local Princetown brewery. There is a good choice of foreign bottled beers too. Oh, and it serves traditional Redaways cider. If you can drag yourself away from the bar, then the coast (Paignton, Brixham etc.) and the Dartmoor National Park are roughly equidistant. The pub stands in its own garden, enjoying panoramic views over the surrounding countryside. The guest rooms have been recently updated with new en-suite shower rooms, colour TV and tea/coffee making facilities. Bar meals are highly recommended, with vegetarians, fish lovers and carnivores all equally well catered for. A (very) full English breakfast is provided, with a vegetarian option available, too. Children are welcome and pets can be accommodated.

- ⇌ One double, three twin-bedded rooms
- £ £
- 🍺 Beer range varies
- 🍽 Snacks and meals daily, lunchtime (except Monday) and evening
- **CC** not accepted

BUCKFASTLEIGH

White Hart

2 Plymouth Road, Buckfastleigh TQ11 0DA
☎ *(01364) 642337*

This pleasant little pub has an open-plan bar-cum-lounge featuring bare Devon stone walls, a wood-burning stove and open fireplaces. Meals (described by one visiting CAMRA member as 'bloody good!') may be taken here or in the dining area (at weekends). An 18th-century house, just outside Dartmoor National Park, the White Hart offers a good range of ales, plus Inch's cider. The pub has a pleasant courtyard, brightened by pots of flowers. The guest rooms are small and simple (as reflected in the price), but perfectly adequate in terms of comfort, with a shared bathroom. Each room has its own washbasin, TV and tea/coffee making facilities. Guests are offered a choice of a full English or continental breakfast. Children are welcome to stay and might enjoy a ride on the nearby Primrose Line (Devon Steam Railway) or a visit to the Otter sanctuary and Butterfly Farm, just half a mile away. Buckfast Abbey is within walking distance, too.

- ⇌ One double, two twin-bedded rooms
- £ £
- 🍺 Dartmoor Best Bitter; Greene King Abbot; Teignworthy Beachcomber; guest beer
- 🍽 Snacks and meals daily, lunchtime and evening
- **CC** accepted

—— COLEFORD ——

New Inn

Coleford, Crediton EX17 5BZ
☎ *(01363) 84242;* FAX *(01363) 85044*
Directions: one and a half miles off the A377 between Exeter and Barnstaple

'New Inn' in this case is certainly a misnomer; I've come across some pretty ancient 'new' inns in my time with CAMRA, but rarely as old as this. This spacious thatched free house dates back to the 13th century, and stands in a peaceful village that was first settled by the Romans. Now full of rural charm with beams, chintz curtains and much brass and other bric-a-brac, visitors can enjoy a restful drink by the log fire, interrupted only by the talkative parrot, 'Captain'. The pub boasts a pleasant garden with benches by a stream, and there are amenities locally for outdoor pursuits such as fishing, riding and golf. The food is highly recommended, prepared from ingredients sourced locally as much as possible. Fish is delivered fresh from Brixham, while cheeses, cream and ice cream also come from nearby producers. The guest rooms (all en-suite) are large and airy and have the usual modern facilities.

⊨ Four double and one family room
£ ££
🍺 Badger Best; Otter Ale; Wadworth 6X; guest beer
🍴 Snacks and meals daily, lunchtime and evening
CC accepted

—— DODDISCOMBSLEIGH ——

Nobody Inn

Doddiscombsleigh, near Exeter EX6 7PS

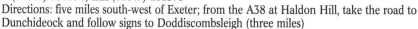
BRITISH INSTITUTE of INNKEEPING
🔷MEMBER
SETTING *professional* STANDARDS

☎ *(01647) 252394;* FAX *(01647) 252978*
Directions: five miles south-west of Exeter; from the A38 at Haldon Hill, take the road to Dunchideock and follow signs to Doddiscombsleigh (three miles)

This remarkable old inn was once famous for turning away travellers, and so giving rise to its name. It is now equally famous for quite the opposite reason – splendid hospitality. A beautiful 16th-century whitewashed building, it stands in a rather isolated spot, yet only six miles from Exeter and within easy reach of Dartmoor and the coast. The inn enjoys a formidable reputation for its food – its cheese board is a frequent award-winner. Meals can either be taken in the bar, which has antique furnishings, stone floors and stained glass windows, or the dining room (open most evenings). A house beer is brewed by Devon's own Branscombe Vale brewery; local ciders are also stocked. There are four letting rooms in the pub itself (two with private shower); additional, more spacious rooms are available at Town Barton, a Georgian manor house in the grounds of the parish church (150 yards). Here just a continental breakfast is served, but guests may pay a supplement for the full English option at the pub. No children under 14 can be accommodated. No pets are allowed but horses can be stabled nearby.

⊨ One single, three doubles
£ £ – ££
🍺 Draught Bass; guest beers
🍴 Snacks and meals daily, lunchtime and evening (restaurant closed Sunday and Monday lunchtimes)
CC accepted

—— DOLTON ——

Union Inn

Fore Street, Dolton, near Winkleigh EX19 8QH
☎ *(01805) 804633;* FAX *(01805) 804633*

Directions: from the A377 Exeter-Barnstaple road take the B3220 Winkleigh turn. Five miles on from Winkleigh, turn left on to the B3217 to Dolton

Of mainly cob and slate construction, the Union, which dates from the 17th century, was converted to an hotel around 1850 to serve the local cattle market. The market is long gone, and Dolton is now a pretty village on the Tarka Trail in good walking country. Nearby is the Halsdon Nature Reserve, a beautiful wooded area bordering the River Torridge, and at Stafford Moor, keen anglers can enjoy one of the best still water fisheries in the country. A slightly longer drive (six miles) takes the visitor to the RHS Gardens at Rosemoor. With so much to do, it is a good idea to take advantage of the inn's special three-day breaks (children under 12 sharing a parent's room and taking meals are charged half price). The Union has just three individually decorated rooms, all with en-suite bath or shower.

- Three double rooms
- £ (££ for the largest room)
- St Austell HSD, guest beer
- Snacks and meals daily (except Wednesday) lunchtime and evening
- **CC** accepted

—— DUNSFORD ——

Royal Oak Inn

Dunsford, near Exeter EX6 7DA
☎ *(01647) 252256*
Directions: just off the A30/B3212

This attractive, stone-built Victorian pub has a comfortable bar, frequented by friendly locals, which leads to the games and dining areas. It is set in a lovely, tranquil village of the Teign Valley, an area of outstanding natural beauty on the edge of the Dartmoor National Park. If it should get too peaceful for you, then the lively city of Exeter is within easy reach as is the east Devon coast. The quiet, well-appointed bedrooms, five of which are en-suite, are in a nicely converted stable block. A full English breakfast is provided and the main meals are recommended. The regular beer list is supplemented by one or two local brews and traditional English cider.

- Six double, one twin-bedded, two family rooms
- £ (single occupancy ££)
- Flowers IPA, Original; Fuller's London Pride; Greene King Abbot or Badger Tanglefoot
- Snacks and meals daily, lunchtime and evening

—— EAST ALLINGTON ——

Fortescue Arms

East Allington, Totnes TQ9 7RA
☎/FAX *(01548) 521215*
Directions: take the A381 from Totnes, then take left turn signed Kingsbridge (eight miles)

This wonderfully preserved 19th-century pub, which takes its name from the local landowner, boasts many original features. The flagstone floored bar displays an impressive collection of brewery memorabilia, including old posters and mirrors. Many of the tables, benches and other fittings have been there since the pub first opened. The lounge and restaurant area promotes an informal atmosphere, warmed by a splendid open fire and decorated with hunting prints. East Allington is a secluded village within easy reach of the coast and the Dartmoor National Park. Children are welcome to stay in the guest rooms; the two double rooms have en-suite facilities. Pets can be accommodated.

🛏 Two double, one twin-bedded room
£ £
🍺 Palmers IPA; Princetown Dartmoor IPA, Jail Ale; guest beer (occasionally)
🍴 Snacks and meals daily, lunchtime and evening (not Mondays in winter)
CC accepted

—— HEXWORTHY ——

Forest Inn

Hexworthy, Princetown PL20 6SD
☎ *(01364) 631211;* FAX *(01364) 631515*
Directions: signed off the B3357 Two Bridges-Bartmeet road; OS654728

The Forest in the name refers to the Dartmoor Forest, where the inn is a haven for walkers, riders, canoeists and others taking advantage of the natural beauty of this area. It provides a wide range of facilities and accommodation, including a 20-bedded bunk house equipped with showers and kitchenette. Choosing the more basic sleeping option doesn't mean you have to cater for yourself, especially as the pub provides good home-cooked meals in the restaurant (open evenings only), based on local produce, and an extensive range of light snacks, served in the less formal Huccaby Room. Afterwards guests can relax on the comfy Chesterfields and enjoy a locally brewed ale by the open fire in the lounge area. For guests who prefer a few more creature comforts the inn also provides 11 guest rooms (four with private bathrooms). Pets can be accommodated.

🛏 Three single, three double, three twin-bedded and two family rooms
£ £ (££ en-suite, £££ single en-suite)
🍺 Teignworthy Reel Ale, Spring Tide; guest beer
🍴 Snacks and meals daily, lunchtime and evening
CC accepted

—— HOLNE ——

Church House Inn

Holne, near Ashburton TQ13 7SJ
☎ *(01364) 631208*
Directions: off the A38 Plymouth-Exeter road, follow Two Bridges/Princetown signs; after crossing Holne bridge, take left fork to village

Away from the tourist hordes, this unspoilt village inn in the Dartmoor National Park, offers the opportunity for a peaceful break. The pub's atmosphere is undisturbed by canned muzak or games machines. The food, based on fresh local ingredients, is recommended, although the landlady points out that this is not a fast food outlet and a little patience may be required at busy times. Booking is advised for the (no-smoking) restaurant, but there is also a bar menu. The 14th-century inn, now a listed building was probably built to provide accommodation for craftsmen building the village church, or as a resting place for visiting clergy. Latterday visitors come for the more leisurely pursuits of hiking, sightseeing and golf (there are several courses in the area). Although a car is advisable, it is not essential as the owners, Mr and Mrs Bevan, can arrange collection from Exeter or Newton Abbot. Four of the six bedrooms have en-suite bathrooms; all have TV and tea/coffee making facilities. Residents also have the use of a pretty sitting room offering books and writing materials. Children are welcome; pets can be accommodated. As well as a choice of real ales, Gray's Farm cider is available at the bar.

- One single, three doubles, one twin-bedded room
- £ ££ (£ not en-suite)
- Butcombe Bitter, Wilmot's; Dartmoor Best Bitter, Legend; Morland Old Speckled Hen; guest beers (occasionally)
- Snacks and meals daily, lunchtime and evening
- CC accepted

—— HORNS CROSS ——

Hoops Inn

Horns Cross, near Clovelly, Bideford EX39 5DL
☎ *(01237) 457222;* FAX *(01237) 451247*
Directions: on the A39, midway between Bideford and Clovelly

Pardon the cliché, but this pub really is a 'real gem'. Built under a thatched roof in the 13th century, it was once the haunt of smugglers, later becoming a coaching inn. Raleigh and Drake number among its former customers. The two bars, featuring beamed ceilings, slate floors and inglenooks with log fires blazing in winter, create a superb atmosphere, which is complemented by the (no-smoking) restaurant which boasts an original terracotta floor and an award-winning menu. Overnight guests have a choice of rooms, either in the old thatch (which is definitely for non-smokers) where all the rooms have either antique four-poster or tester beds, or in the Coachhouse, where the rooms are smaller, but well appointed and include spa baths. All the rooms are en-suite and some can accommodate guests with disabilities. The pub stands in 16 acres of gardens, with plenty of possibilities for outdoor activities locally. The picturesque fishing village of Clovelly nearby is always popular with visitors.

- One single, seven double, three twin-bedded, one family room
- £ £££ (some rooms ££££)
- Beer ranges varies; always at least six ales, many from local breweries
- Snacks and meals daily, lunchtime and evening
- CC accepted

—— LYNMOUTH ——

Rising Sun Hotel

Harbourside, Lynmouth EX35 6EQ
☎ *(01598) 753223;* FAX *(01598) 753480*

When I got married 25 years ago, my husband and I were poor students and could only afford one night in a 'posh' hotel and another few days in a somewhat down-at-heel boarding house with (horror of horrors) brushed nylon sheets. Can you still buy brushed nylon sheets, I wonder? I rather feel that if I were getting married now, I would still like to revel in luxury for at least one night and my choice would be somewhere like the Rising Sun – it is not cheap, but it is quite charming. Newlyweds frequently choose the hotel's Shelley's Cottage, where the poet honeymooned with his bride in 1812. It has a four-poster bed, a sitting room and a private garden with spectacular views. The rest of the hotel's 16 bedrooms are all of a very high standard too, having recently been refurbished, and all with en-suite facilities. This 14th-century thatched former smugglers' inn, with its crooked ceilings and uneven floors is just right for that special occasion (special mid-week breaks are available). Children over seven are welcome.

- 🛏 Two single, 13 double and 1 twin-bedded room
- £ *£££ – ££££*
- 🍺 Exmoor Fox, Gold; Theakston XB, Old Peculier; guest beers
- 🍴 Snacks and meals daily, lunchtime and evening
- CC accepted

—— MARY TAVY ——

Mary Tavy Inn

Lane Head, Mary Tavy, near Tavistock PL19 9PN
☎ *(01822) 810326*
Directions: on the A386, Tavistock–Okehampton road

Bed and breakfast here is a real bargain, and what's more they cater for children and pets too. This traditionally furnished, whitewashed inn stands right on the main road in the Dartmoor National Park. A friendly welcome awaits in the two bars, one of which is warmed by an open fire in winter. There is a proper family room, with traditional games, rather than electronic gizmos; children also appreciate the large garden which overlooks fields and moorland. Good value meals can be enjoyed at the bar or in the dining room, which offers a traditional Sunday carvery. Local facilities include riding stables, fishing, a gliding club and, of course, good long walks. Tavistock (three and a half miles), the birthplace of Sir Francis Drake, has an excellent market and other attractions. The four bedrooms share a bathroom. Children under four years of age are accommodated free of charge; under 15-year-olds are half price.

- 🛏 Two singles, one twin-bedded, one family room
- £ *£*
- 🍺 Draught Bass; St Austell XXXX Mild, HSD; guest beer
- 🍴 Snacks and meals daily, lunchtime and evening
- CC not accepted

—— RINGMORE ——

Journey's End

Ringmore, near Kingsbridge TQ7 4HL
☎ *(01548) 810205*
Directions: off the A379 Kingsbridge-Modbury road

Your journey's end is at a dead end, at the foot of a hill at the bottom of a delightful hamlet in an attractive part of the South Hams. There you will find this charming, 13th-century free house, originally built to accommodate workers on the local parish church. It later became one of the chain of 'new inns' established by Elizabeth I across the country, to encourage travellers and merchants. Several footpaths near the pub link up with the Coastal Path, a mile away, and the nearby coastline (now NT controlled) was once renowned for smuggling. Burgh Island is just a mile away, and there are two golf courses within four miles. Very well preserved, the pub has an oak-panelled bar with bare boards and flagstones, enhanced by soft lighting and, in winter, an open fire. Some of the beers are still brought up from the cellar, while others are served by handpump on the bar which stocks the occasional traditional cider. There is also a tiny snug, a TV lounge (children welcome), a conservatory and a large, well-maintained garden. Home-cooked meals are served in the bar or dining room. The three comfortable, en-suite bedrooms have TV and tea/coffee making facilities. Children under 14 are charged half price. Pets can be accommodated.

- ⇔ One double, one twin-bedded and one family room
- £ **££**
- 🍺 Adnams Broadside; Exmoor ale; Otter Ale; guest beer
- 🍽 Snacks and meals daily, lunchtime and evening
- **CC** accepted

—— SHEEPWASH ——

Half Moon Inn

Sheepwash, Beauworthy EX21 5NE
☎ *(01409) 231376;* FAX *(01409) 231673*
Directions: one mile north of A3072 (at Highampton), between Hatherleigh and Holsworthy

Owned and run by the Inniss family for over 40 years, the Half Moon is a traditional village inn with slate floors and open fires in the heart of rural north Devon. The village lies on the River Torridge, famous for its salmon and trout fishing; the inn provides a rod room, drying facilities and a tackle shop where you can buy licences – it also has its own stillwater fishery on three lakes. There is also plenty to interest non-anglers locally, including the Dartington Glass factory at Torrington and the RHS Rosemoor Gardens. The inn's dining room provides traditional English cuisine after an active day, while Benjie's Bar offers a huge selection of malt whiskies to enjoy afterwards. The 14 guest rooms all have en-suite facilities. Pets can be accommodated.

- ⇔ Two single, four double, six twin-bedded rooms and two family rooms
- £ **£££**
- 🍺 Courage Best Bitter; Marston's Pedigree; local guest beer
- 🍽 Snacks lunchtime, meals daily lunchtime and evening
- **CC** accepted

—— SOUTH MOLTON ——

George Hotel
Broad Street, South Molton EX36 3AB
☎/FAX *(01769) 572514*

Listed by English Heritage as being of architectural and historical importance, the George suffered a roof fire in 1995, which was not as disastrous as it may seem – while the restoration work was going on many hidden features were revealed. Now fully renovated, but retaining its original charm and character, the hotel offers ten guest rooms (six with en-suite bathrooms). The lounge, bar and restaurant are popular with local people – in the past the hotel was connected with such local characters as the hunting parson, Jack Russell, who gave his name to the terrier breed, and Tom Faggus and Betsy Paramore who featured in *Lorna Doone*. The hotel is popular for its live folk and jazz sessions.

⊨ Two single, six double and two family rooms
£ ££ (£ not en-suite)
🍺 Barum Original; Jollyboat Mainbrace
🍽 Snacks and meals daily, lunchtime and evening (except Sunday lunch)
CC accepted

—— SOUTH ZEAL ——

Oxenham Arms
South Zeal, near Okehampton EX20 2JT
☎ *(01837) 840244;* FAX *(01837) 840791*
Directions: just off the A30, four miles east of Okehampton

This delightful old inn is believed to have been built by lay monks, and was later acquired by the Oxenham family, hence the name. Licensed in 1477, it has featured frequently in literary works over the years: one novelist called it 'the stateliest and most ancient abode in the hamlet'. Many distinctive original features have been retained, including a splendid granite fireplace and heavily beamed ceilings. Nonetheless, the prettily furnished guest rooms have up-to-date amenities, and most have a private bathroom. Pets can be accommodated. South Zeal is a very attractive village and there are plenty of opportunities for outdoor pursuits locally, including golf, fishing and rambling (the inn stands at the foot of Cawsand Beacon). There are several castles and NT properties to visit in the vicinity for those whose interests are of a more historic nature.

⊨ Three double, three twin-bedded and two family rooms
£ ££
🍺 Princetown Dartmoor IPA, Dartmoor Gold
🍽 Snacks and meals daily lunchtime and evening
CC accepted

—— SPREYTON ——

Tom Cobley Tavern
Spreyton EX17 5AL
☎ *(01647) 231314*
Directions: from the A30 at Merrymeet roundabout, follow the B3219 for one mile

Between Exeter and Okehampton, the little hamlet of Spreyton may take some finding, but don't give up the search or you will miss this charming white-washed pub fronted by a delightful floral display in summer. Behind the pub is an equally splendid garden offering fine views over the Dartmoor tors. This quiet village local has a good family room (also used for functions) and children are welcome to stay overnight. Pets can be accommodated. All the food is prepared on the premises (even the ice cream is home-made) and there is a choice of a good bar menu or full meals (which must be booked). A children's choice is also available. No food is served on Monday and the pub is closed altogether at lunchtime on that day. The four guest rooms have shared facilities, but make up for that by being well-priced, with a full English breakfast included. This cosy pub is just four miles from the Dartmoor National Park.

- Two single, two double rooms
- £ £
- Draught Bass; Cotleigh Tawny; guest beer (occasionally)
- Snacks and meals, lunchtime and evening Tuesday-Sunday
- **CC** not accepted

—— TORQUAY ——

Chelston Manor Hotel
Old Mill Road, Torquay TQ2 6HW
☎ *(01803) 605142;* FAX *(01803) 605267*

Chelston is a fine old manor house dating back to the 17th century. Although it has lost its thatched roof, it has retained many original features, especially in the bar which used to be the dairy and stables. It enjoys a good reputation locally for its selection of real ales and excellent food. Summer visitors make full use of the garden with its suntrap terrace and heated swimming pool. The hotel is within walking distance of the beach and the town's many other attractions. Most of the guest rooms have en-suite facilities. Children over 12 are welcome to stay and small dogs can be accommodated.

- One single, ten double, three twin-bedded and one family room
- £ £
- Boddingtons Bitter; Flowers IPA, Original; Fuller's London Pride; Marston's Pedigree; Wadworth 6X; Whitbread Fuggles IPA; guest beers
- Snacks and meals daily, lunchtime and evening
- **CC** accepted

Try Also:

Check Inn
14 Castle Street, Barnstaple E31 1DR
☎ *(01271) 375964*

Good value B&B in an old fashioned ale-house, North Devon CAMRA's Pub of the Year in 1998. B&B £

The Tors
Belstone, near Okehampton EX20 1QZ
☎ *(01837) 840689*

Just one double/family room is available in this moorland pub. B&B £

George Inn
Chardstock, near Axminster EX13 7BX
☎ *(01460) 220241*

This 15th-century, characterful thatched is reputedly haunted. Four double en-suite rooms. B&B £ (£££ single occupancy)

Old Inn
Halwell, Totnes TQ9 7JA
☎ *(01803) 712329*

Oriental cuisine is the speciality at this friendly family-run village pub, eight miles from Dartmouth. Three en-suite rooms. B&B £

Plume of Feathers Inn
The Square, Princetown, Yelerton PL20 6QG
☎ *(01822) 890240;* FAX *(01822) 890780*

In the heart of Dartmoor, ideal for families; the pub also has 42 beds in hostel accommodation. B&B £

Black Horse Inn
High Street, Torrington EX38 8HN.
☎ *(01805) 622121;* FAX *(01805) 624763.*

Over 500 years old, the Black Horse featured in the last big battle of the Civil War. Three en-suite rooms. B&B £

DORSET

Pickwick's Inn.
4 The Square, Beaminster DT8 3AS
☎ *(01308) 862094*
Directions: midway between Bridport and Crewkerne

Dominating the town square, the Pickwick is a popular meeting place in this small market town.. I do not think there is any direct connection with the Dickens character, but he would certainly have approved of the service here, particularly in the restaurant which is highly recommended. The extensive menu is complemented by daily specials which includes a good vegetarian selection; meals can also be taken in the bar. Pickwick's is an ancient hostelry, dating back to the beginning of the 16th century, if not earlier. Now a freehouse, this attractive, heavily beamed, stone building lies just seven miles from the coast and within easy reach of tourist attractions such as Parnham House, Forde Abbey, and the Fleet Air Arm Museum at Yeovilton. The four guest rooms (which have shared facilities) are at the top of the building. They are simply furnished, but are light and airy with views over the surrounding countryside. The Thornes say all are welcome here, including 'children, pets and muddy boots'. Beaminsters is surrounded by good walking country

- 🛏 One single, one double, one twin bedded,
- £ B&B £
- 🍺 Brakspear Bitter; Morland old speckled hen; guest beer
- 🍴 Snacks and meals daily, lunchtime and evening

—— MOTCOMBE ——

Coppleridge Inn
Motcombe, near Shaftesbury SP7 9HW
☎ *(01747) 851980;* FAX *(01747) 851858*
Directions: take right turn off the Shaftesbury-Gillingham road to Motcombe, drive through the village, turn left at top of hill, follow signs

A converted 18th-century farmhouse, the Coppleridge is surrounded by 15 acres of private meadow, woodland and gardens, which include tennis courts, a cricket pitch, a safe playground and a nature trail for youngsters. The guest rooms have been converted from former stables and cow stalls around a courtyard, and are attractively furnished with en-suite bathrooms. Guests with disabilities can be catered for. All the rooms enjoy country views. In the house itself there is a galleried bar, a lounge with log fire and flagstone floor and a candlelit restaurant. A fine old barn has been converted for functions and the hotel is licensed to hold weddings. The village of Motcombe has good facilities for visitors including a riding centre, a swimming-pool and fitness centre. Although you could manage here without a car (Gillingham station is four miles distant), there are plenty of opportunities for local excursions, such as Stourhead Gardens, Stonehenge and Longleat. Pets can be accommodated.

- 🛏 Eight twin-bedded/double rooms, two family rooms
- £ £££
- 🍺 Butcombe Bitter, Hook Norton Best Bitter; guest beers
- 🍴 Snacks and meals daily, lunchtime and evening
- CC accepted

—— NETTLECOMBE ——

Marquis of Lorne

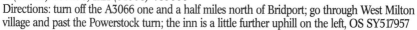

Nettlecombe, Bridport DT6 3SY
☎ *(01308) 485236;* FAX *(01308) 485666*
Directions: turn off the A3066 one and a half miles north of Bridport; go through West Milton village and past the Powerstock turn; the inn is a little further uphill on the left, OS SY517957

This pub – CAMRA regional *Pub of the Year* 1996 – is not the easiest to find, but a warm welcome awaits those who make the effort to do so. Nestled in the Dorset hills and protected by Egardon Hill, an Iron Age earth fort, the 16th-century inn is very popular for country weekends, and bargain breaks are available out of season. Once you have explored the immediate locality, an area of outstanding natural beauty, you can take off to the market town of Bridport or Beaminster, the local beaches at West Bay or Charmouth, or venture further afield to Lyme Regis, Dorchester and Weymouth. When you return, this large, stone-built pub offers good food and comfortable, en-suite bedrooms, all with TV, tea/coffee making facilities, direct dial telephone and hairdryer. The Palmers 200 is served direct from the cask. No children under ten years old can be accommodated.

⋈ Four double, two twin-bedded rooms
£ ££
🍺 Palmers BB, IPA, 200
🍴 Snacks and meals daily, lunchtime and evening
CC accepted

—— NORTH WOOTTON ——

Three Elms

North Wootton, Sherborne DT9 5JW
☎ *(01935) 812881*
Directions: on the A3030, Sturminster Newton road, two miles east of Sherborne

The Mannings took over the Three Elms in 1986, but within two years trade (and Howard's model vehicle collection – now numbering over 1200) had grown so much that the building had to be extended to cope with demand. This homely roadside inn overlooks the picturesque Blackmoor Vale with superb views towards Bulbourne Hill. The garden is popular in summer, with its panoramic vista. The pub enjoys a reputation for good food (meals are served in the bar), with a menu that includes an excellent vegetarian selection and good traditional British dishes as well as some more exotic choices, inspired by far-flung places. Burrow Hill cider accompanies the wide choice of ales (the house beer is Ash Vine Bitter rebadged). The three guest bedrooms are decorated in country style, and one boasts a four-poster bed. The bathroom is shared, but all the rooms have tea/coffee making facilities – and if you require anything else, just ask and it will be supplied if at all possible. Pets can be accommodated.

⋈ Two doubles, one family room
£ £ (££ single occupancy)
🍺 Butcombe Bitter; Fuller's London Pride; Shepherd Neame Spitfire; guest beers
🍴 Snacks and meals daily, lunchtime and evening
CC accepted

—— OSMINGTON MILLS ——

Smugglers Inn

Osmington Mills, near Weymouth DT3 6HF
☎ *(01305) 833125;* FAX *(01305) 832219*
Directions: one mile off the A353

Affectionately known locally as 'Smuggs', this charming old inn lies right on the Dorset coastal path with spectacular clifftop views. Its reputation as a smugglers' haunt is well-founded, as it once was the refuge for one of the most notorious, Pierre Latour. Despite being a very spacious pub, its popularity with holidaymakers means it can still get crowded in summer, not least with diners who have sniffed out its reputation for good food, which is served both in the bar and restaurant. Families like it too; the accommodation provides a choice of bunk beds in the family room, or an adjoining room. The pub itself also has a room set aside for families and a garden with a play area. It was from the beach below that John Constable painted Weymouth Bay which now hangs in the National Gallery. The four prettily furnished bedrooms are all en-suite and have tea/coffee making facilities and TV. A choice of full English or continental breakfast is available.

🛏 One double, two twin-bedded and one family room
£ ££
🍺 Badger Dorset Best, Tanglefoot; guest beers
🍽 Snacks and meals daily, lunchtime and evening
CC accepted

—— PUNCKNOWLE ——

Crown Inn

Puncknowle, Dorchester DT2 9BN
☎ *(01308) 897711;* FAX *(01308) 898282*
Directions: turn off the B3157 to Weymouth at Swyre

Puncknowle (pronounced Punnel) is a charming West Dorset village in the Bride Valley. It has been well preserved (to the extent of retaining its old red telephone box) and many of the stone-built cottages are thatched, as is the pub itself. The garden, which offers fine views, is often used in summer for functions, making use of a marquee and outside bars. The Crown also stages occasional music nights. Good value meals are available, and a full English breakfast is included in the room price. The pub has a public bar, lounge and family room. It is just a mile and a half to Chesil Beach and Weymouth is also just a few minutes' drive. This is Hardy's Wessex and a visit to Dorchester is a must for fans of the author. Only one of the pub's three rooms has en-suite facilities (as is reflected in the reasonable prices), but all have TV and radio and tea/coffee making facilities. Children are welcome and dogs can be accommodated by arrangement.

🛏 Two double, one twin-bedded room
£ £
🍺 Palmers BB, IPA, 200, Tally Ho! (occasionally)
🍽 Snacks and meals daily, lunchtime and evening
CC no

—— SEATOWN ——

Anchor Inn

Seatown, Bridport DT6 6JU
☎/FAX *(01297) 489215*
Directions: at Chideock turn south off the A35; Seatown is three miles west of Bridport

Situated almost on the beach below 'Golden Gap', the highest point (617 feet) on the south coast, the Anchor is surrounded by NT land, with the coastal path running alongside. Seatown is tiny – in winter there are just 25 residents, but the numbers swell considerably in summer. The inn caters well for visitors, all year round; in winter its cosy bars are warmed by real fires. At weekends the pub is a venue for live bands. The two bedrooms above the pub have handbasins, TV and radio, and share a bathroom opposite. Instead of the traditional English breakfast, guests take their breakfasts in a room overlooking the beach, from the supplies of cereals, milk, juice and bread etc. that are stored in the refrigerator in their rooms. The B&B rates are reduced for stays of more than two nights. At lunchtime and in the evening, a basic 'pub grub' menu is supplemented by a daily specials board. A Z-bed is available for children staying with parents.

⊨ One double, one twin-bedded room
£ £
🍺 Palmers BB, IPA, Tally Ho!, 200
🍴 Snacks and meals daily, lunchtime and evening (except Sunday evening in winter)
CC accepted

—— TARRANT MONKTON ——

Langton Arms

Tarrant Monkton, near Blandford Forum DT11 8RX
☎ *(01258) 830225;* FAX *(01258) 830053*
Directions: off the A354, north east of Blandford Forum

This is Thomas Hardy country, and this picturesque village has changed little since he wrote his novels at the end of the last century. Surrounded by the spectacular countryside of the Tarrant valley, it makes an ideal base for visiting Wessex, particularly the nearby towns of Shaftesbury, Salisbury, Sherborne and Poole. Voted *Pub of the Year* by local CAMRA in 1997, the delightful Langton Arms, thatched like many of the houses here, is at the heart of the village. It dates back to the 17th century, but the guest rooms, built in rustic brick around an attractive courtyard, are a more recent addition. All on the ground floor, which makes them accessible to wheelchair-users, each room has its own private entrance and full en-suite bathroom, plus TV and tea/coffee making facilities. With windows overlooking the peaceful surrounding Dorset countryside, you are guaranteed a good night's sleep. Children are welcome to stay – an extra bed can be provided – and pets can be accommodated. Special rates apply for short breaks of two-four nights. A full English breakfast is provided A free house, the pub offers a wide range of real ales. Bar meals are available and a bistro-style restaurant, situated in a converted stable and conservatory, is open Wednesday to Saturday evenings

⊨ Three doubles, three twin-bedded rooms
£ ££(single occupancy £££)
🍺 Ringwood Best Bitter, plus four regularly changed guest beers
🍴 Snacks and meals daily, lunchtime and evening
CC accepted

TRY ALSO:

George Hotel
4 South Street, Bridport DT6 3NQ
☎ *(01308) 423187;* FAX *(01308) 459018*

This Georgian town house is popular with the locals. Four rooms (not en-suite) **££**

Half Moon Inn
Melplash, Bridport DT6 3UD
☎ *(01308) 488321*

Four miles from the sea, the inn's restaurant specialises in fish and vegetarian dishes – 'where Melplash meets the Mediterranean!' Unfortunately, only one room. B&B **£**

Antelope Hotel
Greenhill, Sherborne DT9 4EP
☎ *(01935) 812077;* FAX *(01935) 816473*

Upmarket hotel with 19 rooms. B&B **££** (**£££** single room)

Crown Inn,
Puncknowle,
Dorset

DURHAM & TYNE & WEAR

—— CHESTER-LE-STREET ——

Butcher's Arms
Middle Chare, Chester-le-Street DH3 3QD
☎ *(0191) 388 3605*
Directions: off Front Street, opposite Lambton Arms Hotel

This traditional family-run pub, reputedly the oldest in the town, has a very friendly atmosphere, and a strong local following – it is particularly popular with young people at weekends. Traditional pub games are played, but there is no pool table or jukebox. Its single bar (where meals are served) features a wonderful collection of porcelain, and is comfortably furnished. The same is true of its nicely decorated bedrooms which share a bathroom but are each equipped with colour TV and tea/coffee making facilities. The pub is within 15 minutes' drive of many of the north-east's major tourist site such as the Beamish Open Air Museum, Durham City with its superb cathedral, the Metro Centre, and, the newest attraction, the Angel of the North sculpture at Gateshead. The coast is also just ten miles away, and the pub is within five minutes' walk of the local station.

⇔ Two doubles, two family rooms
£ £
🍺 Camerons Bitter, Strongarm; guest beer
🍴 Meals daily, lunchtime and evening (except Sunday evening)
CC not accepted

—— DURHAM CITY ——

Victoria Inn, 86
Hallgarth Street DM1 3AS
☎ *(0191) 386 5269;* FAX *(0191) 386 0465*

I lived for a year in Durham city (right opposite the prison!) in the early 1970s when my husband was a post-graduate student. We thought it was a magical place and never tired of the wonderful walk around the meandering river and the magnificent Palace Green. Durham Cathedral remains my favourite of all those I have visited in Europe. We have often hoped that circumstances would lead us back there, but so far it hasn't happened. We shall have to make do with a stay at the Victoria, a friendly, family-run pub, popular with locals and students, which boasts authentic Victorian fixtures and fittings. Snacks are available at the pub, but it serves no meals other than breakfast. However, as it is so central you don't have to go far for an evening meal. Alongside a good choice of real ales, the Victoria offers a selection of over 70 whiskies. The three guest rooms offer en-suite facilities; children are welcome and pets can be accommodated. Private car parking is available (rather necessary in the city centre).

⇔ One single, one double and one twin-bedded room
£ £ (££ single room)
🍺 Hodges Original; McEwan 80/-; Marston's Pedigree; Ruddles County; Theakston Best Bitter; guest beer
🍴 Snacks daily lunchtime and evening
CC not accepted

—— NEWBURN ——

Keelman's Lodge,
Grange Road, Newburn, Newcastle-upon-Tyne NE15 8NL
☎ *(0191) 267 1689;* FAX *(0191) 267 7387*
Directions: off the B6085, next to the leisure centre

The independent brewery, Big Lamp has helped to regenerate this part of Newcastle. After moving the brewery into a former water pumping station (a Grade II listed building), they then built the Keelman's Lodge in the grounds. It enjoys an enviable position, alongside the Tyne Riverside Country Park, popular with walkers and cyclists (mountain bikes can be hired from the nearby leisure centre), yet it is just five miles from Newcastle's city centre and even closer to the Metro centre. The airport and mainline station can both be reached within ten minutes. Happily, the en-suite guest rooms are accessible to guests with disabilities. Children are welcome (£10 per child, under three's stay free). All the rooms have one single and one double bed; cots are available on request. Breakfasts are served next door in the Keelman pub which has built up a good local following, both for its beers and bar meals. Alongside the regular Big Lamp beers, a house beer is produced by the pub's own micro-brewery (ask for a tour). Regular theme nights are held, featuring entertainment and special menus.

- Six double rooms
- ££ (£££ single occupancy)
- Big Lamp Bitter, Keelmans, Prince Bishop Ale, Premium, Summerhill Stout, guest beers (occasionally)
- Snacks and meals daily lunchtime and evening
- CC accepted

—— NORTH HYLTON ——

Shipwrights Hotel

BRITISH INSTITUTE of INNKEEPING
MEMBER
SETTING *professional* STANDARDS

Ferryboat Lane, North Hylton, Sunderland SR5 3HW
☎ *(0191) 549 5139;* FAX *(0191) 549 7464*
Directions: take the A1231 turn to Sunderland, north of A19, turn right at next round-about, pub is 400 yards further on

Standing right by the river, with enviable views, the Shipwrights has an interesting history. This listed building served as a ships chandler for the best part of 300 years and at low tide you can still see the slipway where sailing ships were launched. From here too, men were pressganged into the navy. In the more recent past it was the local post office – having the only telephone in the area during World War II. Nowadays it is popular with visitors both to Sunderland city centre (four miles) and Newcastle-upon-Tyne (six miles). There is also much to interest the naturalist, with wildlife, wetlands and wildfowl centres in the vicinity. The bar meals are highly recommended, with a menu offering some very exotic dishes, including crocodile, kangaroo and even locust! Popular with CAMRA members, the pub has been listed in almost every edition of the *Good Beer Guide*. The guest rooms (all en-suite) are furnished in keeping with the pub's character; children are welcome.

- Two singles, one double, one twin-bedded and one family room
- £ (single ££)
- Vaux Samson, Waggle Dance; guest beers
- Snacks and meals daily, at all times
- CC accepted

—— PITY ME ——

Lambton Hounds

Front Street, Durham DH1 5DE
☎ *(0191) 386 4742*
Directions: on the A167

The Lambton Hounds has often appeared in CAMRA's *Good Beer Guide* and I have always been intrigued about the origins of the unusual name of the village – Pity Me seems such a mournful description to be saddled with. There is nothing depressing however about this 18th-century former coaching inn which stands on the old Great North Road at the edge of the village. It features a village bar and a snug with bell-push service, as well as a lounge with an open fire. Good food is served either in the bar or the restaurant. It has a garden – where quoits are played in summer. Families are generally well catered for here and children are welcome to stay overnight. Three of the guest rooms have en-suite bathrooms. The village is a handy base for discovering the treasures of the north-east. Durham, with its splendid castle and cathedral, is a five-minute drive, and it is just a little further to the fantastic open-air Beamish Museum and, for shopoholics, the Metro Centre. Weekend breaks at special rates are available. Pets can be accommodated.

- One single, one double, two twin-bedded and one family room
- £ £
- Vaux Lorimer's Best Scotch, Ward's Best Bitter, guest beer
- Snacks and meals daily, lunchtime and evening
- CC accepted

—— SHINCLIFFE ——

Seven Stars Inn

Shincliffe DH1 2NU
☎ *(0191) 384 8454;* FAX *(0191) 386 0640*
Directions: on the A177, between river and High Shincliffe

By the innkeeper's own admission, the Seven Stars is not a place you are likely to stumble across by accident. Tucked away on the edge of the village, it is worth seeking out and you are assured of a warm welcome. Popular with locals, this attractive, former coaching inn has been well preserved over the last 250-plus years. The well-appointed guest rooms all offer en-suite facilities. It has a comfortable lounge and meals may be taken there or in the restaurant. Both a full English or continental breakfast is available. The pub has a garden and car park. Shincliffe is convenient for historic Durham City and the other main attractions of this delightful area. Although there are no special facilities, children are welcome. Pets can also be accommodated.

- Seven double, one twin-bedded room
- £ (££ single occupancy)
- Vaux Samson, Waggledance; guest beers
- Snacks and meals daily, lunchtime and evening
- CC accepted

—— WOLSINGHAM ——

Bay Horse Hotel
59 Uppertown, Wolsingham DL13 3EX
☎ *(01388) 527220;* FAX *(01388) 528721*
Directions: from the A1(M) follow the A68, then the A689, signed Weardale

The Wear Valley is a largely unspoilt, agricultural area, recently designated as an Area of Outstanding Natural Beauty. This hotel, at the edge of Wolsingham, benefits from views of the dale, and offers rural pursuits such as fishing in the Tunstall reservoir and exploring Hamsterley Forest, a haven for naturalists. A more unusual tourist attraction is the Killhope Leadmining Centre, Britain's most complete and best preserved site of its kind, dominated by a huge working waterwheel. A traditional hostelry, the Bay Horse is described by its landlady as 'a pub with rooms'. She observes that the guest rooms are of differing standards owing to the nature of the building – some are light and airy, others are smaller and darker, but most have fine views of the Pennines. All have en-suite showers, with TV and tea/coffee making facilities. Irons, trouser presses and a drying room are all available on request. Children (and pets) can be accommodated. The basic, popular pub menu is supplemented by a specials board.

- ⊨ Four double, four twin-bedded rooms
- £ ££
- ◖ Ruddles County; Tetley Bitter
- ◉ Snacks and meals daily, lunchtime and evening
- CC accepted

TRY ALSO:

William IV
Durham Road, Birtley DH3 2PF
☎ *(0191) 410 2739*

Convenient for people with business in Newcastle and the Team Valley industrial estate. Ten en-suite rooms offering good value bed and breakfast. B&B £

Strathmore Arms
Holwick, Middleton-in-Teesdale, Barnard Castle DL3 0NJ
☎ *(01833) 640362*

Small country pub in the Teesdale Hills, an excellent walking area. As well as bed and breakfast, there are camping facilities at the pub. Two rooms (one for families). B&B £

Mill Race Hotel
West End, Wolsingham, Bishop Auckland
☎/FAX *(01388) 526551*

Warm, friendly, family-run traditional village pub where food is available at all times. Three en-suite rooms. B&B £

ESSEX

—— BURNHAM-ON-CROUCH ——

Olde White Harte Hotel
The Quay, Burnham-on-Crouch CM0 8AS
☎/FAX*(01621) 782106*
Directions: near the B1010 and the town clock tower

This spacious, comfortable, 17th-century hotel is right by the river and very popular with yachtsmen and women as well as the locals, who number several retired seafarers among them. In keeping with its quayside position, the two panelled public rooms are decorated with charts and chandlery. The atmosphere is enhanced by the lack of any electronic machines. In summer, it is pleasant to take your pint outside on to the private jetty and watch the activity on the river. Good food is served in both the bar and restaurant, at all sessions. The bedrooms vary in quality – eleven of them are fairly basic and have shared bathroom facilities, but most of the double rooms are excellent and many have superb river views. The staff are very friendly and helpful, the breakfasts are nice and the beer is excellent. Pets can be catered for.

🛏 Ten double, seven twin-bedded and two family rooms
£ £ (££ en-suite)
🍺 Adnams Bitter; Crouch Vale Best Bitter; Tolly Cobbold Bitter
🍽 Snacks and meals daily, lunchtime and evening
CC accepted

Ship Inn
52 High Street, Burnham-on-Crouch CM0 8AA
☎ *(01621) 785057;* FAX *(01621) 785547*
Directions: town centre, opposite the clock tower

The Ship is Adnams most distant tied house from the brewery, a fact that happily does not adversely affect the beer quality. This 16th-century inn has recently been extensively restored and refurbished, but has retained its cheerful character. The three bar areas bear a nautical theme and excellent, home-cooked meals can be enjoyed here or in the restaurant. The three guest rooms are extremely well-appointed, each with a private bathroom: the Captain's Cabin is suitable for families (children are charged £10 per night), the Crouch Room is a double and the Burnham Room has twin beds. A choice of full English or continental breakfast is offered. The Ship is situated in the picturesque High Street, a few minutes walk from the historic quayside and its yacht clubs.

🛏 One double, one twin-bedded, one family room
£ ££ (£££ single occupancy)
🍺 Adnams Best Bitter, Regatta, Broadside, seasonal beers
🍽 Lunchtime snacks; meals daily, lunchtime and evening
CC accepted

—— COLCHESTER ——

Rose & Crown Hotel
East Street, Colchester CO1 2TZ
☎ *(01206) 866677;* FAX *(01206) 866616*
Directions: from the A12, follow signs in town for Rollerworld

Colchester is Britain's oldest recorded town, and the Rose & Crown is a pretty ancient inn. It is situated on the edge of Colchester, which is a sizeable place, so it is a fair walk into the town centre, but the splendid castle is just a mile away. The surrounding area is famous as being 'Constable Country' and has much to offer visitors, with the historic towns of Lavenham and Long Melford within easy reach. Most of the en-suite bedrooms are in the hotel's modern extension; three of them feature four-poster beds, and some are adapted to the needs of guests with disabilities. They are all well-equipped and comfortable, although a touch on the pricey side, particularly for single occupancy, but this is after all a four-star standard hotel. The prices indicated here are the room rates only, breakfast is charged as taken. The hotel has an atmospheric beamed Tudor Bar (part of the original building) which is popular with locals, where you can try the house beer, brewed by Tolly Cobbold. Meals can be taken here or in the restaurant (closed on Sunday evening). If you want to pamper yourself a little, visit the hotel's beauty salon.

- ⊨ One single, 23 doubles, four twin-bedded and one family room
- £ Room rate ££ (single ££££)
- 🍺 Adnams Broadside; Tetley Bitter; guest beer
- 🍽 Snacks and meals daily, lunchtime and evening

CC accepted

—— DEDHAM ——

Sun
High Street, Dedham CO7 6DF
☎ *(01206) 323351*

Directions: off the A12, midway between Colchester and Ipswich

The Sun Inn stands opposite the church in what was once an important wool town. Many of the buildings in this pretty village have historic connections with the wool trade and the pub itself dates back to the 15th century. Dedham is on the river Stour and makes an excellent base for touring 'Constable Country', with the major towns, Colchester and Ipswich both within ten miles. The coast, too, is easily accessible. The Sun is very spacious, boasting attractive features such as an inglenook with open log fire, and an extensive garden. The food here, served in both the bar and restaurant, is recommended; if you do not wish to drink beer with your meal, the pub offers a pretty comprehensive wine list. The four guest rooms are beautifully appointed and all have en-suite bathrooms. Children are welcome to stay – it is up to parents whether or not to tell them about the reputed ghost of the last witch to have been burned in this country who apparently haunts the place. Pets can be accommodated.

- ⊨ One single, three double rooms
- £ ££ (single £££)
- 🍺 Adnams Bitter; Courage Directors; Greene King IPA; Theakston Best Bitter, Old Peculier; Wells Bombardier; guest beer
- 🍽 Snacks and meals daily, lunchtime and evening

CC accepted

—— FINCHINGFIELD ——

Red Lion

6 Church Hill, Finchingfield CM7 4NN

☎ *(01371) 810400;* FAX *(01371) 851062*

Directions: leave the M11 at jct 9 (Stansted), follow A120 signs to Dunmow, then Finchingfield (signed)

Finchingfield boasts a reputation as being possibly the prettiest village in the county, some would even say the country! Its quintessential Englishness is certainly admired by the many foreign visitors who have the luck (or foresight) to spend their first night here after arriving at nearby Stansted airport. This 'chocolate box' village is, as one might expect, full of antique shops, craft shops and tea rooms to cater for the tourists. The pub itself dates back to the first quarter of the 16th century, although it was extensively remodelled 300 years later. The friendly bar is replete with old oak beams, exposed brickwork and brass. Meals, based as much as possible on local produce, can be taken here or in the more formal Georgian-style restaurant. The en-suite bedrooms feature hand-painted pine furniture made locally. Children are welcome to stay, although there are no special facilities. Pets can be accommodated.

   Two double, one-twin-bedded room

£ £

   Ridleys IPA, Rumpus, plus a Ridleys guest beer

   Snacks and meals daily, lunchtime and evening

CC accepted

—— HALSTEAD ——

Dog Inn

37 Hedingham Road, Halstead CO9 2DB

☎ *(01787) 477774;* FAX *(01787) 474754*

Directions: at top of High Street, turn left at roundabout

Situated on the very edge of town, benefiting from views over the Colne Valley, the Dog enjoys a strong local following. This friendly, traditional, 17th-century establishment offers comfortable, en-suite accommodation in a quiet extension at the rear. Reasonably priced bar meals are usually available, and a full English breakfast is served. Local places of interest include Hedingham Castle, Gosfield Lake and the Colne Valley Steam Railway – all within four miles. Also within easy reach, visitors can enjoy the beautiful countryside and the delightful villages that abound in this part of Essex. The pub has a garden and a family room.

   One single, two double, one twin-bedded and one family room

£ ££

   Adnams Bitter; Nethergate Bitter

   Snacks and meals, lunchtime and evening from Monday evening-Saturday evening

CC accepted

— RADWINTER —

Plough Inn

Samford Road, Radwinter CB10 2TL
☎ *(01799) 599222*
Directions: at B1053/B1054 junction, four miles north-east of Saffron Walden

A large open-plan bar with original beams and studding, log fires and a wood burner are features of this lovely old Grade II listed former ale house. Real ale is still an important feature – the range varies but you'll usually find local breweries, such as Nethergate and Crouch Vale represented here. The only pub in the village it enjoys a quiet atmosphere in a peaceful situation with delightful views across open countryside. In summer, guests can enjoy the large garden with its fish pond and patio clad with wisteria and vines. Home-made specialities feature on the menu which is served in recessed areas of the bar. The en-suite bedrooms (which can accommodate guests with disabilities) are in a thatched ground floor extension; a third room has just been added. Children are welcome (£10 per night is charged for an additional Z-bed and breakfast). Close to the ancient towns of Saffron Walden and Thaxted, which are well worth a visit, it is also convenient for Cambridge and Newmarket (both approximately 16 miles away). Pets can be accommodated.

⇥ Three double rooms
£ £
🍺 Beer range varies
🍽 Snacks and meals daily, lunchtime and evening
CC accepted

—— RICKLING GREEN ——

Cricketers Arms
Rickling Green, Saffron Walden CB11 3YG
☎ *(01799) 543210;* FAX *(01799) 543512*
Directions: just off B1383 at Quendon, two miles north of Stansted Mountfichet

I had intended to book into the Cricketers last time I flew from Stansted, but my schedule didn't allow me an overnight stop. I really regret it now as I could have basked in the luxury of the newly refurbished 'premier' room, complete with four-poster bed and double jacuzzi and indulged in a Champagne breakfast! The whole pub has just undergone a massive refurbishment programme. There are now ten lovely rooms, all en-suite. The best room has a splendid view over the village green, so in summer you can sit in comfort and watch the cricket. The green is one of the oldest in Essex and plays host once a year to the County CC. The pub itself is comfortable and the bar and restaurant have also benefited from the revamp, without spoiling their olde-worlde charm. After this major overhaul the owners, the Proctors have decided to open all day, offering bar snacks at any time, with full meals available at lunchtime and evening. A continental breakfast is the norm here, a full English option is available for a £3 supplement. Arrangements can be made for people arriving from the airport (15 miles away) at odd hours. Children are welcome and dogs can be accommodated by arrangement.

ᕼ **££ (£££** premier room)
£ Ten double rooms
🍺 Beer range varies, featuring local brews
🍽 Snacks at all times, meals daily lunchtime and evening
CC accepted

—— THAXTED ——

Rose & Crown
31 Mill End, Thaxted CM6 2LT
☎ *(01371) 831152*

It has been suggested that a pub with just two rooms to let is really too small to be in *Room at the Inn*. However, I make no apology for including this one – you'll just have to take the trouble to book in advance. It will be worth it, not only for the friendly welcome you'll receive at the pub itself, but also for the opportunity to explore the lovely old town of Thaxted which boasts a 14th-century Guildhall, and a fine tower windmill housing a small museum. The local church is famous, not least for its annual music festival, inspired by Gustav Holst, a one-time resident of Thaxted. The town claims to be the original home of Morris Dancing and between 150 and 300 dancers gather every year to put on a spectacular display. The pub, said to have been built on the site of a monastic hostelry, offers its guests a variety of real ales and excellent meals (taken either in the bar or cosy dining room). There is also a small garden and patio. One of the bedrooms is en-suite, the other has an adjoining bathroom. Children are welcome.

ᕼ Two twin-bedded rooms
£ **£**
🍺 Ridleys IPA, guest beers
🍽 Snacks and meals daily, lunchtime and evening
CC not accepted

—— TILLINGHAM ——

Cap & Feathers

8 South Street, Tillingham, Southminster CM0 7TH
☎/FAX *(01621) 779212*
Directions: on the B1021, Burnham–Bradwell on Sea road in the Dengie Marshes, 10 miles east of Latchingdon

The Cap & Feathers is a perennial CAMRA guide entry, and ten years on from being voted CAMRA National *Pub of the Year*, its popularity is undiminished. This unspoilt, 15th-century pub really does qualify for the description 'traditional', in its atmosphere, furnishings, its games, such as shut the box, cribbage and bar billiards, and the lack of electronic music. The main bar has been converted from several smaller rooms, but the little snug at the back has been retained and well restored. Outside, hanging baskets adorn the attractive weatherboarded walls and there is a nice little garden. Meals are served in the informal dining room and many visitors turn up just for the food, particularly the meats and fish which are smoked in the pub's own smokery. The pub is said to be haunted, but you are still guaranteed a peaceful night – the ghost, known as 'Captain Cook' appears only at breakfast time, dressed as a sailor. The accommodation, although not luxurious, with shared bathroom, does get very heavily booked, so with just three rooms available, an early reservation is strongly advised. Dogs can be accommodated.

- ⊨ One double, one twin-bedded and one family room
- £ £
- 🍺 Crouch Vale IPA, Best Dark Ale, Best Bitter, SAS, seasonal beers; guest beers
- 🍽 Snacks and meals daily, lunchtime and evening
- CC accepted

TRY ALSO:

Hanover Inn, 65 Church Street, Harwich CO12 3DR
☎ *(01255) 502927*
Convenient for ferry travellers, this old pub offers budget accommodation in four rooms. B&B £

Queen's Head, High Street, Littlebury, near Saffron Walden CB11 4TD
☎ *(01799) 522251*
Ancient inn, dating back 600 years, offering a good standard of accommodation and good. Six rooms. B&B ££ (£££ single)

Waggon & Horses, High street, Great Yeldham CO9 4EX
☎ *(01787) 237936*
Simple accommodation in six rooms with continental breakfast B&B £

GLOUCESTERSHIRE & BRISTOL

—— BLEDINGTON ——

Kings Head
The Green, Bledington OX7 6XQ
☎ *(01608) 658365;* FAX *(01608) 658902*
Directions: on the B4450, six miles from Stow-on-the-Wold

BRITISH INSTITUTE *of* INNKEEPING
MEMBER
SETTING *professional* STANDARDS

'Idyllic' is a much over-used term, especially in guide books! However, in this instance, it truly describes the setting of the Kings Head. Standing opposite the green with its brook and ducks, in a picturesque village in one of the most beautiful parts of England, scarcely any other epithet would do justice to the scene. What's more, Bledington is a frequent *Best Kept Village* award winner. As to the inn itself, it is full of character, with old oak beams, inglenook and exposed stone walls; the lounge is furnished with pews and settles and the restaurant has a real rustic feel about it. The bedrooms, all en-suite, are equally delightful, furnished with care to reflect the age of this 15th-century pub, but with all the necessary accessories for modern life: TV, hospitality tray and telephone. There is a residents' lounge and private patio. There has to be a price for all this antique charm and luxury, and that is reflected in the room rates, but it's still very good value compared to many faceless hotels. And, of course, the pub is ideally situated for touring the Cotswolds, with Stow-on-the-Wold, Burford and Bourton-on-the-Water all within easy reach.

⇄ One single, 10 doubles, two twin-bedded and one family room
£ £££
🍺 Adnams Broadside; Buckley's Reverend James; Hook Norton Best Bitter; Shepherd Neame Spitfire; Wadworth 6X; Uley Old Spot; two guest beers
🍽 Snacks and meals daily, lunchtime and evening
CC accepted

The Old Crown Inn,
Uley, Glos.

—— BROCKWEIR ——

Brockweir Country Inn

Brockweir, near Tintern, Monmouthshire NP6 7NG
☎ *(01291) 689548*
Directions: on the A466

Despite its Welsh postal address, the Brockweir Inn is geographically in Gloucestershire. The peaceful, somewhat scattered village of Brockweir lies on the east bank of the River Wye and to see it now, it is difficult to believe that it was once a busy port and centre for boat building. Cargo used to be transferred from the sailing boats into flat-bottomed barges at the quay, and at that time the village had quite a seedy reputation due to the number of cider houses that served the dock workers and sailors. That's all changed now and the 400-year-old inn is more likely to welcome walkers, as Offa's Dyke path passes close by. The pub does bear some reminders of its past though, since some of the huge beams in the lounge came from an old sailing barge. There is also a smaller, simply furnished bar with a pool table. Walkers are encouraged to leave muddy boots outside, but in the summer the garden and covered courtyard come into their own for *al fresco* dining and drinking. The inn offers a good range of meals, including a vegetarian choice, that are freshly cooked to order. The guest rooms are simply furnished with shared facilities, and a cooked breakfast is provided. Children are welcome.

- ⇔ Two double, one twin-bedded room
- £ £ (££ single occupancy)
- 🍺 Fuller's London Pride; Greene King Abbot; Hook Norton Best Bitter; Thwaites Bitter; guest beer
- 🍽 Snacks and meals daily, lunchtime and evening
- **CC** not accepted

—— CHIPPING CAMPDEN ——

Volunteer Inn

Lower High Street, Chipping Camden GL55 6DY
☎ *(01386) 840688;* FAX *(01386) 840543*
Directions: just off main High Street

Paul Sinclair and his mother took over the Volunteer in 1985 and over the years have worked hard improving and developing all aspects of the business, including the choice of ales, food and the accommodation. Their diligence has paid off and in 1998 the Volunteer was voted Gloucestershire CAMRA's *Pub of the Year*. They have not sat back on their laurels, and are still adding to their investment – by March 1999 all the guest rooms are due to have en-suite facilities (at the time of writing only three do so); one ground-floor room is suitable for guests with disabilities. The 17th-century, former coaching inn lies just off the High Street, once described as 'the most beautiful village street now left in the island'. It stands at the start of the Cotswold Way so is ideal for hikers and for anyone wishing to discover this delightful area, with Stratford-on-Avon just 12 miles away and other attractions such as Hidcote Gardens and the Elizabethan Stanway House even closer. Children are welcome. Pets can be accommodated.

- ⇔ Three double, two twin-bedded rooms
- £ ££
- 🍺 Highgate Saddlers; Hook Norton Best Bitter, Stanway Stanney Bitter; three guest beers
- 🍽 Snacks and meals daily, lunchtime and evening
- **CC** not accepted

—— DIDMARTON ——

Kings Arms

The Street, Didmarton, Badminton GL9 1DT
☎/FAX *(01454) 238245*
Directions: on the A433, six miles west of Tetbury

Just pipped at the post by Chipping Campden's Volunteer (see above), the Kings Arms came in as runner-up in the 1998 battle for the title of Gloucestershire CAMRA *Pub of the Year*. The latest *Good Beer Guide* describes it as having 'a low key exterior which belies the warm and welcoming interior of this tastefully refurbished 17th-century coaching inn'. Set at the edge of the Badminton estate, the pub is leased from the Beaufort family – the rent was set in 1760 for the next 1,000 years at six pence a year! The restaurant has an excellent reputation and comes under the command of chef, Cyrille Portier, who in the best French tradition, offers a regularly changing menu based on seasonal produce sourced locally as much as possible. The main bar (where food is also served) has an open log fire, whilst darts and bar billiards are played in the back bar. The four guest rooms have recently been refurbished and are all en-suite. Local attractions include Westonbirt Arboretum and golf course, and Bath is just 20 minutes away by car.

- ⊨ One single, two double/twin-bedded and one family room
- £ ££ (£££ single room)
- ◖ John Smith's Bitter; Uley Hogshead; guest beers
- ◉ Snacks and meals daily, lunchtime and evening (no main meals Sunday evening)
- CC accepted

—— GLOUCESTER ——

Linden Tree

73-75 Bristol Road, Gloucester GL1 5SN
☎/FAX *(01452) 527869*
Directions: on the A430, three-quarters of a mile south of the city centre

BRITISH INSTITUTE *of* INNKEEPING
◆MEMBER
SETTING *professional* STANDARDS

A country pub in the city, the Linden Tree's only real disadvantage is the tiny car park, but there is public parking a few yards away, and the pub is just a five minute taxi ride from both the rail and bus stations. A Grade II listed building, set at the end of a Georgian terrace, this pub really does aim to give an atmosphere of a rural retreat with its open fire, timber beams and home-cooked food. There is a quiet lounge and a skittle alley which can be carpeted to double as a function room. Many of Gloucester's attractions are within easy walking distance, including the Historic Docks and the Cathedral. The Forest of Dean is 17 miles distant and the Cotswolds just ten minutes by car. All eight rooms have private showers, and all but three also have their own WC. They feature pine furnishings, TV, hot drinks facilities and trouser press. The good value accommodation includes a full English breakfast. Pets can be accommodated by prior arrangement.

- ⊨ Three single, two double, two twin-bedded and one family room
- £ £
- ◖ Adnams Broadside; Badger Tanglefoot; Butcombe Bitter; Farmer's Arms Oddas Light; Wadworth 6X; guest beer
- ◉ Snacks and meals daily, lunchtime and evening (except Sunday evening)
- CC accepted

—— GREAT RISSINGTON ——

Lamb Inn

Great Rissington, near Cheltenham GL54 2LP
☎ *(01451) 820388;* FAX *(01451) 820724*
Directions: in the village, six miles off A40 via Barrington

Set at the heart of the Cotswolds, between Bourton-on-the-Water and Burford, the Lamb is ideally situated for tourists. Overlooking the Windrush Valley, this picturesque pub, which dates in part back to the 17th century, offers comfortable accommodation in its pretty individual bedrooms decorated with chintz and antique furnishings. All of them have en-suite bath or shower, and modern amenities, but TV and radio are not generally available in the rooms, so a peaceful night can be enjoyed by all. There are, however, four suites which each have a lounge or lounge area, with colour TV, and there is a residents' lounge with TV and a log fire. A travel cot is available for families. The pub offers a good bar menu, but you may prefer to eat in the delightful candlelit restaurant in the converted barn (booking advisable). The extensive gardens are very attractive and good use is made of the herb garden for the kitchen. Pets can be accommodated.

   13 double, one twin-bedded room
£ ££
   Hook Norton Best Bitter; Wadworth 6x; guest beer
   Snacks and meals daily, lunchtime and evening
CC accepted

—— HYDE ——

Ragged Cot Inn

Cirencester Road, Hyde, near Stroud GL6 8PE
☎ *(01453) 884643;* FAX *(01453) 731166*
Directions: off the A419, on the Cirencester-Minchinhampton road

This lovely old stone-built free house is set in a private walled garden at the heart of the Cotswolds, close to Minchinhampton Common and Gatcombe Park. Dating from the 17th century, the main part of the pub is a large bar featuring flagstone floors, beams, settles, two open fires and a fine selection of over 30 malt whiskies – a 'malt of the month' is always featured. Its friendly local atmosphere is enhanced by the range of traditional games available and the reference library for the pub's crossword and quiz addicts. Bar meals are available and the pub also has a newly refurbished restaurant. The guest rooms, all en-suite, are situated in a recently converted stable block. They have been attractively furnished and offer all the usual modern amenities. The Bridal Suite has a four-poster bed. Children are welcome and pets can be accommodated. Ask the landlord about the grisly story of his 18th-century predecessor, Bill Clavers – but maybe not just before retiring to bed!

   Three double, seven twin-bedded rooms
£ ££ (£££ single occupancy)
   Draught Bass; Theakston Best Bitter; Uley Old Spot; Wadworth 6X; guest beers
   Snacks and meals daily, lunchtime and evening
CC accepted

—— KINGSCOTE ——

Hunters Hall
Kingscote, near Tetbury GL8 8XZ
☎ *(01453) 860393;* FAX *(01453 860707)*
Directions: on the A4153

This rambling, ivy-covered inn which dates back to the 16th century has a wealth of charm with its beamed ceilings, stone floors, ubiquitous bric-a-brac and no less than three open fires. Old settles and sofas add to the atmosphere of a bygone era. The guest rooms, however, are bang up-to-date, with modern facilities and en-suite bathrooms. They are situated in a separate building which once served as the stables and blacksmith's shop. Several of the rooms are on the ground floor and specially designed for guests with disabilities. One room has a four-poster. An extensive range of bar meals is served in all three bars and there is also an informal restaurant with no-smoking area. The hotel's residents can benefit from reduced green fees at the local golf course, while other outdoor pursuits such as riding and rambling can be enjoyed nearby. The nearest town, Tetbury is a haven for antiques-addicts, while Bath, Cheltenham and Gloucester are all within 18 miles. Pets can be accommodated.

⊨ Six double, five twin-bedded and one family room
£ ££
⊈ Draught Bass; Courage Directors; Theakston Best Bitter; Uley Hogshead
⦿ Snacks and meals daily, lunchtime and evening
CC accepted

—— LITTLETON-UPON-SEVERN ——

White Hart
Littleton-upon-Severn, near Thornbury, Bristol BS35 1NR
☎ *(01454) 412275*
Directions: leave the M4 at jct 21, follow Thornbury, Old Down and Elberton village signs; Littleton is signed from Elberton

The White Hart was built in the 1680s, originally as a farmhouse, and many of the building's old features have been carefully preserved, including two large fireplaces and a lovely old staircase. An extension has been added to the pub but designed to blend in with the existing buildings – CAMRA was so impressed by the attention to detail that it awarded its coveted *Best Refurbishment* prize on completion of the work. The guest rooms at the White Hart are in a converted barn, and the same care has been taken here in giving each room its own individual character and equipping them to a high standard with TV, telephone tea/coffee making equipment and en-suite facilities. Children are welcome to stay and pets can be accommodated. Residents enjoy substantial breakfasts and during the week the home-cooked meals are much appreciated by business customers. The tranquil village stands on the route of the Avon Cycleway and the pub gets very busy in summer with cyclists, ramblers and holidaymakers, when its garden and large car park can get quite full. Just across the River Severn from Wales, there is plenty to see and do locally; real ale lovers may wish to take a look at the nearby Wickwar Brewery, situated in an old cider mill (tours by arrangement, tel 01454 294168)

⊨ Two single, one double and one twin-bedded room
£ ££ (£ in double room)
⊈ Greene King Abbot; Smiles Golden Brew, Heritage; guest beer
⦿ Snacks and meals daily, lunchtime and evening
CC accepted

—— LOWER ALMONDSBURY ——

Old Bowl Inn & Restaurant

16 Church Road, Lower Almondsbury, North Bristol BS32 4DT
☎ *(01454) 612757;* FAX *(01454 619910*
Directions: one mile from the M5 jct 16

When the rooms at the Bowl Inn were being refurbished as guest accommodation, many original features, such as fireplaces, huge ceiling beams and stonework niches, were uncovered and restored as attractive elements in the decor, very much in keeping with the rustic appeal of the rest of the building. The rooms are all individually styled, with modern amenities such as telephone, tea/coffee making facilities, trouser press, satellite TV and VCR. All rooms have either en-suite bath or shower and some feature a four-poster bed, one is adapted to suit guests with disabilities. Children are welcome to stay and pets can be accommodated. The three-night weekend breaks represent good value. The pub comprises an attractive bar (where meals and snacks are served), an oak-beamed conference room and the Lilies Restaurant. The inn, which takes its name from the bowl-shaped land surrounding the Severn estuary, has a long history. Three cottages, built to house monks in the 12th century form part of the original building, which was licensed in 1550. The inn was later used by James II's sherrifs to try supporters of the Duke of Monmouth. It is said to be haunted by a 'Grey Lady'. For tourists, Bristol, Bath and the Slimbridge Wildfowl Reserve are all within easy reach.

- ⊨ Nine double, five twin-bedded rooms
- £ **£££** (**££** at weekend sharing a double room)
- 🍺 Courage Best Bitter, Directors; Wadworth 6X; guest beers
- 🍽 Snacks and meals daily, lunchtime and evening
- **CC** accepted

—— PARKEND ——

Fountain Inn

Fountain Way, Parkend, Royal Forest of Dean GL15 4JD
☎ *(01594) 562189;* FAX *(01594) 564438*
Directions: on the A48, three miles west of Lydney

Set right at the heart of the Forest of Dean, this pub, whose exposed stone walls are bedecked with bric-a-brac, is a delight. Built 200 years ago to serve the local mining community, it was enlarged when the Great Western Railway reached the village in 1868. Although not so many people arrive by train now, the Fountain is still very popular with tourists, who come to roam in the 23,000 acres of the Royal Forest and visit local attractions such as Chepstow Castle, Tintern and Gloucester. The pub itself has eight well-appointed rooms, all en-suite and offering all the usual facilities. One, on the ground floor, has been specially designed for disabled use and is registered with RADAR as being suitable for a wheelchair user with a helper. Various half-board breaks are offered during the year (prices on application). Hostel accommodation in the Fountain Lodge is also available to groups of up to 30, who should book in advance. It enjoys a good reputation locally for its meals,. Pets can be accommodated.

- ⊨ Five double, two twin-bedded and one family room
- £ **£** (**££** single occupancy)
- 🍺 Draught Bass; Freeminer Bitter; guest beer
- 🍽 Snacks and meals daily, lunchtime and evening
- **CC** accepted

—— ULEY ——

Old Crown

The Green, Uley, Dursley GL11 5SN
☎ *(01453) 860502*
Directions: village centre

The Old Crown is a charming old stone pub standing right by the green in a quintessential Cotswold village. The welcoming single bar has recently been sympathetically renovated and there is a games room upstairs. The menu, served in the bar, offers reasonably priced, home-cooked food with a good range of vegetarian options. There are always five real ales available, usually from small independent breweries; the landlady makes a point of changing the guest beers frequently, generally weekly, whilst the regular ales come from the local Uley brewery. The three bedrooms all have en-suite bathrooms, TV and tea-coffee making facilities. Children are charged at half price and there is a 10% discount for CAMRA members staying three nights or more. An excellent breakfast is provided. Uley lies in beautiful rambling country, just 10 minutes' walk from the Cotswold Way long-distance footpath, and makes an ideal overnight stop for walkers. People with an interest in ancient history can walk (one mile) to the Uley Tumulus.

⇥ One single, one double and one family room
£ £ (££ single room)
🍺 Uley Bitter, Pig's Ear; three guest beers
🍴 Snacks and meals daily, lunchtime and evening
CC accepted

—— WATERLEY BOTTOM ——

New Inn

Waterley Bottom, North Nibley, Dursley GL11 6EF
☎ *(01453) 543659*
Directions: follow signs to Waterly Bottom from North Nibley village (OS map recommended, ref 758964)

The New Inn is rather remote, so a good map is recommended for first time visitors – it will be a good investment as you'll be sure to want to return. This spacious pub enjoys an enviable setting, in a valley protected by steep hills. Woods and footpaths offer plenty of scope for ramblers, while naturalists can enjoy a trip to Slimbridge Wildfowl Trust. Berkeley Castle, with its Butterfly House is also a popular tourist destination. There are also two golf courses within a two mile radius. As a free house, the New Inn is able to offer a wide range of ales and traditional cider, including a house beer (WB) from the West Country's Cotleigh Brewery. Note the antique beer engines. A full English breakfast is included in the room price and other meals can be taken in the bar. The fairly simple accommodation is reasonably priced; the two rooms share a bathroom.

⇥ One double, one twin-bedded room
£ £
🍺 Berkeley Dicky Pearce; Cotleigh Tawny; Greene King Abbot; Smiles Best Bitter; Theakston Old Peculier; guest beers
🍴 Snacks and meals daily, lunchtime and evening
CC not accepted

TRY ALSO:

Fox & Hounds
Great Wolford, near Moreton-in-the-Marsh CV36 5NQ
☎/FAX (01608) 674220

Pub of olde-worlde charm dating back to the 16th century, serving eight ales. Four en-suite rooms. B&B £

Old Station Inn
Wells Road, Hallatrow, near Bristol BS39 6EN
☎ (01761) 452228

Conveniently situated on the A39 Bath road, the inn offers five en-suite rooms (price on application)

HAMPSHIRE & ISLE OF WIGHT

—— ALVERSTOKE ——

Alverbank Country House Hotel

Stokes Bay, Alverstoke, Gosport PO12 2QT
☎ *(01705) 510005;* FAX *(01705) 520864*

The Alverbank is by no means cheap, but if you want to push the boat and be spoiled by luxurious surroundings for a change, this upmarket hotel could fit the bill. Secluded in 100 acres of woodland, you can still enjoy the sea breezes as it overlooks Stokes Bay – the beach is 400 yards away. Local CAMRA members report that usually a quiet, relaxing atmosphere prevails, but it does sometimes get busy with wedding receptions and other functions. It also stages an annual Autumn beer festival. At one time, Lille Langry, the beautiful actress with royal connections was a regular guest – I don't suppose she came for the beer. Today's guests enjoy all the usual amenities in nine guest rooms; all but one have en-suite bathrooms. Meals can be taken in the bar or restaurant.

- ⊨ Two single, five double, two twin-bedded, one family room
- £ £££ (££££ single en-suite)
- ◨ Ringwood Best Bitter; three guest beers
- ❡ Snacks and meals daily, lunchtime and evening
- CC accepted

—— CHALE ——

Wight Mouse Inn

Clarendon Hotel, Newport Road, Chale, Isle of Wight PO38 2HA
☎/FAX *(01983) 730431*
Directions: on the B3399 which is off the B3055, Military Road

In a child-centred resort, this hotel is ideal for families, as no less than seven of its 15 bed-rooms are suitable for families and the garden is a children's paradise with apparatus, ballpond, bouncy castle, sandpit and even tricycles, oh and not forgetting the pets corner, starring Arthur the Shetland pony who is available for rides. So what's in it for the grown ups? Well, for a start, atmosphere – the Clarendon is a 17th-century coaching inn of much charm and character standing in its own grounds overlooking the west Wight coastline. Together with the adjoining pub, the Wight House (also run by John and Jean Bradshaw) excellent food, service and accommodation are assured. For whisky buffs, there is a differ-ent whisky for every night of the year (it has been a previous winner of the *Whisky Pub of the Year award*). The pub also offers a good selection of real ales and stages live entertain-ment nightly. All but two of the 15 hotel rooms have en-suite bathrooms, all have TV and hairdryers are provided. Pets can be accommodated.

- ⊨ One single, seven doubles, seven family rooms
- £ £££ (££ between 1st March and 1st November, excluding Bank Holidays)
- ◨ Boddingtons Bitter; Gales HSB; Marston's Pedigree; Morland Old Speckled Hen; Wadworth 6X; Whitbread Fuggles Imperial; guest beers
- ❡ Snacks and meals daily from midday-10 pm
- CC accepted

—— CHERITON ——

Flower Pots Inn

Cheriton, Alresford SO24 0QQ
☎ *(01962) 771318*
Directions: between the A272 and B3046, 7 miles east of Winchester

This unpretentious village pub is a must for real ale fans; it has its own purpose-built brewery, which now supplies many other outlets as well as the pub itself. They also produce their own cider. A CAMRA regional award-winner, the Flower Pots started life as a farm in the early 19th century, being converted to a pub in the mid-1950s. It has a simply furnished public bar where the farmhouse origins are still evident in the tiled floor and large open fireplace, and a covered well can be spotted. There is also a cosy lounge. The guest accommodation is in a converted cow byre between the pub and the brewery, offering five comfortable bedrooms, all with en-suite facilities, TV and hospitality tray. The bar food is simple, straightforward pub fare of jacket potatoes, hotpots and sandwiches, representing good value for money. The inn stands at the head of the Itchen Valley on the edge of the pretty village of Cheriton, within easy reach of many popular tourist haunts, such as Winchester, the New Forest and the Watercress Line steam railway, which sells some of the pub's beers. Pets can be accommodated.

- ⊨ Two double; three twin-bedded rooms
- £ B&B £ £
- ◫ Cheriton Pots Ale, Best Bitter, Diggers Gold; guest beers (occasionally)
- ◖ Snacks and meals daily, lunchtime and evening (except Sunday evening)

—— DUNBRIDGE ——

Mill Arms

Barley Hill, near Romsey SO51 0LF

☎ *(01794) 340401*; FAX *(01794) 340401*
Directions: opposite Dunbridge station (12 minutes by rail from Southampton)

The guest rooms are a new addition at the Mill Arms, and it is very pleasing to note that they have taken the trouble to make the accommodation accessible to people with disabilities. It would be a shame to think that anyone might miss out on the delights that this excellent free house has to offer. In the centre of a picturesque village at the heart of the Test Valley, the pub is frequented by locals and passing ramblers and cyclists. The lounge bar is comfortably furnished with big shabby sofas and refectory tables, complete with newspapers and magazines to enjoy by the blazing log fires. Good bar food is served here and there is also a restaurant with a no-smoking area, offering a an inventive seasonal menu. Two house beers are supplied by local breweries, Hampshire and Itchen Valley. The pub boasts a skittle alley and is working hard to resurrect old traditions such as an annual tug o' war competition, rural sports day, morris dancing, etc. All the guest rooms offer en-suite accommodation. Pets can be catered for.

- ⊨ One double, four twin-bedded, one family room
- £ £ (££ in the double room)
- ◫ Beer range varies
- ◖ Snacks and meals daily, lunchtime and evening
- CC accepted

EASTON

Cricketers Inn

Easton, Winchester SO21 1EJ

☎ *(01962) 779353*

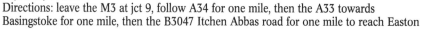

BRITISH INSTITUTE *of* INNKEEPING
MEMBER
SETTING *professional* STANDARDS

Directions: leave the M3 at jct 9, follow A34 for one mile, then the A33 towards Basingstoke for one mile, then the B3047 Itchen Abbas road for one mile to reach Easton

The Cricketers was closed by Whitbread in 1992 but has been built up again into a thriving village free house which serves the local community well. Traditional pub games, such as shove ha'penny and cribbage are still played in a bar cluttered with agricultural implements and cricketing memorabilia. Other pleasing features of the L-shaped bar are the open fireplace and the terrific selection of (mainly local) ales and traditional cider. Meals, served either in the bar or restaurant are very popular, which is not surprising, given the quality and value. The three bedrooms have recently been redecorated and updated to provide en-suite facilities. Although there is no special room, children are welcome to stay. Easton is a pretty little village of thatched cottages, bordering the river Itchen and convenient for country walks. Historic Winchester, famous for its Cathedral and Law Courts is just two miles away, whilst other local attractions include the Watercress Railway Line at Alresford (five miles) and Southampton's Ocean Village (15 miles).

⇥ Two double, one twin bedded room

£ ££

🍺 Beer range varies, with always five on tap

🍴 Snacks and meals daily, lunchtime and evening

CC accepted

HORNDEAN

Ship & Bell Hotel

6 London Road, Horndean PO8 0BZ

☎ *(01705) 592107;* FAX *(01705) 571644*

BRITISH INSTITUTE *of* INNKEEPING
MEMBER
SETTING *professional* STANDARDS

Directions: just off the A3(M)

A former coaching inn dating back to the 17th century, but now a family-run hotel offering good service in friendly, comfortable surroundings, this pub was the original home of Gale's Brewery, when it was established in 1847 by Richard Gale. The brewery has since moved next door (the pub is the brewery tap) and the hotel is pleased to offer brewery tour breaks. The pub itself is spacious with two nicely contrasting bars, featuring the history of the brewery, plus a restaurant. Meeting rooms and conference facilities are also available. The hotel accommodation is in a separate annexe, thus assuring a peaceful night's sleep. The 14 guest rooms all have en-suite bathrooms, and a cot and extra bed can be added for children. The 'Honeymoon' suite has a four-poster bed. All rooms have TV (with satellite options), direct dial telephone, and all the usual amenities. Chichester, Portsmouth and Southampton are all roughly 30 minutes' drive from Horndean, other attractions include Queen's Park (two miles away) and Marwell Zoo.

⇥ One single, six doubles, five twin-bedded rooms

£ ££ (single £££)

🍺 Gale's Butser, GB, HSB, seasonal beers; guest beers

🍴 Snacks and meals daily, lunchtime and evening (except Sunday evening)

CC accepted

—— MILFORD-ON-SEA ——

Red Lion,
32 High Street, Milford-on-Sea, Lymington SO41 0QD
☎ *(01590) 642236*

Situated on the fringes of the New Forest, this pub has welcomed travellers since it originally opened as a coaching inn 200 years ago. The accommodation is limited, with only three rooms, but these have recently been upgraded and offer private amenities,-for adults only. The dining area has also been refurbished and offers a smoke-free atmosphere for customers to enjoy their meals (those addicted to the evil weed may eat in the bar). Food and service is good and the atmosphere friendly, enhanced in winter by open log fires. This attractive old pub has a games area, a large garden and private car park. The elegant resort of Bournemouth which is good for shopping is 40 minutes' drive, as is Southampton, so the Red Lion would be a good stopover before embarking on a long sea voyage. Amateur sailors can take advantage of the facilities at nearby Lymington.

- ⇔ Three double rooms
- £ £
- ⑨ Flowers Original; Fuller's London Pride; Ringwood Best Bitter, True Glory
- ⑩ Snacks and meals daily, lunchtime and evening (except Sunday evening October-May)
- CC accepted

—— TOTFORD ——

Woolpack Inn
Totford, near Alresford SO24 9TJ
☎ *(01962) 732101;* FAX *(01962) 732889*
Directions: on the B3046 Alresford–Basingstoke road

A very pretty, flint-faced pub near Winchester, the Woolpack enjoys a rural setting, yet is convenient for the M3. Totford is reckoned to be the smallest hamlet in England, so will not take long to explore, leaving you free to spend time rambling along the Wayfarers Walk, and to visit other local attractions such as The Grange (one of Europe's great neo-classical monuments), Abbotstone lost village, the Watercress Steam Railway at Alresford and, of course, Winchester itself, once the capital of England. The pub has been carefully restored to retain its heavily beamed interior (even in the bedrooms), and the pleasant garden features a duck pond and a few amusements for children, who are welcome to stay overnight. Meals can be taken in the bars or restaurant, which offers an extensive menu. All ten bedrooms have ensuite shower and WC, TV, telephone and tea/coffee making facilities. Pets can be catered for. A courtesy car service is available for guests arriving by train (between 8am and 6pm)

- ⇔ Two double, eight twin-bedded rooms
- £ £ (single occupancy £££)
- ⑨ Cheriton Pots Ale; Gale's HSB; Palmers IPA; guest beer
- ⑩ Snacks and meals daily, lunchtime and evening
- CC accepted

—— VENTNOR ——

Spyglass Inn

Esplanade, Ventnor, Isle of Wight PO38 1JX
☎ *(01983) 855338*
Directions: on the seafront

The bed and breakfast accommodation at the Spyglass is a little different to most featured in this book. All the guest rooms are self-contained suites. Each has a double bedroom with en-suite bathroom, plus a lounge with French windows and a terrace overlooking the bay. The suites are well furnished and include a TV, as well as a sofa bed for additional guests. Breakfast is prepared by the guests themselves (so there is no restriction on time), in a kitchenette, with everything provided. You are not expected to do all your own cooking though – the Spyglass has an excellent restaurant, with a recommended seafood menu, or you can eat in the bar. Rosie Gibbs the owners' daughter is in charge of the kitchen, and she gets her much requested crabs and lobsters locally. At the bar you can try the local brew from the recently revived Ventnor Brewery. The inn dates back to 1870, and its original purpose was to serve as a bath house to the Royal Hotel. As befits a pub so close to the sea, every nook and cranny is given over to nautical artefacts and memorabilia.

- ⇥ Three doubles
- £ From £
- 🍺 Badger Dorset Best, Tanglefoot; Ventnor Golden Bitter; guest beer (occasionally)
- 🍴 Snacks and meals daily, lunchtime and evening
- **CC** accepted

—— WINCHESTER ——

Wykeham Arms

75 Kingsgate Street, Winchester SO23 9PE
☎ *(01962) 853834;* FAX *(01962) 854411*
Directions: Between the college and cathedral

In the last edition I described the Wykeham as quite possibly the perfect pub – a view confirmed by some very satisfied customers that took the trouble to write to me. Truly delightful, with scarcely an inch of its bare brick walls visible behind paintings, coats of arms and other memorabilia, it has retained two bars and many small rooms, heated only by log fires. Its attractive old furniture, much of it passed on from Winchester College, adds to its appeal. The food, which has won many accolades, is superb and imaginative, and the service is excellent. Above the pub are seven somewhat small but stylish bedrooms. However, since our last edition, a further six, more spacious and luxuriously appointed bedrooms, plus a suite on two floors, have been opened in a 16th-century annexe opposite, which overlooks Winchester College Chapel. All the rooms (in both buildings) have en-suite bathrooms, colour TV, mini bar and tea/coffee making facilities. Children are not catered for, but pets can be accommodated. Once you find the Wykeham, in Winchester's maze of narrow streets, you may encounter a parking problem, but really, you can't have everything!

- ⇥ Ten doubles, two twin-bedded rooms
- £ £££
- 🍺 Draught Bass; Gales Butser, GB, HSB
- 🍴 Snacks lunchtime; meals daily, lunchtime and evening (except Sunday)

TRY ALSO:

Milburys
Beauworth, Alresford SO24 0PB
☎ *(01962) 771248; FAX (01962) 771910*

Two rooms with shared facilities in the pretty village of Alresford at the head of the River Itchen. Good range of local ales. B&B £ (££ single occupancy)

Trout Inn
Itchen Abbas, near Winchester SO23 1BQ
☎ *(01962) 779537*

This smart country pub in the Itchen Valley changed hands just before we went to press, so any reports will be welcome. Six en-suite rooms

Bugle Hotel
The Square, Titchfield PO14 4AS
☎ *(01329) 841888*

17th-century hotel and restaurant, with a honeymoon suite. Ten rooms. B&B ££

HEREFORDSHIRE & WORCESTERSHIRE

—— AYMESTREY ——

Riverside Inn

Aymestrey, near Leominster, Herefordshire HR6 9ST
☎ *(01568) 708440;* FAX *(01568) 709058*
Directions: on the A4110, one mile north of Mortimers Cross

The evening before I sat down to write up this entry to the guide, I had enjoyed a memorable evening watching George Melly perform live. By coincidence, this consummate entertainer has delighted many people at the outdoor concerts staged in the grounds of this pub – his photo hangs in the bar. The 'stage' is an old bowling green in the grounds of a lovely half-timbered inn on the banks of the River Lugg, on the Welsh border. It is set in glorious countryside, at the start of the 25-mile waymarked Mortimer Trail. The old wool town of Leominster (six miles) is noted for its antique shops, whilst the medieval town of Ludlow (eight miles) is also well worth a visit. The Inn serves as the tap for the Woodhampton Brewery, which opened in 1997 on a neighbouring farm. To accompany your ale, you can choose from a mouthwatering seasonal menu presented by a French chef. There are four guest rooms at the inn (all but one are en-suite), plus two suites in a converted stable block. Each of these can sleep four people and has a private bathroom. Guests with disabilities are catered for, as are children. Pets can also be accommodated.

🛏 Three double, one twin-bedded room, plus two suites
£ £ – ££
🍺 Otter Bitter; Woodhampton Old Rooster, Jack Snipe, Kingfisher Ale, Ravens Head Stout, seasonal beers; guest beers
🍴 Snacks and meals daily, lunchtime and evening
CC accepted

—— BEWDLEY ——

George Hotel

Load Street, Bewdley, Worcestershire DY12 2AW
☎ *(01299) 402117;* FAX *(01299) 401269*

The George is a most attractive former coaching inn dating back to the 15th-century. Its bow-fronted windows look out on to a picturesque street at the centre of historic Bewdley. A warm welcome is assured at this family-run pub, with its cosy bars, coffee shop and award-winning restaurant. There are eleven guest rooms with en-suite facilities and all the usual modern amenities such as TV, telephone and tea/coffee making equipment. After exploring Bewdley itself, you could take off to Worcester (45 minutes' drive). Children, who are welcome to stay at the pub, will enjoy the steam train and safari park, which are both close by. Excellent fishing can be had on the River Severn which is just a few minutes' walk, or on the lakes which are a five-minute drive from the hotel. The George offers special rates (including dinner) for a two-night stay. Pets cannot generally be catered for, but an exception is made for guide dogs.

🛏 Two single, four double and five twin-bedded rooms
£ ££ (£££ single room)
🍺 Ind Coope Burton Ale; Tetley Bitter; guest beer
🍴 Snacks and meals daily, lunchtime and evening
CC accepted

—— BISHOP'S FROME ——

Chase Inn
Bishop's Frome, Herefordshire WR6 5BP
☎ *(01885) 490234;* FAX *(01885) 490547*
Directions: turn off the A4103, midway between Hereford and Worcester, on to the B4214 in the direction of Bromyard for one mile

This well-established, 19th-century hotel at the heart of a small, but thriving village, is painted in the traditional black and white of the locality. Well situated for touring the area, it stands opposite the village green with the Malvern Hills to the east, the Black Mountains to the west and in the south the Wye Valley and Symonds Yat. Rural pursuits such as bird watching, horse riding, fishing, cycling and rambling can all be enjoyed locally. More unusually, tours of a local hop farm are available. A relaxed, informal air is the norm at the pub which stages many special events and quizzes (not taken too seriously) are held twice a week. Its two bars maintain a good balance, with neither the drinking nor the dining areas dominating – diners can enjoy a wide-ranging menu and regular food theme evenings. The Chase is also popular with local business people for meetings and with foreign students on language courses who want to experience how the British people live in rural areas. The whole pub was refurbished in the early 1990s and while two of the bedrooms lack private bathrooms, they are all comfortable with the usual facilities. Guests have the choice of a full English or continental breakfast. The inn is accessible by public transport with mainline stations at Ledbury (eight miles) and other nearby towns. Children are welcome to stay.

ᾩ Three double, two twin-bedded rooms
£ £
🍺 Marston Best Bitter; SP Sporting Ales Winner; Wye Valley Bitter; guest beer (occasionally)
🍽 Snacks and meals daily, lunchtime and evening (residents only Sunday evening)
CC accepted

WHAT CAMRA DOES FOR BEER AND WHAT YOU CAN DO!

Thousands of pubs are being closed or ruined.
The Campaign for Real Ale campaigns
• locally to save individual pubs
• nationally on planning, licensing and tax laws
• with official bodies to extend 'listing' to historic pubs
• to encourage people to use their local pub

The grip of the multi-nationals and nationals is tightening
CAMRA campaigns against monopoly and national brands
• CAMRA promotes the independent brewers and publicises the many interesting new companies entering the market
• in 1997 CAMRA saved the vital guest beer law, threatened with abolition
• CAMRA acts as a vigorous consumer voice in Westminster, Whitehall and Brussels.

CAMRA is a non-profit making body run by an elected panel of volunteers. Add your voice and help safeguard your beer and your pub!

—— BROADWAY ——

Crown & Trumpet

Church Street, Broadway, Worcestershire WR12 7AE
☎ *(01386) 853202*
Directions: behind the village green

Broadway is a picture postcard village, full of honey-coloured buildings, of which the Crown & Trumpet is a fine example – the warm stone positively glows on a sunny day. In winter, its old oak beams and log fires provide an equally warm atmosphere in which to dine and sample the extensive range of real ales. An excellent bar menu, of mostly home-made dishes based on local produce, is served daily. This lively pub offers many attractions in the way of regular live entertainment, alongside a good selection of traditional pub games, including Evesham quoits. Broadway is popularly known as the 'Gateway to the Cotswolds' and provides an excellent base for touring. Evesham is just five miles away whilst Cheltenham and Stratford-on-Avon, both a short hop at 15 miles, are very popular with visitors. All the guest rooms have en-suite bathroom as well as TV and tea/coffee making facilities. There are no particular amenities for children, but they are welcome to stay. Pets can be accommodated by arrangement. Visitors staying out of season, or for an extended period, can usually benefit from more favourable rates (enquire when booking).

🛏 Three doubles, one twin-bedded room
£ £ – ££
🍺 Boddingtons Bitter; Flowers IPA, Original; Morland Old Speckled Hen; Stanway Stanney Bitter; Wadworth 6X; guest beer (occasionally)
🍴 Snacks and meals daily, lunchtime and evening
CC accepted

—— CLEOBURY MORTIMER ——

Kings Arms Hotel

Cleobury Mortimer, Worcestershire DY14 8BS
☎/FAX *(01299) 270252*
Directions: on the A1447, Kidderminster to Ludlow road

The Kings Arms presents a very pleasing appearance, its white-washed exterior is replete with hanging baskets and window boxes and it occupies a central position in the picturesque village of Cleobury Mortimer. Dating back to the 16th century, this former coaching inn enjoys a good local reputation for its excellent home-made food. Meals are served both in the delightful bar with its exposed beams and inglenook, and in the restaurant. Those staying two nights at the hotel can take advantage of the special dinner, bed and breakfast deals. There is plenty to occupy visitors for at least a two-day stay here, including two golf courses, a safari park and several NT properties to discover. There are also excellent local walks for ramblers. Beer buffs might enjoy a tour of Hobsons brewery, situated in a characterful building, once a farm granary, in the village. This would have to be arranged in advance (telephone Hobsons on 01299 270837). You can then repair back to the Kings Arms and enjoy their produce in comfort. The hotel has four en-suite rooms, all very well-appointed, with the usual amenities. Children are catered for.

🛏 Two double, two twin-bedded rooms
£ £
🍺 Hobsons Best Bitter, Town Crier; Taylor Landlord; guest beers
🍴 Snacks and meals daily, lunchtime and evening
CC accepted

—— DUNLEY ——

Dog Inn

Dunley, Stourport-on-Severn, Worcestershire DY13 0UE
☎/FAX *(01299) 822833*
Directions: two miles from Stourport on the A451 to Great Witley

In early summer, the Dog Inn is practically obscured behind the glorious wisteria that covers the front of the building – people came from far and wide just to see it. It certainly creates a good landmark for this pub in a quiet rural hamlet. Summer visitors can also enjoy the garden which overlooks open countryside, while their children (who can be accommodated for overnight stays) amuse themselves in the safe play area. The pub also boasts a crown bowling green. There is a snug in the pub, too, where families can retreat if the weather turns chilly. This two-bar inn is also known locally for its food, offering a traditional English menu with vegetarian options, washed down with either real ale or cider. The north Worcestershire countryside, opportunities for walking and fishing. Other attractions include the Severn Valley Steam Railway, the West Midland Safari Park and the magnificent ruin of Great Witley Court (where English Heritage has recently spend £1 million restoring its remarkable fountains). The reasonably priced accommodation includes two en-suite rooms, with either a bath or shower, and a further two that share a bathroom.

🛏 One double, three twin-bedded rooms
£ £
🍺 Banks's Bitter; Hobsons Best Bitter; Theakston Best Bitter; guest beers
🍽 Snacks and meals daily, lunchtime and evening
CC not accepted

—— KNIGHTWICK ——

Talbot

Knightwick, Worcester WR6 5PH
☎ *(01886) 821235;* FAX *(01886) 821060*
Directions: just off the A44, between Worcester and Leominster

The Talbot boasts a unique feature – it is the only pub in the country that brews its own beer from its own hops. Owned by the Clift family who have lived in the Teme Valley for 150 years, the pub is run by sisters Annie and Wiz, whilst brother Philip, is responsible for the 150-acre hop farm. The beer is not the only reason to come here though; the Talbot enjoys a delightful setting in possibly the most beautiful part of Worcestershire, on the banks of the River Teme, an area much favoured by naturalists (especially since otters have been reintroduced to the river). Cultural attractions of the area include the NT's Great Witley Court, the fine 15th-century half-timbered moat house at Lower Brockhampton – a rare example of its kind, and the Sculpture Trail in Brockhampton itself. The pub itself is a fine building, dating from the 14th century, with a lovely oak-panelled dining room. A more lively atmosphere prevails in the lounge bar, where an extensive menu is also served. The guest rooms are attractively decorated with period furniture; seven of them have en-suite bathrooms and two can accommodate an additional child's bed. Dogs can be catered for by arrangement.

🛏 Three single, five double and two twin-bedded rooms
£ ££ (£££ single room)
🍺 Hobsons Best Bitter; Teme Valley T'Other, This, That, Wot?
🍽 Snacks and meals daily, lunchtime and evening
CC accepted

—— LEDBURY ——

Royal Oak Hotel
Southend, Ledbury, Herefordshire HR8 2EY
☎ *(01531) 632110;* FAX *(01531) 634761*

This pub also has its own brewery – but not the hops to supply it. A brewery was first established on this site in 1841, but was closed down in 1921. It was reopened in 1997 and now supplies many other outlets as well as the Royal Oak. The resurrection of the brewery went hand in hand with a complete refurbishment of the hotel, after a change of ownership. The bar downstairs, although a bit pricey, is now very popular with a wide range of clientele, whilst redecoration of the upstairs lounge led to the exposing of wooden beams which had been covered up when the place was modernised in 1836. The pub has 15th-century origins, so has undoubtedly seen many changes over the years. The guest rooms have also been updated, and all but two of them offer en-suite facilities. Children are welcome to stay (they are charged £10 per night sharing their parents room), and pets can be accommodated. Ledbury is equidistant (15 miles) from Worcester, Gloucester and Hereford, while Cheltenham and Tewkesbury are just a little further, giving plenty of scope for places to visit.

🛏 Ten double rooms
£ ££
🍺 Ledbury Challenger, SB, seasonal beers; guest beers (occasionally)
🍴 Snacks lunchtime, meals daily, lunchtime and evening
CC not accepted

—— MALVERN ——

Malvern Hills Hotel
Wynds Point, Malvern, Worcestershire WR13 6DW
☎ *(01684) 540690;* FAX *(01684) 540327*
Directions: on the A449 between Malvern-Ledbury and the junction with the B432

High on the western slopes of the Malvern Hills, the hotel stands on a site where a hostelry was first built over 500 years ago (not early enough for the soldiers at the hill fort opposite which is one of the finest pre-Roman examples in the country). The 1999 *Good Beer Guide* describes the hotel as a 'comfortable, upmarket weekend retreat', an apt enough description. The oak-panelled Jenny Lind lounge is very stylish as is the candlelit Nightingales restaurant which offers a full menu, based on local produce. A simpler bar menu is also available, and a hot and cold buffet is served at lunchtime. The comfortable guest rooms are decorated in fresh country style; all have en-suite bathrooms, plus radio, TV, telephone and a welcome tray. The honeymoon suite boasts a four-poster bed. Local attractions include Eastnor Castle, Malvern Theatre and Elgar's birthplace at Lower Broadheath. The pub welcomes walkers who come to enjoy the breathtaking views. Pets can be accommodated.

🛏 Two single, eight double, four twin-bedded and two family rooms
£ £££ (reduction for children)
🍺 Hobsons Best Bitter; Morland Old Speckled Hen; Webster's Yorkshire Bitter; Wood Shropshire Lad; guest beer
🍴 Snacks and meals daily, lunchtime and evening
CC accepted

—— ST OWENS CROSS ——

New Inn

St Owens Cross, Hereford HR2 8LQ
☎ *(01989) 730274*
Directions: at the A4173/B4521 junction

You can't miss the New Inn at St Owens Cross – its half-timbered frontage is almost completely covered with hanging baskets – a presentation that has won awards for the publicans, Jane and Nigel Donovan. The pub has a plush but friendly lounge bar where informal meals are served. The second bar has been converted to a restaurant where the menu offers home-made meals based on local produce; a chef's daily specials board provides seasonal variety. The pub has an attractive, completely enclosed garden, which is ideal for families (children are welcome to stay overnight). Although there are only two letting rooms, they are both very well appointed with four-poster beds and full en-suite facilities, TV, etc. There are plenty of local attractions for country-lovers, including golf, fishing, horse-riding and rambling. The county town of Hereford itself is also well worth visiting, particularly for the cathedral (built by King Offa) and the famous Mappa Mundi, one of the earliest maps of the world (circa 1300).

    Two double rooms
£   £££
    Draught Bass; Bateman XB; Smiles Best Bitter; Tetley Bitter; Wadworth 6X; guest beers
    Snacks and meals daily, lunchtime and evening
CC accepted

—— TENBURY WELLS ——

Ship Inn

Teme Street, Tenbury Wells, Worcestershire WR15 8AE
☎ *(01584) 810269*

This attractive, bow-fronted, white-washed pub, a floral delight, stands on a pedestrianised street at the heart of the old market town of Tenbury Wells. A free house, it has been welcoming visitors to the town since the 17th century. I don't know if the menu was as good way back then, but certainly these days, the Ship has an excellent reputation for its food. The restaurant is a no-smoking area, but meals can also be taken in the bar. Unusually for a town-centre pub, the Ship has a large garden (ideal for any children who may be staying here). Set on the borders of Shropshire, Herefordshire and Worcestershire, there is plenty to see and do in the area, and some beautiful countryside to explore. The three, well-appointed guest rooms share a bathroom but they do have individual washing facilities and a TV. A full English breakfast is served. Pets can be accommodated.

    One single, two double rooms
£   £
    Hobsons Best Bitter, plus two or three different guest beers each week
    Snacks and meals daily, lunchtime and evening
CC accepted

——— WHITNEY-ON-WYE ———

Rhydspence Inn

Whitney-on-Wye, Herefordshire HR3 6EU
☎ *(01497) 831262;* FAX *(10497) 831751*
Directions: on the A438, one mile west of Whitney

Much altered since it was built as a manor house in the 14th century, the Rhydspence justly enjoys a fine reputation for its food and accommodation. This striking, timbered building lies on the border between England and Wales (the stream in the garden is the dividing line) and was as popular with drovers of ancient time as it is now with tourists. Both the public and the guest rooms are furnished and maintained to a very high standard. All the bedrooms have their own character, some featuring exposed timbers and one has a four-poster bed; others, in the newer part of the building, are generally larger and more modern in appearance. They all have en-suite bathrooms, TV and tea/coffee making facilities. Bargain breaks (minimum two nights) of dinner bread and breakfast are offered either Sunday-Thursday or Friday and Saturday. Both the bars are in the older part of the house and a variety of meals and snacks may be taken here. There is also a smart restaurant for more formal occasions but where service is friendly nonetheless and food is of high quality. The nearest town, Hay-on-Wye, is now world famous for its second-hand bookshops and the annual Literary Festival.

⛉ One single, six double rooms
£ *£££*
🍺 Draught Bass; Felinfoel Bitter; Robinson's Best Bitter
🍽 Snacks and meals daily, lunchtime and evening
CC accepted

TRY ALSO:

Three Kings Inn

Hanley Castle, Worcester WR8 0BL
☎ *(01684) 592686*

This unspoilt village pub has only one room to let but had to be included as it is such a CAMRA favourite. B&B £

HERTFORDSHIRE

— ALDBURY —

Greyhound Inn
19 Stocks Road, Aldbury, near Tring HP23 5RT
☎ *(01442) 851228;* FAX *(01442) 851495*
Directions: take Tring exit off the A41; Aldbury is signed from Tring

Aldbury is a charming little village right by the NT's Ashridge Forest and near the start of the Ridgeway long distance footpath. Ridgeway is also the name given to one of the beers brewed at the nearby independent Tring Brewery, who also supply the Greyhound with its house ale, Aldbury Ale. The pub is very traditional in style in keeping with the village which has a 13th-century church, a duckpond and ancient stocks to keep the villagers in order! The public bar has a huge inglenook, which is very effective in winter, the oak-beamed restaurant is ideal for intimate dining, and the characterful bedrooms, furnished with old pine and period pieces, are a delight to retire to. All ten rooms have en-suite bath or shower, TV and tea/coffee making facilities. The room rate does not include breakfast, leaving guests free to choose from the continental or full English available. Catering very much for tourists and weekenders, the room rates here are cheaper Monday-Thursday, but dinner bed and breakfast packages are available Friday-Sunday. Children under two are accommodated free. Local attractions include the Tring branch of the National History Museum, Whipsnade Zoo and Pendley

- ⊨ Seven double, two twin-bedded, one family room
- £ £ (££ weekend); single occupancy £££ (££££ weekend)
- ⊄ Draught Bass; Tring Ridgeway Bitter; fortnightly guest beer
- ⦿ Snacks and meals daily, lunchtime and evening
- CC accepted

— ARRINGTON —

Hardwicke Arms Hotel
Ermine Way, Arrington, near Royston SG8 0AH
☎ *(01223) 208802;* FAX *(01223) 208885*
Directions: five miles from Royston on the A1198 to Huntingdon

The Hardwicke Arms is an ancient inn – dating back to the 13th century – at the northern fringe of the county. It stands opposite Wimpole Hall which the NT describes as 'the most spectacular mansion in Cambridgeshire' and has a fine interior and landscaped grounds. Also worth a visit is Wimpole Home Farm, built in 1794 and now a favourite with families who enjoy the rare breeds and the adventure playground. Cambridge is just 15 minutes away by car, and Newmarket is only a little further. The hotel has attractive public rooms in its bars and the more formal, oak-panelled restaurant which offers a Sunday lunchtime carvery and fresh fish as a speciality on Thursdays. All but one of the guest bedrooms has en-suite bathrooms, and all have TV and tea/coffee making facilities. Pets can be accommodated by arrangement.

- ⊨ Two single, six double, two twin-bedded and two family rooms
- £ ££
- ⊄ Adnams Best Bitter; Greene King Bitter; Hook Norton Old Hooky
- ⦿ Snacks and meals daily, lunchtime and evening (except Sunday evening)
- CC accepted

—— HERTINGFORDBURY ——

Prince of Wales
244 Hertingfordbury Road, Hertingfordbury, near Hertford SG14 2LG
☎ *(01992) 581149*
Directions: 400 yards from the A414

The Prince of Wales is a good beer drinkers' pub, with at least six real ales on tap at all times. It can get very busy, but local CAMRA members recommend that visitors make way for Buster the dog when he gets thirsty! The patio area is particularly popular in summer. The seven guest rooms also get quite booked up, so it is worth reserving ahead. All the rooms are nicely furnished and comfortable with tea/coffee making facilities and TV; bathroom facilities are shared. Pets can be accommodated. There is a varied menu, with most of the food being prepared on the premises. Hertingfordbury is an ancient village, mentioned in the Domesday Book and set just a mile from Hertford, the attractive county town and home of McMullen's brewery. Other local places worth a visit are Hatfield House, the erstwhile home of Elizabeth I, and Knebworth House.

⊨ Three singles, four doubles
£ £ (££ single)
🍺 Dark Horse Sunrunner; Fuller's London Pride; McMullen AK; Wadworth 6X; guest beers
🍽 Snacks and meals daily, lunchtime and evening (residents only Sunday evening)

—— ST ALBANS ——

Lower Red Lion
36 Fishpool Street, St Albans AL3 4RX
☎ *(01727) 855669*
Directions: off the High Street, via George Street

A delightful old pub in one of the most charming old streets in St Albans, where once as many as 40 stage coaches a day clattered through, en route for London from the north. Historic in itself, this old beamed pub is surrounded by relics of the Roman city of Verulamium; part of the old city wall is preserved in Verulam Park nearby which also houses the Roman Museum with its fine collection of artefacts and mosaics. Just 20 minutes from London by train, the city of St Albans with its notable Abbey and market, is a popular spot with tourists. Many choose to stay in the traditional surroundings of the family-run Lower Red, whose bar is free of electronic interference and justly popular with locals. As one of the city's few free houses, it offers a good range of regularly changing guest ales. Two beer festivals are also hosted annually on May Day and August Bank Holiday. No evening meals are served (but the home-cooked lunches are very good) and there is a good choice of restaurants within walking distance. The guest rooms are cosy and comfortable, just two of them have en-suite facilities. Children are welcome to stay.

⊨ Two single, two double, three twin-bedded and one family room
£ £
🍺 Fuller's London Pride; Oakham JHB; four guest beers
🍽 Snacks and meals lunchtime, Monday to Saturday.
CC accepted

—— WARESIDE ——

Chequers Inn

Wareside, near Ware SG12 7QY
☎ *(01920) 467010*
Directions: on the B1004 between Ware and Much Hadham

Guests are not exactly provided with 'B&B' here, but rather 'E & B' as the very reasonable prices include an evening meal rather than breakfast. This 400-year old pub has a cottagey feel to it, helped by an open fire and friendly atmosphere. There are three bars as well as a snug, complemented by a 40-seater restaurant. A house beer is brewed specially for the pub by the Dark Horse Brewery, based in nearby Hertford, which is also home to the bigger independent, McMullen's, and is worth a visit for its antique shops and castle. The Chequers is very popular with ramblers, and there is a choice of a three or five-mile waymarked circuit that starts from the pub. The three guest rooms share a bathroom. Children can be accommodated although there are no special facilities.

- ⇔ Two single, one twin-bedded room
- £ £
- 🍺 Adnams Bitter; Greene King Abbot; guest beers
- 🍽 Snacks and meals daily, lunchtime and evening (except Sunday evening)
- **CC** accepted

ISLE OF MAN: SEE OFFSHORE BRITAIN
ISLE OF WIGHT: SEE HAMPSHIRE & ISLE OF WIGHT

KENT

—— CANTERBURY ——

Old Gate Inn

162-164 New Dover Road, Canterbury, Kent CT1 3EL
☎ *(01227) 452154; FAX (01227) 456561*
Directions: off the A2 and the junction with the Old Dover Road

BRITISH INSTITUTE *of* INNKEEPING
MEMBER
SETTING *professional* STANDARDS

My husband discovered this pub for me just after Christmas, when travelling with our teenage son. They were beginning to give up hope of finding anywhere serving lunch at 4 o'clock in the afternoon, when my sharp-eyed son spotted the pub's notice saying food served all day. They kept going on about the great food for days afterwards. They were made to feel very welcome and found it hard to leave, having settled themselves in front of one of the three open fires. The pub has a good atmosphere enhanced by mismatched furnishings, beamed ceilings and wooden floors. The comfortable guest rooms are attractively furnished and have TV, telephone, hot drinks facilities and a hairdryer. All but two of the rooms have en-suite bathroom. Unfortunately, children are not accepted as overnight guests. It is just a few minutes into the centre of Canterbury, which can get very busy with tourists, especially French people on day trips, and students on foreign exchanges, but there is also some delightful countryside and villages to explore in this corner of Kent.

- ⊨ One single, seven double, two twin-bedded rooms
- £ £ (single ££)
- ◉ Draught Bass; Hancock's HB
- ◉ Snacks and meals daily, at any time
- CC accepted

—— CHIDDINGSTONE CAUSEWAY ——

Little Brown Jug

Chiddingstone Causeway, near Tonbridge TN11 8JJ
☎ *(01892) 870318; FAX (01892) 870563*
Directions: on the B2027 Tonbridge–Edenbridge road, opposite Penshurst station

This family-owned and -run free house is well situated for exploring the 'Garden of England', being very close to such historic houses as Penshurst Place, Hever Castle and Chartwell, former home of Winston Churchill. The pub itself is an imposing building of much architectural interest, dating from the time of the railway boom, but enjoying very rural surroundings. It is set in a large garden, with a safe play area which is a boon for any families staying. The pub enjoys a good reputation for its food, the extensive menu includes a vegetarian selection and a choice of roast meats on Sunday. Meals can be enjoyed either in the spacious bar or dining room. The bedrooms are completely self-contained, allowing guests to be free to come and go as they wish. They all have en-suite bathrooms, TV and tea/coffee making facilities. One room on the ground floor may be suitable for guests with mobility problems, although it has no special facilities. Pets can be accommodated.

- ⊨ Two double, four twin-bedded rooms
- £ ££
- ◉ Courage Best Bitter; Morland Old Speckled Hen; guest beers
- ◉ Snacks and meals daily, lunchtime and evening
- CC accepted

—— CLAYGATE ——

White Hart
Claygate, Marden, near Tonbridge TN12 9PL
☎ *(01892) 730313*
Directions: on the B2162, midway between Yalding and Horsmonden

A Victorian inn, set in open countryside amongst the hop gardens and orchards, this pub provides an ideal base for tourists. One of the country's most visited stately homes, Leeds Castle, is ten miles away and even closer is the fairytale Scotney Castle. Gardening addicts can visit Vita Sackville-West's famous gardens at Sissinghurst Castle (ten miles), or the more unusual Yalding Organic Garden, just three miles away. Home-cooked food, including choices from the daily specials board, is served in the bar or restaurant (booking advised). Meals can also be enjoyed in good weather in the large garden. Local Biddenden cider complements the three cask ales, two of which are Kentish brews. The four bedrooms have en-suite facilities with either a bath or shower, plus TV and tea/coffee making facilities. An iron, trouser press and hairdryer are available on request. The reasonably priced accommodation is not suitable for children, but pets can be catered for. A full English breakfast is served.

🛏 One single, one double, two twin-bedded rooms
£ £
🍺 Goacher's Light; Shepherd Neame Master Brew Bitter; Wadworth 6X
🍴 Snacks and meals daily, lunchtime and evening
CC not accepted

—— ELHAM ——

Rose & Crown
High Street, Elham, near Canterbury CT4 6TD
☎ *(01303) 840226;* FAX *(01303) 840141*
Directions: turn off the M20 at jct 12, follow the A20 signs to the Channel Tunnel, at first roundabout take Elham turn

One of my favourite antique shops in this area of Kent is in Elham, so I always have two good reasons for visiting this charming little village when I'm down this way. The second reason is a good lunch – either at the Kings Arms in the square or at the Rose and Crown, I've not personally tried the pub's accommodation (my mum puts me up for nothing!), but I have peeked through the windows and it looks fine. The rooms were only converted in 1997 from a stable block around the courtyard behind the pub; they all have en-suite bathrooms and are large enough to add an extra bed for a child. As they are all on the ground floor, they are accessible to guests with disabilities. The Rose and Crown served for many years as a coaching stop on the way to Dover, and was apparently frequented by the man Baroness Orczy used as a model for the hero in her novel, *The Scarlet Pimpernel*. It still is an ideal stopover to travellers to the continent, particularly for the Channel Tunnel. The comfortable, half-timbered bar and (no-smoking) restaurant are warmed by open fires, and offer a varied menu.

🛏 Five double, one twin-bedded room
£ ££
🍺 Beer range varies, usually four on top
🍴 Snack and meals daily, lunchtime and evening
CC accepted

—— EASTLING ——

Carpenters Arms

The Street, Eastling, near Faversham ME13 0AZ
☎ *(01795) 890234;* FAX *(01795) 890654*
Directions: leave the M2 at jct 6 and follow signs from A2 in Faversham

I grew up in Kent, when hops were just beginning to fade from much of the rural landscape. Now, sadly, very few hopfields are left at all, leaving just the photographs and other memorabilia recording the days when teams of hop-pickers travelled down from London to join in the harvest. A collection of old hop-picking photos is one of the highlights of the Carpenters Arms. This 14th-century brick and timbered country pub oozes character: both the delightful bar and the restaurant feature inglenooks – the one in the brick-floored, candlelit dining room boasts a bread oven. Good food, on a menu which combines traditional English and continental dishes, is served both in the restaurant and the bar. A hearty English breakfast is provided. The beers come from Shepherd Neame in nearby Faversham which celebrated its tercentenary in 1998 and is believed to be the oldest brewery in continuous operation in the country. The guest bedrooms are in a detached, weatherboarded lodge next to the pub, offering a quiet night's rest with en-suite bathrooms, TV, radio and tea/coffee making facilities. Children over 12 years old are welcome. Local attractions include Leeds Castle and Belmont House (clock collection).

🛏 Three double rooms
£   £ (single occupancy £££)
🍺 Shepherd Neame Master Brew Bitter, Spitfire, Bishops Finger, seasonal beer
🍴 Snacks and meals daily, lunchtime and evening (except Sunday evening)
CC accepted

—— FOLKESTONE ——

Clifton Hotel

The Leas, Folkestone CT20 2EB
☎/ FAX *(01303) 851231*
Directions: on the seafront; from M20 follow signs for the seafront

Folkestone's heyday as a family resort, when people used to flock from London to spend a week at the seaside, are sadly long gone, and its grand hotels have been converted into elegant apartment buildings. The Clifton is one of the few sizeable hotels to have survived, and that is partly due to its position on The Leas, a very wide, attractive promenade overlooking the English Channel (on a clear day you can see France). Although cross Channel ferries no long use Folkestone Harbour, the town is only 15 minutes from the port of Dover and passengers using the Channel Tunnel find this privately owned hotel a useful overnight stop. Families are welcome; there is a children's room and garden. The bar is comfortable and quiet and serves an excellent pint of Bass, whilst the lounge is slightly more plush and boasts sea views. The bar menu offers standard pub fare at reasonable prices. The comfortable, nicely decorated bedrooms all have en-suite facilities, and some can accommodate guests with disabilities. Special rates for short breaks on request. Pets can be accommodated.

🛏 17 single, 39 doubles, 15 twin-bedded and nine family rooms
£   £££ (single ££££)
🍺 Draught Bass; Courage Directors
🍴 Snacks and meals daily, lunchtime and evening
CC accepted

—— LITTLEBOURNE ——

King William IV
4 High Street, Littlebourne, Canterbury CT3 1ST
☎/FAX *(01227) 721244*
Directions: on the A257 road to Sandwich from Canterbury

This well maintained village inn stands on the main road, just a little way outside Canterbury. The public bar has a good local following, and hosts league darts matches and quiz nights. Meals can be taken here or in the restaurant, and can be washed down with the Kentish ales from Shepherd Neame or traditional cider. Visitors can easily while away a day or more in Canterbury. The cathedral of course has been a major draw ever since the first pilgrims came to worship at the shrine of St Thomas Becket (famously murdered in the cathedral because of his disagreement with Henry II). Today's visitors can experience some of the conditions early pilgrims encountered by visiting the Canterbury Tales exhibition which brings to life some of Chaucer's stories. Canterbury is also good for shopping, with a pedestrianised main street, where you will find an abundance of gift shops, antique shops and tea rooms. Its main drawback is the parking, so try if you can, to leave your car at the King William. The pub has seven en-suite guest rooms, and is popular with ramblers.

- ⇥ One single, three double, two twin-bedded and one family room
- £ £ (££ single room)
- 🍺 Draught Bass; Fuller's London Pride; Shepherd Neame Master Brew Bitter
- 🍽 Snacks lunchtime; meals daily, lunchtime and evening
- CC accepted

—— WINGHAM ——

Dog Inn,
Canterbury Road, Wingham CT3 1AB
☎ *(01227) 720339*
Directions: five miles east of Canterbury on A257 to Sandwich

BRITISH INSTITUTE of INNKEEPING
MEMBER
SETTING *professional* STANDARDS

Just a mile further on from Littlebourne towards Sandwich, you come to the little village of Wingham where the early 13th-century Dog Inn is ready to receive pilgrims (or tourists). Overnight accommodation at this characterful inn is offered in quaint little rooms, but they do all have en-suite bathrooms. A full English breakfast is served, whilst main meals can be taken in either a smoking, or non-smoking dining area (or outside in the garden in good weather). Wingham is convenient for Canterbury and the coast. Other local attractions include Goodnestone Gardens (three miles away) and the delightful old town of Sandwich, with its weatherboarded houses. Sandwich is one of the original Cinque Ports, as is nearby Deal, which is well worth a visit to see Walmer Castle, once the home of the Duke of Wellington (indeed he died there), and is full of Wellington memorabilia – including his boots! Julius Caesar landed with his troops on the beach at Deal, and children especially would enjoy a trip to the White Cliffs Experience at nearby Dover, which vividly tells the story of this part of Kent from the Roman invasion to the building of the Channel Tunnel. Children are welcome to stay at the pub, and pets can also be accommodated.

- ⇥ One single, two double, one twin-bedded and two family rooms
- £ £
- 🍺 Flowers Original; Shepherd Neame Master Brew Bitter; Wadworth 6X; guest beer (occasionally)
- 🍽 Snack and meals daily, lunchtime and evening
- CC accepted

Lancashire

—— Balderstone ——

Myerscough

Smithy Road, Balderstone, Blackburn BB2 7LE
☎ *(01254) 812222*
Directions: from jct 31 of the M6 follow signs for Clitheroe (two miles)

This pub in the Ribble Valley might make a good choice for travellers with business in Blackburn, but who would rather stay in a country inn than the town itself. Close to the entrance of Salmesbury Aerodrome (and very convenient for the M6), the Myerscough has a cosy atmosphere in its wood-panelled lounge and separate room for non-smokers, which has an open fire. Good quality meals can be served in either room (evening meals finish at 8.30). The guest rooms are a recent addition to the pub and all have en-suite facilities. The prices quoted are for the room only – breakfast is charged separately.

The accommodation is not suitable for children.
⇥ Three double rooms
£ Room rate £
🍺 Robinson's Hatters Mild, Hartleys XB, Best Bitter
🍴 Snacks and meals daily, lunchtime and evening
CC accepted

—— Belmont ——

Black Dog

2-4 Church Street, Belmont, near Bolton BL7 8AB
☎ *(01204) 811218*
Directions: follow the A666 from Bolton, then the A675 (also accessible via the M65, jct 3)

Belmont is a moorland village five miles north of Bolton, surrounded by excellent fell walking country in beautiful scenery. Originally a farm, the Black Dog became a tavern in 1825, brewing its own beer (alas no more). Today it is a popular, homely pub, where Jim Pilkington, the landlord, eschews a jukebox, but whistles along to tapes of classical music. There is a rare treat if you happen to visit on New Year's Day, as the pub hosts an annual Viennese concert with a live ten-piece orchestra. The inn has several rooms; none of them is designated as a restaurant, but lunches and evening meals are available for residents. You are assured of a peaceful night's sleep as none of the rooms is above the bar. They all have en-suite bathrooms, as well as TV and tea/coffee making facilities. One is suitable for use by families (children under 11 years old stay free). With a full English breakfast included in the price, the Black Dog represents good value. If you have business in Manchester (the city centre is 12 miles away) you may prefer to stop off here.

⇥ One double, one twin-bedded and one family room
£ £ (single occupancy ££)
🍺 Holt Mild, Bitter
🍴 Snacks and meals daily, lunchtime and evening
CC not accepted

—— BLACKPOOL ——

Ramsden Arms Hotel

204 Talbot Road, Blackpool FY1 3AZ
☎ *(01253) 623215*
Directions: near the town centre on the A586

Local CAMRA members describe the Ramsden Arms as a rare, unspoilt, classic. The proprietors, the Caffreys describe it as a 'country' style pub on the fringe of Blackpool town centre. The imposing Tudor-style exterior opens into an oak-panelled interior crammed with bric-a-brac and memorabilia. A favourite with American visitors, it feels like a real pub, not a town bar. It offers an unrivalled range of real ales, and a terrific selection of pub games. Children are welcome in the games room until 8 pm and can also be accommodated overnight. Convenient for non-drivers as it is close to both the rail and bus stations, it is also just a five-minute stroll away from Blackpool's famous attractions. The pub does not serve evening meals, but there's plenty of restaurants nearby to choose from. Only one of the rooms has an en-suite bathroom, and the owners point out that the prices stay the same all year round, and do not take a hike in the summer. They say "be different, not disappointed, stay at an English pub at a fraction of hotel prices". Hear, hear.

🛏 Three twin-bedded rooms
£ £
🍺 Boddingtons Bitter; Ind Coope Burton Ale; Marston's Pedigree; Morland Old Speckled Hen, Tetley Mild, Bitter; Ushers Rascals Bitter; guest beers
🍽 Snacks and meals Monday-Saturday lunchtime
CC not accepted

—— BURNLEY ——

Sparrow Hawk

Church Street, Burnley BB11 2DN
☎ *(01282) 421551;* FAX *(01282) 456506*
Directions: on the A682 inner ring road

Although this hotel, on Burnley's ring road, looks rather imposing, the main bar has a good atmosphere and is tended by friendly, helpful staff. The oldest pub in the town, it is well liked by local CAMRA members not just for its ale – there is a constantly changing range of three guest beers – but also for the occasional traditional cider in summer. All the guest bedrooms are en-suite and are well-appointed with radio, TV, telephone and tea/coffee making equipment. The Sparrowhawk has conference facilities for up to 80 delegates, making it popular with business folk. I'm told the home-cooked lunchtime bar meals are 'superb', whilst the more formal restaurant is open in the evenings. A full English breakfast is served to set you up for the day.

🛏 Ten single, 15 double, nine twin-bedded and two family rooms
£ ££
🍺 Moorhouse's Premier, Pendle Witches Brew; Theakston Best Bitter; guest beers
🍽 Snacks and meals daily, lunchtime and evening
CC accepted

——— ENTWISTLE ———

Strawbury Duck Hotel

Overshores Road, Entwistle, Bolton BL7 0LU
☎ *(01204) 852013*
Directions: from the A676 Bolton–Burnley road, take the B6391 towards Turton, then follow signs to Entwistle

In a secluded spot, in a lovely rural area near the Pennine moors, the Strawbury Duck is a homely country pub and hotel, parts of which date back 300 years. Despite its relative isolation it is always busy, particularly with visitors on walking holidays. There are several country parks and nature conservation areas nearby. Turton Tower, which has connections with Oliver Cromwell, is also worth a visit. Situated just yards from the station (indeed it was formerly the Station Hotel), the pub is easily accessible by rail from Manchester and Blackburn. Three of the bedrooms feature four-poster beds; all the rooms have private bathrooms. There is an extensive menu, including a good choice of Indian and Balti dishes and a special section for children. Children are welcome in the pub itself until 8.30 pm and can stay overnight. A choice of full English or continental breakfast is available.

- ⇆ Three double, one twin-bedded rooms
- £ £ (single occupancy ££)
- ⌷ Moorhouse's Pendle Witches Brew; Taylor Landlord; guest beer
- ⌷ Snacks and meals daily, lunchtime (except Monday), and evening (food served all day Saturday and Sunday)
- CC accepted

——— GARSTANG ———

Royal Oak Hotel

Market Place, Garstang, Preston PR3 1ZA
☎ *(01995) 603318;* FAX *(01995) 606529*
Directions: off the A6 on the one-way system in the town centre

The Royal Oak is a small, family-run hotel, with its origins in the 15th century when it was a farmhouse. It was extended in the late 17th-century to become a coaching inn and has recently been sympathetically refurbished with care taken to retain its character. The overnight accommodation is in nine well decorated and comfortably appointed guest rooms (all en-suite) with the usual amenities, including TV. Some rooms are suitable for guests with disabilities. There is a 40-seat restaurant, and an attractive lounge bar, where meals may also be taken. Garstang is popularly thought of as the 'Gateway to the Lake District'. It is a pleasant little market town, near the picturesque Forest of Bowland, so there is plenty to see and do locally, and Preston is easily accessible via the M6. Children are welcome to stay and pets can be accommodated.

- ⇆ Two single, five double and two twin-bedded rooms
- £ £ (££ single room)
- ⌷ Robinson's Hatters Mild, Hartleys XB, Best Bitter
- ⌷ Snacks and meals daily, lunchtime and evening (food available all day Sunday)
- CC accepted

—— GREAT HARWOOD ——

Royal Hotel

Station Road, Great Harwood BB6 7BA
☎ *(01254) 883541*
Directions: three miles from the M65 and ten miles from the M6 (jct 31), half a mile from the town centre

At this friendly free house, the owners, Pamela and Martin Hughes make a point of buying their beers from smaller independent breweries (there's usually four on tap). The same care is taken in the kitchen – Pamela does most of the cooking for the pub, using fresh local produce whenever possible. The Royal is a well maintained, open-plan Victorian pub, a regular CAMRA award-winner which enjoys a good local following (particularly with the athletics and cycling clubs). Blackburn Rovers fans can be at the ground in five minutes, and it is convenient for Manchester Airport (45 minutes). Great Harwood itself is a small mill town surrounded by the Pennine moors, including Pendle Hill (famous for its 17th-century witches). The lovely Ribble Valley and the Trough of Bowland are also easily accessible. The guest rooms are modern, with all but one having en-suite facilities and all have TV. There is no accommodation for children. Pets can be catered for by prior arrangement – Martin says the bar is dog friendly as long as the house cat doesn't object.

- ⊨ Two single, two twin-bedded rooms
- £ ££
- ⊪ Black Sheep Best Bitter; Moorhouse's Premier; guest beers
- ⦿ Snacks and meals lunchtime (except Monday and Tuesday) and evening
- CC not accepted

—— HAWKSHEAD ——

Red Lion Hotel

81 Ramsbottom Road, Hawkshead, near Bury BL8 4JS
☎ *(01204) 852539;* FAX *(01204) 853998*
Directions: on the A676 from Burnley

The Red Lion makes a good choice for business people as it offers favourable corporate rates and is very convenient for Manchester City centre (eight miles) and Bolton (three miles). It is within easy reach of all the regional motorways (M62, M6, M56 and M66). This upmarket country inn is decorated to a high standard and the same goes for the guest rooms, which all offer en-suite facilities. A full English breakfast is provided and other meals can be taken in either the bar or restaurant. Set in the Pennine Valley, there is much to offer tourists too, with the East Lancs steam railway station at Ramsbottom (two miles away) a popular attraction. The hotel offers reduced weekend and long-stay rates. Children are welcome.

- ⊨ Two double, three twin-bedded rooms
- £ £££
- ⊪ Jennings Dark Mild, Bitter, Cumberland Ale; guest beer
- ⦿ Snacks and meals daily, lunchtime and evening (food available all day Sun)
- CC accepted

—— LITTLE ECCLESTON ——

Cartford Hotel
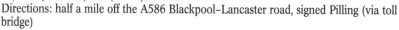

Cartford Lane, Little Eccleston, near Preston PR3 0YP
☎ *(01995) 670166;* FAX *(01995) 671785*
Directions: half a mile off the A586 Blackpool–Lancaster road, signed Pilling (via toll bridge)

The Cartford, perennially popular with CAMRA members, is delightfully situated by the toll bridge over the River Wyre in one of the most picturesque parts of the Fylde. It boasts one and a half miles of fishing rights, and there's lots of scope for riverside and country walks. Also nearby are Blackpool (15 minutes' drive), historic Lancaster and the scenic Trough of Bowland. The pub is over 200 years old and offers a good selection of real ales, including those from the Hart Brewery which opened in 1994. Situated behind the hotel, this is the only brewery on the Fylde (tours are available by prior arrangement, telephone 01995 671686). The hotel also offers a good range of meals (many home-cooked), including daily specials, either in the bar or the gallery dining area. A pizza menu is available in the evenings too. Families are made very welcome here, children staying overnight are charged reduced rates. The garden, overlooking the river, has a play area. All the rooms have modern furnishings and en-suite bathrooms, TV, etc. Small pets can be accommodated.

🛏 One single, two double, one twin-bedded and two family rooms
£ £ (££ single room)
🍺 Boddingtons Bitter; Hart Brewery beers (variable); guest beers
🍽 Snacks and meals daily, lunchtime and evening
CC accepted

—— WHALLEY ——

Swan Hotel
62 King Street, Whalley, near Clitheroe BB7 9SN
☎ *(01254) 822195;* FAX *(01254) 824875*
Directions: off the A59, near the M6 jct 31

In a recent biography, the Queen mentioned that given the choice, she would like to retire to the Ribble Valley, which is certainly a beautiful area. Given her love of the turf, maybe the Swan would become her local. Horse racing is the main theme at the Swan; indeed, the hotel owns no less than six racehorses, and their exploits are followed with great interest by the locals. Visitors with other sporting interests are also well provided for here. There are six golf courses and three rivers for angling within three miles of the hotel, while football fans can get to either Blackburn Rovers or Burnley grounds quite easily from Whalley. The Swan is a 17th-century coaching inn, family-run and offering excellent ale (the landlord is a CAMRA member), an occasional traditional cider, good food and accommodation. The five spacious bedrooms all have en-suite bathrooms and are comfortably appointed. Children are welcome to stay.

🛏 Two double, three twin-bedded and one family room
£ £ (single occupancy ££)
🍺 Boddingtons Bitter; Moorhouse's Premier; Thwaites Bitter; Wadworth 6X; guest beer
🍽 Snacks and meals daily, from noon-9 pm
CC accepted

TRY ALSO:

Saddle Inn
Sidgreaves Lane, Lea Town, near Preston PR4 0RS
☎ *(01772) 786982*

A Thwaites house, 15 minutes from Blackpool, yet a real country pub with two letting rooms.
B&B £

WHAT CAMRA DOES FOR BEER

Thousands of pubs are being closed or ruined.
The Campaign for Real Ale campaigns
• locally to save individual pubs
• nationally on planning, licensing and tax laws
• with official bodies to extend 'listing' to historic pubs
• to encourage people to use their local pub

WHAT CAMRA DOES FOR YOU
• All CAMRA members receive our monthly newspaper, What's Brewing. It gives hard news from the world of beer and pubs – advance notice of festivals and events as well as information about new beers and breweries.
• We sell a wide range of books, including local guides.
• CAMRA branches run beer festivals, brewery trips, pub visits and other social activities.

Members of CAMRA are ordinary drinkers motivated solely by a love of good beer – they are all ages, both sexes, and from all walks of life.

JOIN TODAY
You're welcome to get involved.
CAMRA has been called 'Europe's most successful consumer organisation' – but we still need your help.
CAMRA is run locally and nationally by elected, unpaid volunteers.
CAMRA is a not-for-profit body and is completely independent of any commercial interest.
CAMRA relies totally on people like you for funds and support.
Help us stand up for the rights and choice of ordinary drinkers.

LEICESTERSHIRE, RUTLAND AND NORTHAMPTONSHIRE

—— BARNWELL ——

Montagu Arms

Barnwell, near Oundle, Northants PE8 5PH
☎/FAX *(01832) 273726*
Directions: off the A605, by the River Oundle

As I write this, my son has just been telling me about his school English project on ghost stories. Some of his tales have made my flesh crawl, and not a few of them concern pubs, so it may be some while before I want to try this particular hostelry, which is said to be haunted. However, that will be my loss as the Montagu Arms is, according to local CAMRA members, a fine stone-built 17th-century house. It features a spacious, characterful, heavily timbered bar (where meals can be taken), as well as a no-smoking restaurant, offering an adventurous menu, and a games room. The large garden has a play area, with a recently built adventure playground and a crazy golf course which appeals to 'children' of all ages. There is also a campsite, but families are welcome to stay overnight in the pub itself. The guest rooms are all en-suite and are well equipped with TV, radio, tea/coffee making facilities, etc. The pub is situated on the Nene Way, which is popular with walkers, and one of its nearest neighbours is Royal Barnwell, home of Princess Alice, the Queen Mother's sister.

🛏 Five twin-bedded rooms
£ £
🍺 Adnams Bitter, Broadside; Bateman XB, XXXB; Flowers IPA, Original; Hop Back Summer Lightning; guest beers
🍽 Snacks and meals daily, lunchtime and evening
CC accepted

—— BELTON ——

George Hotel,

Market Place, Belton, near Loughborough, Leics LE12 9UH
☎/FAX *(01530) 222426*
Directions: off the B5324, three miles from the junction of the M42 with the M1 (jct 23a)

This attractive inn stands on what was believed to be the old Burton-Nottingham coaching route in the charming village of Belton. Sympathetically restored, the beamed bar features an unusual raised central fireplace, while the intimate restaurant displays a mural signed by A Johnson and dated 1852 which was uncovered during the renovations. Bar meals are available and in fine weather they can be eaten outside under the shadow of the village maypole (which is still put to use every May Day). The majority of the comfortable guest rooms have en-suite bathrooms, and all have TV, radio, telephone and tea/coffee making facilities. Pets can be accommodated. The pub is very convenient for the East Midlands Airport and Donington Park with its race track and Motor Museum. Other tourist destinations within easy reach include Twycross Zoo and Melbourne Hall, while both Derby and Nottingham would be worth of a day trip.

🛏   One single, nine double, 11 twin-bedded and two family rooms
£   £ (££ single)
🍺   Courage Directors; Marston's Pedigree; John Smith's Bitter
🍽   Snacks and meals daily, lunchtime and evening
CC accepted

—— BLAKESLEY ——

Bartholomew Arms

High Street, Blakesley, Towcester NN12 8RE
☎ *(01327) 860292*
Directions: four miles off A5; three miles off A43 at Silverstone

As we went to press, the guest rooms at the Bartholomew Arms were in the process of being upgraded to feature all en-suite facilities, recarpeted and redecorated. Everything is planned to be complete for the summer season of 1999. The prices may therefore change from those quoted below, so check when booking. Whatever you pay for your room includes one of the pub's renowned breakfasts. Extremely hearty, they will set you up for a day's race-going at nearby Towcester (for horse lovers) or Silverstone for the four-wheeled variety. This unspoilt village local has a very friendly atmosphere. Children are welcome to stay and pets can be accommodated.

🛏   Two double, two twin-bedded rooms
£   £
🍺   Ansells Bitter; Marston's Pedigree; Tetley Bitter; guest beer
🍽   Snacks and meals daily, lunchtime and evening (except Sunday evening)
CC accepted

—— GLOOSTON ——

Old Barn Inn

Andrews Lane, Glooston, near Market Harborough, Leicestershire LE16 7ST
☎/FAX *(01858) 545215*
Directions: Glooston can be reached from the A47 (via Hallaton, or from the A6 (via Langtons and Stanton Wyville)

The mouthwatering, imaginative menu which changes on a monthly basis would be enough to make me want to stay here (once a month possibly!). Owners Charles Edmondson-Jones and Stewart Sturge have won many awards for their restaurant, and rightly so. Another major factor in the inn's favour is the lack of passing traffic – it stands in a tiny hamlet on an old Roman road, which now has no through route. That, and the absence of piped music, make it ideal as a peaceful rural retreat. Dating back to the 16th century, replete with oak beams and an open fire, the Old Barn stands in an area steeped in history. It is within easy reach of ancient battle grounds and the old town of Stamford, whilst more energetic pursuits can be enjoyed on nearby Rutland Water and there are ample opportunities for country walks. The owners stipulate that 'well-behaved' children are welcome (those sharing their parents' room are charged just for breakfast). Pets can also be accommodated. The guest rooms have en-suite showers, TV and the usual amenities.

- ⇔ Two double and one family room
- £ **££** (**£££** single occupancy)
- 🍺 Theakston Best Bitter; three guest beers
- 🍽 Snacks and meals available weekend lunchtimes and every evening except Sunday
- **CC** accepted

—— SUDBOROUGH ——

Vane Arms

Main Road, Sudborough, Northants NN14 3BX
☎ *(01832) 733223*
Directions: just off the A6116, between Brigstock and Thrapston

Perennially popular – indeed often packed out – this village pub really lives up to the definition of a free house. A regular local CAMRA award-winner, it offers no less than nine real ales at all times, which are changed frequently and include some pretty rare brews, plus draught Belgian beers and a range of country wines. This delightful stone and thatched house has a small upstairs restaurant that has an excellent home-cooked menu, specialising in Mexican dishes (the licensees are American) and bar meals are also available. Traditional games such as skittles, darts and pool are played. The three pleasant guest rooms all have en-suite facilities, featuring whirlpool spa baths, plus TV, telephone and tea/coffee making equipment. Sudborough is a conservation village featuring several other thatched houses.

- ⇔ One double, one twin, one family room
- £ **£** (single occupancy **££**)
- 🍺 Beer range varies
- 🍽 Snacks and meals daily, lunchtime and Tuesday-Saturday evening
- **CC** accepted

—— SULGRAVE ——

Star Inn

Manor Road, Sulgrave, Oxon OX17 2SA
☎ *(01295) 760389;* FAX *(01295) 760991*
Directions: From M40 jct 11 or M1 jct 15a, follow brown tourist signs for Sulgrave Manor

Despite the Oxfordshire postal address, the Star is actually in Northamptonshire – but only just. It is on the doorstep of Sulgrave Manor, the ancestral home of George Washington. Americans making a pilgrimage there would find in the Star, exactly the kind of place they might imagine an 'olde Englishe pub' to be. Stone-built it has retained all the character that was admired by America's Chief Justice, William Taft, when he visited in 1889, and wrote that it 'is a relic of bygone days when comforts were plain and ale was plenty'. With its flag-stone floors, beamed ceilings and inglenook, the bar is quite charming. Meals can be taken here or in the equally attractive restaurant. There is still ale aplenty, but the 'comforts' have been updated somewhat. The guest rooms (one of which is actually a small suite) all have private bathrooms and the usual modern amenities. Decorated to a high standard, in keeping with the character of the place, the rooms are unfortunately not suitable for families. Apart from the nearby Manor, other attractions in the area include Warwick Castle, and Silverstone race circuit, while the Cotswolds, Oxford and Stratford are also within easy reach.

🛏 Three double rooms, one suite
£ ££
🍺 Hook Norton Best Bitter, Old Hooky, Generation
🍽 Snacks and meals daily, lunchtime and evening
CC not accepted

—— WAKERLEY ——

Exeter Arms

Main Road, Wakerley, Oakham, Rutland LE15 8PA
☎ *(01572) 747817;* FAX *(01572) 747100*
Directions: west of the A43, Stamford-Corby road

In the recently resurrected little county of Rutland, the village of Wakerley lies in the Rockingham Forest, in the Welland Valley. The Exeter Arms enjoys a tranquil setting, ideal for woodland walks (Walkerley Great Wood is close by). It is also convenient for Burghley House and Rockingham Castle and for all the amenities offered by Rutland Water, said to be Europe's largest man-made lake. You are assured of a warm welcome at the pub from Margaret and Dave Docherty who offer good, simple bar meals (including home-cooked daily specials) at reasonable prices. A full English breakfast is served to overnight guests. The bedrooms are a new feature here. In a newly renovated annexe, they provide peaceful accommodation in en-suite rooms, furnished and equipped to a high standard. While not having special facilities for guests with disabilities, some rooms are on the ground floor and may be suitable for less mobile visitors. Children are welcome and pets can be accommodated.

🛏 Three double, two twin-bedded rooms
£ £ (££ single occupancy)
🍺 Adnams Broadside; Bateman XB; Marston's Pedigree; guest beer (occasionally)
🍽 Snacks and meals daily lunchtime (except Monday) and evening
CC accepted

—— WEEDON ——

Globe Hotel

High Street, Weedon, Northants NN7 4QD
☎ *(01327) 340336;* FAX *(01327) 349058*
Directions: three miles west of M1 jct 16, at the A5/A45 crossroads

Originally an 18th-century post house, which served cavalry officers from the nearby training centre, this 18-room hotel now offers all the modern comforts, but manages to keep a real pub atmosphere in the bar. The service is friendly but also efficient and professional. The restaurant is highly recommended, but you can also dine less formally in the bar. The bedrooms (all en-suite) are well appointed with TV (including film channel) and tea/coffee making facilities. Pets can be accommodated. Weedon is very handy for many tourist attractions, such as Sulgrave Manor (ancestral home of George Washington). It is also close to the Grand Union Canal, and the Canal Museum at Stoke Bruerne, the National Hunt course at Towcester which stages a monthly antiques fair, and Silverstone Grand Prix circuit.

⋈ Four single, nine double, two twin-bedded and three family rooms
£ ££ (££££ for some single rooms)
🍺 Marston's Bitter, Pedigree; Webster's Yorkshire Bitter; guest beers
🍽 Snacks and meals daily, lunchtime and evening (restaurant closed Sunday evening)
CC accepted

Heart of England

Daventry Road, Weedon NN7 4QD
☎ *(01327) 340335*

Weedon is reckoned to be at the very centre of England, so this hotel is aptly named. Built in the 1740s to serve the Grand Union Canal on whose bank it stands, the hotel boasts military connections, dating back to the Napoleonic Wars. This substantial building comprises an oak-panelled bar, a lounge, a number of smaller rooms and a restaurant which is divided into four more intimate areas. For children there are play facilities in the pub as well as out in the canalside garden. The hotel has comfortable bedrooms with en-suite facilities, where guests with disabilities can be catered for. One room has a four-poster bed, and all have tea/coffee makers, direct dial telephone and TV. Children are welcome to stay and pets can be accommodated by arrangement. This Mansfield house offers a good selection of real ales from other breweries, alongside a menu of traditional English dishes (served in the bar and restaurant). Tourist attractions in the area include the NT's Canons Ashby, built in the 1550s by John Dryden and home to his family for over 400 years. In Upper Stowe the Old Dairy Farm Centre has something for everyone from the rare breeds on the farm, to the working craftsmen and women displaying their skills and the shop selling antiques, clothes and gifts.

⋈ Five single, three double, and five twin-bedded rooms
£ ££ (£££ single room)
🍺 Mansfield Bitter, Riding Bitter, Old Baily; guest beers
🍽 Snacks and meals daily, lunchtime and evening
CC accepted

—— WHISSENDINE ——

White Lion

38 Main Street, Whissendine LE15 7ET
☎/FAX *(01664) 474233*
Directions: two miles from the A606 Oakham–Melton Mowbray road

Whissendine is an ancient village, listed in the Domesday Book as Witchingdine. This 200-year-old family-run inn is well situated between Rutland Water – popular for water sports – and the delightful Vale of Belvoir. An extensive renovation and redecoration programme, sympathetic to the pub's age and character, has just been completed. The eight en-suite guest rooms have individually controllable central heating, TV and hot drinks facilities. The rooms are strictly for non-smokers, but there is a residents' lounge on the same floor, with TV and video, where smoking is permitted. The two family rooms have either a double or two single beds, a double bunk and a cot. The rates given are for room only, giving guests the option of choosing a continental breakfast (£2.95) or the full English variety (£5.95). Home-cooked food on a wide-ranging menu is served in the bar (warmed in winter by open fires), and the restaurant. There is also a carvery on Friday night and Sunday lunchtime. The pub has a function room which opens on to a floodlit garden, bordered by willow trees, with a climbing frame and Wendy house for children and a petanque piste. Guide dogs can be accommodated, other pets can be housed if necessary at a nearby kennel/cattery.

- ⛵ Six double, two family rooms
- £ £ (single occupancy ££)
- 🍺 Everards Beacon, Tiger, Old Original, seasonal beers
- 🍴 Snacks and meals Tuesday-Sunday lunchtime and Tuesday-Saturday evening
- CC accepted

TRY ALSO:

Bulls Head

Church Hill, Wolvey, Leicestershire LE10 3LB
☎/FAX *(01455) 220383*

Inexpensive bed and breakfast in two twin-bedded rooms with shared facilities. B&B £

LINCOLNSHIRE

— BOSTON —

Olde Magnet Tavern
South Square, Boston PE21 6HX
☎ *(01205) 369186*
Directions: just off the market square in the town centre

Boston is famous as the place where the Pilgrim Fathers were tried and imprisoned in what is now the Guildhall Museum, before setting sail to America to found the other Boston in 1620. They departed just a few years before the Magnet was built (around 1650) – its beamed ceilings and stone floors have worn well. Standing by the river, the Magnet is surrounded by old warehouses which have recently been converted to residential use and include an arts centre. Friendly and popular, this free house offers a public bar, lounge, dining area and a games room for pool, darts and dominoes. The four en-suite guest rooms are of a high standard and offer the usual amenities of TV, tea/coffee making facilities, etc. Children can be accommodated by prior arrangement (one of the double rooms has an additional single bed), as can pets. The prices are for room only, breakfast is charged extra. The food, mainly home-cooked, is recommended. Boston has a thriving market, held Wednesday and Saturday, and another point of interest is the Boston 'Stump' – the largest parish church in the country.

- ⊨ One single, two double, one twin-bedded room
- £ £ (single ££)
- 🍺 Draught Bass; Bateman XB; Stones Best Bitter; Taylor Landlord; Theakston Old Peculier; Worthington BB
- 🍴 Snacks and meals daily, lunchtime and evening (Sunday lunch only by arrangement)
- **CC** accepted

The Magnet Tavern,
Boston, Lincs.

—— DYKE ——

Wishing Well Inn

Main Street, Dyke, near Bourne PE10 0AF
☎ *(01778) 422970;* FAX *(01778) 394508*
Directions: off the A15, one mile north of Bourne

Barely visible behind a curtain of foliage, this charming village inn is extremely popular. And its not just the greenery that's growing. At the time of writing it has eight guest rooms, but five more are due to open by the time this guide is published. All offering en-suite bathrooms, the traditionally furnished rooms are equipped with TV and tea/coffee making facilities. Some rooms are adapted to the needs of guests with disabilities. The Wishing Well's public rooms are delightful, featuring exposed stone walls, heavily beamed ceilings and huge inglenooks (put to good use in winter). With two restaurants (the smaller one features the wishing well in the pub's name), the pub enjoys a good reputation locally for its food, but not, say local CAMRA, at the expense of its beer trade. It offers something like 250 guest ales a year and stages an annual beer festival in August. Children are welcome here (the pub has a children's certificate) and the garden has an enclosed activity area for them to enjoy. The historic town of Stamford and Rutland Water with its many amenities, are just a short drive away, and there are several other places of tourist interest within easy reach.

- ⊨ Eight double, five twin-bedded rooms
- £ ££ – £££
- 🍺 Beer range varies with always five ales on tap
- 🍽 Snacks and meals daily, lunchtime and evening
- CC accepted

—— FULBECK ——

Hare & Hounds

The Green, Fulbeck, Grantham NG32 3JJ
☎ *(01400) 272090;* FAX *(01400) 273663*
Directions: just off the A17, at junction with the A607 Grantham–Lincoln road

This lovely old pub overlooks the green of one of Lincolnshire's prettiest villages. With its steep streets and old stone houses, Fulbeck is very popular with visitors who enjoy the Manor Stables Craft Workshops there and Fulbeck Hall, home of the Fane family since 1632, which is open to the public for most of the summer. The spacious inn (extensions were added in the 18th and 19th centuries to the 16th-century original) is now Grade II listed. The pub has been upgraded again in the last few years, including a revamp of the restaurant and improvements to the guest rooms which are situated in the former mews. The bedrooms are all en-suite with bath or shower, colour TV and tea/coffee making facilities, some are on the ground floor and may suit guests with mobility problems – the bar and restaurant are both accessible to wheelchairs. Children are welcome; the pub has its own garden with a popular boules pitch. Tourist attractions within easy reach include Rutland Water, Lincoln, with its cathedral and the NT's Belton House, a fine example of Restoration country house architecture.

- ⊨ Four double, two twin-bedded and two family rooms
- £ £ (single occupancy ££)
- 🍺 Bateman XB; Fuller's London Pride; Marston's Pedigree; John Smith's Bitter; guest beer (summer)
- 🍽 Snacks (lunchtime) and meals daily, lunchtime and evening
- CC accepted

GRANTHAM

Angel & Royal Hotel
High Street, Grantham NG31 6PN
☎ *(01476) 565816;* FAX *(01476) 567149*
Directions: off the A1, in the town centre

According to *Good Beer Guide* editor, Roger Protz, the Angel and Royal is one of the most important historical pubs in the whole of England. Built on land once owned by the Knights Templar, the 'Royal' part of its name is most appropriate, since King John held his court there in 1213 and Richard III wrote out the death warrant for the then Duke of Buckingham in 1483 in the Chambre du Roi, which is now the dining room. The 'Angel' appeared in the 19th century, when a visit by Edward III and his wife was marked by the erection of a stone angel carrying a crown over the archway. This arch certainly presents a splendid entry to the hotel and Roger suggests that the inn may once have been part of a never completed castle. Over the years the building was transformed into an inn catering for visiting Lords and Ladies. Today all are welcome to enjoy the magnificent surroundings. Two splendid bars are warmed in winter by open fires; there is also a no-smoking lounge and the beautiful restaurant with its stone walls. The 29 en-suite bedrooms are spacious and comfortable with modern amenities. Children are welcome to stay (high chairs, cots and even a baby listening service can all be provided). Popular local tourist destinations include Belvoir Castle and Belton House.

🛏 11 single, 10 double and eight twin-bedded rooms
£ £ (single £££)
🍺 Courage Directors; Marston's Pedigree; Theakston Best Bitter; occasional guest beer
🍴 Lunchtime snacks; evening snacks and meals daily
CC accepted

GRIMSTHORPE

Black Horse Inn
Grimsthorpe, Bourne PE10 0LY
☎ *(01778) 591247;* FAX *(01778) 591373*

Standing in the shadow of Grimsthorpe Castle, the Black Horse is anything but grim, since the owners Brian and Elaine Rey go out of their way to give you a warm welcome and a pleasant stay. Built to serve the coaching trade in the early 18th century, the inn has been well renovated and modernised. It boasts an award-winning (no-smoking) restaurant, but if you prefer, you can eat in the less formal bar, whilst relaxing in front of an open fire. Here you can try the house ale, brewed to the landlord's own recipe, by local brewery, Bateman. There is also a smaller, intimate lounge. Summer visitors can enjoy the private, but extensive walled garden. The well-equipped guest rooms all have private facilities. If you want a touch of luxury, book the executive (honeymoon) suite, with its four-poster bed, private sitting room and spa bathroom. The accommodation is not suitable, however, for families. This area has plenty to offer in the way of cultural and leisure pursuits; Grimsthorpe Castle itself has extensive grounds including gardens, a lake and a nature trail. Historic Stamford, which found international fame as *Middlemarch* in the TV series, is within easy reach.

🛏 Four double, two twin-bedded rooms
£ ££ (£££ single occupancy)
🍺 Bateman XXXB; guest beer (occasionally)
🍴 Snacks and meals daily, lunchtime and evening
CC accepted

—— HORNCASTLE ——

Admiral Rodney Hotel
North Street, Horncastle LN9 5DX
☎ *(01507) 523131;* FAX *(01507) 523104*

I have never been to Horncastle, but I shall certainly be planning a trip there soon, not just because local CAMRA members have recommended the admirable Admiral Rodney, but also because, so the licensee tells me, this market town is well known for its antique shops. It's not that I see myself as a budding Lovejoy, it's just the fascination of what unusual, long-forgotten objects one might find. Judging by the number of TV programmes on the subject these days, I'm obviously not alone. So all you fellow delvers, head off to Horncastle and book in at the Admiral. Recently refurbished, the hotel has no less than 31 rooms (enough for the full *Antiques Roadshow* crew). All are en-suite and some rooms are suitable for guests with disabilities. Children can be catered for (at reduced prices), but I won't be taking mine – they both sigh heavily when their dotty parents make a beeline for (yet another) antique shop. The popular Rodney Bar bears a nautical theme and offers a monthly changing guest beer (usually from a small brewer). You can eat here or in the courtyard restaurant.

- 🛏 18 double, ten twin-bedded and three family rooms
- £ ££ (£££ single occupancy)
- 🍺 Courage Directors; John Smith's Bitter; guest beer
- 🍽 Snacks and meals daily, lunchtime and evening
- **CC** accepted

—— LINCOLN ——

Barbican Hotel
St Marys Street, Lincoln LN5 7EQ
☎ *(01522) 543811*
Directions: near station

This Victorian edifice looks somewhat forbidding on the outside, but it has been freshly renovated inside and is centrally situated (indeed it is billed as the city's most central hotel). The refurbishment has not been overdone and many of the original Victorian features have been retained. It offers spacious bars (where meals may also be taken) and a quiet restaurant. All the guest rooms have en-suite bathrooms and modern amenities. Standing opposite the station, it is convenient for non-drivers and this ancient city is small enough to explore on foot. Its crowning glory is the cathedral, which over the years has survived fire, earthquake and civil war. Opposite the cathedral is the castle, which also dates from Norman times. A more unusual tourist venue is the National Cycle Museum. If you are mobile, there are plenty of places in the surrounding area to visit, including Gainsborough Old Hall, and the NT's splendid Belton House with its landscaped park. The hotel can cater for families and pets are also accommodated by arrangement.

- 🛏 Seven single, three double and four twin-bedded rooms
- £ £ (££ single room)
- 🍺 Two guest beers which are changed every few days
- 🍽 Snacks and meals, lunchtime and evening, Monday-Saturday
- **CC** accepted

—— LOUTH ——

Masons Arms
Cornmarket, Louth LN11 9PY
☎ *(01507) 609525*
Directions: near the town centre, off the A157

Dating back to 1730, this imposing building was a former post house, but had been left empty and derelict for some years, before being recently restored as the characterful inn it now is. Open all day, serving coffee and tea as well as the more usual liquid refreshment, the pub offers comfortable bars (where informal meals are served) and an upstairs restaurant. It is now run by a father and son team, Roger and Justin Goldsmith; Justin is the chef and Roger ensures that there are always six real ales on tap. The newly renovated bedrooms (five of which are en-suite) promise a very comfortable stay. Children are welcome (although there is no designated family room). Louth is a fine Georgian town, with some handsome buildings, listed in the *Domesday Book* as a prosperous market town. The ancient market rights have been fiercely preserved and a very well-attended market is still held three times a week. Lying between the coast and the unspoilt countryside of the Wolds, it is an excellent choice for a short break. For sporting enthusiasts, the Market Rasen racecourse and Caldwell Park Racing Circuit are both within 20 minutes' drive.

🛏 Three single, five double and two twin-bedded rooms
£ £
🍺 Draught Bass; Bateman Dark Mild, XB, XXXB; Marston's Pedigree; Highwood Tom Wood Best Bitter; guest beer
🍽 Snacks and meals daily, lunchtime and evening (except Sunday evening)
CC accepted

—— OASBY ——

Houblon Arms Inn
Village Street, Oasby NG32 3NB
☎/FAX *(01529) 455215*
Directions: midway between Grantham and Sleaford, two miles north of the A52

Houblon is the French word for hops, and I was interested to know if there was any connection between the pub and hop growing, so I asked the landlord. However, he told me to look at the back of a £50-note which depicts John Houblon, the first governor of the Bank of England and the local landowner in the 18th-century. The name of this 16th-century pub was changed in his honour. This friendly old stone-built pub is a local CAMRA favourite, featuring oak beams, cosy antique furnishings, open fires and masses of ornaments. It is popular for its table top games (there are no electronic machines or pool) and its live music (Thursday evening), when jazz and folk bands alternate weekly. Children can be accommodated (Z-beds are available, and they are only charged for breakfast), but very young children cannot be catered for in the restaurant. The motel-style rooms are all on the ground floor and so may be suitable for less mobile guests. They are all en-suite and two have four-poster beds. At present all are double rooms, but are being converted to give the accommodation listed below.

🛏 Two double, two twin-bedded, one family room
£ £
🍺 Draught Bass; Bateman XB; guest beers
🍽 Snacks lunchtime, meals daily lunchtime and evening (except Monday lunch)
CC accepted

—— OSBOURNBY ——

Whichcote Arms

London Road, Osbournby, Sleaford NG34 0DG
☎ *(01529) 455239;* FAX *(01529) 455500*
Directions: just off the A15

Standing alone, this fine substantial yellow brick Victorian pub is just off the A15, a popular route for travellers between York, Lincoln, Cambridge and East Anglia. It makes an ideal overnight stop, or for a longer stay to explore the area which abounds with stately homes and museums, such as Coningsby, commemorating the Second World War (lots of airforce bases were built in the region). Also within easy reach are Boston and Spalding – famous for its flower festival. The pub offers a warm, friendly atmosphere, free from piped music, although landlord, Mike can sometimes be persuaded to take up the guitar or harmonica and sing. He and his wife Belinda concentrate on real beers and ciders from independent producers – he sent a note to me saying 'sorry no nitrokeg'! They offer a limited, but wholesome, home-cooked menu, based as much as possible on fresh local produce – diners may eat in either the bar or restaurant. The five guest rooms all have en-suite showers, plus TV and tea/coffee makers. The family room can accommodate up to two children who are charged £10 per head, including breakfast – which is always the full English variety.

 ⊨ One double, three twin-bedded, one family room
 £ £ (££ single occupancy)
 🍴 Oakham JHB, plus a continuous rotation of guest beers
 🍽 Snacks and meals daily, lunchtime and evening (except Tuesday)
 CC not accepted

—— RAITHBY-BY-SPILSBY ——

Red Lion

Main Street, Raithby-by-Spilsby PE23 4DS
☎ *(01790) 753727*
Directions: take the Lincoln road out of Spilsby, via Hundleby, then turn right for Raithby

This attractive, friendly pub stands in a pretty Wolds village within easy reach of Bolingbroke Castle and John Wesley's Chapel. The Wolds themselves are very popular for outdoor pursuits, with the Snipe Dales Nature Reserve just a mile away. It is also very convenient for the coast ('bracing' Skegness is 13 miles distant), and for exploring 'Tennyson country'. Other places of interest nearby include potteries, water mills and a heavy horse centre. The Red Lion has had a change of ownership since our last edition, but has lost none of its appeal. On the plus side, the pub now stocks local Highwood beers, and there are rumours that the new owners, Roger and Maggie Smith are intending to install a microbrewery. The tastefully decorated bedrooms are comfortable and cosy, and two have en-suite bathrooms. There is no family room, but children are welcome. Pets can be accommodated.

 ⊨ Two double; one twin-bedded room
 £ £ (££ single occupancy of double en-suite)
 🍴 Highwood Tom Wood Best Bitter, Harvest; John Smith's Bitter; Tetley Bitter
 🍽 Snacks and meals daily evenings, plus weekend lunchtimes
 CC not accepted

—— SKEGNESS ——

Vine Hotel

Vine Road, Seacroft, Skegness PE25 3DB
☎ *(01754) 610611;* FAX *(01754) 769845*
Directions: take Lumley Road from the Clock Tower, turn left into Drummond Road, then right after one mile into Vine Road

After St Clements Church, the Vine is the oldest building in 'Skeggy'. It was built as a farmhouse, converted to an inn in the mid-19th century, and acquired by the local brewery, Batemans in 1921. Both the bars now offer Batemans 'Good Honest Ales' which are regular CAMRA award winners. The Vine had a somewhat murky past, linked with smugglers, robbers and disappearing customs officials! However, this has been redeemed by its later connections with Alfred Lord Tennyson who used to sit in the garden writing poetry. The leafy gardens and the hotel's secluded woodland setting might inspire anyone to verse; the hotel offers a tranquil refuge from this busy resort's attractions. The Tennyson Bar and the panelled Oak Room both convey a pleasant, almost rural, atmosphere. The bar has warming open fires, a good following for its traditional games and an extensive bar menu. More formal meals are served in the olde-worlde restaurant. All the guest rooms have en-suite facilities. The hotel is popular for weddings and the spacious Honeymoon Suite is particularly appealing with its four-poster bed. Pets can be accommodated by arrangement

 ⇥ Three single, ten double, three twin-bedded and five family rooms
 £ ££ (£££ single room)
 ◗ Bateman Mild XB, Valiant, XXXB, seasonal beers; Marston's Pedigree; guest beer (occasionally)
 ◖ Snacks and meals daily, lunchtime and evening
 CC accepted

—— STAMFORD ——

Dolphin

60 East Street, Stamford PE9 1QE
☎/FAX *(01780) 757515*
Directions: just off the A1, 200 yards from the town centre

This lovely old inn is characterised by its many small, intimate rooms. One of the oldest pubs in Stamford, the Dolphin boasts a fine collection of prints of the old town. It offers a good range of real ales all year round, but July is the high spot, when it hosts its own beer festival. The pub has a new 40-seater restaurant, where steaks and grills are a speciality. The overnight accommodation is in a guest house, opposite the pub (under the same ownership) where eight en-suite bedrooms offer modern amenities. Pets can be catered for. Stamford is convenient for travellers on the A1, and for non-drivers, the station and bus park are both within easy reach. The pub is just two minutes from the centre of this charming old town, which fans will recognise as the setting for the TV production of *Middlemarch*. Popular tourist destinations in the locality include Burghley House (one mile) and Rutland Water.

 ⇥ One single, four double; two twin-bedded and one family room
 £ £
 ◗ Wells Eagle, Bombardier; three regularly changing guest beers
 ◖ Snacks and meals daily, lunchtime and evening
 CC accepted

—— SOUTH WITHAM ——

Blue Cow Inn and Brewery
South Witham, near Grantham NG33 5QB
☎/FAX *(01572) 768432*
· Directions: between Grantham and Stamford, signed from the A1

Now here's something different for would-be brewers. CAMRA member landlord, Dick Thirlwell offers two-day residential brewing courses here. He should know what he's talking about as he built up the Blue Cow Brewery from scratch. He installed the four-barrel plant himself in 1997 and launched his beers to a very appreciative clientele – not least because of his low prices. From this small scale operation he manages to produce enough beer to supply his own pub (including, usually a monthly special brew) plus two other local outlets. If you don't actually want to learn how to brew yourself (and you do have to be up by 7am on Saturday morning to do so!), you're welcome just to have a look around the brewery. The Blue Cow is a 13th-century, unspoilt inn, boasting exposed beams, stone-flagged floors and open log fires. Meals can be taken in any of the bars or in the restaurant. All the guest rooms have en-suite facilities. Children are welcome and pets can be accommodated. Set between historic Stamford and Grantham, the pub is just five miles from the vast Rutland Water with its nature trails, cycleways and water sports.

🛏 One double, two twin-bedded rooms
£ £ (££ single occupancy)
🍺 Thirlwell's Best Bitter, Templars Tipple, Premium
🍽 Snacks and meals daily, lunchtime and evening
CC accepted

TRY ALSO:

Queens Arms Hotel
Wrawby Street, Brigg DN20 8BS
☎ *(01652) 653174*

Market town local, with its own microbrewery (Brigg). Four rooms (not en-suite), including one for families. B&B £

Habrough Hotel/Horse & Hounds
Station Road, Habrough DN40 3AY
☎ *(01469) 576940*

Good en-suite accommodation in a hotel with 23 en-suite rooms; real ale is in the adjoining pub. B&B ££££

Carre Arms Hotel
1 Mareham Lane, Sleaford NG34 7JP
☎ *(01529) 303156;* FAX *(01529) 303139*

Upmarket, refurbished Bass house, with excellent daily changing menu. Thirteen en-suite rooms (including family facilities). B&B ££ (£££ single)

Ship Albion
37 Albion Street, Spalding PE11 2AJ
☎ *(01775) 76944*

Friendly edge of town pub, near the huge Geest factory. Seven rooms including one for families. B&B £

GREATER LONDON

—— BATTERSEA ——

Raven
140 Westbridge Road, Battersea SW11
☎ *(0171) 228 1657*

Dating back to the 16th century, the Raven is the oldest pub in Battersea, and must offer some of the best value accommodation in the capital. The rooms are fairly basic, but are ideal for tourists on a limited budget. Half of the rooms have en-suite amenities; for the rest there are shower facilities close by on the same level. Children are welcome to stay. A full English breakfast is provided. No other food is served on a regular basis, but if you require an evening meal, this too can be provided. The The beer range is limited to two real ales in summer. The pub is very convenient for trips into central London with Clapham Junction mainline station and tube about ten minutes' walk away, and good bus services. The pub has no car park and street parking can be tricky.

⇥ eight double rooms
£ ££
🍺 Fuller's London Pride, plus either Boddingtons Bitter, Courage Best Bitter or Young's Bitter (on rotation) and an occasional guest beer
🍽 See above
CC not accepted

The Sanctuary House
Hotel,
London SW1

── CLAPHAM COMMON ──

Windmill on the Common

Clapham Common South Side, Clapham SW4 9DE
☎ *(0181) 673 4578;* FAX *(0181) 675 1486*
Directions: on the A24, midway between Clapham Common and Clapham South underground stations

The first of Young's hotels (and once the home of the brewery's founder), this old coaching inn stands right on the common. Advertised by Youngs as a 'country hotel in London', the recently refurbished large single bar with its conservatory-cum-family room, does have a comfortable feeling. It can get very busy, especially in summer when the crowd spills out over the common. Food is available in the bar, and there is a good value restaurant for both hotel guests and others. For hotel residents there is a separate lounge for out of hours use, without a bar, but with night porter service. Whilst the majority of weekday guests are on business, there remains a good business/leisure mix with many overseas visitors using the hotel for holidays. Reduced rates are available for weekend guests. The en-suite rooms are all furnished to a very high standard – as one would expect in an ETB four-crown establishment – and equipped with satellite TV, writing tables and all the usual amenities. One room is adapted for guests with disabilities and there are rooms available for non-smokers. There are no designated family rooms, but children are welcome (cots are provided free of charge). Pets can be accommodated. Breakfast is a choice of full English or a continental option.

- ⊨ 19 double, 10 twin-bedded rooms
- £ ££££
- ⌾ Young's Bitter, Special
- ⦿ Snacks and meals daily, lunchtime and evening
- CC accepted

WHAT CAMRA DOES FOR BEER

Has your pint lost its flavour?

CAMRA promotes high-quality, tasty, distinctive beers
- through positive awards
- we also monitor and criticise the increasing blandness of many brands
- through 145 beer festivals a year
- by running campaigns for higher standards in breweries and pubs – we even publish a guide to keeping cask-conditioned ale called *Cellarmanship*

—— EAST SHEEN ——

Plough
42 Christchurch Road, East Sheen SW14 7AF
☎ *(0181) 876 7833;* FAX *(0181) 392 8801*
Directions: just off the South Circular road

The Plough originated as a row of farmer's cottages over 200 years ago, when this was still the countryside, a fair way out of the city. Now London is within easy reach by modern public transport (Waterloo in 15 minutes, but the station is a few minutes' walk), and the long since redundant cottages have become a comfortable inn, which aims, in its decor and atmosphere, to preserve a reminder of its rural beginnings. It also aims to offer accommodation at reasonable prices (at least in comparison with most of nearby Richmond's hotels). However, its bar prices reflect its position in a somewhat exclusive residential area. The seven subtly decorated rooms have been refurbished with up-to-date facilities; all are en-suite. Pets are accepted. Food at the Plough comes highly recommended, including the substantial breakfasts. The pub is just a couple of minutes' walk from Richmond Park and the Thames, with Kew Gardens just a mile away.

- ⊨ Three double, three twin-bedded and one family room
- £ **£££** (single occupancy **££££**)
- 🍺 Brakspear Bitter; Courage Best Bitter, Directors; occasional guest beer
- 🍽 Snacks and meals daily, lunchtime and evening
- **CC** accepted

—— ISLINGTON ——

Lamb Hotel
46 North Road, Islington N7 9DP
☎ *(0171) 609 0253;* FAX *(0171) 609 1380*

I worked in Islington many years ago, before it became trendy, and there were very few pubs that I cared to visit then, let alone stay in. All that has changed and the area is now the haunt of the MPs and media folk. The Lamb too, has had a facelift. This fine Italianate building, built by the Lord Mayor of London in 1855 is now a real landmark. Inside, a Victorian theme has been recreated in its traditional-style Tavern bar and a cosy wine bar has been established in the cellar where weekday lunches are served. All but two of the guest rooms offer en-suite facilities, and they all have telephone and TV. Children are welcome to stay. Outside a paved yard is used for summer drinking. Islington is close to King's Cross mainline station has good transport links with the centre (just two miles away) and the city. There is one proviso – the Lamb changed hands just before we went to press, which would normally lead to it being excluded, but such is the paucity of pub accommodation in London, we have taken the risk of keeping it in the guide and would welcome any feedback from readers.

- ⊨ Four double, four twin-bedded and ten family rooms
- £ **££**
- 🍺 Fuller's London Pride
- 🍽 Snacks and meals lunchtime Monday-Friday
- **CC** accepted

—— KEW ——

Coach & Horses
8 Kew Green, Kew, Richmond TW9 3BH
☎ *(0181) 940 1208*
Directions: over Kew Bridge, opposite the Botanic Gardens

Tourists to London will rarely find as good value as this pub offers, and in such a good position. It stands right opposite Kew gardens, on the 'village' green. Kew Bridge mainline rail station and Kew Gardens tube are in walking distance. Hampton Court Palace is easily accessible by road (20 minutes' drive) or by boat. Kew Village is, in estate agents' parlance 'highly sought after' and the Coach and Horses is as close as you'll get to a village pub atmosphere in London. Popular and friendly, it stages regular darts matches and quizzes and occasionally hosts live music. It has a good reputation for its home-cooked meals, prepared under the supervision of the landlady, Betty Bamford. It has a large, pleasant garden at the back and a few tables out the front facing Kew Green. The six guest rooms all have en-suite showers, hospitality tray and TV. A full English breakfast is provided. Well behaved pets can be accommodated.

- ⇥ One single, four doubles, one family room
- £ £ (£££ single)
- 🍺 Young's Bitter, Special, Winter Warmer, seasonal beers
- 🍴 Snacks and meals daily, lunchtime and evening (except Sunday evening)
- CC accepted

—— WANDSWORTH ——

Brewers Inn

147 East Hill, Wandsworth SW18 2QB
☎ *(0181) 874 4128;* FAX *(0181) 877 1953*
Directions: on the A3

If you arrive at the Brewers Inn by car, do try not to miss it as you approach down East Hill, because then you can turn into St Annes Hill for the car park. Once past the pub you are locked into the Wandsworth one-way system, which is not the most fun you can have in a car. Wandsworth Town mainline station is roughly a ten-minute walk, and there are good bus services from Clapham Junction (opposite the main St John's Hill entrance). This substantial house has recently been refurbished in traditional style and has three areas: a bar with bare boards and wooden tables, a more comfortable, carpeted saloon, and an oak-panelled, candlelit restaurant. There is a bistro menu with daily specials for more informal dining. The 16 guest rooms all have their own bath or shower, TV, trouser press and telephone. Air conditioning has recently been installed in half of the rooms (which are let at a higher rate). Children under 12 and sharing their parents room are just charged for breakfast; over twelves pay £15 bed and breakfast. Cots can be provided. Weekend rates are considerably cheaper than the weekday tariff.

- ⇥ Four singles, seven doubles, three twin-bedded and two family rooms
- £ £££ (weekend ££); single room ££££
- 🍺 Young's Bitter, Special, seasonal beer; guest beer (occasionally)
- 🍴 Snacks and meals daily, lunchtime and evening
- CC accepted

——— WESTMINSTER ———

Sanctuary House Hotel

31-35 Tothill Street, Westminster SW7H 9LA
☎ *(0171) 799 4044;* FAX *(0171) 799 3657*
Directions: by St James's Park tube station

Very convenient for our honourable Members of Parliament, this new hotel, owned by the London brewery, Fuller's is centrally situated for anyone coming to London for business or pleasure. Just two minutes' walk from the Houses of Parliament and Westminster Abbey and 10 minutes from Buckingham Palace and St James's Park, the Sanctuary is within reach of all London's major sights and shopping centres. Fully air-conditioned, the hotel offers a choice of smoking or no-smoking rooms; all are of course en-suite and have satellite TV, radio, and many other facilities. Laundry and dry cleaning services are also available. There are rooms adapted to the needs of guests with disabilities, and there is a lift to all floors. The hotel has no designated family rooms as such but children are welcome to share their parent's room for an additional £12. Reduced rates apply at the weekend (Friday and Saturday nights). Cots are provided free of charge. On the ground floor, a Fuller's Ale and Pie House aims to provide good home cooking and real ales in a traditional setting (the hotel has no other restaurant).

- ⊨ 24 double, ten twin-bedded rooms
- £ *££££*
- ◖ Fuller's Chiswick, London Pride, ESB, seasonal beers
- ◗ Snacks and meals daily, lunchtime and evening
- CC accepted

TRY ALSO:

Kew Gardens Hotel

292 Sandycombe Road, Kew, Richmond TW9 3NG
☎ *(0181) 940 2220;* FAX *(0181) 332 6231*

Recently refurbished hotel in Kew 'village' a few minutes' walk from the Royal Botanic Gardens. 18 en-suite rooms. B&B *££££*

Mitre

130 Mitcham Road, Tooting SW17 9NH
☎ *(0181) 672 5771*

This large pub changed hands just before we went to press. Five minutes' walk from Tooting Broadway tube station it offers 16 rooms with en-suite showers. B&B *££*

GREATER MANCHESTER & MERSEYSIDE

—— DELPH ——

Old Bell Hotel

Huddersfield Road, Delph, Saddleworth, near Oldham OL3 5EG
☎ *(01457) 870130; FAX (01457) 876597*
Directions: on the A62 Huddersfield road, seven miles from Oldham

The Old Bell is an upmarket country hotel with some very stylish rooms which feature leaded windows and Laura Ashley furnishings; some have four poster or half-tester beds. All ten rooms have en-suite facilities and are well equipped. The inn dates back to the 16th century and its spacious bar has welcomed such famous guests as Princess (later Queen) Victoria and Charles Dickens. Less illustrious visitors have included Dick Turpin. Informal meals can be taken in the bar, while the restaurant offers a more extensive and adventurous menu. Vegetarians are always catered for. Delph still bears reminders of its involvement in the textile trade in its old weavers cottages. The hotel is convenient for the Peak District National Park and Saddleworth Moor, and within easy reach of areas made famous by literature and TV: Brontë country, Herriot country and Last of the Summer Wine's Holmfirth. Children are welcome and pets can be accommodated. Weekend discounts are available.

- ⋈ Three single, six double and one twin-bedded room
- £ ££ (single room £££)
- 🍺 Taylor Golden Best, Dark Mild, Porter (Christmas), Landord; guest beer (occasionally)
- ⬤ Snacks and meals daily, lunchtime and evening

—— DIGGLE ——

Diggle Hotel

Station Houses, Diggle, Saddleworth, near Oldham OL3 5JZ
☎ *(01457) 872741; FAX (01457) 875274*
Directions: just off the A62

This stone-built, 200-year-old pub is very popular and particularly busy in summer when the garden comes into its own. The Diggle stocks a traditional cider alongside the real ales. To build up a thirst (or appetite for the pub's splendid bar food), you could take a turn around one of the many local golf courses. Diggle is a small hamlet within easy reach of Manchester and its airport (20 miles), Huddersfield (ten miles) and Oldham (five miles). It is close to the Huddersfield Narrow Canal and a good base for walkers on Saddleworth Moor. The pub has been redecorated not so long ago, with care has been taken to preserve its character. The three double rooms are comfortably furnished and, although lacking private facilities, they each have a vanity unit, TV and telephone. There is a residents' lounge for guests. Children are welcome to stay, although there are no special facilities for families.

- ⋈ Three double rooms
- £ ££
- 🍺 Boddingtons Bitter; Taylor Golden Best, Landlord; Flowers Original; guest beer (occasionally)
- ⬤ Snacks and meals daily, lunchtime and evening
- CC accepted

—— LOWTON ——

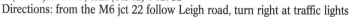

Red Lion Hotel

Newton Road, Lowton, Warrington WA3 1HE
☎ *(01942) 671429;* FAX *(01942) 741781*
Directions: from the M6 jct 22 follow Leigh road, turn right at traffic lights

The Red Lion is a big, friendly pub which attracts customers of all ages, and stands in its own garden which leads down to a bowling green. Bowling matches are staged every week-end in the summer months and the pub is also a popular venue for small functions. The main bar serves the lounge and a smaller room, whilst the pool room has a small bar of its own. There is a restaurant which is open daily at lunchtime and in the evening until 9.30. A children's menu is served and bar snacks are available, too. The guest rooms all have en-suite showers. The room rate includes continental breakfast. The Red Lion's situation allows for easy access to the North-west's motorway network and is convenient for Haydock Park (horse racing), Wigan Pier and Pennington Country Park.

⋈ One single, one double and one family room
£ £ (single room ££)
▣ Davenports Bitter; Greenalls Mild, Bitter, Original; Tetley Bitter; guest beer
⋈ Snacks and meals daily, lunchtime and evening
CC accepted

—— MANCHESTER ——

Crown Inn

321 Deansgate, Manchester M3 4LQ
☎/FAX *(0161) 834 1930*
Directions: within walking distance of Deansgate mainline station and G.Mex metro

The Crown is in the Castlefield area of Manchester which has been designated a City Centre Urban Park. It offers easy access to many of Manchester's attractions, including the G.Mex Centre, museums, the Castlefield Canal Basin and the Granada Studios Tour (beloved of *Coronation Street* fans). Sports-lovers can quickly reach the Old Trafford cricket ground and Man. United football club via the A56. The Crown is a thriving pub, rebuilt in late Victorian style. According to local CAMRA members, this is the only outlet for mild in the area. The single bar manages to combine the atmosphere of both a lounge and vault. The bar food is good value, as is the accommodation, in spacious, comfortable rooms. None of the guest rooms has a private bathroom, but they all have washbasins, Sky TV and tea/coffee making facilities. The rooms are not suitable for families.

⋈ One single, one double, seven twin-bedded rooms
£ £
▣ Vaux Mild, Samson; monthly guest beer
⋈ Snacks and meals daily, lunchtime and evening
CC not accepted

Smithfield Hotel

37 Swan Street, Manchester M4 5JZ
☎ *(0161) 839 4424*
Directions: on the A665, between the A62 and A664

A good choice for an inexpensive night's stay in the city centre, the Smithfield is close to both Piccadilly and Victoria stations. The old Smithfield market used to stand right behind the pub (it was originally called the Smithfield Vaults). A comfortable one-roomer today, it is more of a pub than a hotel; chatty, convivial and offering its ales at keen prices. It is very popular both with locals and CAMRA members, and offers very good value for money. Almost café-bar in style, the single narrow bar has a drinking end and a dining end – and the food is recommended. The guest beers usually include a mild. The nine guest rooms are large and fairly basic (three bathrooms are shared by all the guests), but they are comfortable nonetheless. Each has a TV and tea/coffee making facilities. A full English breakfast is provided.

- ⊨ One single, six doubles, two family rooms
- £ £
- ◧ Matthew Clark Twelvebore Bitter; Fuller's London Pride; Highgate Dark; guest beers
- ◖ Snacks and meals daily, lunchtime and evening (until 8.30pm)
- CC not accepted

—— MARPLE ——

Pineapple Inn

45 Market Street, Marple, Stockport SK6 7AA
☎ *(0161) 427 3935*
Directions: on the A626

As England's waterways are increasingly being restored for leisure use, so villages such as Marple become more popular with visitors and tourists. The Pineapple is just a short walk from Marple canal which is famous for its 16 locks. Another feature of aquatic interest are the Roman lakes nearby. The pub draws much of its trade from the canal, just as I guess it used to a couple of centuries ago, with narrow boat users and hikers stopping for a pint of local ale or a meal in the bar or dining room. This friendly, traditional inn at the village centre offers straightforward accommodation, in two rooms with shared facilities. Although the licensees say they can usually meet all reasonable needs their guests may have, the accommodation is not suitable for families. The rooms are all centrally heated and have TV and tea/coffee making facilities. The pub is convenient for Stockport and Manchester and, being south-east of the city is well situated to use as a base for the Peak District National Park.

- ⊨ Two twin-bedded rooms
- £ £ (££ single occupancy)
- ◧ Robinson's Hatters Mild, Hartleys XB, Best Bitter, Frederics, Old Tom
- ◖ Snacks lunchtime, meals daily, lunchtime and evening
- CC accepted

—— PRESTWICH ——

Woodthorpe

Bury Old Road, Prestwich, Manchester M25 0EG
☎ *(0161) 795 0032;* FAX *(0161) 795 0351*
Directions: near the junction of the A665 and A6044

Originally the home of the Holt brewing family (and still stocking that brewery's beers), this lovely building, set in its own private grounds, stands opposite the entrance to Heaton Park and is within walking distance of Heaton Park metro. There is a bus service practically to the door, with Manchester city centre being about 10 minutes' drive, and the M62 motorway accessible in just five minutes. Surrounded by lawns and trees, the hotel offers ample parking. In World War Two the house was commandeered by the Ministry of Defence, but then remained empty until 1953 when it was turned into an hotel. It remained largely unchanged until 1993, when it was stylishly restored. Although only one of the guest rooms has a private bathroom – it also features a four-poster bed – they are all spacious and well equipped. The service here is very good and the home-cooked food is served in the spacious, popular bar and the restaurant. Children are welcome to stay. The room price include a full English breakfast.

- ⇥ Two double, one family room
- £ £ (££ en-suite, or single occupancy)
- 🍺 Holt Mild, Bitter
- 🍽 Snacks and meals daily until 7pm
- **CC** accepted

—— SOUTHPORT ——

Blakes Hotel

19 Queens Road, Southport PR9 9HN
☎ *(01704) 50081;* FAX *(01704) 500949*
Directions: take the Manchester road north from the Promenade, Queens Road is on the left (junction after Lord Street)

Our entry for Southport is an unusual combination – but one that works very successfully – for the full name of this establishment is Blakes Hotel and Pizza Pub. The pizza restaurant is open daily from 5-11 pm, but hotel guests can if they prefer order a 'takeaway' via room service. The menu does include other choices, but pizzas are the speciality here. There is a children's menu and the pub has a comfortable family room at the rear. Beer lovers are not neglected either as the hotel bar offers no less than ten real ales at all times. The comfortable guest rooms are traditionally furnished and all have en-suite facilities, plus TV and tea/coffee making equipment. A travel cot is available for the smallest guests. Pets can be accommodated, but if you do not have your own, the hotel's two dogs are usually happy to take you for a walk to nearby Hesketh Park. Southport's Lord Street, with its shops and restaurants is a two minute walk in the opposite direction. Golfers are completely spoilt for choice here with four championship courses within the town itself and ten more courses in the surrounding area.

- ⇥ Three single, five double, two twin-bedded and one family room
- £ £
- 🍺 Adnams Bitter; Fuller's London Pride; Marston's Bitter; Moorhouse's Black Cat, Premier, Pendle Witches Brew; guest beers
- 🍽 Snacks and meals every evening
- **CC** accepted

—— STALYBRIDGE ——

Church Inn
422 Huddersfield Road, Millbrook, Stalybridge SK15 3JL
☎ *((0161) 338 2813*
Directions: on the B6175, between Stalybridge and Mossley

This fine old Victorian pub boasts many original features, including a 'baronial' staircase and tiled walls and floor. Its many rooms include a large lounge and a games room, plus a small dining room where good quality food at reasonable prices is served all day. There is also a sizeable function room, which is much in demand as a venue for a folk club and a base for the Carrbrook Brass Band, the Mossley Morris Men and the Milltown Cloggies! There is also a regular live singer who performs every Thursday evening. If it all gets too lively for you, you can retreat in good weather to the garden. Situated on the edge of the Pennines, this is an ideal spot for outdoor pursuits, with the Stalybridge Country Park and the Leeds-Huddersfield canal both nearby. Children are welcome. One of the family rooms sleeps five, one has four beds, and the other three. All the rooms have shower facilities, but share toilets. A full English breakfast is provided. Pets can be accommodated.

- ⊨ One double, two twin-bedded, three family rooms
- £ £
- 🍺 Banks's Mild, Marston's Bitter
- 🍴 Snacks and meals served daily noon-10 pm (9 pm on Sunday)
- CC not accepted

—— STOCKPORT ——

Southlands Hotel
Beech Road, Cale Green, Stockport SK3 8HF
☎ *(0161) 480 5681;* FAX *(0161) 476 2143*

This hotel comes fairly highly recommended. Most of CAMRA's National Executive stayed here for a meeting and seemed pretty satisfied – particularly on the beer front. The ales here are competitively priced, even by the standards of the the Manchester region, and to find Robinson's Dark Mild on the bar nowadays is a very rare treat indeed. The hotel's public bar is called Copperfields and is accessible via the hotel and also has a direct street entrance. This low-ceilinged room has built up a good local following, especially with darts and dominoes players. Half of the guest rooms have en-suite bathroom, those with shared facilities are naturally, cheaper. A five percent surcharge is made for bills settled by credit card.

- ⊨ Eight single, eight double, four twin-bedded and one family room
- £ £
- 🍺 Boddingtons Bitter; Marston's Pedigree; Robinson's Dark Mild, Best Bitter; John Smith's Bitter
- 🍴 Snacks and meals daily, lunchtime and evening (except Sunday evening)
- CC accepted

—— WORTHINGTON ——

Crown Inn

Platt Lane, Worthington, Standish, Wigan WN1 2XF
☎ *(01257) 421354;* FAX *(01257) 428981*
Directions: Worthington lies on a minor road between the A49 and A6, a few miles north of Wigan

The guest rooms at the Crown are all still fresh and sparkling, having been part of a £250,000 refurbishment and expansion plan that was completed early in 1998. Furnished and equipped to a high standard and all en-suite, the rooms are suitable for families, but sadly none have been adapted to the needs of less able guests. Breakfast is served in an attractive conservatory, and the hotel's restaurant is open for evening meals, and all day Sunday. The refurbishment also created a 100-seat function room for business or social occasions. This 150-year old free house has a friendly bar where a selection of real ales and lunchtime snacks or meals are available. The Crown is centrally situated in the north-west, roughly equidistant from the M6 (jct 27) and the M61 (jcts 6 and 8), so would make an ideal stopover for weary travellers.

🛏 Four single, six double rooms
£ £ (£££ single room)
🍺 Draught Bass; Boddingtons Bitter; Chester's Mild; Taylor Landlord; Tetley Bitter; guest beers
🍽 Snacks and meals daily, lunchtime and evening
CC accepted

TRY ALSO:

Albany Hotel

87-89 Rochdale Road East, Heywood OL10 1PX
☎ *(01706) 369606*

Privately owned hotel between Rochdale and Bury with 19 en-suite rooms. B&B ££

Black Swan

13 Bottom o'th'Moor, Oldham OL1 3HH
☎ *(0161) 624 4977*

Spacious pub, locally known as the 'Mucky Duck', near the town centre, offering good value accommodation in six guest rooms with shared facilities. B&B £

NORFOLK

CLEY-NEXT-THE-SEA

George & Dragon Hotel
High Street, Cley-next-the-Sea, Holt NR25 7RN
☎ *(01263) 740652;* FAX *(01263) 741275*
Directions: on the A149 coast road

This pub on the north coast stands beside one of the best birdwatching reserves in the country. It has its own comfortable hide on the second floor overlooking the hotel's own scrape (lake) and offering a clear view of the salt marshes and the sea. A 'Bird Bible' in the lounge bar is used for noting unusual sightings. In 1926 the Norfolk Naturalists Trust was formed in the hotel and a close association has remained. Special winter weekend breaks are available to enthusiasts. Many other outdoor pursuits can be enjoyed here, too, such as riding, windsurfing and golf, and for those with a more cultural bent, several stately homes can be visited in the vicinity. Cley is a tranquil village, boasting a fine early 18th-century windmill, a working pottery and an excellent delicatessen with its own smokehouse. The George and Dragon features polished parquet floors throughout the large, relaxing bars and the dining room where the food, based on fresh local ingredients, is highly recommended. All but two of the guest rooms are en-suite; one has a four-poster bed. Pets are catered for. Children under ten are charged £5 per night, older children £10.

- ⊨ One single, four doubles, two twin-bedded, one family room
- £ ££ (££££ single en-suite)
- ◧ Greene King IPA, Abbot, seasonal beers; guest beers
- ⦿ Snacks and meals daily, lunchtime and evening
- CC not accepted

—— DERSINGHAM ——

Feathers Hotel

Manor Road, Dersingham PE31 6LN
☎/FAX *(01485) 540207*
Directions: off the A149 between King's Lynn and Hunstanton

According to the 1999 *Good Beer Guide* the Feathers has something for everyone: two quiet, comfortable, wood-panelled bars for ale-lovers, a separate bar for games and live music, a large safe, landscaped garden with playthings for children and a restaurant. On top of that, there are the five en-suite bedrooms. This fine carstone building, is a mere quarter of a mile from Sandringham. Formerly a coaching inn boasting connections with visiting royalty, the hotel extends its opening hours on summer afternoons to cater for the tourist trade. Family run, the Feathers offers a good value set menu (lunchtime and evening), with plenty of home-cooked choices in the restaurant, as well as a grill menu served in the bar in the evenings. There is a thoughtful selection of vegetarian dishes (including a Sunday lunch) and a children's menu. A full English breakfast is provided. On the real ale front, the bar stocks three guest beers a week, many from small independent breweries. Pets can be accommodated.

⊨ Four twin-bedded, one family room
£ ££
🍺 Adnams Bitter; Draught Bass; guest beers
🍽 Snacks and meals daily, lunchtime and evening
CC accepted

—— DOWNHAM MARKET ——

Crown Hotel

Bridge Street, Downham Market PE38 9DH
☎ *(01366) 382322;* FAX *(01366) 386194*
Directions: Downham Market is on the B1057 Ely-Kings Lynn road; Bridge Street is off the High Street

It would be very easy to pass by the old-fashioned market town of Downham Market and equally easy to dismiss the unassuming facade of the Crown in the old market square. But it would be a mistake. The Crown's small frontage hides a fine 17th-century coaching inn which extends way back. The comfortable, oak-panelled bar, with its roaring fire has scarcely changed in 100 years. Go through the bar and you come to the old stables, now converted into the restaurant, but retaining its bare brick walls and floor; solid elm tables now stand in place of horses in the loose boxes! Meals are also served in the Fox Room, a low-beamed 'Dickensian' parlour. Upstairs the guest rooms are spacious and well-equipped; seven have en-suite bathrooms. Downham Market is a good base for touring north and west Norfolk, with its fens, lavender fields and the fine coastline featuring on the landscape. A few miles in one direction takes you to Sandringham, or go the other way to Ely and its cathedral. Houghton Hall is just one of the many NT properties to visit in the area.

⊨ Two single, four double, four twin-bedded and one family room
£ ££ (£££ single room)
🍺 Bateman XB; Courage Best Bitter, Directors; Theakston Mild, Best Bitter
🍽 Snacks and meals daily, lunchtime and evening
CC accepted

—— HAPPISBURGH ——

Hill House
Happisburgh NR12 0PW
☎ *(01692) 650004*
Directions: next to the church

I would love to stay here, if only to be able to respond to the question, "where did you spend your holidays" with the most original reply ever: "oh, in a railway signal box by the sea"! Indeed one of the rooms offered here really is in a converted signal box, and what's more it benefits from splendid sea views. This double room has its own bathroom (I guess you would not want to trek back to the pub in the middle of the night); the other two rooms in the pub itself, share a bathroom. The Hill House dates back to the 16th century when it was called the Windmill (the name was changed in the 1700s). Once a coaching inn, it has strong connections with Sherlock Holmes, as Sir Arthur Conan Doyle wrote *The Dancing Men* here. The pub boasts a lovely big garden. In summer an outdoor bar is set up for children, who are also welcome as overnight guests. Pets can be accommodated. This coastal village, with the cheerful name, has a useful landmark – its own lighthouse.

⊨ Two double, one family room
£ £
🍺 Adnams Bitter; Fuller's London Pride; Marston's Pedigree; Shepherd Neame Spitfire; guest beers
🍽 Snacks and meals daily, lunchtime and evening
CC accepted

—— INGHAM ——

Swan Inn
Ingham NR12 9AB
☎ *(01692) 581099*
Directions: on the B1151 Stalham-Sea Palling road

The Swan is the newest acquisition to the small tied estate of the local Woodforde's Brewery. This 14th-century thatched pub is situated next to the imposing village church in an unspoilt area of north-east Norfolk. The pub originally formed part of Ingham Priory which was destroyed under Henry VIII – the village is more famous nowadays for its cricket club. The Swan's spacious bars have a genuinely rustic feel, where brick and flint walls combine with oak beams and log fires to create a warm, friendly atmosphere. Alongside Woodforde's own ales you'll find a selection of guests from other, mostly independent, breweries. Home-cooked meals and breakfast are served in the bars. The guest accommodation is in a separate building, a beautifully converted stable block, where again bare brick walls and solid beams give real character to the rooms. All en-suite, the comfortable rooms feature hand-built pine four-poster beds and country furnishings. Modern amenities include TV, radio and tea/coffee making facilities. Children are welcome to stay, but please give prior notice. Equally, pets can be accommodated by arrangement. The inn offers lower rates in winter. Ingham is just a few miles from both the Norfolk Broads and the coast.

⊨ Five double rooms
£ ££
🍺 Adnams Bitter; Woodforde's Mardler's Mild, Wherry, Great Eastern, Nelson's Revenge; guest beers
🍽 Snacks and meals daily, lunchtime and evening
CC accepted

—— KINGS LYNN ——

Stuart House Hotel
35 Goodwins Road PE30 5QX
☎ *(01553) 772169;* FAX *(01553) 774788*
Directions: follow signs for town centre; once through Southgate Arch fork right, after 150 yards fork right again at Lord Napier PH

Stuart House is a family-run establishment, standing in its own grounds in a quiet, but central part of town. It is worth taking the time to properly explore this town which was established in the 12th century; the Tuesday market place has some fine medieval and Georgian buildings (and naturally a market on Tuesday). Use the town as a base and you will find Sandringham, the Norfolk Lavender Farm at Heacham and Burnham Thorpe, Admiral Nelson's birthplace, within easy reach. The hotel offers comfortable, recently refurbished accommodation in 18 en-suite rooms. All are individually furnished – the Honeymoon Suite features a four-poster bed and a jacuzzi. The rooms are equipped with satellite TV, telephone and tea/coffee making facilities. The hotel bar displays the building's Victorian origins and offers bar meals, an extensive selection of malt whiskies (and of course real ales) and a cosy fire. A full a la carte menu is also served in the restaurant, where gourmet nights are a feature. Live entertainment is regularly staged too. The hotel has private parking and gardens.

⋈ Four single, eight double, four twin-bedded and two family rooms
£ ££ (£££ single room)
🍺 Adnams Bitter; Taylor Landlord; Woodforde's Wherry; guest beers
🍽 Snacks and meals daily, lunchtime and evening
CC accepted

—— LARLING ——

Angel Inn
Larling, Norwich NR16 2QU
☎ *(01953) 717963*
Directions: on the A11 between Thetford and Norwich

You can't miss this whitewashed inn as its stands directly on the main road, where it was established in the 17th century to serve the burgeoning coaching trade. Still attracting passing travellers, the pub is also frequented by visitors to the Snetterton race circuit a mile up the road, where a weekly market is held on Sunday. It is very popular with local CAMRA members who hold their annual beer festival at the pub, and come to try the regularly changing guest ales. Morning coffee is available and children are welcome – the pub has its own garden. An extensive menu is served, both in the bar and the restaurant. The overnight accommodation is of a good standard, in five en-suite guest rooms. Larling is close to Thetford, with its extensive forest, and a short drive in the opposite direction (around 15 miles) will take you to the county town of Norwich, with its splendid castle museum, cathedral and other places of interest such as the Sainsbury Art Centre at the University.

⋈ One double, four twin-bedded rooms
£ ££
🍺 Adnams Bitter, plus three changing guest ales
🍽 Snacks and meals, daily, lunchtime and evening
CC accepted

—— MUNDESLEY ——

Royal Hotel

30 Paston Road, Mundesley NR11 8BN
☎ *(01263) 720096;* FAX *(01263) 722055*
Directions: on the main coast road

The Royal is ideal for families with young children as it stands directly across the road from a good beach. Several of the guest rooms can be used for families (the price varies according to the family group). All the hotels rooms offer en-suite facilities, with TV, telephone and teamakers; several of them feature four-poster beds. A full English breakfast is served. A free house, the hotel's main bar has a comfortable olde-worlde charm, enhanced by the fire in the inglenook and leather chairs. Dedicated to Lord Nelson, a local as well as a national hero, the bar features much Nelson memorabilia, and attracts real ale drinkers. Meals can be taken here or in the hotel restaurant. Centrally situated along Norfolk's extensive coastline, with the popular resort of Cromer just a few miles up the road, Mundesley is convenient for trips along the Broads, just to the south, and for visiting Norwich, roughly 20 miles away.

- 🛏 32 double rooms
- £ £ (££ single occupancy)
- 🍺 Adnams Bitter; Greene King IPA; guest beers
- 🍴 Snacks and meals daily, lunchtime and evening
- CC accepted

—— NEATISHEAD ——

Barton Angler Country Inn

Irstead Road, Neatishead, Wroxham NR12 8XP
☎ *(01692) 630740; (01692) 631122*
Directions: on a minor road between Irstead and Neatishead villages

Standing opposite Barton Broad, at the heart of the Norfolk Broads, this rural inn would suit those wanting to holiday near, but not actually on the water. Boat traffic on the Broads in high season can, I am told, get a bit like Piccadilly Circus, so the Barton Angler might be a more relaxing choice. Boats and cycles can be hired by the day locally. For those who prefer to come out of season, the inn offers three or four day breaks at special rates between October and Easter. Over 400 years old, the pub has a pleasant bar which opens on to a patio and extensive gardens. Home-prepared meals can be enjoyed either in the bar or the restaurant. Although there is no specific family room, children are welcome to stay. All but two of the guest rooms have en-suite facilities; two rooms feature four-poster beds, one has a shower and the other a bathroom. A continental breakfast is included in the price, the full English option is available for a supplement. The pub lies roughly equidistant between the Norfolk coast and Norwich – both a 20-minute or so drive and well worth a day trip.

- 🛏 Three single, one double and one twin-bedded room
- £ ££ (£££ for the four-poster room with bath)
- 🍺 Greene King IPA, Abbot
- 🍴 Snacks and meals daily, lunchtime and evening (restaurant closed Monday evening)
- CC accepted

—— NORTHREPPS ——

Parson's Pleasure
Church Barn, Northrepps, Cromer NR27 0LG
☎ /FAX *(01263) 579691*
Directions: next door but one to Northrepps church

At the Parson's Pleasure the accommodation is described as 'celestial' and the food 'divine'. I haven't had the pleasure myself (if you'll pardon the expression), but I shall certainly make the effort in the near future to seek out this splendid establishment. The building is a beautiful old brick and flint barn (which belonged presumably to the neighbouring church), that has been brilliantly converted to provide a bar, restaurant and guest rooms. As many of the original features as possible have been retained internally, with, as one would expect, much exposed timber and bare brick walls. The guest rooms are all en-suite and equipped with TV and tea/coffee making facilities; some may be suitable for guests with disabilities. Pets can be accommodated. The Church Barn enjoys a pleasant rural setting, and is just a mile from the nearest beach. Cromer, which was a very popular resort in Victorian times and has a charming, old-fashioned air, is the nearest town, and Norwich is within easy reach at 22 miles. Golfers can choose from four courses within a six-mile radius, and there are several stately homes and NT properties within striking distance.

- ⊨ One single, four double and one family room
- £ ££
- ◖ Greene King IPA, Abbot
- ◉ Snacks and meals daily, lunchtime and evening
- CC not accepted

—— NORTH WOOTTON ——

Red Cat Hotel
Station Road, North Wootton, King's Lynn PE30 3QH
☎/FAX *(01553) 631244*
Directions: off the A148/A149

The Red Cat has been in the same family for three generations, and I can quite understand what has kept them there. Although friendly and informal, both the public and guest rooms are furnished and maintained to a high standard. The spacious bars are very traditional and the lovely oak-beamed dining room boasts a beautiful latticed bay window and a carved open fireplace. The eight prettily decorated bedrooms all have en-suite bathrooms with electric showers and shaving points; each room also has a TV, hairdryer and the usual facilities. North Wootton is within easy reach of the historic medieval port of King's Lynn, the royal estate at Sandringham and of course the coast, with all its attractions for naturalists. Pets can be accommodated.

- ⊨ Three singles, four double/twin-bedded, one family room
- £ £ – ££
- ◖ Adnams Bitter; Draught Bass; Highgate Dark; guest beer (occasionally)
- ◉ Snacks and meals daily, lunchtime and evening

—— REEDHAM ——

Railway Tavern
17 The Havaker, Reedham NR13 3HG
☎/FAX *(01493) 700340*
Directions: from the A47 at Acle, take the B1140; Reedham is six miles south

Reedham lies in quiet surroundings about half a mile from the river and ferry at the heart of the Norfolk Broads. As the name implies, the pub stands right next to the station, with a regular service from Norwich (20 minutes away). One CAMRA member recommends the train as the village 'lies several T-junctions off a cat's cradle of unclassified roads...if you choose to drive from Lowestoft, at one point you have to take a tiny ferry across the Yare'. The adventurous souls who do discover the tavern will be delighted. The guest rooms are situated in the pub's old stable block and have been refurbished to a very high standard, complete with antique furnishings and en-suite facilities. Access has been provided for guests with disabilities. The two double rooms each have their own shower, while the family room has a full bath, and bunk beds for children. A free house, this friendly pub features a large selection of malt whiskies and lots of games in the bar; there are no fruit machines or jukebox, but the pool room has Sky TV. Daily newspapers are available for customers. The food is recommended, from substantial bar snacks to a full four-course meal in the intimate restaurant. The courtyard garden is the setting for summer barbecues. Pets can be accommodated. By the time you read this the pub may have an added attraction – an on-site brewery is planned.

- ⊨ One double, one twin-bedded, one family room
- £ ££
- ⬛ Up to six real ales, changing regularly
- ⦿ Snacks and meals daily, lunchtime and evening

—— RUSHALL ——

Half Moon Inn
The Street, Rushall IP21 4QP
☎/FAX *(01379) 740793*
Directions: six miles north east of Diss

Largely food oriented, this welcoming 16th-century former coaching inn between Diss and Norwich, enjoys an excellent local reputation for its home-cooked meals. Tables can be reserved for diners in the no-smoking conservatory or in the mellow-beamed bar which boasts a fine inglenook. Food is served all day on Sunday. The pub offers a reasonably-priced wine list and a good choice of real ales, including one produced specially for the pub by Norfolk brewers, Woodforde's. Three of the guest rooms can accommodate families, and some are suitable for guests with disabilities. Two of the older rooms do not have private bathrooms, but they are particularly characterful with a wealth of exposed beams, and very cosy. This quiet corner of Norfolk is well situated as a base for exploring East Anglia as a whole. A couple of miles away the Waveney Valley is noted for its delightful scenery and picturesque old villages. A short drive (17 miles) takes you into Norwich for excellent shopping facilities and the Castle museum.

- ⊨ Seven double/twin-bedded rooms
- £ £
- ⬛ Adnams Bitter, Hoskins Bitter; guest beers
- ⦿ Snacks and meals daily, lunchtime and evening (all day Sunday)
- CC accepted

—— SEA PALLING ——

Old Hall Inn
The Street, Sea Palling NR12 0TZ
☎ *(01692) 598323*
Directions: on the B1159 coast road between Cromer and Great Yarmouth

Those of nervous disposition may not wish to stay here – the inn is reputedly haunted by the ghost of the 'Grey Lady'. Some people, of course, automatically expect England's ancient inns to come complete with resident spirits. However, the Old Hall has only become a pub within the last 30 years; this old manor house was built in the 18th-century and had previously been a farm. Now a free house, it has been well preserved, retaining low ceilings, exposed beams and an inglenook. There are two simply furnished bars, one of which features traditional pub games, and a small restaurant. The food is home-made on a menu which features daily specials alongside locally caught fish and the sought-after Cromer crabs. Reasonably priced accommodation is available in six guest rooms; four are en-suite, the other two have washbasins. All rooms have TV and tea/coffee making equipment. The pub has a large car park and a garden. Sea Palling is a small village, whose fine beach has won a cleanliness award, making it popular with families. The nearest of Norfolk's famous Broads is two miles distant.

- ⇥ One single, one double, one twin-bedded and three family rooms
- £ £
- ◖ Adnams Bitter, Broadside; Elgood's Bitter; Woodforde's Broadsman; guest beer
- ⦿ Snacks and meals daily, lunchtime and evening
- CC not accepted

—— SMALLBURGH ——

Crown Inn
Smallburgh NR12 9AD
☎ *(01692) 536314*
Directions: on the A149 between Stalham and North Walsham

This attractive, thatched and whitewashed pub stands on the main road to Great Yarmouth. Its 15th-century origins have been well preserved in its comfortable, beamed interior. The bar offers a good selection of real ales and meals cooked to order, from freshly prepared ingredients sourced locally as much as possible. If you prefer you may eat in the dining room. The games room opens on to an attractive garden. This part of Norfolk is very popular with visitors, and there is easy access to the 200-plus miles of waterways that make up its best known natural asset, the Broads. The resort of Great Yarmouth is 20 miles away and Norwich, even closer at 14 miles. The Crown has only two rooms to offer, and neither of which are suited to families. Both offer en-suite facilities and there is a private residents' lounge with TV and tea/coffee making facilities. A special winter weekend break of bed and breakfast for Friday and Saturday night and Sunday lunch before departure is available.

- ⇥ One double, one twin-bedded room
- £ £
- ◖ Greene King IPA, Abbot; Marston's Pedigree; Tetley Bitter; fortnightly guest beer
- ⦿ Snacks and meals daily, lunchtime and evening (except Sunday evening)

—— THORNHAM ——

Lifeboat Inn
Ship Lane, Thornham PE36 6LT
☎ *(01485) 512236;* FAX *(01485) 512323*
Directions: follow the A149 coast road from Kings Lynn to Cromer; Thornham is six miles after Hunstanton

An old smugglers' inn, but now a large and busy pub, the Lifeboat's Smugglers Bar, lit by oil lamp aims to recreate the atmosphere that would have prevailed when it was built in the 16th century. The old game of Pennies (which was outlawed by George III) is still played in this characterful bar. Complementing the bar is a spacious lounge with a grand fireplace, and a vine-covered conservatory leading on to a walled patio garden. Traditional country fare is the main feature of the menus here – the local mussels being particularly popular. Meals are served in the bar or restaurant. Most of the 14 guest rooms enjoy sea views and are comfortably furnished and equipped with TV, tea/coffee makers, etc. Children are charged £12 per night. Hearty breakfasts will set you up for a day's walking or birdwatching. You are welcome to bring your dog to accompany you. A short drive will take you to Holkham Hall, Sandringham and other historic sights.

- ⇔ Four double, six twin-bedded and three family rooms
- £ £££ (££££ single occupancy)
- ⌻ Adnams Bitter; Draught Bass; Greene King IPA, Abbot' Woodforde's Wherry; guest beer
- ⦿ Snacks and meals daily, lunchtime and evening
- CC accepted

—— WARHAM ALL SAINTS ——

Three Horseshoes
Bridge Street, Warham All Saints, Wells-next-the-Sea NR23 1NL
☎ *(01328) 710547*
Directions: half a mile from the A149 coast road, between Wells and Stiffkey

The CAMRA member who recommended this village pub for the first edition described it as a 'genuine time warp' and happily, it remains so. The walls are adorned with old posters and photographs, even a case of clay pipes. A grandfather clock and gas lighting in the public bar add to the atmosphere, and, in keeping with the period feel, the beers here are all gravity dispensed, served through a 'hole-in-the-wall' bar. The second room, a step down from the bar boasts some antique one-armed bandits. There is an emphasis on home cooking, featuring many old-fashioned dishes, with daily specials. Cider is available in summer. The accommodation is next door in the old post office, a Grade II listed building, where the residents' lounge, dominated by its inglenook, is charming and very cosy – the only modern concession is the TV. The furnishings in the bedrooms are traditional, even down to the proper white bedlinen (oh, bliss). One double room is en-suite and as it is on the ground floor, may suit less mobile guests. The other rooms all have washbasins. The accommodation is unsuitable for children under 14, but dogs are welcome.

- ⇔ Two single, three double rooms
- £ £
- ⌻ Greene King IPA; Woodforde's Mardler's Mild, Wherry; guest beers
- ⦿ Snacks and meals daily, lunchtime and evening
- CC not accepted

—— WELLS-NEXT-THE-SEA ——

Crown Hotel
The Buttlands, Wells-next-the-Sea NR23 1EX
☎ *(01328) 710209;* FAX *(01328) 711432*
Directions: off the A149

This hotel, with its imposing Georgian facade, overlooks a large tree-lined green, known as The Buttlands, which was used by townsmen in the middle ages to practise their archery skills. Wells is pretty little fishing port, where Lord Nelson, who was born in a neighbouring village, returned in his later years, to set up home with his wife. Some say it has not changed much since his time. The Crown is also convenient for other tourist sites, such as Holkham Hall and the Sandringham Estate, and there are miles of sandy beaches for families to enjoy. The food is highly recommended, prepared by award-winning chefs for the restaurant and bar. Children are catered for in a south-facing sun lounge, and there are no less than four guest rooms suitable for families. Ten of the rooms have en-suite bathrooms and special two-night breaks are available in the winter and midweek during the spring. Pets are catered for by arrangement.

⋈ One single, six doubles, four twin-bedded and four family rooms
£ ££ (££££ single en-suite)
🍺 Adnams Bitter; Draught Bass; fortnightly guest beer
🍴 Snacks and meals daily, lunchtime and evening
CC accepted

TRY ALSO:

White Horse Hotel
4 High Street, Blakeney, Holt NR25 7AL
☎ *(01263) 740574*

Good quality en-suite accommodation in a creekside village opposite Blakeney Point
B&B £ – £££

White Horse Inn
Fakenham Road, East Barsham, Fakenham NR21 0LH
☎ *(01328) 820645*

Three en-suite rooms in a 17th-century free house near Little Walsingham. B&B ££

NORTHAMPTONSHIRE: SEE LEICESTERSHIRE, RUTLAND & NORTHAMPTONSHIRE

NORTHUMBERLAND

—— ALLENDALE ——

King's Head Hotel

Market Place, Allendale, Hexham NE47 9BD
☎ *(01434) 683681*
Directions: on the B6295, just south of Hexham

It is hard to believe, but Allendale, up by Hadrian's Wall claims to be at the geographical centre of Great Britain. This large picturesque village in the Northumberland National Park is certainly a central spot from which to tour the north of England. Set in a designated area of outstanding natural beauty, it offers a wealth of outdoor pursuits or you can head off for Newcastle and Tyneside's Metro Centre. The King's Head is a lovely, traditional old inn, with a comfortable bar. Free from electronic machines, it offers a tranquil atmosphere in which to enjoy a good selection of ales (some from local brewers) and the excellent home-cooked food from a regularly changed menu. Vegetarians are catered for in an imaginative fashion and children can pick from their own menu or opt for a smaller portion of an adult dish. Aware how fierce the weather can be up here, the licensees go out of their way to make your stay comfortable. The four en-suite guest rooms are centrally heated (with extra back up for when it's really cold) and electric blankets are also provided. All rooms have a television and coffee/tea makers. Pets can be accommodated.

- ⇔ Three double, one family room
- £ £
- 🍺 Beer range varies, with always six or seven real ales on tap
- 🍽 Snacks and meals daily, lunchtime and evening
- **CC** accepted

—— CORBRIDGE ——

Wheatsheaf

St Helens Street, Corbridge NE45 5HE
☎ *(01434) 632020*
Directions: off the A69/A68

Solidly built out of stone to withstand the Northumbrian winters, this lovely old inn dates back to the 14th century, while the village itself has a far more ancient history. It was built up around the Roman fort of Corstopitum, which was a supply depot for Hadrian's troops. Many of the major sites along Hadrian's Wall are within just a few minutes' drive; while Newcastle-upon-Tyne and Kielder Water, Europe's largest man-made lake, are within 30 minutes' drive. A warm welcome is assured at the Wheatsheaf which has a comfortable bar and lounge. The conservatory restaurant offers spectacular views over the Tyne valley and the river. There is also a large garden. The six guest rooms all have en-suite bathrooms, telephone and tea/coffee making facilities.

- ⇔ Two singles, three doubles, one family room
- £ £ (£££ single)
- 🍺 Vaux Samson; Wards Best Bitter
- 🍽 Snacks and meals daily, noon–9.30pm (9pm Sunday)
- **CC** accepted

—— FALSTONE ——

Blackcock Inn

Falstone, Hexham NE48 1AA
☎/FAX *(01434) 240200*
Directions: off the A69 at Hexham; follow Kielder Water signs

The Blackcock Inn, originally a single-storey thatched house, has been modernised and enlarged over the years, but has retained many interesting features, including the blackleaded range in the bar and a rather grand black marble fireplace in the small dining room that once graced a country mansion, Allerwash Hall. Food is available all day in the bar and dining room, and there is a good, often changed, selection of real ales, including a house beer from Whitbread. Three of the four bedrooms have en-suite bathrooms, and all have TV and hospitality tray. A stair lift makes the guest rooms accessible to most visitors, although none of the rooms is specifically adapted for guests with disabilities. Children are welcome to stay (the garden has a play area) and pets can be accommodated. The Blackcock attracts many customers taking advantage of the local facilities for activity holidays. Falstone lies at the southern end of Kielder Water, with its superb amenities for water sports and fishing. Two cycling routes also pass near the inn: the Reivers and the Coast to Coast routes.

ᕫ One single, three doubles, one twin-bedded room
£ £
🍺 Ruddles Best Bitter; John Smith's Magnet; Theakston Best Bitter; Wells Bombardier; guest beers
🍽 Snacks and meals daily, served from 11.30 am-9.30 pm
CC accepted

—— SEAHOUSES ——

Olde Ship Hotel

Seahouses NE68 7RD
☎ *(01665) 720200;* FAX *(01665) 721383*
Directions: by the harbour

I've not been to Seahouses since I lived briefly in Durham in the 1970s, and left from Seahouses pier on a fascinating trip to the Farne Islands. I remember the Olde Ship being absolutely crammed with nautical memorabilia, and apparently that is still the case – which is not really surprising since the hotel has been run by the same family for well over 80 years. The guest rooms, however, have recently been upgraded, very stylishly and gained four-crown highly commended status from the ETB. Some of the rooms enjoy a sea view, and they all have en-suite bathrooms, satellite TV and all the other amenities you would expect in a hotel of this class. Attractively furnished, some bedrooms feature four-poster beds. Children over ten years old can be accommodated. The characterful main bar boasts stained glass windows, and there is another snug, low-beamed bar and a small family room. In the harbourside garden you can try your hand at quoits.

ᕫ One single, nine double and six twin-bedded rooms
£ £££ (££ low season)
🍺 Draught Bass; McEwan 80/-; Marston's Pedigree; Morland Old Speckled Hen; Ruddles Best Bitter; John Smith's Bitter; Theakston Best Bitter; guest beer (occasionally)
🍽 Snacks and meals daily, lunchtime and evening
CC accepted

—— SLALEY ——

Rose & Crown Inn

Main Street, Slaley, Hexham NE47 0AA
☎ *(01434) 673263;* FAX *(01434) 673305*
Directions: take the Slaley turn (B6306) off the A68

The rooms at the family-run Rose & Crown have also recently had a face lift and offer comfortable en-suite accommodation with TV and coffee/tea making equipment. By the time this guide is published a brand new fourth (double) room should be ready. The inn has a cosy, traditional bar which stocks a house ale, and an attractive dining room. All the food is prepared on the premises under the supervision of landlady, Margaret Pascoe, and includes full meals, tasty bar snacks and a full English breakfast. A 200-year-old listed building, the pub is just five miles from the historic town of Hexham and within easy driving distance of Kielder Forest, the Roman wall (including the forts at Vindolanda and Housesteads) and the Metro Centre. A mile away, Slaley Hall Golf complex is a popular championship course, while arrangements can be made at the pub for other sporting activities, such as horse-riding, sailing and fishing. The lovely Northumbrian coast and the Holy Island are also well worth a visit. Children can be accommodated in a double room, the pub itself has a family room and a garden.

- One single, three doubles
- £ £
- Black Sheep Special; Theakston Best Bitter; two guest beers
- Snacks and meals daily, lunchtime and evening

CC accepted

—— STAGSHAW BANK ——

Fox & Hounds

Stagshaw Bank, Corbridge NE45 5QD
☎ *(01434) 633024*
Directions: on the A68, two miles north of Corbridge

This welcoming Grade II listed building dates back 400 years and is built out of local stone to withstand harsh winters. Well situated for visitors to the north-east, it is five miles from the lovely market town of Hexham, noted for its abbey, 15 miles from Gateshead's Metro Centre and 17 miles from one of the country's best open-air museums at Beamish. If you still have any energy after visiting that lot, there are five golf courses within a five-mile radius. All the eight bedrooms are en-suite and the room price includes a full English breakfast. Children are welcome at this ETB three-crown establishment. There is always a good reason to come back here as the three handpulls on the bar offer a regularly changing range of real ales; traditional cider is also stocked. Meals are taken in the spacious conservatory/restaurant.

- One single, six doubles, one family room
- £ ££
- Guest beers (always three on tap)
- Snacks and meals daily, lunchtime and evening

CC accepted

TRY ALSO:

Dyvels Hotel
Station Road, Corbridge NE45 5AY
☎ *(01434) 633633;* FAX *(01434) 632461*

Five en-suite rooms in this lovely old village near Hadrian's Wall.
B&B £ (££ single occupancy)

All lovers of good pubs should keep an eye out for outlets
bearing the British Institute of Innkeeping logo and membership plaques, as its aims are to promote high standards
of professionalism in licensed retailing and to provide the
skills, training and nationally recognised qualifications to
help members run some of the best pubs in the country.

WHAT CAMRA DOES FOR YOU

• All CAMRA members receive our monthly newspaper, What's Brewing. It gives hard news from the world of beer and pubs – advance notice of festivals and events as well as information about new beers and breweries.
• We sell a wide range of books, including local guides – you'll find a list of national titles at the end of this book. Ring the CAMRA HQ telephone number to enquire about local publications.
• CAMRA branches run beer festivals, brewery trips, pub visits and other social activities.

Members of CAMRA are ordinary drinkers motivated solely by a love of good beer – they are all ages, both sexes, and from all walks of life.

JOIN TODAY

You're welcome to get involved.
CAMRA has been called 'Europe's most successful consumer organisation' – but we still need your help.
CAMRA is run locally and nationally by elected, unpaid volunteers.
CAMRA is a not-for-profit body and is completely independent of any commercial interest.
CAMRA relies totally on people like you for funds and support.
Help us stand up for the rights and choice of ordinary drinkers.

You will find a subscription form at the end of this book. It's only £14 for a single subscription and there are discounts for young people, over 65 and joint subscriptions.

NOTTINGHAMSHIRE

—— BARNBY-IN-THE-WILLOWS ——

Willow Tree Inn
Front Street, Barnby-in-the-Willows NG24 2SA
☎ *(01636) 626613*
Directions: off the A17

The delightfully-named Barnby-in-the-Willows is a quiet village, not far from Newark (which still holds a popular market almost every day) and the Sherwood Forest, famous of course, for the legend of Robin Hood. The Willow Tree was not built until long after Robin and his Merry Men had ceased holding up wealthy travellers to give up their money to the poor, but this 17th-century inn was established to serve that same coaching trade. A comfortable free house, the Willow Tree boasts an open log fire in every room and features stone floors and exposed beams. It offers freshly cooked food in the bar or restaurant in the evening and at weekends, a good wine list and a choice of real ales, including a house beer from Bateman and a weekly changed guest beer. Families are welcome (the pub has a garden) and pets can be accommodated. The guest rooms are en-suite, and offer all the amenities one would expect in an ETB three-crown establishment, including a full English breakfast.

- ⛃ Four double, three twin-bedded and two family rooms
- £ £ (££ single occupancy)
- ⛾ Marston's Pedigree; guest beer
- ⦿ Snacks and meals daily, evenings plus Saturday and Sunday lunchtime
- CC accepted

—— EDWINSTOWE ——

Forest Lodge Hotel
Church Street, Edwinstowe, Mansfield NG21 9QA
☎/FAX *(01623) 824443*
Directions: on the A6034, just off the A614

Edwinstowe bills itself as 'Robin Hood's Village', and indeed it does lie at the heart of Sherwood Forest, near the famous Major Oak. The hotel itself stands opposite St Mary's Church, where, according to legend, Robin and Maid Marion were wed. The Forest Lodge has been completely refurbished to a high standard since being taken over by John and Carol Henshaw in 1997. They have taken care to carry out the work sympathetically, and the guest rooms, comfortably furnished in country style, are all en-suite, and one has a four-poster bed. All have TV and tea/coffee making facilities. The bar, with its beamed ceiling and exposed brickwork always stocks two guest beers, and offers a varied menu. The Hayloft bar caters for large parties and business entertaining (up to 80 people). Local amenities include horse-riding, golf and a swimming-pool, while other attractions (particularly popular with children) include the World of Robin Hood, the castle at Nottingham (a 35-minute drive), and Sherwood Forest Farm Park.

- ⛃ Four double, two twin-bedded, one family room
- £ £ (££ in four-poster room)
- ⛾ Marston's Pedigree; Ruddles Best Bitter; guest beers
- ⦿ Snacks and meals daily, lunchtime and evening
- CC accepted

—— KEGWORTH ——

Station Hotel
Station Road, Kegworth DE74 2GE
☎ *(01509) 672252;* FAX *(01509) 670648*
Directions: two minutes from the M6 (jct 24), off the A6, a mile outside the village towards Bonington

The Station Hotel was built 1847 to serve the burgeoning railway trade. That business has dwindled all over the country and in Kegworth has ceased altogether since the trains no longer stop here at all. The pub, has however, survived and is popular both with locals and road travellers, particularly for the quality of its cuisine. All food is home made, using fresh ingredients where possible, including local game and herbs from the pub's own herb garden. The restaurant is upstairs, but meals can also be taken in the bar or the other two traditionally furnished rooms downstairs. The pub is surrounded by countryside with good local walks. Its large garden is popular with families and has splendid views. The four bedrooms, also traditionally furnished, are particularly spacious and have TV and tea/coffee making facilities, but no private bathrooms. A full English breakfast is provided. Children are welcome to stay, and would probably enjoy a trip to the American Adventure (15 miles away). Another attraction, Donnington Park, is closer at five miles.

- ⋈ Two single, one double, one twin-bedded room
- £ £
- 🍺 Draught Bass; M&B Mild; guest beers
- 🍽 Snacks and meals daily, lunchtime and evening

TRY ALSO:

Turks Head
Grove Street, Retford DN22 6LA
☎ *(01777) 702742*

Friendly 1930s pub with mock-Tudor frontage and a very friendly, cosy atmosphere. Simple, good value accommodation, including a family room. B&B £

—— KIMBERLEY ——

Nelson & Railway Inn
Station Road, Kimberley NG16 2NR
☎ *(0115) 938 2177*
Directions: one mile north of the M1 jct 21

BRITISH INSTITUTE *of* INNKEEPING
MEMBER
SETTING *professional* STANDARDS

This homely pub has featured in almost every edition of the *Good Beer Guide*, a tribute to its consistent high standards (particularly on the beer front) for over 25 years. Originally two inns (hence the somewhat odd name), the pubs were joined some time ago to form a single unit, although happily keeping separate bars. It looks on the outside almost more like a Victorian cottage than a pub and the entrance is via the garden path. The Nelson is also in the fortunate position of standing right next door to Hardys & Hansons brewery (no wonder the beer's always in such perfect condition). An electric pump is used for serving the Best Bitter, whilst the Kimberley Classic is handpulled. The food is highly recommended – much of it is home made, using vegetables and herbs grown in the pub's own garden, and there is an emphasis on game dishes. Meals can be taken in the wood-panelled bar or the small restaurant. Relax afterwards in the a well restored, beamed lounge. There are just three guest rooms with shared bathroom facilities. They are simply, but comfortably furnished and inexpensive, with an excellent, full English breakfast included in the price. This is DH Lawrence country and Nottingham – where the author's birthplace is now a museum – is just 20 minutes' drive away, whilst dedicated fans can make a pilgrimage to nearby Eastwood to the DH Lawrence Centre.

🛏   One double, one twin-bedded, one family room
£   £
🍺   Hardys & Hansons Best Bitter, Kimberley Classic, seasonal beer
🍽   Snacks and meals daily, lunchtime and evening
CC accepted

—— NETHER LANGWITH ——

Jug & Glass
Queens Walk, Nether Langwith, Mansfield NG20 9EW
☎/FAX *(01623) 742283*
Directions: on the A632 between Cuckney and Bolsover

Good value bed and breakfast is offered in this unspoilt village inn. There has been a hostelry on this site since the 12th century and the present house is over 300 years old. The guest accommodation is a relatively new addition to the pub; one of the rooms has en-suite facilities. This is a traditional inn, situated on the village green, with a quiet public bar, where pub games are played around the open fire. Meals can be taken here or in the restaurant. As at the Nelson (above), the Best Bitter is dispensed here by electric pump, with Kimberley Classic served via handpump. The garden, with a little stream running nearby, is a popular venue for outdoor drinking in summer. It is close to Sherwood Forest visitor centre and Clumber Park (both approximately eight miles away). Other local attractions are Cresswell Craggs (four miles) and Bolsover Castle (five miles).

🛏   One twin-bedded, one family room
£   £
🍺   Hardys & Hansons Best Bitter, Kimberley Classic, seasonal beer
🍽   Snacks and meals daily, lunchtime and evening (except Sunday evening)
CC not accepted

NEWARK

Mail Coach
Beaumond Cross, 13 London Road, Newark NG24 1TN
☎ *(01636) 605164*

The Mail Coach was obviously built to serve the coaching trade, but these days attracts a good regular local following, who are a friendly, welcoming bunch. Set just off from the centre of this historic town, a five-minute walk takes you to the cobbled square where a market is still held almost daily. Newark, whose castle is famous for its connections with the Civil War and Robin Hood, has become better known in recent years for the popular antiques fair held on the Newark showground and as the site of the first Center Parcs holiday village in the UK. The pub's guest rooms are all comfortable and well serviced, although only three offer en-suite facilities. The rooms are unsuitable for children, but group rates are offered for party bookings. If you feel in party mood, book in on a Thursday when regular live music – everything from blues and jazz to folk – is staged. The bands play outside in good weather in summer.

- ⊨ Two single, one double and four twin-bedded rooms
- £ £ (££ single room)
- 🍺 Boddingtons Bitter; Flowers IPA, Original, Glentworth Dizzy Bonde; Marston's Pedigree; guest beer
- 🍽 Snacks and meals daily, lunchtime and evening
- CC accepted

NORMANTON-ON-TRENT

Square & Compass
Eastgate, Normanton-on-Trent, Newark NG23 6RN
☎ *(01636) 821439*
Directions: three miles from the A1, signed off the B1164, south of Tuxford

Standing on the edge of the village, this popular pub has been well converted from three cottages, with care taken to preserve its low timbered ceilings and traditional character. Cosy and friendly, it boasts a large wood-burning stove in the central fireplace, and encourages intimacy with several snug areas and alcove. The restaurant, called the Gun Room, is decorated with game shooting memorabilia and stuffed birds, and (not surprisingly) specialises in game dishes. Vegetarians may prefer to eat in the bar where they are also well catered for. Children are made very welcome, with a family room next to the main bar and a good-sized garden with play equipment. Adults can enjoy playing pool and nine pin skittles. The single en-suite bedroom has its own entrance, giving visitors some independence, and pets can be accommodated. Christmas is a good time to visit for beer lovers as Adnams seasonal Tally Ho is always bought in a year in advance to 'lay down' for the following winter. Lincoln, with its cathedral and other attractions, is an easy drive at 12 miles. Breakfast is not included in the room price, but is an optional extra.

- ⊨ One family room
- £ £ Room rate
- 🍺 The beer range (from Adnams) changes weekly
- 🍽 Snacks and meals daily, lunchtime and evening (Sunday: traditional roast lunch only served)
- CC not accepted

OXFORDSHIRE

——— BABLOCK HYTHE ———

Ferryman Inn
Bablock Hythe, Northmoor OX8 1BL
☎ *(01865) 880028;* FAX *(01865) 881033*
Directions: by the Thames, between Stanton Harcourt and Standlake

By an ancient old ferry crossing on the River Thames, the Ferryman occupies a site where an inn has stood for over a thousand years, serving river traffic and tourists. There is still a working ferry here and visitors can also hire rowing boats and steam launches. Day fishing tickets are available, and hotel guests can take advantage of free fishing on the Thames. There is always something going on at the Ferryman, which has a nine-acre field for outdoor events which range from car rallies, raft races and regattas to a beer festival in mid-July. The function room has a skittle alley with an Aunt Sally. The pub intends to open its own brewery in 1999. The spacious public rooms include the Riverside Lounge Bar and the Fishermans Bar with a pool table and dartboard. Meals can be taken in either bar or the restaurant. The pub itself (including the WC) is accessible to customers in wheelchairs, but none of the guest rooms is adapted to their needs. The six en-suite rooms all have river views and access to a large balcony at the rear. The have tea and coffee making facilities and TV, but are strictly for non-smokers.

🛏 Three double, one twin-bedded and two family rooms
£ £ (single occupancy £££)
🍺 Greene King IPA, Abbot; guest beer (occasionally)
🍴 Snacks and meals daily, lunchtime and evening
CC not accepted

——— BAMPTON ———

Romany Inn
Bridge Street, Bampton OX18 2HA
☎ *(01993) 850237*
Directions: on the A4095 Witney–Faringdon road

The Romany has only been a pub since the 1960s, having been a grocer's store and a café before that. The building, however, is 17th century, built over a Saxon cellar. Now a very well established hostelry, it is just one of the many attractive buildings in this Cotswolds village in an area which has much to offer the visitor. Other local tourist haunts include Witney (famous for its blankets), Kelmscot (erstwhile residence of William Morris of the Arts & Crafts movement) and the delightful towns of Burford and Bibury. Children are welcome to stay, and the pub's extensive, but secluded garden has a good play area. The Romany has a friendly atmosphere, serving excellent ale, including a couple of beers from the independent Wychwood Brewery in Witney. Food, both in the bar and the restaurant is recommended. The guest rooms are comfortable (all but one are en-suite), and pets can be accommodation by arrangement. The rates vary according to season.

🛏 One single, five doubles, four family rooms
£ £ (single en-suite ££)
🍺 Archers Village; Courage Directors; guest beers
🍴 Snacks and meals daily, lunchtime and evening
CC accepted

—— BLEWBURY ——

Red Lion at Blewbury
Nottingham Fee, Blewbury, Didcot OX11 9PQ
☎ *(01235) 800403;* FAX *(01235) 850142*
Directions: 300 yards north of the A417

Simple, but reasonably priced accommodation, including a full English breakfast, is available at this unspoilt, picturesque pub which was established in the late 18th century. None of the rooms has a private bathroom, but they are all spacious and comfortable and offer firm beds. The pub itself also has a cosy, comfortable feel to it and is full of character, featuring exposed beams and brasses, old clocks and a large inglenook. It enjoys a good reputation locally for its meals, which can be enjoyed either in the restaurant, where there is a no-smoking area, in the main bar, or the wine bar. The menu includes daily specials and a vegetarian choice. The pub has its own garden, and children are welcome to stay overnight. Blewbury is south of Oxford and convenient for anyone with business in Reading. For race-lovers, Newbury is just a little further south, via the A34.

🛏 One single, one double and one twin-bedded room
£ £
🍺 Brakspear Bitter, Special, seasonal beers
🍴 Snacks and meals daily, lunchtime and evening (Sunday evening for residents only)
CC not accepted

—— BURFORD ——

Lamb Inn
Sheep Street, Burford OX18 4LR
☎ *(01993) 823155;* FAX *(01993) 822228*
Directions: off the High Street

The Lamb, in the appropriately-named Sheep Street is a famous old inn in a Cotswolds town that is extremely popular with tourists, and therefore can get very busy at peak times. I would advise anyone visiting the Cotswolds to try and go out of season (if you can work out when that is!). Then, providing your budget allows, I would suggest making a reservation at this inn (special weekend and mid-week breaks are available). Dating back to the 15th-century, the Lamb sits very comfortably in its surroundings, the mellow stone looks like it almost grew there. In keeping with its setting, the flagstoned bar and panelled lounge are beautifully furnished with old settles and comfy armchairs and sofas. Bar meals are served at lunchtime, whilst in the evening, the pretty restaurant offers adventurous menus that are changed daily – expect to pay around £24 a head for a choice of three courses or £19 for two courses. The guest rooms, all en-suite, are individually styled, most of them having a cottagey feel, although some offer four-poster or half-tester beds. Children are welcome to stay and pets can be accommodated. The pub has a delightful garden. Burford, by the River Windrush, is a very attractive town, often called the 'Gateway to the Cotswolds', and makes a good base for touring.

🛏 Fifteen double and twin-bedded rooms
£ ££££
🍺 Adnams Bitter; Hook Norton Best Bitter; Wadworth 6X; guest beer (occasionally)
🍴 Snacks and meals daily lunchtime; evening meals daily (except Sunday)
CC accepted

—— FIFIELD ——

Merrymouth Inn

Stow Road, Fifield OX7 6HR
☎ *(01993) 831652;* FAX *(01993) 830840*
Directions: on the A424 Burford–Stow-on-the-Wold road, opposite the Fifield turn

Mentioned in the *Domesday Book*, this historic, 13th-century coaching inn is an ideal choice for touring the Cotswolds. Its heavily beamed bar with stone floor is so typical of the region, what better way could there be to absorb the atmosphere of this beautiful area? You will quickly feel at home in this family-run inn, with its log fires and good food prepared daily on the premises, served in the bar or restaurant. The bedrooms are in a separate building with TV, tea/coffee making facilities and telephone. All but one of the rooms has an en-suite bathroom. Special breaks with bed, breakfast and evening meal are available – phone for details. Major tourist attractions such as Blenheim Palace, Warwick Castle and the Cotswold Wildlife Park are within easy reach of the pub and the centres of Oxford, Stratford-on-Avon, Cheltenham and Warwick make good day trips. The pub has its own garden and a family room, so children are made very welcome.

⋈ Two single, three double, five twin-bedded and one family room
£ **££** (single room **£££**)
🍺 Banks's Bitter; Donnington BB, SBA; Wadworth 6X; guest beer (occasionally)
🍽 Snacks and meals daily, lunchtime and evening

—— GORING ——

John Barleycorn

Manor Road, Goring, Reading RG8 9DP
☎ *(01491) 872509*
Directions: turn off the B4009 at the Miller of Mansfield pub

This Brakspear pub just squeaks into the Oxfordshire listings, although its postal address is actually Berkshire. It stands on the Ridgeway long distance footpath, very popular with hikers, on the Oxfordshire side of the River Thames and is tucked away from the main street of pretty Goring village. The low-ceilinged, 17th-century house has a proper public bar as well as a cosy lounge, although there is no price differential between them. Meals are served in the lounge/restaurant, which can accommodate families. The extensive menu features home-made, freshly prepared dishes, including daily specials. There is a limited choice for vegetarians. The guest beer is from the brewery's own selection. Pool and bar billiards are played here and there is a garden for sunny days. None of the rooms have en-suite bathrooms, but they do all have TV and tea/coffee making facilities and pets can be catered for.

⋈ One single, two double, one family room
£ **£** (**££** single)
🍺 Brakspear Bitter, Special; guest beer
🍽 Snacks and meals daily, lunchtime and evening
CC accepted

—— GREAT TEW ——

Falkland Arms

Great Tew, Chipping Norton OX7 4DB
☎ *(01608) 683653;* FAX *(01608) 683656*
Directions: off the B4022, five miles east of Chipping Norton

Great Tew is a rarity – a quite unmodernised village of thatched cottages. The Falkland Arms has its rightful place opposite the green and the village school. It, too, is reminiscent of days gone by and has been left untouched as far as possible, boasting heavy beams, oak settles, flagstone floors and an inglenook. To make you believe you have truly stepped back in time, you can even buy snuff and clay pipes at the bar, where incidentally you can choose from no less than eight real ales, or a traditional cider. And the pub should never run short of drinking vessels as the ceiling is hung with an enormous collection of them. The pub's tiny dining room opens in the evening to serve award-winning food – the licensees warn that bed and breakfast guests have to reserve a table as they get heavily booked. Lunches are available in the bar. The guest rooms have recently been refurbished to a high standard and decorated in keeping with the rest of the building. All the rooms are en-suite and two feature four-poster beds; the large room on the top floor offers the best view of the garden and beyond. The bedrooms (like the dining room) are for non-smokers only. The pub does not accept children under 14. Special winter midweek breaks are available, but early booking is advised.

- ⇆ One single, five double rooms
- £ ££ (£££ single room)
- 🍺 Adnams Broadside; Badger Tanglefoot; Hook Norton Best Bitter; Wadworth 6X, SummerSault, Farmer's Glory; guest beers
- 🍽 Snacks and meals daily, lunchtime, evening meals daily (except Sunday)
- CC accepted

—— HOOK NORTON ——

Sun Inn

High Street, Hook Norton OX15 5NH
☎ *(01608) 737570;* FAX *(01608) 730770*
Directions: opposite the church

You shouldn't have any reason to complain about beer quality here – the ale has only has to travel a matter of yards along the road from the brewery. This welcoming village pub attracts a good mix of customers of all ages who enjoy its warm, relaxed atmosphere and the fact that there is ample seating. Hops, flagstone floors and open fires add charm to this traditional inn. It has a skittle alley that doubles as a function room (capacity 60 people), and a recently refurbished restaurant offering an inventive menu of freshly made meals, cooked to order. There are six en-suite bedrooms (for non-smokers only), with TV, telephone and tea/coffee making equipment. The pub does not accept bookings from families with children. A full English breakfast is included in the price. Hook Norton is a picturesque village in the Cotswolds, half an hour's drive from both Oxford and Stratford-on-Avon.

- ⇆ One single, three double, two twin-bedded rooms
- £ ££
- 🍺 Hook Norton Mild, Best Bitter, Generation, Old Hooky; guest beers
- 🍽 Snacks and meals daily, lunchtime and evening
- CC accepted

—— LONG WITTENHAM ——

Machine Man Inn
Fieldside, Long Wittenham OX14 4QP
☎/FAX *(01865) 407835*
Directions: between Abingdon and Didcot, one mile off the A415 at Clifton Hampden, follow signs

The Machine Man derives its unique name from its 19th-century owner, the local mechanic. He used to dispense his home-brewed cider while repairing farm machinery, aided by his steam-powered traction engine. Obviously an engine fanatic, he also founded (in 1865) a museum for model railways in the village. This down-to-earth local enjoys a pleasant setting, overlooking farmland, just off the village centre. There is good fishing to be had and some pleasant Thamesside walks. Any visitors in springtime who happen to be *Winnie the Pooh* fans can take a walk to Little Wittenham for the annual Pooh Sticks competition (in March) at the bridge. Good value, home-made food is listed on a short but frequently changed menu; the steaks from the local butcher are said to be excellent, but there is also a vegetarian choice. The dining area, which is separated from the bar by archways, can accommodate children, who are also welcome to stay. All six guest rooms have en-suite facilities, TV and coffee/tea making equipment. Pets can be catered for.

⋈ Six double rooms
£ £ (single occupancy ££)
🍺 Abbey Bellringer; Hop Back Summer Lightning; West Berkshire Good Old Boy; guest beers
🍽 Snacks and meals daily, lunchtime and evening
CC accepted

—— NORTH LEIGH ——

Woodman Inn
New Yatt Road, North Leigh, Witney OX8 6TT
☎ *(01993) 881790*

BRITISH INSTITUTE of INNKEEPING
MEMBER
SETTING *professional* STANDARDS

Directions: off the A4095 Woodstock road, two miles west of Witney

This cosy country inn sits at the edge of the village, benefiting from panoramic views over the Evenlode Valley. Very pretty and well maintained, it is convenient for the busy market town of Witney and Burford, the 'Gateway to the Cotswolds'. The magnificent Blenheim Palace, five miles away is well worth a day trip and one could easily spend several days exploring Oxford, with its wealth of attractions, which is just ten miles from North Leigh. Although the pub itself is not very big, it does have a large, terraced garden which plays host to the twice-yearly Oxfordshire Beer Festival at Easter and the August Bank Holiday. Although neither of the guest bedrooms has its own bathroom, they are attractively decorated and feature comfortable, antique Victorian furnishings. One room can accommodate a family. The home-made food is highly recommended, and overnight guests are served a full English breakfast. Pets can be accommodated.

⋈ One double, one twin-bedded room
£ £ (single occupancy ££)
🍺 Hook Norton Best Bitter; Wadworth 6X; two guest beers
🍽 Snacks and meals daily, lunchtime and evening (except Monday evening)
CC accepted

—— SOULDERN ——

Fox

Fox Lane, Souldern, near Bicester OX6 9JW
☎ *(01869) 345284*
Directions: take the Aynho turn off the B4100; the Souldern turn is two miles on the left

An attractive pub, built of the local Cotswold stone in the centre of an extremely picturesque village, the Fox is easily accessed from the M40 (jct 10). Within a 20-mile radius of the village you can reach Oxford, Stratford-upon-Avon, Warwick and Blenheim Palace. This friendly inn, which has won awards for its food and hospitality, is thus central to some of England's most visited tourist destinations. Two of the four bedrooms offer en-suite bathrooms, and all are comfortably appointed. The village has no through traffic, so a peaceful night's sleep is assured. Although there are no family rooms as such, children are welcome to stay. Pets can also be accommodated. The pub boasts open fires in the bar which serves a good range of real ales and also offers a selection of traditional games (but not electronic ones), and there is a garden. Meals are served in either the bar or restaurant.

- Three double, one twin-bedded room
- £ £ (single occupancy ££)
- Draught Bass; Fuller's London Pride; Hancock's HB; Hook Norton Old Hooky; guest beer
- Snacks and meals daily, lunchtime and evening
- CC accepted

—— WATLINGTON ——

Fox & Hounds

13 Shirburn Street, Watlington OX9 5BU
☎ *(01491) 612142;* FAX *(01491) 614571*
Directions: on the B4009, three miles from the M40 (jct 6)

According to local CAMRA members, the Fox & Hounds boasts an unusual food speciality: it offers a selection of over 40 chili dips! I can't imagine how you can make that many different dips, but I am assured it is correct. The rest of the home-made menu is recommended too, meals can be taken in either the bar or the no-smoking dining room. This traditional 17th-century inn has been extended into the neighbouring former butcher's shop, giving three drinking areas. There is also a patio which is a suntrap in fine weather. Families are welcome and children can be accommodated. The rooms are simply furnished and equipped; neither is en-suite. Watlington is a pleasant little town at the edge of the Chilterns, half a mile from the Ridgeway long distance footpath. There are some good walks to be had around here and the keen-eyed bird lover may spot a Red Kite which are apparently abundant in the locality. You don't have to walk alone as dogs can be catered for at the pub. The Fox & Hounds is almost equidistant from Oxford and Henley, where the landlord's lovingly kept Brakspear's ales come from.

- Two twin-bedded rooms
- £ £
- Brakspear Bitter, Old (winter), Special, seasonal beers
- Snacks and meals daily, lunchtime and evening
- CC accepted

TRY ALSO:

Angel
14 Witney Street, Burford OX18 4SN
☎ *(01993) 822438;* FAX *(01993) 822714*

16th-century inn, once a smugglers' den, but now a respectable hostelry with an award-winning restaurant. En-suite rooms. B&B ££

George Hotel
Main Street, Lower Brailes OX15 5HN
☎ *(01608) 685223*

Ten minutes from the Hook Norton brewery, this pub offers full English breakfast and accommodation in five en-suite rooms. B&B ££

RUTLAND: SEE LEICESTERSHIRE, RUTLAND & NORTHAMPTONSHIRE

The Lamb Inn,
Burford, Oxon.

SHROPSHIRE & STAFFORDSHIRE

—— BISHOPS CASTLE ——

Castle Hotel
The Square, Bishops Castle, Shropshire SY9 5BN
☎/FAX *(01588) 638403*
Directions: in the market square

Situated on the main square of a small market town on the Welsh border, this 18th-century inn enjoys a good local following. The front entrance opens into a snug bar which boasts much original woodwork. This leads into a larger room and a public bar at the rear, where there is a good selection of traditional games. The pub has a large garden and serves excellent food. All the guest rooms have en-suite bathrooms and a full English breakfast is included in the price. Children cannot be accommodated here. The handpumps in the bar offer a choice of real ales, including one from the Six Bells Brewery, which was established at the pub of the same name in the town in 1997 (although as an independent business) and now supplies some 25 local outlets. The Castle is convenient for walkers wishing to explore Offa's Dyke and Wild Edriks Way.

- ⊨ One single, three double and one twin-bedded room
- £ ££
- 🍺 Fuller's London Pride; Hobsons Best Bitter; Six Bells Big Nev's; Worthington Bitter; guest beer
- 🍽 Snacks lunchtime; meals daily, lunchtime and evening
- CC accepted

—— BRIDGNORTH ——

Bear
Northgate, Bridgnorth, Shropshire WV16 4ET
☎ *(01746) 763250*
Directions: from the High Street, follow Broseley signs (B4373)

This attractive pub stands near the historic Northgate in the busy market town of Bridgnorth. Comfortable and friendly, it retains the traditional two-bar layout, which is mercifully free from juke box and slot machines. Popular with local and visiting CAMRA members for its daily changing guest beer, it also enjoys a reputation for its excellent, home-cooked meals, based on fresh produce, including daily specials. Thursday is 'gourmet evening' when the lounge bar becomes a restaurant for the night and booking is essential. Both the bar and the lounge have access to a charming cottage garden. The well appointed accommodation at the pub has been refurbished sympathetically, in keeping with the character of the pub, and to a high standard. All the rooms have en-suite bathrooms, TV and tea/coffee making equipment. Children are welcome to stay and would surely enjoy a trip on the Severn Valley Steam Railway – the station is close by, and trains operate daily in summer, weekends out of season. Also of interest in and around the town are the castle ruins, many half-timbered buildings and the Stanmore Motor Museum. A short drive takes the visitor to Ironbridge, designated a World Heritage Site and well worth a day trip.

- ⊨ One single, two double, one twin-bedded room
- £ £ (££ single room)
- 🍺 Batham Mild, Best Bitter; Holden's Bitter; Ruddles Best Bitter; at least two guest beers
- 🍽 Snacks lunchtime; meals lunchtime and evening, Monday-Saturday
- CC not accepted

—— BURSLEM ——

George Hotel

Swan Square, Burslem, Stoke-on-Trent, Staffordshire ST6 2AE
☎ *(01782) 577544; 6 (01782) 837496*
Directions: on the A50 in the town centre

The George is a smart hotel at the heart of the 'Potteries', in a town famous for its connections with Arnold Bennett, whose novels, such as *Anna of the Five Towns* and *Clayhanger*, were set in the area. Many of the famous potteries still active today have shops or visitor centres in the town, such as Royal Doulton (right next to the hotel), Crown Burslem and Wade. You can also visit the Gladstone working pottery museum at nearby Longton. Children, however, might be more interested in the leisure amenities at nearby Festival Park which include Waterworld, Superbowl and a multi-screen cinema complex. The George, which has been awarded an ETB four-crown rating, has 38 immaculate en-suite guest rooms which all have Sky TV, hairdryer, trouser press and hospitality tray. It has good conference/meeting facilities, with each function room having its own bar. The Carvery is ideal for a quick lunch, or you can linger longer in the elegant dining room.

🛏 Nine singles, 12 doubles, 13 twin-bedded and two family rooms
£ ££ (single ££££)
🍺 Marston's Bitter, Pedigree; Morland Old Speckled Hen; guest beer (occasionally)
🍽 Snacks and meals daily, lunchtime and evening
CC accepted

—— CANDY ——

Old Mill Inn

Candy, near Oswestry, Shropshire SY10 9AZ
☎ *(01691) 657058*
Directions: follow the B5479 to Oswestry, turn left after the bridge to Trefonen, first right after Ashfield, then first right

If you drive down the hilly roads to the west of Oswestry in the delightfully named Candy valley, you will come across this friendly, family-owned inn. In a picturesque setting, in its own extensive, peaceful grounds, this old stone inn stands right on Offa's Dyke Walk. The original pub has been extended to provide a large L-shaped lounge, replete with beams and log fires. There is always a choice of real ales, and a creative menu offers freshly cooked meals most days. The accommodation is simple, but inexpensive, with a choice of full English or continental breakfast. The guest rooms share bathroom facilities and a residents' lounge with a TV. The market town of Oswestry on the Welsh border is two miles away, while a half hour drive takes you to the historic city of Chester, where the zoo is a popular attraction. Nearby Llangollen is also well worth a visit. Children are welcome, although there are no particular facilities for them.

🛏 Two single, one double, two twin-bedded rooms
£ £
🍺 Beer range varies
🍽 Snacks and meals, lunchtime and evening Wednesday-Monday
CC accepted

—— ECCLESHALL ——

George Hotel
Castle Street, Eccleshall, Staffordshire ST21 6DF
☎ *(01785) 850300;* FAX *(01785) 851452*
Directions: from the M6 jct 14, take the A5013, or the A519 from jct 15

There is an added incentive to spend a night at the George – the owners have installed their own brewery behind the pub (the first in the town for more than a century), serving up a range of real ales, including some seasonal additions. The brewery has expanded considerably since opening in 1995 and now supplies some 450 outlets. Even without the its own beers, this former coaching inn at the town centre has enough traditional character to attract plenty of visitors. The bar features exposed brick, heavy beams and a delightful inglenook. Meals can be taken here or in the Bistro. The ten en-suite bedrooms are furnished to a high standard and are pleasantly decorated in keeping with the age of the building. They have all the usual facilities, including satellite TV. Pets can be accommodated. Eccleshall is a market town in the Vale of Trent, offering plenty to see and do in the locality, including the Wedgwood Centre at Barlaston, Ironbridge, the home of the Industrial Revolution, and, for families, Alton Towers theme park. Special weekend breaks rates apply and pets can be accommodated.

- ⇥ two single, six double, one twin-bedded and one family room
- £ £££ (££££ single) midweek; ££ weekend
- 🍺 Slaters Bitter, Original, Premium, Supreme, seasonal beers; two guest beers
- 🍽 Snacks and meals daily, lunchtime and evening (all day Saturday and Sunday)
- CC accepted

—— IRONBRIDGE ——

Golden Ball Inn

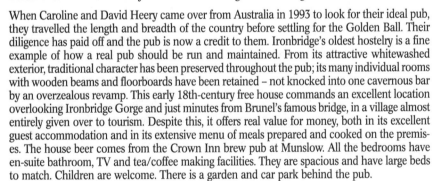

BRITISH INSTITUTE *of* INNKEEPING
🍺 MEMBER
SETTING *professional* STANDARDS

1 Newbridge Road, Ironbridge, Shropshire TF8 7BA
☎ *(01952) 432179;* FAX *(01952) 433123*
Directions: take the Madeley road from Ironbridge then first right

When Caroline and David Heery came over from Australia in 1993 to look for their ideal pub, they travelled the length and breadth of the country before settling for the Golden Ball. Their diligence has paid off and the pub is now a credit to them. Ironbridge's oldest hostelry is a fine example of how a real pub should be run and maintained. From its attractive whitewashed exterior, traditional character has been preserved throughout the pub; its many individual rooms with wooden beams and floorboards have been retained – not knocked into one cavernous bar by an overzealous revamp. This early 18th-century free house commands an excellent location overlooking Ironbridge Gorge and just minutes from Brunel's famous bridge, in a village almost entirely given over to tourism. Despite this, it offers real value for money, both in its excellent guest accommodation and in its extensive menu of meals prepared and cooked on the premises. The house beer comes from the Crown Inn brew pub at Munslow. All the bedrooms have en-suite bathroom, TV and tea/coffee making facilities. They are spacious and have large beds to match. Children are welcome. There is a garden and car park behind the pub.

- ⇥ One single, three double and one twin-bedded room
- £ £ (££ single)
- 🍺 Courage Directors; Marston's Pedigree; Ruddles Best Bitter; guest beers
- 🍽 Snacks and meals daily, lunchtime and evening
- CC accepted

—— LUDLOW ——

Bull Hotel

14 The Bull Ring, Ludlow, Shropshire SY8 1AD
☎ *(01584) 873611;* FAX *(01584) 873666*
Directions: in the town centre, near the railway station

Right at the heart of the town, the Bull is one of the oldest buildings in Ludlow. Though the frontage is Georgian, the rear of the inn boasts a black and white facade, which is typical of the area. The earliest record of the building is in the mid-14th century, but it could well be older. The Bull is just one of some 500 listed structures in this splendid old town, which is well worth a visit in its own right, but also convenient for other tourist destinations such as Ironbridge, Powis Castle and the Severn Valley. The pub's four guest rooms are comfortable and well appointed, with TV and hospitality tray, and they all have en-suite facilities. One twin-bedded room can accommodate a child's bed (for a £10 supplement) and pets can be catered for, too. The bedrooms overlook the pub's yard, which is lively in summer when it hosts the Ludlow Fringe, staged alongside the famous Ludlow Festival. Other events at the pub include theatre, music and children's entertainment.Live music in winter, too. Meals are served at lunchtime in the bar and the upstairs dining room.

⇥ Two doubles, three twin-bedded rooms
£ £
🍺 Marston's Bitter, Pedigree; guest beer (occasionally)
🍽 Snacks and meals daily, lunchtime (Sundays from Easter-September only)
CC accepted

WHAT CAMRA DOES FOR BEER AND WHAT YOU CAN DO!

Thousands of pubs are being closed or ruined.
The Campaign for Real Ale campaigns
• locally to save individual pubs
• nationally on planning, licensing and tax laws
• with official bodies to extend 'listing' to historic pubs
• to encourage people to use their local pub

The grip of the multi-nationals and nationals is tightening
CAMRA campaigns against monopoly and national brands
• CAMRA promotes the independent brewers and publicises the many interesting new companies entering the market
• in 1997 CAMRA saved the vital guest beer law, threatened with abolition
• CAMRA acts as a vigorous consumer voice in Westminster, Whitehall and Brussels.

CAMRA is a non-profit making body run by an elected panel of volunteers. Add your voice and help safeguard your beer and your pub!

—— NORTON ——

Hundred House Hotel

Bridgnorth Road, Norton, Shifnal, Shropshire TF11 9EE
☎ *(01952) 730353;* FAX *(01952) 730355*
Directions: on the A442, midway between Bridgnorth and Telford

This stunning hotel will not fit everyone's budget, but visitors from all over the world have praised it so highly, we couldn't leave it out. 'Romantic' is one of the most apt descriptions, either for the Georgian inn itself or its most delightful garden, which produces 50 varieties of herb for the hotel's highly regarded kitchen. Another guest described her stay as 'fragrant' – well that might have been the garden or the characterful bar which is hung with bunches of drying flowers and herbs, adding to the atmosphere created by the exposed brick walls, wood panelling and open log fires. The recommended meals, which are based as far as possible on fresh seasonal produce, can be enjoyed in the bar or restaurant. The guest rooms come in two categories, standard and superior. All are en-suite with TV, telephone, coffee/tea makers, etc. The superior rooms are larger and more sumptuously furnished with period pieces; some have half-tester beds, and for additional amusement, some feature a decorative swing hanging from the ceiling beam! The hotel is convenient for visitors to Ironbridge, and guests can take advantage of the 'Ironbridge Travel Back in Time' package which includes two days dinner, bed and breakfast, plus passports to the sites in Ironbridge. Pets can be catered for by arrangement.

- ⛁ One single, three double, two twin-bedded and four family rooms
- £ ££££
- ⛃ Everards Tiger; Wood Shropshire Lad; guest beers
- ⛾ Snacks and meals daily, lunchtime and evening
- CC accepted

—— SHREWSBURY ——

Castle Vaults

16 Castle Gates, Shrewsbury, Shropshire SY1 2AB
☎ *(01743) 358807*

Convenient for non-drivers, the Castle Vaults is just a minute's walk from the main line station. A free house, this family-run pub stands in the shadow of the castle, which now houses a Regimental Museum. Shrewsbury is a Tudor town with many well preserved black and white buildings typical of the period. The *Brother Cadfael* stories are based around the town and visitors to the Shrewsbury Quest can experience something of a monk's lifestyle in the 12th century and see 'Brother Cadfael's' workshop. A flower show is held in the town in August and a CAMRA beer festival in September (the Castle Vault's rooms get booked up very early for this event). The bedrooms all have en-suite facilities, with TV and tea/coffee making equipment, and a full English breakfast is included in the price. Pets can be accommodated. The pub specialises in Mexican cuisine, served in the bar or dining room (which offers a no-smoking area). There is always a choice of four guest beers, including local brews. In summer take your drink up to the unusual roof garden, which is a suntrap in good weather.

- ⛁ one single, three double, one twin-bedded and one family room
- £ £ (££ single occupancy)
- ⛃ Hobsons Best Bitter; Marston's Pedigree; guest beers
- ⛾ Snacks and meals lunchtime and evening, Monday-Saturday
- CC not accepted

—— TELFORD ——

Albion Inn
Station Hill, St Georges, Telford, Shropshire TF2 9AD
☎ *(01952) 614193*
Directions: take the M54 exit to Telford Centre, head for railway station, then follow signs for St Georges/Oakengates

Conveniently situated for visitors heading for central Wales, or for those with business in Telford itself (three minutes' drive), this friendly village local is comfortable and welcoming. The refurbished single bar offers three distinct areas with darts at one end and a dining area at the other, where a black-leaded range is a feature. It offers a good value, varied menu of mainly home-cooked fare; the steaks are particularly recommended, and the breakfasts are hearty. Special weekend breaks including bed, breakfast and evening meal are available at reduced rates, and there are also reductions for long stays. The guest rooms offer high standards of comfort and facilities, and are both en-suite. The pub boasts an award-winning garden with views over the Shropshire plain. Ironbridge is just ten minutes' drive away and Shrewsbury can be reached in 20 minutes.

╞═ One double, one twin-bedded room
£ £ (££ single occupancy)
◖ Banks's Mild; Marston's Bitter, Pedigree, Head Brewer's Choice
◉ Snacks and meals daily, lunchtime and evening
CC not accepted

TRY ALSO:

Swan Inn
Knowle Sands, Bridgnorth, Shropshire WV16 5JL
☎ *(01746) 763424*

Overlooking Bridgnorth and the Severn Valley, five rooms in a traditional roadside pub. B&B ££

White Lion
West Castle Street, Bridgnorth, Shropshire
☎ *(01746) 763962*

Inexpensive bed and breakfast; three of the five rooms are en-suite. B&B £

Shrewsbury Hotel
Bridge Place, Shrewsbury, Shropshire SY1 1PU
☎ *(01743) 236203*

En-suite rooms at one of JD Wetherspoons' new Wetherlodges, attached to a traditional Wetherspoons free house. B&B £

Cock Hotel
148 Holyhead Road, Wellington, Telford, Shropshire TF1 2DL
☎ *(01952) 244954;* FAX *(01952) 248965*

The Cock is being refurbished as this guide is being compiled, to provide seven en-suite rooms. Prices (before refurbishment): B&B £ (££ single en-suite)

SOMERSET

—— BISHOPS LYDEARD ——

Lethbridge Arms
Gore Square, Bishops Lydeard, Taunton TA4 3BW
☎ *(01823) 432234;* FAX *(01823) 433982*
Directions: on the A358, between Taunton and Williton

You can't miss this whitewashed 16th-century former coaching inn standing on a crossroads at the edge of the Quantocks. Originally a stopping place for watering cattle, the Lethbridge became the magistrate's court in the first half of the 19th century and later housed the local library. The CAMRA member that recommended this rural inn, told me sternly, it was 'overdue for inclusion'. He praised the landlord, Trevor Evans, for his excellent ales (better kept than many in the area) and traditional cider and the home-cooked food, served in the two bars and restaurant, which includes a good value carvery on Sunday. There is a selection of pub games and a skittle alley. The overnight accommodation is comfortable, although only two of the rooms have private bathrooms. Children are welcome to stay (the extensive garden features a large play area), and pets can be catered for. The surrounding area offers amenities for good walks, fishing and golf. It is a five-minute walk to a station of the West Somerset railway line.

- ⇔ three double, one twin-bedded and three family rooms
- £ £
- 🍺 Boddingtons Bitter; Cotleigh Tawny; Marston's Pedigree; Morland Old Speckled Hen; guest beer (occasionally)
- ◉ Snacks and meals daily, lunchtime and evening
- **CC** accepted

—— CLEVEDON ——

Campbells Landing Hotel
The Beach, Clevedon BS21 7QT
☎ *(01275) 872094;* FAX *(01275) 342595*
Directions: opposite the pier

This comfortable hotel stands right opposite Clevedon's recently restored pier, and is convenient for many of the area's tourist attractions, such as the SS Great Britain and Cheddar Gorge. Clevedon is seven miles from Bristol and the suspension bridge and the M5 motorway are also easily accessible. Quiet and restful, the hotel offers a chance to take the bracing sea air, whilst enjoying good food and an excellent choice of real ales. Meals are served in the bar or restaurant and the extensive menu features daily specials. All the guest rooms are en-suite and have up-to-date amenities including cable TV. Four of the rooms offer views over the Bristol Channel. A full English breakfast is provided. Children are welcome to stay and pets can be accommodated by prior arrangement.

- ⇔ Six double, two family rooms
- £ ££ (single occupancy £££)
- 🍺 Draught Bass; Courage Best Bitter; Exmoor Gold; Fuller's London Pride, ESB; guest beers
- ◉ Snacks and meals daily, lunchtime and evening (except Sunday evening)
- **CC** accepted

—— COMBE HAY ——

Wheatsheaf

Combe Hay, Bath BA2 7EG
☎/FAX *(01225) 833504*
Directions: turn off the A367 from Bath to Shepton Mallet by the Odd Down 'park and ride', take left turn for Combe Hay, pub is two miles down lane

Built in 1576, but only becoming a pub in the 18th century, the Wheatsheaf is a characterful, spacious inn, replete with solid timber beams and log fires. Set in its own delightful terraced garden where the plentiful tables are regularly cleared and cleaned during busy summer sessions, the inn enjoys panoramic vistas over the north Somerset countryside. The large, airy guest rooms are in fact in a separate building in the grounds of the pub, and benefit from the same views. Newly built in cottage style, they are tastefully furnished with country pine; all the rooms have en-suite bathrooms, TV and tea/coffee making facilities. The family room has an extra single bed for a child (over ten's only accepted). The pub has a good reputation for its traditional English fare, which is all prepared on the premises, based on fresh local ingredients – game and fish dishes are a speciality. Combe Hay itself is a charming village, boasting a grand Georgian manor house and rectory. There are good local walks to be enjoyed, particularly following the towpath of the old Somerset Coal Canal. For cultural diversion, Bath is just a 15-minute drive away.

⊨ Two double, one family room
£ ££
🍺 Butcombe Bitter; Courage Best Bitter; Morland Old Speckled Hen; guest beers
🍽 Snacks and meals daily, lunchtime and evening
CC accepted

—— CORTON DENHAM ——

Queen's Arms Inn

Corton Denham, near Sherborne DT9 4LR
☎ *(01963) 220317*
Directions: four miles south-west of Sherborne, three miles south of A303

Local CAMRA members describe the Queen's Arms as a 'superb country inn' which has established a well-deserved reputation for its cask ales (a monthly guest features), freshly prepared food on a regularly changing menu, and comfortable overnight accommodation. This fine pub stands in glorious countryside, much beloved of ramblers. An 18th-century hamstone building, it nestles in the Cadbury Hills in the peaceful village of Corton Denham, on the Dorset border. Country pine furniture, log fires and bare stone floors all add to the pub's attractive, welcoming atmosphere. The five en-suite bedrooms, enjoying pleasant views, are equally well appointed. The pub does not accept children as overnight guests. In the bar, chalkboards are used to display real ales and the good choice of daily specials on the food menu. Thatchers and Kingston Vale ciders are also stocked. Local attractions include the abbey town of Sherborne, Haynes Motor Museum and Wincanton race course.

⊨ One single, two double, two twin-bedded rooms
£ ££
🍺 Archers Best Bitter; Cotleigh Tawny; Smiles Golden Brew; guest beers
🍽 Snacks and meals, lunchtime and evening, Monday evening-Sunday lunchtime
CC not accepted

—— CROWCOMBE ——

Carew Arms

Crowcombe, Taunton, TA4 4AD
☎ *(01984) 618631*
Directions: just off the A358, ten miles from Taunton

A few years ago CAMRA compiled a National Inventory of Heritage Pubs – only those that had been little altered over the years were eligible, and the list is certainly not very long, considering the tens of thousands of pubs in the country as a whole. The Carew Arms appears on the list and is a typical example of the type of pub that CAMRA would like to see saved for posterity (or at least for future generations to enjoy). This unspoilt, stone-built 'gem' was built in the 17th century and retains its flagged stone floors, original windows and three open fireplaces. The bedrooms, as one might expect, are not en-suite, and are described as 'cosy'; the only modern concessions being the provision of a TV and tea/coffee making facilities. Children are welcome to stay and pets can be accommodated. The pub boasts a skittle alley and an untamed garden. Good quality food is available, including a full English breakfast. Crowcombe is a lovely village at the southern edge of the Quantocks, in a good area for walking, cycling and horseriding. The West Somerset railway, which runs between Bishops Lydeard and Minehead for most of the year, stops at Crowcombe Heathfield station.

🛏 Two double, one twin-bedded room
£ £
🍺 Butcombe Wilmot's, Exmoor Ale
🍽 Snacks and main meals, lunchtime and evening daily
CC not accepted

—— EAST LYNG ——

Rose & Crown

East Lyng, Taunton TA3 5AU
☎ *(01823) 698235*
Directions: on the A361 Glastonbury road, seven miles from Taunton

A splendid stone fireplace dominates the bar in this ancient (13th century) former coaching inn. Popular with locals and visitors alike, it has the friendly, civilised atmosphere of a village local. The owners of this free house say that their top priorities are food, drink and service. For evening meals in the little restaurant area that adjoins the bar, it is necessary to book, but good bar meals are also available. There is also a skittle alley and an attractive garden. The two comfortable guest rooms have en-suite bathrooms. The pub does not accept children as overnight guests. A short drive takes you to Street, probably Britain's (indeed Europe's) largest village, now famous for its 'factory' shops. Glastonbury, where the energetic can climb the Tor, is also close by.

🛏 Two double rooms
£ £ (single occupancy ££)
🍺 Ansells Bitter; Butcombe Bitter, Wilmot's; Eldridge Pope Royal Oak; Tetley Bitter
🍽 Snacks and meals daily, lunchtime and evening
CC accepted

—— KNAPP ——

Rising Sun
Knapp, North Curry, Taunton TA3 6BG
☎ *(01823) 490436*
Directions: signed off the A361, Glastonbury road, or turn off the A358, Taunton-Langport road at Thornfalcon garage, signed North Curry

Architecturally stunning, this 15th-century longhouse boasts many original features: exposed beams, carved wood panelling, an old bread oven and inglenooks. The terraced garden offers views over the surrounding countryside of the Somerset Levels. A free house, the pub offers a good selection of wines and, in summer, local farmhouse cider, to complement its well-kept real ales. There are just two guest bedrooms, which share a bathroom, but I do not think most people stay here for luxurious accommodation, just for the luxury of not having to go anywhere after dining well. The pub has won awards for its food – a blackboard menu usually offers at least a dozen different fish dishes, all freshly brought in from Brixham and St Mawes. Meat-eaters and vegetarians are not forgotten either, and offered a varied menu. If, however, you do not wish to avail yourself of the full restaurant facilities, snacks are also served in the bar. Children are welcome overnight and pets can be accommodated.

⋈ Two double rooms
£ £ (single occupancy ££)
🍺 Draught Bass; Boddingtons Bitter; Exmoor Ale
🍽 Meals daily, lunchtime and evening; snacks at lunchtime and Sunday-Thursday evenings
CC accepted

—— LUXBOROUGH ——

Royal Oak
Luxborough, near Dunster TA23 0SH
☎ *(01984) 640319;* FAX *(01984) 641298*
Directions: six miles from Dunster

In the first edition of this guide, the rooms at the Royal Oak were described as quaint and unmodernised, but in keeping with the unspoilt atmosphere of the pub. Well, the pub is still unspoilt, a true rural inn of great charm, featuring exposed beams and flagstone floors. However, the guest rooms have had a facelift and been upgraded. They all now have private bathrooms and are attractively furnished in country-style. Children and guests with disabilities are catered for, and there is a honeymoon suite. Most of the rooms are situated in a new extension above the dining area of the pub to ensure a peaceful night for anyone retiring early. There are two dining rooms, the main one leading off from the bar, and a second, more intimate 'Green Room' for candelit dinners. The food, from simple bar snacks to the extensive menu specialising in fish and game, is all excellent. Traditional cider is available here too. This family-run rural village inn nestles in the Brendon Hills at the edge of the Exmoor National Park, ideal for ramblers. Famous for its connections with *Lorna Doone*, the area also offers spectacular coastal scenery (the sea is within walking distance) and picturesque villages. The Royal Oak can cater for pets.

⋈ Six double, two twin-bedded, one family room
£ ££
🍺 Cotleigh Tawny; Exmoor Gold; Flowers IPA; two guest beers
🍽 Snacks and meals daily, lunchtime and evening
CC not accepted

NORTH BREWHAM

Red Lion
North Brewham, Bruton BA10 0JL
☎ *(01749) 850287*
Directions: three miles east of Bruton on the Maiden Bradley road

The owners of the Old Red Lion, Anne and Tom O'Toole list ten reasons on their publicity leaflet about why visitors would enjoy staying at their free house. The CAMRA member that recommended the pub, said he had to agree with all of them! One aspect that particularly appealed to me was that guests are given their own key and have access to their rooms during the day – something that not all establishments offer. The pub has a cosy cellar bar, boasting beams, a flagstoned floor and an open fire, where you can enjoy local ales and traditional Somerset cider. Freshly cooked meals can be eaten here or in the comfortable dining room. The day's special dishes and snacks are listed on a blackboard, and the O'Tooles are happy to cater for special diets by arrangement. The pub has ample parking space and its gardens and meadow offer unspoilt views. The only disadvantage that I can see is that the pub only has two rooms! These are both en-suite with TV and tea/coffee making equipment. Both rooms offer views across the valley to Alfred's Tower, which marks the start of the 28-mile footpath to Ham Hill near Yeovil. This part of Somerset offers plenty of opportunities for ramblers and there are many historic houses and gardens in the area. Bruton itself (three miles) is 600 years old and well worth a visit. Children can be accommodated at the inn, although there are no special facilities.

ᕮ   One double, one twin-bedded room
£   £
🍺   Butcombe Bitter; guest beer
🍽   Snacks and meals daily, lunchtime and evening
CC   accepted

The Royal Oak Inn,
Winsford, Somerset

—— STOGUMBER ——

White Horse Inn

Stogumber, Taunton TA4 3TA
☎ *(01984) 656277*
Directions: take turn off the A358, 12 miles north of Taunton, pub is two miles down lane to Stogumber

The White Horse is a traditional local standing opposite the 12th-century church in the conservation village of Stogumber. This little inn is basically one bar, with an extra room available for private parties. Good wholesome meals are served; and breakfast can be a choice of a full English fry-up, fish or just the continental variety. There are only two guest rooms, which are not suitable for families. They are both en-suite with bath and shower, TV and tea/coffee making facilities. The White Horse is set in open countryside so there are plenty of opportunities for gentle walks or more strenuous hill-walking. It is handy for the West Somerset railway which offers visitors an easy way to get around the local area. Other attractions include Dunster Castle and a cider museum. Local Lane's cider is sold at the pub in the summer.

⨤ one double, one twin-bedded room
£ £
◗ Cotleigh Tawny; Otter Ale; guest beer (occasionally)
▮◗▮ Snacks and meals daily, lunchtime and evening
CC accepted

—— TAUNTON ——

Masons Arms

Magdalene Street, Taunton TA1 1SG
☎ *(01823) 288916*
Directions: in the town centre, opposite St Mary's Church

I would not normally include in this guide a pub such as the Masons Arms as the only accommodation it offers is self-catering. However, the CAMRA member (from Merseyside) that recommended it put in a plea for Somerset's county town to be included and suggested that the Mason's Arms was the best option. He says this free house offers good local beers and the accommodation is second to none. Available all year round, this comprises a well furnished, self-contained flat with its own separate entrance. It has two bedrooms, a spacious lounge with TV and telephone, a well-equipped kitchen and a bathroom with shower. Bed linen is provided and a charge for electricity is included in the rental. Children (and pets) can stay in the flat by prior arrangement. Just because it is self-catering, does not mean that you have to cook for yourself as the pub offers good bar snacks and meals – their speciality is Grillstone dishes with meals served on a pre-heated stone tray. The pub itself offers a quiet retreat, away from the main streets of the town, yet within walking distance of the main shopping area and the bus station. Its newly renovated skittle alley doubles as a function room. For non-drivers, the main line station is just a mile away. The town has its own theatre, the Brewhouse, and other attractions in and around the area include Hestercombe House and gardens, Somerset County Cricket Ground and museum, and the race course.

⨤ One single, one twin-bedded room
£ Rates on application
◗ Draught Bass; Exe Valley Bitter; Juwards Premium; guests
▮◗▮ Snacks and meals Monday-Saturday, lunchtime and evening
CC not accepted

—— WILLITON ——

Foresters Arms
55 Long Street, Williton, Taunton TA4 4QY
☎ *(01984) 632508;* FAX *(01984) 633692*
Directions: on the A39, near Williton station

There are two things to bear in mind before deciding to book in at the Foresters Arms, one: don't stay the night if you are of a nervous disposition – it is rumoured to be haunted; two: don't challenge the local quiz team – one of its members is a *Mastermind* winner! The ghost, incidentally, is reputed to be that of a girl from the old local workhouse. This 17th-century pub on the edge of town gets busy in summer as it plays host to touring cricket teams. For other tourists, it is convenient for the Quantocks and the Brendon Hills and is six miles from Dunster Castle. If you wish, you can leave the car behind and explore the area on the West Somerset railway. The pub offers a good choice of real ales and Rich's traditional cider. Meals are served in both the bar and restaurant. Half of the guest rooms have en-suite facilities, and a full English breakfast is included in its reasonable prices.

🛏 Three single, five double, three twin-bedded and three family rooms.
£ £
🍺 Ash Vine Hop and Glory; Cotleigh Tawny, Harrier; John Smith's Bitter; guest beers
🍽 Snacks and meals daily, lunchtime and evening
CC accepted

—— WINSFORD ——

Royal Oak Inn

Winsford, Exmoor National Park TA24 7JE
☎ *(01643) 851455;* FAX *(01643) 851009*
Directions: off the A396 between Tiverton and Minehead

The Royal Oak is a glorious old thatched inn, dating from the 12th century. It has been well maintained and sympathetically restored to retain its original character while providing modern comforts. A log fire crackles in the old stone fireplace in the beamed bar, while easy chairs and sofas add a homely touch to the lounges. Good food is served in both the restaurant and the bar, offering a daily changed menu of seasonal English fare. Some of the real ales are served direct from the barrel, and traditional cider is also stocked. The inn has eight en-suite bedrooms, some with four poster beds, decorated in elegant country-style, while an annexe offers a further five larger, en-suite rooms. These rooms, which can accommodate an additional child's bed, are set around the courtyard, where there is also a family cottage to let. Picturesque Winsford was described in the early 20th-century by writer, W Hudson as 'second to no English village in beauty', but the Exmoor National Park boasts many other lovely villages, as well as some fascinating historic and natural sites, such as the Caratacus Stone on Winsford Hill, thought to have been inscribed in the Dark Ages, and the Tarr steps, considered to the finest bridge of its type in the country. Children are welcome to stay at the Royal Oak, and pets can be accommodated.

🛏 Eleven double, two twin-bedded and one family room
£ £££ – ££££ (rates vary according to room and season)
🍺 Exmoor Ale; Flowers IPA, Original; Shepherd Neame Spitfire
🍽 Snacks and meals daily, lunchtime and evening
CC accepted

TRY ALSO:

Nettlebridge Inn
Nettlebridge, Oakhill, near Bath BA3 5AA
☎ *(01749) 841360*

Big roadside pub on the A367, convenient for visitors to Bath (30 minutes by car). Six en-suite rooms with family facilities. B&B £

Malt Shovel Inn
Blackmoor Lane, Bradley Green, Cannington, Bridgwater TA5 2NE
☎ *(01278) 653432*

Family-run free house overlooking the Quantocks. Three doubles, one family room. B&B £ (single occupancy ££)

Who'd 'a' Thought It
17 Northload Street, Glastonbury BA6 911
☎ *(01458) 834460;* FAX *(01458) 831039*

This unusually named pub boasts an equally unusual interior – it is stuffed with all kinds of ephemera, including a collection of old advertising signs. Five en-suite rooms. B&B £ – ££ (££ – £££ single occupancy)

Rock Inn
Waterrow, near Taunton TA4 2AX
☎ *(01984) 623293*

Old inn, built against a rock face which is exposed in the bar area. Seven en-suite rooms. B&B ££

Bear Inn
Market Place, Wincanton BA9 9LP
☎ *(01963) 32581*

Simple, inexpensive B&B in a 17th-century coaching inn, just off the busy A303, in the centre of Wincanton. Seven rooms (three en-suite; two suitable for families). B&B £

STAFFORDSHIRE: SEE SHROPSHIRE & STAFFORDSHIRE

SUFFOLK

—— BROME ——

Cornwallis Arms

Brome, Eye, Suffolk IP23 8AJ
☎ *(01379) 870326; FAX (01379) 870051*
Directions: off the A140, Ipswich-Norwich road

The Cornwallis Arms really is something else – well worth saving up for a special occasion. It was built in the 16th century as the dower house to Brome Hall on the Cornwallis estate, and later served as a rectory. It became a country house hotel in the 1970s and was acquired in 1995 by the new St Peter's Brewery, based in Suffolk, and extensively refurbished. The bar is in the original Elizabethan house and serves the brewery's real ales, including the more unusual speciality fruit and wheat beers. There is an elegant restaurant, a most attractive conservatory and a conference room. The guest rooms are quite luxurious, furnished in Tudor or Regency style, featuring four poster beds, exposed beams and en-suite bathrooms. Pets can be catered for. The Cornwallis stands in 20 acres of grounds which include some wonderful topiary and water gardens. If you can drag yourself away from the hotel, it is well worth taking a trip to have a look at St Peter's Brewery, which itself is based in a fine medieval hall at South Elmham, near Bungay. Tours are available (tel 01986 782322) and there is a bar and restaurant open at weekends and bank holidays.

- 13 double, two twin-bedded and one family room
- £ £££ (children £; single occupancy ££££)
- St Peter's Best Bitter, Strong and speciality beers
- Snacks and meals daily, lunchtime and evening
- CC accepted

—— BURY ST EDMUNDS ——

Bushel Hotel

St Johns Street, Bury St Edmunds IP33 1SN
☎ *(01284) 754333*
Directions: off the A14, follow town centre signs

The Bushel is one of the few pubs in this Georgian town to offer accommodation. Clean and homely, all five rooms have TV, tea/coffee making facilities and washbasins, one room has its own shower. The pub is very convenient for the town centre (five minutes' walk), and has its own car park at the back (entrance in St Andrews Street). When this 15th-century former coaching inn was refurbished in the late 1980s care was taken to make the most of the original features of the building. There is a separate area for games – pool and darts are played. Bar meals are available or there is a restaurant which has a carvery. A full English breakfast is served. There is a reduced rate for children.

- Two double, two twin-bedded and one family room
- £ £ (single occupancy ££)
- Greene King IPA, Abbot, seasonal beers
- Snacks and meals daily, lunchtime and evening (except Sunday evening)
- CC accepted

—— CLARE ——

Clare Hotel and Restaurant
19 Nethergate Street, Clare CO10 8NP
☎/FAX *01787) 277449*
Directions: near the town centre

Clare is home of the little independent Nethergate Brewery whose 'Umbel' beers are brewed according to ancient traditions and infused with coriander seeds. The new owner of the Clare Hotel, Richard Herring, has developed a close association with the brewery and you can sample the beers, dispensed by gravity direct from the cellar, in his comfortable bar. This pretty country inn, which is happily devoid of electronic games, jukeboxes, etc., stands on the imposing Nethergate Street (the main road to Cambridge), close to the town centre where filming for TV's *Lovejoy* series took place. Not surprisingly, antiques hunters will find plenty of places to browse around, including an antiques warehouse. Much of the hotel has recently been refurbished, including the conservatory restaurant which looks out on to a secluded walled garden. Food is also served in the lounge bar. All the meals are prepared with fresh produce and the menu includes vegetarian dishes. Morning coffee and afternoon tea are available, and a full English breakfast is provided. The cosy guest rooms were part of the refurbishment programme and they all have en-suite shower and toilet, TV, hot drinks facilities and hairdryer. The rates vary according to season, with a discount available to CAMRA members. Stretch your legs in the nearby Country Park which offers riverside walks and an ancient priory, or explore the ruins of Clare Castle.

- ⊨ Two double, three twin-bedded rooms
- £ £ (££ high season); single occupancy ££ (£££ high season)
- ❶ Nethergate IPA, Augustinian, guest beers (occasionally)
- ⦿ Snacks and meals daily, lunchtime and evening
- **CC** accepted

Cornwallis Arms,
Brome, Suffolk

——— LAVENHAM ———

Angel
Market Place, Lavenham CO10 9QZ
☎ *(01787) 247388;* FAX *(01787) 248344*
Directions: off A1141

This ancient (14th-century) hostelry just oozes charm and character at the heart of an extremely well preserved medieval wool town. The Angel is only one of the beautiful timber-framed buildings in Lavenham where you can also see the magnificent Guildhall which stands opposite the pub, the Priory and lots of smaller domestic dwellings. Inside, the pub has a wealth of exposed beams, and the bar boasts a Tudor double inglenook, scrub-topped tables and an excellent selection of board games – apart from catering for visitors, it is also a well-used village local. If you pick a quiet time, the owners will give you a tour of the medieval vaulted cellars. An award-winning menu, based on fresh local produce is changed daily and caters for children. Meals are served in the bar and restaurant. The guest bedrooms are comfortable, all en-suite, and equipped with TV, telephone and tea/coffee making facilities. There is also a residents' lounge on the first floor which boasts a fine pargeted ceiling. The family bedroom is situated on the ground floor and has its own entrance, with a ramp, so this may suit less mobile guests.

⊨ Six doubles, one family room
£ £££ (single occupancy ££££)
🍺 Adnams Bitter; Greene King IPA; Mauldons White Adder; Nethergate Bitter; guest beer (occasionally)
🍽 Snacks and meals daily, lunchtime and evening
CC accepted

——— LONG MELFORD ———

George & Dragon
Hall Street, Long Melford, Sudbury CO10 9JB
☎ *(01787) 371285;* FAX *(01787) 312428*
Directions: off the A134, three miles north of Sudbury

This is *Lovejoy* country, and a Mecca for antique dealers and hunters – Long Melford boasts almost 40 antique shops! The proprietors at the George and Dragon, the Thorogoods, thoughtfully provided me with a most attractive town (sorry, village) plan which gives details of all the shops and other attractions. It is indeed an unusual village – with a church the size of a cathedral, and two Tudor halls open to the public (Kentwell and Melford Hall). After a tour of all that, you may need a bed for the night which can be provided by the friendly hosts at the village inn. The Thorogoods make every effort to make you feel welcome in their traditionally-run pub. The bars are spacious, the restaurant pleasant, with a menu changed daily, specialising in pies, puddings and local game, and there are delightfully secluded gardens to enjoy in fine weather. The seven guest rooms although small, are characterful and attractively furnished, again in traditional style, with all the usual modern conveniences, including en-suite bathrooms; one room is suitable for visitors with disabilities. Pets are accommodated.

⊨ Two double, four twin-bedded and one family room
£ ££
🍺 Greene King IPA, Abbot; Marston's Pedigree; guest beer
🍽 Snacks and meals daily, lunchtime and evening
CC accepted

SOUTHWOLD

Crown Hotel
High Street, Southwold IP18 6DP
☎ *(01502) 722275;* FAX *(01502) 727263*

Southwold, an old-fashioned seaside town, is the home of Adnams Brewery, and the Crown is the slightly cheaper of its two, small, select hotels here. The brewery has put in place a programme of refurbishment for its hotels, and the Crown has been revamped to a high standard. The lounge and restaurant face the main street of this attractive seaside town, whilst the small public bar at the back has a nautical theme. The food is often superb here, with a daily-changed menu served in the bar or restaurant. The nine en-suite rooms are spacious; the other three are smaller, but characterful with shared facilities. There is a parlour for residents' use, although it is used as an extension of the restaurant at busy times. The room price includes continental breakfast. Note: the hotel closes for a week in January.

⊨ Two singles, nine doubles, one family room
£ £££ (single room £££)
🍺 Adnams Bitter, Broadside, Old (winter) or Mild (summer)
🍴 Snacks and meals daily, lunchtime and evening
CC accepted

WALBERSWICK

Bell Inn
Ferry Road, Walberswick, Southwold IP18 6TN
☎ *(01502) 723109;* FAX *(01502) 722728*

Just across the River Blyth from Southwold (accessible by foot or ferry) stands the peaceful village of Walberswick which has always been popular with visitors to the area. The 600-year-old Bell Inn is at the heart of the village, near the green and just a stone's throw from the beach. The bar has a friendly atmosphere, described by the CAMRA member who recommended it as 'buzzing'. Low beams, flagged floors, high-backed wooden settles and open log fires, all add to its character. The guest accommodation is equally pleasant, in six en-suite rooms. Special mid-week breaks are available in winter, offering three nights accommodation for the price of two. A full cooked breakfast is provided and the emphasis on the bar food is also traditionally English. The service is excellent and the landlady, Sue Ireland-Cutting goes out of her way to cater for her guests' needs. Local attractions include the Minsmere Bird Sanctuary and the famous 'Cathedral of the Marshes' at Blythburgh. Pets can be accommodated by arrangement.

⊨ Four double, one twin-bedded and one family room
£ ££
🍺 Adnams Bitter, Extra, Regatta, Broadside
🍴 Snacks and meals daily, lunchtime and evening (except Sunday evening in winter)
CC accepted

—— WESTLETON ——

Crown at Westleton

Westleton, Saxmundham IP17 3A1
☎ *(01728) 648777;* FAX *(01728) 648239*
Directions: off the A12 at Yoxford

This smart, comfortable pub makes an ideal base for touring the area – providing you are not on a tight budget. It is less than two miles from Minsmere, rated as one of Europe's top bird sanctuaries, and is convenient for visitors to Southwold (seven miles) and Snape (nine miles) where the Maltings play host to the annual Aldeburgh Festival. The comfortable bar displays old photos of the village alongside a collection of antique blacksmith's and wheelwright's tools. The restaurant offers a daily-changed table d'hôte menu. The pub has delightful gardens to enjoy in good weather. The bedrooms are small (some being in a converted stable block), but well appointed, with big, thick towels provided in the en-suite bathrooms. Six of the rooms are quite luxurious, featuring four-poster or half-tester beds and jacuzzis. One room on the ground floor has 'class two' facilities for guests with disabilities. Guide dogs can be accommodated, as can your average family hound. Smoking is not permitted in any of the bedrooms. The rates, which include breakfast, vary according to the standard of the room.

- 🛏 One single, 16 doubles, two family rooms
- £ **£££ – ££££**
- 🍺 Beer range varies
- 🍴 Snacks and meals daily, lunchtime and evening (no bar meals Saturday)
- **CC** accepted

TRY ALSO

Swan

Southwold IP18 6EG
☎ *(01502) 722168;* FAX *(01502) 724800*

Adnams' flagship hotel in Southwold, backing on to the brewery itself. Twenty-seven rooms in the main hotel, a further 18 in the garden. B&B **££££**

White Hart

High Street, Aldeburgh IP15 5AJ
☎ *(01728) 453205*

Welcoming, single-bar pub with three small but nice guest rooms. B&B **£**

SURREY

—— CARSHALTON ——

Greyhound Hotel

2 High Street, Carshalton SM5 3PE
☎ *(0181) 647 1511;* FAX *(0181) 647 4914*
Directions: on the A232 between Croydon and Sutton

Dating back to the 16th century, the Greyhound was once (in)famous for its involvement in cock fighting. Originally built as part of the Gaynesford Estate, it underwent renovations when it was acquired by Young's Brewery in the mid-19th century. Still a Young's house today it was updated again in the late 1960s when a 200-year-old mosaic of a greyhound was uncovered. It is said to be haunted by the ghost of a traveller who froze to death on pub's doorstep. The hospitality has improved somewhat since that happened! It offers four well-appointed guest rooms, two with en-suite bathrooms and all having tea/coffee making facilities and TV. The room price includes a continental breakfast. Children are welcome to stay the night, although there are no special amenities for them. The pub has two bars (one with an open fire), where the Young's ales can be accompanied by home-cooked food. Convenient for Croydon for shopping or business, the pub stands by Carshalton ponds at the heart of what is still considered a village, and is close to Honeywood House, a local Heritage Centre.

- Three double, one twin-bedded room
- £ **£££** (**££** double room, not en-suite; **££££** single occupancy of en-suite room)
- Young's Bitter, Special, seasonal beers
- Snacks and meals daily, lunchtime and evening (except Sunday evening)
- **CC** accepted

WHAT CAMRA DOES FOR BEER

Has your pint lost its flavour?

CAMRA promotes high-quality, tasty, distinctive beers
- through positive awards
- we also monitor and criticise the increasing blandness of many brands
- through 145 beer festivals a year
- by running campaigns for higher standards in breweries and pubs – we even publish a guide to keeping cask-conditioned ale called *Cellarmanship*

—— COLDHARBOUR ——

Plough Inn
Coldharbour Lane, Coldharbour, Dorking, RH5 6HD
☎ *(01306) 711793*
Directions: on the Leith Hill-Dorking road, signed from the Dorking one-way system

The beer at the Plough does not have far to travel – much of it comes from Leith Hill Brewery set up in an old barn right by the pub. The Plough's licensees, set up their own tiny brewery in 1996 'through necessity, due to increasing overheads'. Well maybe necessity was the cause, but the customers are the beneficiaries – the beers are much appreciated by local CAMRA members and the other customers who, particularly in summer, fill this pub to bursting. Drinkers, it has to be said, are limited here as much of the bar area is given over to dining, however, they do spill out into the garden in fine weather. The food is excellent and served at all reasonable times. The pub also stocks a good choice of other real ales (up to nine in all) and a traditional cider. Leith Hill is popular spot with walkers and its famous tower affords dramatic views over the surrounding countryside, much of which is owned by the NT and Forestry Commission. The pub has one en-suite room for overnight guests which unfortunately cannot accommodate children.

- ⊨ One double room
- £ ££
- 🍺 Adnams Broadside; Badger Tanglefoot; Leith Hill Crooked Furrow, Tallywhacker; guest beers
- 🍽 Snacks and meals daily, at all times
- CC accepted

—— FARNHAM ——

Duke of Cambridge
East Street, Farnham GU9 7TH
☎ *(01252) 716584;* FAX *(01252) 716549*

BRITISH INSTITUTE of INNKEEPING
◆ MEMBER
SETTING *professional* STANDARDS

This family-owned free house reopened in 1997 following substantial expansion and sympathetic renovations. Dedicated to the aims of CAMRA members everywhere, the bar has no less than seven handpumps offering a high turnover of unusual beers, many from micro-breweries, whilst regulars include brews from Hogs Back, Donnington and Harveys. It also stocks traditional cider in summer and a choice of more than 20 malt whiskies. You may need a bed for the night if you linger too long in the bar here and happily the pub can offer four en-suite rooms of a good standard. Two of the rooms have an additional sofa-bed so children can be accommodated. Good home-made food on an extensive menu is served in a restaurant area. Pool and bar billiards are played here and live music is occasionally staged. There is a sunny patio for summer days. The pub is convenient for the town centre and railway station (ten minutes' walk), and you can walk to The Maltings, which hosts the annual Beerex, in the same time.

- ⊨ Three double, one twin-bedded room
- £ £
- 🍺 Beer range varies
- 🍽 Snacks and meals daily, lunchtime and evening
- CC accepted

—— HERSHAM ——

Bricklayers Arms

6 Queens Road, Hersham KT12 5LS
☎ *(01932) 220936;* FAX *(01932) 230400*
Directions: off the A317, via the M25 jct 10 and the A3

Visitors in summer will easily spot the Bricklayers by its magnificent window box floral displays. This well presented, Victorian village pub is one of the few in the area to have retained two bars. The guest rooms were added just a few years ago; both have en-suite bathrooms, with thermostatically controlled power showers, and are furnished to a high standard (ETB three-crown status), but are not suitable for children. A direct dial telephone, TV, hair dryer, tea/coffee and valet facilities are provided in each room. A short distance from the M25, giving good access to both Heathrow and Gatwick airports, the pub is convenient for visitors to Hampton Court Palace and the Royal Horticultural Society's Wisley Gardens. It enjoys a good reputation locally for its home-cooked bar food. Meals are not available on Saturday and Sunday evenings, but there are several restaurants in the neighbourhood. The room price does not include breakfast which is charged at an additional £5.50.

🛏 Two double rooms
£ Room rate £ (single occupancy £££)
🍺 Badger Tanglefoot; Boddingtons Bitter; Brakspear Bitter; Flowers IPA; Fuller's London Pride; guest beers
🍽 Snacks and meals daily, lunchtime, and Monday to Friday evenings
CC accepted

—— MICKLEHAM ——

Running Horses

Old London Road, Mickleham RH5 6DU
☎ *(01372) 372279;* FAX *(013720 363004*
Directions: on the B2209, off the A24 between Leatherhead and Dorking, five minutes from the M25 (jct 9)

BRITISH INSTITUTE *of* INNKEEPING
MEMBER
SETTING *professional* STANDARDS

The Running Horses is situated on the old road to London, which in the 16th century when this inn was built, would have been the coaching route.The pub was a popular stop and its bar conceals a highwayman's hideaway. Today's visitors are more likely to come in for a pint after a walk in the beautiful surrounding countryside, managed by the NT – the pub stands just below Box Hill – or after a round of golf (there are two courses nearby). The pub has two traditional bar areas, the main one dominated by a large inglenook. Meals can be taken there or in the restaurant which offers an extensive, high quality menu. The guest rooms, all named after race courses, are a recent addition, offering excellent, comfortable en-suite accommodation with TV, direct dial telephone and tea/coffee making equipment. Children are welcome to stay and pets can be catered for by prior arrangement. Considerable reductions are available for weekend guests. The pub is convenient for Gatwick (20 minutes by car) and Heathrow (35 minutes).

🛏 Four double, one twin-bedded room
£ £££ – ££££
🍺 Friary Meux BB; Fuller's London Pride; King & Barnes Sussex; Morland Old Speckled Hen; Young's Bitter; guest beer (occasionally)
🍽 Snacks and meals daily, lunchtime and evening (except Sunday evening)
CC accepted

—— OCKLEY ——

Kings Arms Inn
Stane Street, Ockley RH5 5TP
☎/FAX *(01306) 711224*
Directions: on the A29, nine miles from the M25

The Kings Arms is another old coaching inn – 400 years old to be precise. It stands on the original Roman road, and is very convenient for a quick dash to Gatwick airport for an early plane – the journey should take no more than ten minutes by car. The pub enjoys pleasant, peaceful surroundings by the village green, with views over the Surrey Hills. The guest rooms also have a nice outlook over the pub's own attractive gardens. The six rooms are all en-suite and well-appointed with good quality furnishings and all the necessary amenities required by today's guests. The bar offers a relaxed atmosphere for meals and snacks, while the more formal Cavalier Restaurant features an upmarket menu in surroundings to match. A full English breakfast is provided. The King's Arms does not take bookings from families with children.

- ⇥ Six double rooms
- £ ££ (£££ single occupancy)
- ⬛ Eldridge Pope Pope's Traditional; Flowers IPA; King & Barnes Sussex; Whitbread Fuggles Imperial; guest beer (occasionally)
- ⦿ Snacks and meals daily, lunchtime and evening
- CC accepted

—— PEASLAKE ——

Hurtwood Inn
Walking Bottom, Peaslake, near Guildford GU5 9RR
☎ *(01306) 730857;* FAX *(01306) 731390*
Directions: turn off the A25 at Gomshall, midway between Guildford and Dorking, the pub is 2.5 miles from the junction

I find the address of this hotel intriguing – where is the Bottom walking to I wonder? However, the village name is explained by the licensees – nothing to do with vegetables apparently, it derives from 'Pise Lacu' a small stream which has its source there. The hotel's name comes from the Hurtwood, a privately owned forest of some 4,000 acres which is popular with ramblers and riders. Other local attractions include Leith Hill, the highest in southeast England where a 64-ft viewing tower offers a panoramic view of the Surrey hills and beyond. The splendid Hurtwood Inn offers elegant public rooms and smart, en-suite bedrooms. Eight of the guest rooms are on the ground-floor, overlooking the garden and can accommodate families or guests with mobility problems. The prices given are for room only; a full English breakfast is available for £8.50 or the continental version for £6.95. Snacks and light meals are served in the bar (which incidentally, stocks traditional ciders), whilst the stylish, oak-panelled restaurant offers a full menu. Pets can be accommodated.

- ⇥ Three single, five double, three twin-bedded and six family rooms
- £ Room rate £ – ££ (££££ single room)
- ⬛ Courage Best Bitter; Fuller's London Pride; Hogs Back TEA; guest beer (occasionally)
- ⦿ Snacks and meals daily, lunchtime and evening
- CC accepted

SUSSEX (EAST)

—— HARTFIELD ——

Anchor Inn
Church Street, Hartfield TN7 4AG.
☎ *(01892) 770424*
Directions: on the B2110, midway between Tunbridge Wells and Forest Row

A must for *Winnie the Pooh* fans! This pub lies near the Ashdown Forest and the famous Pooh Bridge, as immortalised in A A Milne's classic children's story. The theme is continued at the Anchor where the spacious Victorian-style bedrooms feature the lovable bear. Both rooms have en-suite shower rooms, TV and tea/coffee making facilities. Children (and teddy bears) are welcome to stay overnight, although there is no family room as such. Originally a 14th-century farmhouse, the pub's oak beams, wood panelling and open fire help create a cosy atmosphere, popular with locals. A more unusual feature is the veranda which overlooks the side street, giving it a rather Antipodean air. A good value menu is served in the bar and restaurant. I imagine there's honey for breakfast. There are some very pretty villages around this area and the Forest itself is good for walks – your dog can also be accommodated at the inn, so give him a treat too.

⊨ One double, one twin-bedded room
£ ££
🍺 Draught Bass; Harveys BB; Flowers IPA, Original; Fuller's London Pride; Wadworth 6X; guest beer (occasionally)
🍽 Snacks and meals daily, lunchtime and evening
CC accepted

—— ROBERTSBRIDGE ——

Ostrich
Station Road, Robertsbridge TN32 5DG
☎ *(01580) 881737;* FAX *(01580) 881325*
Directions: next to the railway station

Initially, the principal function of the Ostrich was to serve as a station hotel. Now rail trade has diminished, this small family-run pub is very popular as a local, and its overnight guests are just as likely to be car-borne. The pub is still slowly being sympathetically restored, taking care to preserve its classic Victorian pub architecture. Two of the guest rooms offer en-suite facilities, the third has private use of a separate bathroom. They have all been refurbished to a high standard, with modern fittings, including TV and hairdryer, in each room. The pub has a public bar, a saloon bar and a function room. A full English breakfast is served, but the pub does not offer much in the way of meals, except by prior arrangement. Robertsbridge is a medieval village, noted for its rural museum and classic motorcycle shop; a station on the Rother Valley steam railway is under construction here. Several NT properties, including Bodiam Castle, Scotney Castle and Bateman's are within easy reach. Children can be accommodated.

⊨ One double, two twin-bedded rooms
£ ££ (£ not en-suite)
🍺 Harveys BB; King & Barnes Sussex; Larkins Chiddingstone Bitter; guest beer
🍽 Snacks daily, lunchtime
CC not accepted

SUSSEX (WEST)

—— ARUNDEL ——

Swan Hotel

27–29 High Street, Arundel BN18 9AG.
☎ *(01903) 882314;* FAX *(01903) 883759*
Directions: in the village centre

Carefully restored to a very high standard in Victorian style, this lovely old hotel also serves as the Arundel Brewery tap. The brewery was set up in 1992, the first in the town for 60 years, and brews beers to authentic old Sussex recipes – ask the landlord about the local legend of Old Knucker. The traditional style bar and tap room has retained its oak flooring and wood panelling. Light meals can be taken here or in the award-winning restaurant which has a good reputation locally for its menu based on fresh, seasonal produce. There is also a comfortable lounge. The 15 guest bedrooms have been exceptionally well decorated in pleasant fresh colours, and are well appointed with en-suite bathrooms, telephone, hair dryer, TV and tea/coffee making facilities. Arundel is a charming old village with much local tourist interest, including the castle, which is open to the public, the Wild Fowl and Wetlands Trust, and the nearby towns of Brighton, Chichester and Petworth (a must for antiques lovers). Children are welcome to stay and the hotel offers special weekend luxury breaks (based on a two-night stay).

🛏 Two single, eight double, three twin-bedded and two family rooms
£ ££ (single £££)
🍺 Arundel Best Bitter, Gold, ASB, Stronghold, Old Knucker, occasional beers; Fuller's London Pride; guest beers
🍴 Snacks and meals daily, lunchtime and evening
CC accepted

—— COCKING ——

Blue Bell Inn

Bell Lane, Cocking, near Midhurst GU29 0HN.
☎ *(01730) 813449*
Directions: on A286 in the village centre

The picturesque village of Cocking enjoys a favoured situation at the foot of the Sussex Downs – famous walking country. The Blue Bell is a traditional country pub at the village centre with lovely views, and here you are assured of a warm welcome from staff and locals alike. The guest rooms do not have en-suite facilities, but are comfortable and have all the usual amenities. Cocking is convenient for Chichester (nine miles) and the coast (12 miles); other local attractions include the Weald and Downland Open Air Museum, and the Goodwood Estate for horse and motor racing and of course Goodwood House itself. The market towns of Midhurst and Petworth are also worth a visit. The pub staff are happy to provide packed lunches before you set off in the morning.

🛏 One double, one twin-bedded
£ B&B £
🍺 Hampshire Lionheart; Whitbread Boddingtons Bitter, Flowers Original; guest beer
🍴 Snacks and meals daily, lunchtime and evening

──── ELSTED MARSH ────

Elsted Inn
Elsted Marsh, Midhurst GU29 0JT
☎ *(01730) 813662*
Directions: off the A272 Midhurst–Petersfield road; four miles west of Midhurst take Elsted Harting road south for 1.8 miles

The Elsted Inn isn't much to look at – a whitewashed Victorian house, built to serve railway passengers, but the station was closed long ago. More recently, it was the home of Ballard's Brewery, but that too has moved on, and the building has now been converted into new guest rooms. If you do stop to sup at the pub, however, you may find it very hard indeed to move on. There are two simple bars, unmodernised, but very congenial, lit by three open fires, where traditional games have not given way to electronic gadgets. For many visitors though, the little candlelit dining room is the unmissable part, since the owners, who have both been employed as chefs around the world, put a huge amount of effort into creating interesting, tasty dishes, making full use of local produce such as hand-made sausages, and bread from the NT's craft bakery at Slindon. As it has become so popular it is advisable to book for the restaurant although the owners say they can often squeeze a couple of big tables in the bar as long as everyone is prepared to 'muck in together'. The bedrooms, which are named after local breweries all have en-suite bathrooms and the use of a private garden. The pub's main garden offers a good view of the Downs. A choice of full English or continental breakfast is available. Pets can be catered for by prior arrangement. There is a drying room for walkers' damp clothes.

🛏 Two double, two twin-bedded rooms
£ ££ (supplement for single occupancy)
🍺 Ballard's Trotton, Best Bitter, Wild, Nywood Gold (summer), Wassail; Fuller's London Pride; guest beer (usually from a local independent brewery)
🍽 Snacks and meals daily, lunchtime and evening
CC accepted

BRITISH INSTITUTE *of* INNKEEPING
MEMBER
SETTING *professional* STANDARDS

All lovers of good pubs should keep an eye out for outlets bearing the British Institute of Innkeeping logo and membership plaques, as its aims are to promote high standards of professionalism in licensed retailing and to provide the skills, training and nationally recognised qualifications to help members run some of the best pubs in the country.

—— FINDON ——

Village House Hotel

Old Horsham Road, Findon BN14 0TE
☎ *(01903) 873350;* FAX *(01903) 877931*
Directions: off the A24, four miles north of Worthing

This hotel stands at the centre of a lovely village, noted for its horse racing connections – silks from the local stables decorate the bar. Goodwood, Fontwell, Brighton and Plumpton racecourses are all within easy reach. Other outdoor pursuits enjoyed locally are golf (six courses within a ten-mile radius) and walking – the South Downs Way is perennially popular and both the Cissbury and Chanctonbury rings are close by. Walkers are kindly asked to leave boots outside. Built of local stone, with a white-painted frontage, the Village House dates back to the 16th century. Apart from the convivial bar, there is a restaurant which enjoys an excellent reputation locally, especially for its curries. A traditional cider is usually stocked alongside a range of real ales. The pub has a children's certificate. Six of the eight bedrooms have en-suite bath or shower and all have telephone, satellite TV, teasmade, trouser press and hair dryer. A full English breakfast is provided. Special weekend bargain breaks are available in winter. Pets can be accommodated. Brighton, famous for its pier, Seaworld, and the 'Lanes' full of bijou shops – a treat for antique hunters – is worth a day trip.

🛏 Three singles, two doubles, two twin-bedded and one family room
£ ££
🍺 Harveys BB; King & Barnes Sussex; Morland Old Speckled Hen; John Smith's Bitter; Webster's Yorkshire Bitter; guest beer
🍴 Snacks and meals daily, lunchtime and evening

—— KIRDFORD ——

Half Moon

Kirdford, near Billingshurst RH14 0LT
☎ *(01403) 820223;* FAX *(01403) 820224*
Directions: off the A272 between Petworth and Billingshurst; follow signs to Kirdford at Wisborough Green

Tile-hung, this 16th-century pub is a typical example of the local Sussex architecture. It stands opposite the 13th-century church in the picturesque village of Kirdford. Inside, its beamed interior has been carefully preserved. Meals are served in the bar or the restaurant which has built up a good reputation locally, particularly for fresh seafood – the licensee's family has been involved in the seafood business for three generations, so he knows what to buy. The Half Moon is ideal for a relaxing weekend, but if you are feeling energetic there are plenty of opportunities locally for walkers, golfers, cyclists and equestrians – all these activities can be arranged via the pub. Although only the double room has en-suite facilities, the other rooms are pleasant and the service friendly without being intrusive. A full English breakfast is provided. Pets can be accommodated.

🛏 One double, one twin-bedded and one family room
£ £ (££ en-suite and for single occupancy)
🍺 Arundel Best Bitter; Boddingtons Bitter; Greene King Abbot; King & Barnes Sussex; Shepherd Neame Spitfire; guest beers
🍴 Snacks and meals daily, lunchtime and evening (except Sunday evening)

—— MIDHURST ——

Crown

Edinburgh Square, Midhurst GU29 9NL
☎ *(01730) 813462*
Directions: in the old part of town, behind the parish church

Be sure to get your timing right here – if your booking includes the first Sunday of the month, you'll be in for a treat, for that is the day the Stevenses offer their increasingly popular spit roasts. The roast in question is usually lamb, as it is the most successful, and it is either served as a traditional roast, or as a 'chunk in a bap'. If you miss the event, don't despair: the Crown does offer a home-cooked menu all week, plus an ever-changing range of up to ten real ales, with some dispensed straight from the cask. There are also occasional ciders. This three-bar pub dates back in part to the 16th century and the guest accommodation is in the older part of the building and hence not en-suite. Ghosts allegedly dwell here, but by all accounts have not been sighted recently. It is popular with visitors thanks to its situation in a quiet part of this bustling market town, and handy for Goodwood, the Chichester Festival and several NT properties. A small courtyard houses a well-used barbecue, but there is no garden. Children are welcome to stay (although there is no family room as such).

🛏 One single, one double, one twin-bedded room
£ £
🍺 Cheriton Pots Ale, Diggers Gold; Fuller's London Pride; guest beers
🍴 Snacks and meals daily, lunchtime and evening
CC not accepted

—— ROGATE ——

Wyndham Arms

North Street, Rogate, near Petersfield GU31 5HG.
☎/FAX *(01730) 821315*
Directions: on the A272 Petersfield road, five miles east of Midhurst

Tim and Gabi Shepherd have successfully built up their business at the Wyndham since they took it on in a severe state of dilapidation – they even had to rebuild the roof. Happily, the original timbers in the bar were sound – they have lasted well, many were salvaged from ships decommissioned during the reign of Henry VIII! Now a very pretty village inn, the Wyndham, rather unusually, has a ground floor 'cellar' where a window has been installed, so customers can observe their beers (all from local independent breweries) being drawn straight from the cask. This CAMRA award-winning pub plays host to a midsummer beer festival every year. The overnight accommodation (strictly for non-smokers) is in comfortably refurbished rooms of which two are en-suite. Little touches like fresh flowers and a selection of books and magazines in the bedrooms make it that bit special. All the food is freshly prepared on the premises under Gabi's supervision, and the restaurant is often heavily booked. Thatcher's cider accompanies the ales on the bar. The NT's recently restored Uppark House, Petworth House, Winchester and Chichester are all within striking distance.

🛏 Three doubles, two twin-bedded, one family room
£ ££ (£ not en-suite; discount for CAMRA members)
🍺 Ballards Wassail; Cheriton Pots Ale; Hop Back Summer Lightning; Ringwood Fortyniner; guest beers
🍴 Snacks and meals daily, lunchtime and evening
CC accepted

—— SINGLETON ——

Horse & Groom
Singleton, near Chichester PO18 0EX
☎ *(01243) 811455*
Directions: on the A286, midway between Chichester and Midhurst

This most attractive pub stands right by the roadside on the A286, but traffic noise should not be a problem for overnight guests as the bedrooms are in a separate building. This friendly, family-run free house enjoys an excellent reputation for its ales and food. Good, home-cooked food is served in the beamed bar with its open fire where darts and billiards give it a real village local atmosphere. There is also a restaurant for non-smokers which hosts monthly theme nights. Singleton is a pretty village, home to the Weald and Downland Open Air Museum. It is just a mile from Goodwood and close to Chichester (six miles). The en-suite guest rooms (all on the ground floor) have recently been created in a listed building in the pub's grounds and equipped to a high standard. A full English breakfast is provided. The pub's large garden features swingboats and a trampoline, popular with children; the pub does not however cater for children as overnight guests.

⋈ Three double, three twin-bedded rooms
£ ££
🍺 Ballards Best Bitter; Cheriton Pots Ale; Gales HSB; guest beers
🍽 Snacks lunchtime, meals daily, lunchtime and evening
CC accepted

Eathorpe Park Hotel,
Royal Leamington Spa,
Warwickshire

WARWICKSHIRE &
WEST MIDLANDS

—— BIRMINGHAM ——

Bull

1 Price Street, Aston, Birmingham B4 6JU
☎ *(0121) 333 6757;* FAX: *(0121) 359 1168*
Directions: off Lancaster Circus, just off New Town Row at the end of Corporation Street, behind the General Hospital

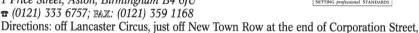

A cottagey interior hides inside this pub which aims for a rural atmosphere even though it is just a stone's throw from the city centre. Next time you need a bed for the night in Birmingham, book in here and make the acquaintance of its friendly regulars who include a theatre group, water polo team, a choir and two sets of local football supporters! If they do not keep you chatting all night in the bar, there is a cosy little snug off the lounge, where customers have been known to doze off in the comfortable armchairs. A charming landlady, who obviously has a passion for porcelain jugs, going by the vast collection here, offers real ales, traditional ciders and good food at all times of the day. The breakfast and service in the morning are particularly recommended. Three of the guest rooms offer en-suite facilities; the prices are very reasonable and the homely atmosphere is appreciated by all who shun the anonymous hotels of the city.

🛏 Two single, two double, one twin-bedded and one family room
£ £
🍺 Ansells Mild; Marston's Pedigree; Wadworth 6X; guest beer (occasionally)
🍽 Snacks and meals daily, noon-10.30 pm
CC not accepted

—— DUDLEY ——

Lamp Tavern

116 High Street, Dudley DY1 8XX
☎ *(01384) 254129*
Directions: on the A459, at the top of the town

The Lamp is a lively, welcoming local with a simple bar, but also a more comfortable lounge, which has recently been refurbished, with an area set aside for diners. The guest rooms (four of which have en-suite bathrooms) and the function room are recent additions. There are discounts for CAMRA members, and reduced rates at weekends. Pets can be accommodated. Children are welcome as overnight guests and the pub has a garden for them to enjoy in good weather. Dudley stands at the highest point in the Black Country and the main attractions for tourists include the zoo, the castle and the Black Country Open Air Museum.

🛏 One single, three doubles, one family room
£ £ (££ single room)
🍺 Batham Mild, Best Bitter, XXX (winter)
🍽 Snacks and meals daily, lunchtime

—— 193 ——

—— EATHORPE ——

Eathorpe Park Hotel
The Fosse, Eathorpe, Leamington Spa CV33 9DQ
☎ *(01926) 632632;* FAX *(01926) 632481*
Directions: on the Fosse Way (B3355) between the A423 and A4425

The Eathorpe Park tends to attract business people during the week. Its location, within 20 minutes' drive of four motorways, two Inter-city rail terminals and Birmingham Airport, makes it very convenient for meetings and conferences. At the weekends, there is quite a different atmosphere, when the hotel is booked for social functions, and special events, including 'Murder Mystery' evenings and live jazz concerts; they stage an annual beer and jazz festival, too. The hotel is also licensed to conduct wedding ceremonies. The beer range mostly comes from local breweries, such as Church End at Shustoke. All food is freshly prepared on the premises and served in the bars or restaurant. The basement houses 'the Dungeon', a bistro/discotheque that is available for private parties. Eathorpe Park's accessibility rather belies the fact that the hotel is surrounded by farmland and stands in its own 11 acres of grounds, so you can be assured of a peaceful stay. The 16 rooms have en-suite bathrooms and all the usual modern amenities. Pets can be accommodated

⇥ Three single, eight double, two twin-bedded and three family rooms
£ ££ (single room ££££)
🍺 Church End Cuthberts, Marston's Pedigree; guest beers
🍽 Snacks and meals daily, lunchtime and evening
CC accepted

—— EDGEHILL ——

Castle
Edgehill, near Banbury OX15 6DJ
☎ *(01295) 670255;* FAX *(01295) 670521*
Directions: on A422 Banbury-Stratford road, (turn opposite Upton House)

Architecturally speaking, this must be one of the most unusual pubs in this guide. A 70-ft high octagonal tower, built in 1742 to commemorate the Battle of Edgehill out of local stone, it was opened in 1750 on the anniversary of Oliver Cromwell's death. It was linked by a wooden draw bridge to a smaller square tower – the original drawbridge has since been replaced by a faithful replica. Designed by Sanderson Miller, based on Guy's Tower at Warwick Castle, it became a pub in 1822 when it was sold by a descendant of Miller. Set right on the border with Oxfordshire, the views from the garden extend across several neighbouring counties, and take in the Civil War battle site. The main tower has two bars offering ale, traditional cider and a good choice of meals and snacks. The guest rooms are in the small tower, and have en-suite bathroom, TV, telephone and tea/coffee making facilities. A continental breakfast is served in the room. Centrally situated for touring the area, Stratford, Warwick with its fine castle, and the NT's Upton House are all within a short drive. For walkers and riders there are many footpaths and bridle paths, several of which pass right by the inn.

⇥ One twin-bedded, one family room
£ ££
🍺 Hook Norton Best Bitter, Generation, Old Hooky, guest beer
🍽 Snacks and meals daily, lunchtime and evening
CC accepted

—— HAMPTON-IN-ARDEN ——

White Lion
High Street, Hampton-in-Arden, Solihull B92 0AA
☎ *(01675) 442833;* FAX *(01675) 443168*
Directions: in the village centre

The White Hart is an ideal choice for visitors to the National Exhibition Centre who would rather be in rural surroundings than at the heart of the city. Both the NEC and the airport can be reached in five minutes from this ancient village pub. Built as a farmhouse 600 years ago, its construction is based on old ships' timbers, which were taken from oaks that were originally grown around the village. Quite unspoilt (the bar has been virtually unchanged for the last 50 years), this is a small, friendly local with a recommended restaurant. Light meals and snacks are also available in the bar; a full English breakfast is served. All eight guest rooms have en-suite facilities. Families are welcome.

- ⊨ Three single, one double, three twin-bedded and one family room
- £ ££
- 🍺 Draught Bass; M&B Brew XI
- 🍴 Snacks lunchtime, meals daily, lunchtime and evening (except Sunday evening)
- CC accepted

—— KENILWORTH ——

Clarendon House Hotel
Old High Street, Kenilworth CV8 1LZ
☎/FAX *(01926) 857668*

The Clarendon, which is rated as a four-crown hotel by the tourist authority, is quite a plush establishment, but it also serves the local community very well in its welcoming bar. It appeals to a more mature clientele, but then according to what one reads in the media, it is the retired generation that have the most leisure time – and the money to enjoy it – and certainly rooms at the Clarendon do not come cheap. The guest rooms are all en-suite and well equipped. Pets can be accommodated. Light meals and snacks can be taken in the bar at lunchtime, whilst evening meals are served in the hotel's restaurant. A full English breakfast is served. This traditional country inn stands in the attractive centre of Kenilworth where the Earl of Leycester famously entertained Elizabeth I at the castle at a cost of £1,000 a day in 1576. Even now it's a lot cheaper to stay at the Clarendon! Kenilworth is just a few minutes from the spa town of Leamington which has some stylish shops.

- ⊨ Ten double, five twin-bedded rooms
- £ ££ (££££ single occupancy)
- 🍺 Boddingtons Bitter; Flowers IPA; Greene King IPA, Abbot; Wadworth 6X; guest beer (occasionally)
- 🍴 Snacks lunchtime, meals daily, lunchtime and evening
- CC accepted

—— LITTLE COMPTON ——

Red Lion Inn

Little Compton, Moreton-in-Marsh GL56 0RT
☎ *(01608) 674397*
Directions: on the A44, Chipping Norton–Moreton-in-Marsh road

This lovely old pub (circa 16th century) is built of warm Cotswold stone and features a low-ceilinged, beamed lounge bar. The public bar, with its dartboard and pool table has a strong involvement with the village community. The Red Lion is the only Warwickshire tied house of the little Donnington brewery, based in Stow-on-the-Wold, in Gloucestershire. The three bedrooms overlook the pub's very pleasant garden, where the old game of Aunt Sally can be played. The rooms are comfortably furnished and have washbasins, and tea/coffee making facilities. The bathroom is shared. Tourists will find the Red Lion very central for visiting Blenheim Palace, Stratford-on-Avon and the many attractions of the Cotswolds, including Bourton-on-the-Water. There are also four golf courses in the vicinity. Two French chefs ensure that the pub's reputation for meals is consistently high. A hearty English breakfast is included in the very reasonable room rates.

🛏 One double, one twin-bedded and one family room
£ £
🍺 Donnington BB, SBA
🍴 Snacks and meals daily, lunchtime and evening
CC accepted

—— RUGBY ——

Three Horse Shoes Hotel

Sheep Street, Rugby CV21 3BX
☎ *(01788) 544585;* FAX *(01788) 546097*
Directions: follow the A4071 to the town centre, passing Sheep Street on the right, the next right turn takes you to the hotel car park

Set right at the heart of Rugby, in a pedestrian zone, this impressive 18th-century former coaching inn is, according to local CAMRA members, an ideal retreat from some of the noisier pubs nearby. Its only disadvantage for overnight guests is the rather limited parking facilities. It is convenient for parents with children at the adjacent Rugby School, which gave rise to the story of *Tom Brown's Schooldays*, and of course is famous for being the birthplace of rugby football. Fans can visit the only museum dedicated to the sport, the Gilbert Museum, in the town. Other nearby attractions include Coventry Cathedral, Warwick Castle, Althorp House and Stratford-on-Avon. The Three Horseshoes features a cosy lounge bar, warmed by a log fire, where the guest beers are usually from local breweries. Meals can be eaten here or in the oak-beamed Twickers Restaurant. For a more lively atmosphere, the hotel offers Lucan's Wine Bar. All the guest rooms are en-suite with modern amenities. The room rate does not include breakfast, which is a choice of full English (£6.50) or the continental variety (£4.50). The room rates are reduced by £10 per room at weekends. Pets can be catered for.

🛏 15 single, ten double, five twin-bedded and two family rooms
£ Room rate ££ (£££ single room); weekend £ (££ single room)
🍺 Greene King IPA, Abbot; weekly guest beer
🍴 Snacks and meals daily, lunchtime and evening
CC accepted

—— WARWICK ——

Old Fourpenny Shop

27-29 Crompton Street, Warwick CV34 6HJ
☎ *(01926) 491360;* FAX *(01926) 411892*
Directions: leave the M40 at jct 15 and follow the A429 into Warwick; turn left at the Wheatsheaf Inn

I am very tempted on my next trip to Warwick to book in here. Although it is an easy day trip from where we live, the last time we visited we spent the whole day in the splendid castle and didn't get to see any of the rest of the town at all. So the Fourpenny Shop, set in a quiet side road, very close to the castle would be ideal, and it comes highly recommended by CAMRA members. The choice of five guest beers may have something to do with it – what is more the locals are so enthusiastic about their real ale that the range has been know to change completely between the lunchtime and evening sessions in the same day! The Fourpenny Shop was transformed in recent years from a run-down local into a flourishing hotel, and now offers a comfortable split-level bar and a dining room (meals are served in both). The accommodation, in eleven well refurbished en-suite guest rooms (with either bath or shower) is of the same high standard that is maintained on the beer and food front. Incidentally, the pub's strange name dates from the time of the building of the nearby canal, when navvies used to call at the then Warwick Tavern for a fourpenny tot of rum with a cup of coffee which was cheaper than the local going rate.

⊨ Two singles, five doubles, three twin-bedded and one family room
£ ££ (single room £££)
🍺 M&B Brew XI, plus five guest beers
🍴 Snacks and meals, lunchtime and evening, Tuesday-Saturday
CC accepted

TRY ALSO:

Crown Inn

16 Holloway Street, Upper Gornal, Dudley DY3 2EA
Tel (01902) 66509

Simple, but inexpensive accommodation with shared bathroom, in a traditional old pub of character. The rates reduce for stays of more than one night. Three twin-bedded rooms.
B&B £

Bulls Head

Church Hill, Wolvey LE10 3LB

Fairly basic, but good value accommodation in a well refurbished pub, handy for the A5 and the M69, not far from Coventry. Three rooms, B&B £

WILTSHIRE

—— AMESBURY ——

Antrobus Arms Hotel

Church Street, Amesbury, Salisbury SP4 7EU
☎ *(01980) 623163;* FAX *(01980) 622112*
Directions: half a mile off the A303

The Antrobus is a fine old hotel, well furnished and maintained, with high standards of service. Originally the home of the Pinckney family, the Georgian building was acquired in 1868 by the Reverend Meyrick who turned it into a school for young gentlemen. A spacious, friendly bar (which stocks a traditional cider), a restaurant and an attractive drawing room, where French windows open on to a terrace and a Victorian walled garden which features a fountain. The hotel also boasts a kitchen garden which produces vegetables for the restaurant where the international menu includes vegetarian dishes. Bar snacks are also available. The best guest room has a four-poster bed, a view over the garden and a private bathroom. Most of the 19 rooms have en-suite facilities (the single rooms share a bathroom), and some have period furnishings. They all have satellite TV, direct dial telephone, and hospitality tray. Stonehenge is within walking distance. Pets can be accommodated. An all-inclusive price per night for dinner, bed and breakfast is available, as well as a special weekend rate.

- ⇥ Three single, eight double, four twin-bedded and one family room
- £ £££ (££££ single occupancy of en-suite room)
- 🍺 Draught Bass; Wadworth 6X; Young's Special; guest beers (occasionally)
- 🍽 Snacks and meals daily, lunchtime and evening

CC accepted

—— BOX HILL ——

Quarrymans Arms

Box Hill, Corsham, Wiltshire SN13 8HN
☎ *(01225) 743569*
Directions: 300 yards south of the A4 at Box Hill

This unassuming little pub barely looks big enough to offer accommodation (and indeed it does only have two rooms). I would be inclined to say it is easy to pass it by, but in fact, despite being just yards from the A4 it is so well hidden in a maze of lanes that the landlord generally advises phoning him for directions once you appear to be getting close. It is definitely worth the search. The stone free house was built 300 years ago to serve the local mining community – it is still popular with those going underground, but nowadays the cavers and potholers do it for pleasure. The dining room has a good local reputation for its freshly produced meals on an inventive menu. The pub stocks local beers, plus a cider in summer. The dining area has a big picture window which offers the same spectacular view as the little garden, looking out over the Colerne Valley. The rooms are both on the ground floor and in the process of being upgraded to include en-suite facilities. Pets can be accommodated.

- ⇥ One double, one family room
- £ ££
- 🍺 Bath Gold; Butcombe Bitter; Mole's Tap; Wadworth 6X; guest beer
- 🍽 Snacks and meals daily, lunchtime and evening

CC accepted

— FORD —

White Hart
Ford, Chippenham SN14 8RT
☎ *(01249) 782213*
Directions: off the A420

I cannot better the 1999 *Good Beer Guide* description of this pub – 'superb 16th-century inn with a fabulous selection of ales (always ten available) and an award-winning restaurant'. The White Hart boasts a delightful setting beside a trout stream, where the patio provides a much needed overspill for drinkers on busy summer weekends. Out of season, the public bar is cosy, with plenty of drinking space around the bar itself. There is also a very spacious restaurant, which is just as well since people come from miles around to eat here. There, and in the bar, enormous portions of well-cooked dishes from a good range are served at very reasonable prices. Three guest rooms are in the pub itself, and these all have en-suite showers, whilst the remaining eight rooms are in a converted stable block and have en-suite bath and shower. All the rooms are equipped with TV, telephone, hairdryer, trouser press and hospitality tray.

⋈ Nine double, two twin-bedded rooms
£ **£££** (single occupancy **££££**)
🍺 Beer range varies
🍽 Snacks and meals daily, lunchtime and evening
CC accepted

— HIGHWORTH —

Saracens Head Hotel
High Street, Highworth, Swindon SN6 7AG
☎ *(01793) 762284; FAX (01793) 861856*
Directions: on the A361

This former coaching inn is just one of several interesting old buildings at the centre of Highworth, which makes an ideal base for touring the Cotswolds. Family-run, with friendly staff, the hotel has 12 comfortable guest rooms, all with en-suite showers, satellite TV, facilities for making drinks and direct dial telephone. The traditionally furnished snug bar is popular with both locals and visitors; meals can be enjoyed here or in the adjacent dining room, where a dress code applies. There is an attractive courtyard with tables and seating. Pets may be catered for, at the discretion of the licensee.

⋈ Five singles, six doubles, one family room
£ **££** (single **££££**)
🍺 Arkell's Bitter, 3B, seasonal beers
🍽 Snacks and meals daily, lunchtime and evening
CC accepted

—— NORTH NEWNTON ——

Woodbridge Inn

North Newnton, near Pewsey SN9 6JZ
☎/FAX *(01980) 630266*
Directions: on the A345, on the roundabout three miles south of Pewsey

Local CAMRA members describe the Woodbridge as a 'smart, foody pub' and if you stay here, you are sure to want to sample the food. Owners, Lou and Terri Vertessy enjoy a good reputation – their spicy dishes are particularly popular – and they have won numerous awards for their international menu and wine list. The 16th-century country pub stands on the banks of the Avon in five acres of meadowland which also serves as a campsite. The garden area features a petanque pitch and children's playground. The pub has angling rights on this stretch of the river and dry-fly fishing can be arranged. Midway between Stonehenge and the Avebury Stone Circles, the Pewsey Vale is designated as an area of outstanding natural beauty. The inn has a cosy, informal atmosphere – the bar boasts a fascinating collection of old signs and china; meals can be taken here or in the restaurant. The cosy feel extends to the overnight accommodation as the comfortable guest rooms are decorated in a cottagey style. All but one of the rooms has an en-suite bathroom. Children can be accommodated.

- ⊨ Three doubles, one twin-bedded room
- £ £ (single occupancy ££)
- ◨ Wadworth IPA, 6X, Farmer's Glory; guest beer
- ⊙ Snacks and meals daily, lunchtime and evening
- **CC** accepted

—— SALISBURY ——

Devizes Inn

53 Devizes Road, Salisbury SP2 7LQ
☎ *(01722) 327842*
Directions: on the A360; turn left into Hartington Road for the pub car park

The Devizes is very centrally situated in Salisbury, indeed a car is not essential as it is within walking distance of the railway station and there is a regular service to the pub from the bus garage. The medieval city of Salisbury certainly lends itself to exploration on foot – guided walks around the splendid Cathedral and Cathedral Close (home of the former prime minister, Sir Edward Heath) are available from the Tourist office. Another interesting, longer walk directly from the inn takes you to the site of Old Sarum Castle. Other attractions, such as Stonehenge (four miles) are easily accessible. The Devizes is a comfortable, friendly, two-bar pub which has a good local following. The landlord, Brendan O'Malley is just completing refurbishment of the whole premises, and the three guest rooms offer en-suite accommodation with TV and tea/coffee making facilities. An excellent breakfast, offering a varied choice, is provided at the time you want it, not as set out by the establishment, but the pub does not offer any other meals. There is however, a good selection of restaurants in the city.

- ⊨ One double, two family rooms
- £ £ (single occupancy ££)
- ◨ Hop Back Summer Lightning, GFB; guest beer (occasionally)
- **CC** accepted

New Inn of Salisbury

39-47 New Street, Salisbury SP1 2PA
☎ *(01722) 327679;* FAX *(01722) 334651*
Directions: adjacent to Cathedral Close

This attractive old inn is in an ideal position for attracting tourists, standing right by the Cathedral Close. The business, which has been run by the Spicer family for over 20 years, includes a tea room and restaurant, where the menu is based on home-made dishes using fresh produce. The heavily beamed Inglenook Lounge is warmed by an open fire, but the atmosphere is healthily 'smoke-free', due to the Spicer's no-smoking policy operated throughout the premises. Four of the guest rooms have en-suite bathrooms and all have TV and tea/coffee making facilities. Some boast cathedral views and the most expensive room features a four-poster bed. The price includes a continental breakfast. There is overnight parking for hotel residents available during the week, and all day at the weekends. In summer, guests can take advantage of the south-facing walled garden which stands in the shadow of the cathedral. Children are welcome to stay, although there are no special facilities for them.

⊨ Three single, four double/twin-bedded rooms
£ £ – ££ (depending on room)
🍺 Badger Dorset Best, Tanglefoot; Wells Eagle; guest beer (occasionally)
🍴 Snacks and meals daily, at all times
CC accepted

—— UPTON LOVELL ——

Prince Leopold

Warminster BA12 0JP
☎ *(01985) 850460;* FAX *(01985) 850737*
Directions: half a mile from the A36, four miles from Warminster

The Prince Leopold has not always been a pub – it was built in 1887 as the local post office and general store to serve the once prosperous local woollen industry. It was named in honour of Queen Victoria's youngest son who frequented the inn when he lived in the village of Boyton nearby. It is now quite an upmarket establishment, although friendly and comfortable and the licensees request that smart, casual dress is adopted by their customers. Light meals and snacks are served from an extensive bar menu and the restaurant is recommended, particularly for its curry and fresh fish dishes which are a speciality of the house. The beer range varies, with always three real ales on tap at any time, as well as Stowford Press cider. The pub has a pleasant riverside garden overlooking the Wylye Valley. Fishing, golf and horse riding facilities are all available and can be arranged at the pub. Other major attractions, such as Bath, Salisbury and Longleat are within easy reach. All the guest rooms have en-suite facilities and children are catered for. A full English breakfast is provided.

⊨ Three double, one twin-bedded room
£ £ (single occupancy ££)
🍺 Beer range varies
🍴 Snacks and meals daily, lunchtime and evening
CC accepted

—— WEST HARNHAM ——

Old Mill

Town Path, West Harnham, Salisbury SP2 8EU
☎ *(01722) 327517;* FAX *(01722) 333367*
Directions: off A3094; right off Harnham Road into Lower Street, second left into Middle Street

The Old Mill at Harnham enjoys a truly delightful setting at the edge of unspoilt water meadows with its own riverside garden. The views across to Salisbury are much the same as when John Constable painted here in the 18th century. Built by the church authorities in the 12th century, the structure became a papermill in 1550; the millraces can still be seen, and the diverted waters of the River Nadder run through what is now the restaurant. Here you will find good quality English cooking, based as much as possible on local produce, with fresh seafood a speciality. Meals can also be taken in the bar which is warmed by log fires in winter and, in keeping with the character of the place, is free from electronic machines, juke box and pool tables. The 11 characterful guest rooms all have private bathrooms as well as hairdryers, direct dial telephones and tea/coffee making facilities. It is a short stroll to Salisbury with its cathedral, Medieval Hall and museums, and a short drive takes you to Longleat or Wilton House.

- ⇥ Two single, five double, one twin-bedded and three family rooms
- £ £££
- ⌷ Hop Back Summer Lightning, GFB; Ringwood Best Bitter; Theakston XB; guest beer (occasionally)
- ▮●▮ Snacks and meals daily, lunchtime and evening
- CC accepted

—— WILTON ——

Wheatsheaf

1 King Street
Wilton SP2 0AX
☎ *(01722) 742267*
Directions: on the A36, next to Wilton Shopping Village

The name of Wilton is synonymous with carpets, and Wilton and Axminster carpets have been made here since the 18th century when two French weavers established the craft in the town. Today the original factory has a visitor centre and museum, and the Wilton Carpet Factory shop is just one of the outlets in the Wilton Shopping Village (which includes factory shops from many other manufacturers), right next door to the Wheatsheaf. Visitors to the town will also not want to miss the splendid Wilton House, built as a nunnery in the 9th century and currently the home of the Earl of Pembroke. It boasts state rooms designed by Inigo Jones and a wonderful collection of some 200 miniature costumed teddy bears. The House is a five minute walk from the Wheatsheaf which enjoys a riverside setting, beside the Wylye. Popular with locals and visitors alike, it comprises two bars, a small restaurant for non-smokers and a pleasant garden. Noted for its home-cooked meals, which are also served in the bar, the pub offers good value, but simple accommodation in three guest rooms with shared bathroom facilities. Children are catered for and made very welcome. A full English breakfast is provided.

- ⇥ Two double, one twin-bedded room
- £ £
- ⌷ Badger Dorset Best, Tanglefoot
- ▮●▮ Snacks and meals daily, lunchtime and evening
- CC not accepted

—— WINTERBOURNE MONKTON ——

New Inn

Winterbourne Monkton, near Avebury, Swindon SN4 9NW
☎ *(01672) 539240*
Directions: off the A4361, north of Avebury (jct 16 exit of the M4)

Winterbourne Monkton is a little village in rural Wiltshire. The New Inn serves its local community well and is welcoming to visitors. It has a bar where in summer a traditional cider complements the real ales, and a restaurant (meals are served in both). Families are well catered for – the guest rooms can be adapted to accommodate children and the garden has a play area. Just north of Avebury, whose famous stone circles are considered to be one of the most important Megalithic sites in Europe, the pub is also convenient for Silbury Hill and the Ridgeway Walk. Salisbury is approximately 45 minutes by car and worth a visit for its many important buildings, including the lovely Queen Anne Mompesson House which featured in Emma Thompson's recent film of *Sense and Sensibility*. The inn has five guest rooms, all with en-suite facilities. A full English breakfast is provided. Pets can be catered for.

🛏 Two double, three twin-bedded rooms
£ £ (single occupancy ££)
🍺 Adnams Bitter; Wadworth 6X; guest beer
🍽 Snacks and meals daily, lunchtime and evening
CC accepted

—— WOOTTON RIVERS ——

Royal Oak

Wootton Rivers, near Marlborough SN8 4NQ
☎ *(01672) 810322;* FAX *(01672) 811168*
Directions: on a minor road between the A345 and A346, north-east of Pewsey

This charming, thatched free house, dating back to the 16th century, is situated close to the Kennet and Avon canal in a picturesque village featuring many other old thatched houses, and a 13th-century church. A friendly, three-bar pub which oozes olde-worlde charm in its oak-beamed interior, the Royal oak offers good beers and food. The comfortable accommodation is in a separate house through the pub's garden, comprising six bedrooms, three of which have en-suite facilities. The whole house can be rented for weekend house parties (children and pets are welcome). A good, full English breakfast is provided. There are amenities locally for golf, fishing, boating and of course, country walks; more unusually microlite flights can also be booked nearby. This area is becoming very popular with those curious about Corn Circles, so if you want to make a study of them, you could do worse than to book into the Royal Oak for a few days. Marlborough, and Avebury are also within easy reach.

🛏 One single, five double, one twin-bedded and one family room
£ £
🍺 Ushers Best Bitter; Wadworth 6X; guest beers
🍽 Snacks and meals daily, lunchtime and evening
CC accepted

—— WROUGHTON ——

Fox & Hounds

1 Markham Road, Wroughton, Swindon SN4 9JT
☎/FAX *(01793) 812217*
Directions: from the M4 (jct 16) follow B4005 into Wroughton

The overnight accommodation at the Fox & Hounds is in an adjacent motel lodge. It would not suit those who like the old-world charms of creaking floors and low beams, but has the advantage of being well away from the noise of the road (and the bar), while benefiting from views of the surrounding countryside. Another advantage of purpose-built accommodation is that it has modern en-suite facilities which make it accessible for guests with disabilities. The pub itself, although much altered and refurbished in the 1980s, retains a cottage atmosphere (it was originally built as a farm cottage under a thatched roof). The bar, where home-cooked meals are served, has a log fire, and there is a large garden.

- ⇔ Four single, four double beds
- £ ££ (single £££)
- 🍺 Arkell's Bitter, 3B, Kingsdown Ale
- 🍽 Snacks and meals daily, lunchtime and evening
- **CC** accepted

TRY ALSO:

Deacon's Alms

118 Fisherton Street, Salisbury SP2 7QT
☎ *(01722) 336409*

Busy town pub with six letting rooms at bargain prices. £

WORCESTERSHIRE: SEE HEREFORDSHIRE & WORCESTERSHIRE

YORKSHIRE (EAST)

—— BEVERLEY ——

Dog & Duck
33 Ladygate, Beverley HU17 8BH
☎ *(01482) 886079;* FAX *(01482) 862419*
Directions: just off the market square

A pub right at the heart of historic Beverley, famous for its Minster, but offering many other attractions too, including the Saturday market. Host Mark McMullen's aim is to keep the Dog & Duck as traditional as possible, in keeping with the locality. It has period decor, plush bench seating, dark wood furniture and real fires, and offers a good range of real ales and whiskies. The guest accommodation was added in 1993 in a new building in the grounds of the pub; each room has its own front door and allocated parking place, giving guests the freedom to come and go as they please. The bright, modern bedrooms all have en-suite bathrooms, TV and tea/coffee making facilities. An additional child's bed is available and some rooms are suitable for guests with disabilities. The pub offers a full English breakfast and a good choice of lunchtime meals and snacks, and although no evening meals are served, there are several local restaurants to choose from. Beverley's main shopping street and the army museum are within walking distance.

🛏 Two singles, two doubles, two twin-bedded rooms
£ £
🍺 Marston's Pedigree; Morland Old Speckled Hen; Theakston XB; guest beer
🍽 Snacks and meals daily, lunchtime
CC not accepted

—— BRIDLINGTON ——

New Crown
158 Quay Road, Bridlington YO16 4JB
☎ *(01262) 401874*
Directions: in the old part of town, near the railway station

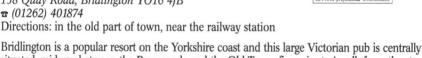

BRITISH INSTITUTE *of* INNKEEPING
🍺 MEMBER
SETTING *professional* STANDARDS

Bridlington is a popular resort on the Yorkshire coast and this large Victorian pub is centrally situated, midway between the Promenade and the Old Town, five minutes' walk from the station and close to the amusement arcades, ten-pin bowling alley and the leisure centre. It offers its own leisure activities in the games room which has a dartboard, pool table and big screen TV for Sky sports fans. If the fresh sea air has more appeal, you can join in one of the fishing boat trips arranged by the hotel from the nearby harbour, or visit the RSPB reserve at Bempton Cliffs (three miles away). A little further afield are Scarborough (15 miles), Whitby (30 miles) and Hornsea, famous for its pottery (20 miles). The guest rooms, situated on the third floor, lack private bathrooms and are priced accordingly; they do have tea/coffee making facilities and there is a residents' lounge with TV. Children are welcome and the pub has a family room with a child-size pool table, playhouse and caged birds.

🛏 One single, two double, three twin-bedded and two family rooms
£ £
🍺 Vaux Lorimer's Best Scotch; Wards Best Bitter, Waggle Dance; guest beer (on occasion)
🍽 Snacks and meals lunchtime and evening Monday-Saturday
CC not accepted

Windsor Hotel

14 Windsor Crescent, Bridlington YO15 3HY
☎ *(01262) 673623*
Directions: opposite the harbour, follow signs for the Spa

Just one minute from the seafront and town centre, this friendly, traditional pub has an open-plan bar area and a spacious children's room. Upstairs a comfortable lounge, furnished with leather Chesterfield sofas and armchairs, affords good views of the sea and harbour. Popular with the locals in winter, in the summer it draws mostly a family trade. A wide-ranging menu is served at lunchtime, and tea and coffee are always available in the bar, which, unusually for a seaside pub, has no jukebox. The overnight accommodation has just been upgraded (the work should be completed by the time this guide is published) to offer en-suite facilities in all rooms. They all have sea views, some offering a wide panorama, and each room has a TV and tea/coffee making facilities. Three day special breaks are available, as well as reduced rates for a week's stay. Children are welcome. The owners, Mick and Jo Waddington also have self-catering flats to let. Nearby the Sewerby Park and Bird Sanctuary is popular with visitors, and the historic city of York makes a good day trip at around 40 miles distant.

🛏 Ten double, three twin-bedded rooms
£ £
🍺 Camerons Bitter; Tetley Bitter; guest beer (occasionally)
🍴 Snacks and meals daily, lunchtime
CC not accepted

—— DRIFFIELD ——

Bell in Driffield

Market Place, Driffield YO25 6AN
☎ *(01377) 256661;* FAX *(01377) 2532228*
Directions: town centre

The Bell was built in the early 1700s when Driffield was no more than a hamlet. With the growth of the canal trade at the end of the century, Driffield prospered and so did the Bell. The present owners have worked hard – and very successfully – to recreate the look and atmosphere of the original pub. What was the old Corn Exchange is now an attractive bar where light meals are served. A lunchtime buffet is also laid out in the panelled Oak Room and there is yet another restaurant for a la carte meals. The Bell, which is now really more of an hotel than a pub, also has a billiard room and more unusually, a new leisure complex housing an indoor swimming-pool, sauna, steam room, a giant whirlpool bath and squash courts. These are all for the exclusive use of the hotel guests. The 14 guest bedrooms are well-appointed with TV, tea/coffee making equipment and other amenities, some feature four-poster beds and all have en-suite bathrooms. Some of the rooms are situated in the inn's former stables, and may be suitable for guest with disabilities (although not all the leisure facilities are accessible). Children over the age of 12 are welcome to stay. The Bell is very music-oriented and hosts live jazz every Tuesday and is the home base of the prize-winning East Riding Brass.

🛏 Two single, 12 double beds
£ £££ (££££ single room)
🍺 Beer range varies – always three, usually local real ales
🍴 Snacks and meals daily, lunchtime and evening
CC accepted

—— HULL ——

Old English Gentleman
Mason Street, Hull HU2 8BH
☎ *(01482) 324659*

This olde-worlde pub has a wonderful theatrical atmosphere. Situated just behind the New Theatre which stages a wide variety of entertainment, the pub is frequented by visiting actors and performers who leave their mark. The pub's walls are covered with signed photographs and other theatrical ephemera. The accommodation is not grand, but has been recently refurbished and gained the approval of the local tourist board. The four rooms have shared bathroom facilities and are let at very reasonable prices. Children are welcome to stay in their parents' rooms, but there are no special facilities for them. This Mansfield tied house is very convenient for the town centre (just a minute's walk) and two minutes from the M62 motorway.

🛏 One single, two double, one triple-bedded room
£ Mansfield Riding Mild, Riding Bitter
🍴 Snacks and meals lunchtime and evening, Monday-Saturday
CC not accepted

—— NAFFERTON ——

Cross Keys
Driffield Road, Nafferton, Driffield YO25 0JJ
☎ *(01377) 254261*
Directions: 400 yards off the A166, York-Bridlington road

Nine miles from the seaside resort of Bridlington, at the northern end of Nafferton village, you will find this solid country inn. Its guest rooms have tea/coffee making equipment, TV and washbasins. A full English breakfast is provided. The bathroom, with bath and shower is shared between the four rooms. Children are welcome to stay (the charge varies, according to size of family and age of children), and they can eat in the restaurant. The bar is also popular for meals, and there is a separate games room where traditional pastimes such as dominoes and pool are complemented by modern video games. Places of tourist interest locally include Burton Agnes Hall and Sledmere House (both within ten miles).

🛏 Two singles, one double, one twin-bedded room
£ £
🍴 Beer range varies
🍽 Snacks and meals, lunchtime and evening, Tuesday-Saturday
CC not accepted

—— NORTH NEWBALD ——

Tiger Inn
The Green, North Newbald, Market Weighton YO4 3SA
☎ *(01430) 827759*
Directions: off the A1034 between South Cave and Market Weighton

The Tiger was built as a farmhouse in this little village on the edge of the Wolds. Overlooking the village green, the interior has been converted to a bar with a matchboarded ceiling, warmed by a log fire, leading into the pool room. There is also a pleasant lounge where the window seat is an attractive feature. The overnight accommodation is in simple rooms without the benefit of en-suite facilities, but it is good value, with a full English breakfast provided. Evening meals are also available. Children are welcome, although there are no particular amenities for them. The pub has a garden and car park.

🛏 One single, one double, one twin-bedded room
£ £
🍺 Black Sheep Bitter; Boddingtons Bitter; guest beer
🍴 Snacks and meals every evening
CC not accepted

TRY ALSO:

Windmill Inn
53 Lairgate, Beverley HU17 8ET
☎ *(01482) 862817*

Free house at the centre of Beverley. Eleven en-suite rooms. B&B £

Goodmanham Arms
Main Street, Goodmanham, Market Weighton YO4 3JA
☎ *(01430) 873849*

This friendly village pub on the Wolds Way has just one letting room. B&B £

Wolds Inn
Huggate, York YO4 2YH
☎ *(01377) 288217*

Comfortable village pub, high up in the Wolds, popular with walkers. Three en-suite rooms. B&B £ (single occupancy ££)

YORKSHIRE (NORTH)

—— BOROUGHBRIDGE ——

Black Bull

6 St James Square, Boroughbridge YO51 9AR
☎ *(01423) 322413;* FAX *(01423) 323915*
Directions: seven miles north of the A59/A1 jct

Standing solidly at the corner of St James Square in the town centre, this attractive Grade II listed building has always been an inn, but has been much extended over the years. The three-roomed original with its small central bar and an inglenook remains the heart of the pub, but the spacious, characterful restaurant, added more recently, has been built with reclaimed timber and bricks and blends in well. The guest bedrooms are in a new extension, and have also been designed sympathetically, whilst offering modern amenities such as en-suite bathrooms, hairdryer, hospitality tray, TV and direct dial telephones. The accommodation is not suitable for children. The Black Bull enjoys a good reputation locally for both its bar meals and the restaurant; this is not surprising since the head chef, the licensee's son Robert, has run some of the best eating establishments in the Antipodes. For those with cultural inclinations, Harewood House and Castle Howard are both within 30 minutes' drive.

- ⇥ Four double rooms
- £ £ (single occupancy £££)
- 🍺 Black Sheep Best Bitter; John Smith's Bitter; guest beer
- 🍴 Snacks and meals daily, lunchtime and evening
- **CC** accepted

—— CLAPHAM ——

New Inn Hotel

Clapham, Settle LA2 8HH
☎ *(015242) 51203;* FAX *(015242) 51496*
Directions: on the A65, five miles north of Settle

BRITISH INSTITUTE of INNKEEPING
MEMBER
SETTING *professional* STANDARDS

Clapham is a most delightful village which straddles both sides of the Clapham Beck, the two halves being linked by three bridges. The church is at the top of the village, the New Inn at the bottom. This friendly, 18th-century former coaching inn has been run by the Mannion family for just over ten years during which time they have carried out a thorough refurbishment. They have added oak panelling to the two comfortable bars and created a no-smoking restaurant where children are welcome. Meals can be taken in the bars if preferred. Upstairs a cosy lounge has been provided for residents, who are accommodated in 16 en-suite guest rooms. Some of the rooms feature antique four-poster or brass beds and the rates vary considerably according to the room, but all have TV, tea and coffee making equipment, etc. Children are welcome and pets can be accommodated, so you can take your dog for a walk along the delightful village Nature Trail.

- ⇥ Eleven double, four twin-bedded and one family room
- £ £ – £££ (££££ single occupancy of some rooms)
- 🍺 Black Sheep Best Bitter; Dent bitter; Tetley Bitter; guest beer
- 🍴 Snacks and meals daily, lunchtime and evening
- **CC** accepted

—— CROPTON ——

New Inn
Cropton, near Pickering YO18 8HH
☎ *(01751) 417330;* FAX *(01751) 417310*
Directions: take the Rosedale turn off the A170 Pickering–Thirsk road

The award-winning New Inn is a *Good Beer Guide* regular, combining two irresistible attractions for CAMRA members: a free house and a brewery. The six pretty, en-suite bedrooms give a cast iron excuse for staying on when the pub gets snowed in – standing as it does at the top of a very steep hill at the edge of the North Yorkshire Moors National Park, this is not an unknown occurrence. Indeed, it was the real threat of not having any beer at all, with supplies blocked in very harsh winter weather, that encouraged the licensees to brew their own in the first place. That was in 1984, and they've not looked back; in fact, after ten years, the brewery had to be moved out of its cellar home into a new purpose-built brewery behind the pub, from where it now serves many other local outlets. The comfortable bar has a beamed ceiling and a log fire; the Victorian-style restaurant serves good quality food; the family room in the conservatory overlooks the two-acre grounds – what more could you ask for? You do not even have to go far to be a tourist, as trained guides are on hand to take you through the brewing process at the brewery's visitor centre (there is a small charge).

🛏 Five double, two twin-bedded/family rooms
£ ££
🍺 Cropton King Billy, Two Pints, Scoresby Stout, Backwoods Bitter, Monkmans Slaughter, seasonal beers; Tetley Bitter
🍽 Snacks and meals daily, lunchtime and evening
CC accepted

—— EASINGWOLD ——

Station Hotel,
Knott Lane, Raskelf Road, Easingwold YO61 3NT
☎ *(01347) 822635;* FAX *(01347) 823491*

CAMRA's food writer, Susan Nowak recommended this hotel to me, so you can rest assured that you'll get good grub – the full English breakfast includes loads of black pudding. Meals are not served at the pub otherwise on a regular basis, but will be provided for residents on request. The beers aren't bad either – in fact most of them come from the award-winning brewery set up by the licensees in redundant stables behind the hotel. The beers have been so popular that the brewery now supplies several other local outlets. Ironically, although the beer names follow a railway theme, there is no longer a station in Easingwold. So, like the majority of other pubs in this guide, the hotel's overnight guests mostly arrive by car. The pub, which was voted *Pub of the Year* by York CAMRA in 1998, has a lively main bar, with a quieter room leading off it. The bar is warmed by open fires in winter and there is a garden for sunny days. The guest rooms have lofty ceilings and have good en-suite facilities. Children are welcome to stay. Pets can be accommodated by arrangement.

🛏 Two double, two twin-bedded, one family room
£ £
🍺 Easingwold Steamcock, Full Steam, Inspector's Special, seasonal beers; John Smith's Bitter; guest beers
🍽 Snacks available, meals by request
CC accepted

—— ELSLACK ——

Tempest Arms Hotel

Elslack, near Skipton BO23 3AY
☎ *(01282) 842450;* FAX *(01282) 843331*
Directions: on the A56, 4.5 miles south-west of Skipton

Acquired by the Cumbrian brewery, Jennings in 1996, the Tempest is a rambling 18th-century inn set in peaceful countryside. The welcoming bar is just perfect – with cosy corners, log fires and quiet areas. The pub is very popular for meals, which can be taken in the bar or the candlelit dining room where wood floors and exposed beams provide an atmospheric background to the quality menu. There is also a club room for meetings, and a rustic barn for functions. Rated three-crown status by the ETB, a high standard of overnight accommodation is provided in the ten guest rooms which all have en-suite facilities (bath and shower), TV, direct dial telephone and tea/coffee making equipment. Special 'Yorkshire Breaks' are available for a minimum of two nights, including a full English breakfast and a three-course evening meal. There are plenty of leisure pursuits to be enjoyed locally, including golf, fishing, swimming and naturally, walking. The Dales, Pennine Way and Ilkley Moor are all within easy reach, and Settle, Leeds and Harrogate are no more than 15-25 miles by car.

- ⛉ Six double, two twin-bedded and two family rooms
- £ ££ (££££ single occupancy)
- ⛃ Black Sheep Best Bitter; Jennings Bitter, Cumberland Ale, Sneck Lifter; guest beer
- ⟒ Snacks and meals daily, lunchtime and evening
- CC accepted

—— GRASSINGTON ——

Black Horse Hotel

Garrs Lane, Grassington, near Skipton BD23 5AT
☎ *(01756) 752770*
Directions: on the B6265, just north of Skipton

Grassington is an attractive Dales village of stone-built houses and country shops, on an old coaching route. Travellers still stop off for refreshment and maybe a bed for the night at the Black Horse, just as they did in the 17th century. The hotel offers bed and breakfast or half board rates. It has a warm, friendly bar where you'll find a log fire, a selection of traditional pub games and generally, a good-natured bunch of locals. A wide range of snacks is served here, whilst the Stables Restaurant offers an extensive menu, of mostly English dishes, including a vegetarian choice. A full English breakfast is provided. The bar stocks mostly local real ales, as well as a traditional cider. The hotel, which is rated four-crown standard by the tourist board, has 15 en-suite bedrooms, all with TV, direct dial telephone and tea-coffee making facilities. Two of the rooms feature modern pine four-poster beds. Children are welcome (the rate charged varies according to age).

- ⛉ Eleven double, three twin-bedded and one family room
- £ ££ (£££ single occupancy)
- ⛃ Black Sheep Bitter, Special; Tetley Bitter; Theakston Old Peculier; Webster's Yorkshire Bitter; guest beer (occasionally)
- ⟒ Snacks daily lunchtime, meals daily, lunchtime and evening
- CC accepted

—— GRINTON-IN-SWALEDALE ——

Bridge Inn
Grinton-in-Swaledale, Richmond DL11 6HH
☎ *(01748) 884224;* FAX *(01748) 884044*
Directions: on the B6270, half a mile from Reeth

Local CAMRA members describe the Bridge Inn as 'an hospitable pub in a peaceful setting on the River Swale'. Its position, in the north-eastern corner of the Yorkshire Dales National Park, affords stunning views over the hills and moors of Swaledale. The pub is owned and run by Trevor and Margaret Hird who have carried out a complete refurbishment to provide two pleasant bars and a light, airy restaurant, which doubles as a family room. There is also an area set aside for residents with a cosy open fire. The six spacious bedrooms all have en-suite bathrooms and all the usual amenities, including double glazing to keep out winter chills. The family room has bunk beds for two children, who are charged at £10 each per night. A full English breakfast is provided and the pub is well known locally for its good bar and restaurant meals which come in generous portions. Pets can be accommodated. The Bridge is within easy reach of Richmond and the A1 at Scotch Corner.

🛏 Four double, one twin-bedded and one family room
£ ££
🍺 Black Sheep Best Bitter; John Smith's Bitter; Tetley Bitter; Theakston Old Peculier; guest beers
🍽 Snacks and meals daily, lunchtime and evening
CC accepted

—— INGLETON ——

Wheatsheaf Inn & Hotel
22 High Street, Ingleton via Carnforth LA6 3AD
☎ *(015242) 41275*
Directions: top end of village which lies on the A65 midway between the M6 (jct 36) and Settle

The Wheatsheaf comes highly recommended by some satisfied customers who have already been back for a second visit. They are particularly enthusiastic about the superb food which comes in 'huge helpings' and includes a vegetarian menu. This very friendly, family-run establishment offers nine comfortable bedrooms, which have recently been refurbished, most of them with king-sized beds and old pine furnishings. Well appointed, the rooms all have en-suite bathrooms, TV, and tea/coffee tray. A family room is available – children are charged half the adult price. The Wheatsheaf was built in the 17th century as a coaching inn and was extended in the 19th century into the blacksmith's shop and the stables (now the restaurant). Here a blackboard menu offers a good range of traditional dishes, with daily specials which may include local game. The dining room is for non-smokers, but meals can also be taken in the pub's long, cosy bar. The picturesque village of Ingleton is surrounded by some impressive scenery and is popular with walkers finishing the 'Waterfalls Walk'.

🛏 Eight double/twin bedded rooms, one family room
£ ££
🍺 Black Sheep Best Bitter, Special (summer), Riggwelter; Moorhouse's Pendle Witches Brew; Theakston Best Bitter; guest beer (occasionally)
🍽 Snacks lunchtime, meals daily lunchtime and evening
CC accepted

—— LONG PRESTON ——

Maypole Inn
Long Preston, Skipton BD23 4PH
☎ *(01729) 840219*
Directions: on the A65 between Settle and Skipton

The pretty, traditional maypole, to which this pub owes its name, stands on the pleasant green in front of the inn at the village centre. Popular with villagers and visitors alike, this regular CAMRA local award-winner has two bars – a comfortable lounge with an open fire on one side with an adjoining restaurant and a larger tap room on the other where traditional games are played. Both bars are warmed by open fires in winter. The six guest rooms are tastefully furnished, each with a private bathroom, TV and tea/coffee making facilities. The rooms are of varying sizes, according to the guests' needs; some feature window seats so you can sit and admire the view. Excellent home-made food is served in generous portions, all freshly prepared to order, and there is a good vegetarian choice. This area is excellent for active outdoor pursuits such as potholing or climbing, pony trekking, fishing and golf. It is popular with both mountain and road cyclists. Walkers will find many footpaths passing right by the pub into the Dales. The lovely old town of Skipton is well worth a visit, while steam train enthusiasts will want to head for Settle (four miles) for a breathtaking ride on the Settle–Carlisle line. Pets can be accommodated.

⊨ One single, two double, one twin-bedded and one family room
£ £ (single ££)
🍺 Boddingtons Bitter; Castle Eden Ale; Taylor Landlord; Worth Alesman; guest beer (occasionally)
🍴 Snacks and meals daily, lunchtime and evening, all day from noon-9pm Sunday
CC accepted

—— LOW ROW ——

Punch Bowl Inn
Low Row, near Reeth, Swaledale DL11 6PF
☎ *(01748) 886233; FAX (01748) 886522*

This very lively pub is at the heart of the community since it also serves as the village shop (where cave lamps can be hired), tea room and restaurant. The energetic and enterprising owner, Pete Roe organises all sorts of activities at the pub, and aims to keep prices as low as possible for enthusiasts. To this end, alongside the traditional B&B accommodation, there is also a bunk house, so altogether there are beds for up to 90 people. Pete keeps a list of experienced and fully qualified instructors, so he is able to help organise all kinds of field trips for student groups, and outdoor pursuits such as potholing, mountain biking, canoeing. Not only that, the Punch Bowl also hosts a beer festival at Easter and August Bank Holiday. The welcoming bar, which is warmed by a log fire and adorned with lead mining and pot-holing equipment, offers no less than 130 malt whiskies, plus a real ale, 'Fred's' brewed only for the pub by 'Fred-up-the-dale'. The guest rooms include five with en-suite facilities and a full English breakfast is provided. Children are charged half price (under fives are free).

⊨ Four double, seven twin-bedded and three family rooms
£ £
🍺 John Smith's Bitter; Theakston Best Bitter, XB, Old Peculier; guest beers
CC accepted

—— MIDDLEHAM ——

White Swan Hotel
Market Place, Middleham DL8 4PE
☎ *(01969) 622093;* FAX *(01969) 624551*
Directions: Middleham is on the A6108 Ripon-Leyburn road; the hotel is just off the market place

This is another Yorkshire pub which has been recommended by a contented customer enthusing about the food. Here it is 'just brilliant and exceptional value'. This assertion is backed up by Brian Pike, the food critic for *Dales Life* who says the pub has 'an enviable reputation with a menu having a distinctly cosmopolitan feel'. The White Swan has a very traditional atmosphere. Both the bar and the comfortable lounge (which overlooks the market place) are warmed by open fires. The pleasant guest rooms all have en-suite bath or shower, plus TV, tea/coffee making equipment and direct dial telephone. Two rooms feature half tester beds and some offer a good view of the ruined castle, once the home of Richard III. Middleham is an interesting little town retaining several Georgian fronted buildings and a cobbled market square. Situated between Wensleydale and Coverdale, visitors will find plenty to do, including stately homes and gardens open to the public, while children beg to be taken to the Lightwater Valley theme park nearby. Pets can be accommodated at the inn.

- ⇔ Eight double, three family rooms
- £ ££
- ⌑ Black Sheep Best Bitter, Special; Hambleton Bitter; John Smith's Bitter; guest beer
- ⦿ Snacks and meals daily, lunchtime and evening
- CC accepted

—— PICKHILL ——

Nags Head Country Inn
Pickhill, Thirsk YO7 4JG
☎ *(01845) 567391;* FAX *(01845) 567212*
Directions: off the A1, approximately eight miles south of Bedale

The Nags Head was established 200 years ago to cater for travellers on the London-Edinburgh road, and is still fulfilling its original function as well as providing a good base for those wanting to tour 'Herriot country'. Run by two brothers, Edward and Raymond Boynton, for more than 25 years now, the Nags Head is both a popular village pub and a comfortable hotel. The pub combines a cosy bar (noted for its huge collection of ties) with a small lounge and a smart restaurant (meals are also served in the bar). The accommodation comprises 15 well-equipped en-suite bedrooms, plus a cottage which can be used for additional bed and breakfast guests, or booked on its own for a self-catering holiday. Pets can also be catered for by prior arrangement. The Bowes Museum and the splendid outdoor Beamish Museum are both within easy reach, as are Jervaulx, Rievaulx and Fountains Abbey. For children, Flamingo Land and the Lightwater Valley theme park are both major attractions.

- ⇔ Two single, eight double, five twin-bedded and one family room
- £ ££ (£££ single room)
- ⌑ Black Sheep Special; Hambleton Bitter; John Smith's Bitter; Theakston Black Bull; guest beer (occasionally)
- ⦿ Snacks and meals daily, lunchtime and evening
- CC accepted

—— RIBBLEHEAD ——

Station Inn
Ribblehead, Ingleton via Cornforth LA6 3AS
☎ *(015242) 41274*
Directions: on the B6255, Ingleton-Hawes road

A pub for railway enthusiasts, standing right next to the Ribblehead station of the Settle-Carlisle line. You can sup your ale in the pub garden while watching the steam trains crossing the famous Ribblehead viaduct. Not surprisingly, the railway theme is continued in the pub itself, the cosy bar is full of paintings and drawings and photographs of rail memorabilia. Warmed by a cast iron stove, the bar offers a good choice of real ales and malt whiskies, and the occasional traditional cider. A good range of meals can either be taken here or in the snug dining room where children are welcome. Giant Yorkshire puddings are a speciality of the house and come with a variety of fillings from chilli con carne to a traditional roast lunch! Vegetarians are also catered for. Produce for the pub kitchen is sourced locally as far as possible, and freshly cooked to order. The inn, which was built at around the same time as the viaduct, enjoys spectacular views and is well placed for outdoor pursuits, including the 'three peaks' walk of Pen-y-Ghen, Whernside and Ingleborough. Four of the guest rooms offer en-suite facilities, and all have TV and tea/coffee making equipment.

    One single, three double, one twin-bedded and one family room
£ £
    Black Sheep Bitter, Special; Theakston Bitter, XB, Old Peculier; guest beer (on occasion)
    Snacks and meals daily, lunchtime and evening
CC accepted

—— RICHMOND ——

Black Lion Hotel
12 Finkle Street, Richmond DL10 4QB
☎ *(01748) 823121*
Directions: side street, off the market square

Richmond in Swaledale is a very attractive old town, dominated by the magnificent ruins of its castle. The Black Lion is just off the cobbled market square and is a popular meeting place for local people. Guests can linger in the traditional old bars which are open all day, or repair to the comfortable residents' lounge. Meals, based on fresh local produce, are served in the restaurant or in the bars. The overnight accommodation is comfortable, but not plush. None of the rooms has a private bathroom, but they do all have washbasins, TV and tea/coffee making facilities. A full English breakfast is provided. You will need to 'stoke up' in the morning for energy as this area has a lot for visitors to explore, not least in the town itself which boasts a Georgian Theatre Museum, built in 1788 which is still in use for public performances. Richmond lies on the Coast to Coast Walk, popular with serious walkers. If you prefer to travel by car (the hotel has a car park), then a short drive will take you to the splendid Castle Howard, Raby Castle with its extensive deer park or Newby Hall which offers miniature steam train rides and river boat trips. Pets can be accommodated at the Black Lion by arrangement.

    Four single, four double, four twin-bedded and two family rooms
£ £
    Cameron Strongarm; Flowers Original; Tetley Bitter, Imperial; guest beer
    Snacks and meals daily, lunchtime and evening
CC not accepted

ROBIN HOOD'S BAY

Victoria Hotel
Station Road, Robin Hood's Bay, near Whitby YO22 4RL
☎ *(01947) 880205;* FAX *(01947) 881170*

This imposing hotel was built a hundred years ago right on the clifftop, overlooking Robin Hood's Bay and the village. Half of the guest bedrooms enjoy the same panorama, so make sure you check when booking if you want a room with a view. Two-crown rated by the ETB, the rooms all have en-suite facilities, and a full English breakfast is provided. The hotel also offers an extensive bar menu and *à la carte* restaurant and they say 'home-made' is the key-word in the kitchens here. The bar stocks traditional cider as well as draught beers in a village where, according to local CAMRA members, all the pubs stock real ale. Robin Hood's Bay is an attractive seaside village, which had a disreputable past due to its involvement with smugglers. Whitby, just north of the bay also has an intriguing history, and stories of witches and Count Dracula abound. Nonetheless, today this picturesque fishing port is well worth a visit – Captain Cook's house is here. Whitby, like the rest of this stretch of coastline is also famous for its seafood. Serious walkers can embark on the Coast to Coast walk or take to the Cleveland Way locally.

- 🛏 Four double, two twin-bedded and three family rooms
- £ ££
- 🍺 Camerons Bitter, Strongarm
- 🍴 Snacks and meals daily, lunchtime and evening
- CC accepted

RUNSWICK BAY

Runswick Bay Hotel
Runswick Bay, near Whitby TS13 5HR
☎ *(01947) 841010*

A good port of call for hikers – the Cleveland Way long distance footpath runs directly through the hotel car park! Set atop the hill overlooking Runswick Bay, the pub benefits from terrific views over the coastline and the surrounding countryside. A warm and friendly atmosphere is to be found in its central bar which serves two further rooms. There is also a dining room, but the extensive menu is also served in the bar if you prefer. A full English breakfast is provided to residents staying in the three en-suite guest rooms. The rooms all have TV and tea/coffee making facilities. Children are welcome – under threes are accommodated free of charge, up to 14 year-olds are charged £8 per night when sharing their parents room. Pets can also be catered for by prior arrangement. Runswick Bay is a pretty little place, boasting many fisherman's cottages, situated eight miles north of Whitby, which gets very busy with tourists in summer. The whole of this area of coast is designated as a 'Heritage' area and other places to visit include Robin Hood's Bay, the undeveloped resort of Ravenscar and Staithes which has connections with Captain Cook.

- 🛏 One double, one twin-bedded and one family room
- £ £
- 🍺 Tetley Bitter; guest beers (summer)
- 🍴 Snacks and meals daily, lunchtime and evening
- CC not accepted

—— THORNTON WATLASS ——

Buck Inn

Thornton Watlass, Ripon HG4 4AH
☎ *(01677) 422461;* FAX *(01677) 422447*
Directions: one mile off the B6268, Masham–Bedale road

The Buck stands on the picturesque village green, with its wall serving as the boundary for the cricket pitch – if the ball hits, it scores a four, whilst a six is over the roof! If the game becomes too violent, spectators can retire to the relative safety of the sheltered back garden, where quoits is a popular pursuit in summer, and there is play equipment for children. This pretty village, with houses built of local stone and a fine 11th-century church, forms part of the Thornton Watlass Estate. The pub itself has a small cosy bar with an open fire, leading into a dining area, and a larger bar, the Long Room, which hosts live music every weekend. All but two of the bedrooms have en-suite bathrooms and there is a residents' TV lounge. Pets can be accommodated. A hearty Yorkshire breakfast is served and the pub offers an extensive lunch and dinner menu, based on fresh local produce. Picnic lunches can also be provided. Various themed breaks can be arranged for golfers, race-goers and anglers.

- One single, three double, two twin-bedded and one family room
- £ ££ (£ not en-suite)
- Black Sheep Best Bitter; John Smith's Bitter; Tetley Bitter; Theakston Best Bitter; guest beer (usually from a local independent brewery)
- Snacks and meals daily, lunchtime and evening
- CC accepted

—— WEAVERTHORPE ——

Star Inn

Weaverthorpe, Malton YO17 8EY
☎ *(01944) 738273*
Directions: off the A64/B1249

Set in a rural Wolds valley, this inn has grown to incorporate a row of eight other cottages, which have been renovated in keeping with the 200-year-old character of the pub. Both the bar and lounge are warmed by open fires from late summer through to the spring. Susan and David Richardson, who have been in charge of the inn for more than ten years now, have built up a formidable reputation for the restaurant, by offering an original dinner menu specialising in local game. CAMRA's food writer, Susan Nowak is a great fan, and another very satisfied customer told me that not only was the food superb – he cited the game casserole, fish chowder and pigeon breasts – but it was matched by the quality of the ale. Three of the five guest rooms have en-suite amenities; the others have washbasins. All have shaver points, TV and tea/coffee making facilities. Guests can have their own keys for independent access at all times. Reduced rates are available for longer stays, and bargain weekend breaks are available on a half board basis. The stately homes of Castle Howard and Sledmere House are nearby.

- One single, two double, one twin-bedded and one family room
- £ £
- Camerons Bitter, Ruby Red,; Marston's Pedigree; Hambleton Stallion; York Yorkshire Terrier; guest beer (occasionally)
- Evening meals Wednesday-Monday
- CC accepted

TRY ALSO:

Crown Hotel (Suddaby's)
Wheelgate, Malton YO17 0HP
☎ *(01653) 692038*

Home of the Malton Brewery. Nine rooms. B&B £

Tiger Inn
The Green, North Newbald, York YO43 3SA.
☎ *(01430) 827759*

Three reasonably priced guest rooms with shared facilities at the village centre, near the Wolds Way long distance footpath. B&B £

Fox & Hounds Inn
Starbotton, near Skipton BD23 5HY
☎ *(01756) 760269*

Pub with just two en-suite rooms at the heart of the Yorkshire Dales National Park. B&B ££

Olde Beehive Inn
Newholm, Whitby YO21 3QY
☎ *(01947) 602703*

Billing itself as 'one mile out of Whitby, the inn where you turn back time', the Beehive offers three en-suite rooms. B&B £

Ship Inn
Rosedale Lane, Port Mulgrave, Hinderwell TS13 5JZ
☎ *(01947) 840303*

Friendly inn with simple accommodation, close to Runswick Bay. B&B £

YORKSHIRE (SOUTH)

—— DONCASTER ——

Wheatley Hotel
Thorne Road, Doncaster DN2 5DR
☎ *(01302) 364092;* ℻ *(01302) 361017*
Directions: take the Edenthorpe road from Doncaster, the hotel is one mile past the hospital

A good choice for families, this friendly hotel has a well-equipped children's play room, as well as a garden with its own play area. Children sharing their parents' room are charged £10 per night and they are well catered for on the hotel's restaurant menu, which represents good value for the mainly home-cooked meals. Adults can choose to dine either in the restaurant or the bar which offers a large screen TV for Sky sports fans. There is a large, comfortable lounge divided by impressive wood and leaded glass doors. Set in the Wheatley Hills area, just outside Doncaster, the pub is within easy reach of the race course (two miles). Four of the guest rooms have en-suite facilities. Discounts are available for long stays or large parties. A full English breakfast is served. Pets can be accommodated by prior arrangement.

⋈ Two single, two double, seven twin-bedded and two family rooms
£   £ (££ en-suite)
◨ John Smith's Bitter, Magnet; guest beer (occasionally)
◉ Snacks and meals daily, lunchtime and evening (except Sunday evening)
CC accepted

—— SHEFFIELD ——

Rutland Arms
86 Brown Street, Sheffield S1 2BS
☎ *(0114) 272 9003;* ℻ *(0114) 273 1425*

The Rutland Arms is handy for those who prefer not to travel by car as it is just five minutes from both the rail and bus stations. This Victorian 'gem' which boasts a distinctive, well-preserved Gilmour's Brewery frontage stands in the city's rapidly expanding cultural quarter – an area that is becoming popular for its nightlife and leisure facilities. The Rutland is increasingly being frequented by locals for early evening weekday meals (food is in fact served all day between noon and 7pm and noon-2.30 at weekends). A comfortable pub, with a single, well-furnished lounge, it is one of the few real ale pubs in the city to offer accommodation. One of the single rooms is fully en-suite with its own bathroom, five have private showers, and the other room just has a washbasin. All the rooms have TV and tea/coffee making facilities. A full English breakfast is served. The pub boasts a colourful, award-winning garden – another unusual feature for a city pub.

⋈ Four single, one double, one twin-bedded and one family room
£   £ (££ single en-suite)
◨ Greene King Abbot; Ind Coope Burton Ale; Marston's Pedigree; Tetley Bitter; guest beer
◉ Snacks and meals daily, noon-7pm Monday-Friday, noon-2.30 weekends
CC accepted

TRY ALSO:

Stanhope Arms
Dunford Bridge, Penistone S30 6TF
☎ *(01226) 763104*

Multi-roomed pub on the Alternative Pennine Way. The five rooms can all accommodate families. B&B £

KEY

Each entry in *Room at the Inn* contains a reference section. The first example given below describes what each icon (pictogram) represents and what kind of information you will find. The second, bottom, example is a real entry from the book to give you and idea of what to expect.

- 🛏 The number of rooms and type of accommodation available
- £ The price guide (see Introduction text)
- 🍺 A list of beers which are regularly available, and occasional guests
- 🍽 The type of food available and what time of day it is served
- **CC** Whether credit cards are accepted or not

- 🛏 Ten double, seven twin-bedded and two family rooms
- £ £ (££ en-suite)
- 🍺 Adnams Bitter; Crouch Vale Best Bitter; Tolly Cobbold Bitter
- 🍽 Snacks and meals daily, lunchtime and evening
- **CC** accepted

 Member of the British Institute of Innkeeping

YORKSHIRE (WEST)

—— BATLEY ——

White Bear

108 High Street, Birstall, Batley WF17 9HW
☎ *(01924) 476212*
Directions: on the B6125, between Huddersfield and Leeds

Local CAMRA members describe the White Bear as 'compact'. It is a traditional corner pub, with a comfortable lounge and a tap room, which usually stages live entertainment at the weekend. The guest rooms offer basic, but good value accommodation, with shared bathroom facilities. Children are welcome and pets can be accommodated. Situated just five minutes from the M62 (junction 27), the pub is very convenient for Leeds, Bradford and Halifax. This is Brontë country and the village has strong connections with the famous literary family. Other local attractions include the excellent weekly markets in the area and, for serious shoppers, the nearby Scopos Mill Centre. This development, set in converted former textile mills, started out as factory outlets, but has become an upmarket retail centre (the owner refers to it as the 'Harrods of the North').

🛏 Two single, two twin-bedded rooms
£ £
🍺 Tetley Mild, Bitter; guest beer (occasionally)
🍽 Snacks and meals daily, lunchtime and evening
CC not accepted

—— BRADFORD ——

New Beehive Inn

171 Westgate, Bradford BD1 3AA
☎ *(01274) 721784*
Directions: on the B6144, half a mile from the city centre

Listed on CAMRA's National Inventory of pubs of outstanding historic interest, this many-roomed, gaslit pub has retained all its original Edwardian character, while offering the high standards of food, accommodation and hospitality demanded by today's guests. It is a very popular choice for local pubgoers; the huge cellar bar with its flagstone floor and bare walls is a regular venue for jazz, blues and folk bands, and also houses a traditional skittle alley. German beers are featured in this bar, although draught ales are also available. Centrally located, the pub is convenient for the Alhambra, St George's Hall and the Museum of Photography, as well as both bus and rail stations. There are 13 guest bedrooms (eight have en-suite bathrooms) which have been refurbished and awarded two-crown status by the English Tourist Board. William Wagstaff is the master of the kitchen as well as the cellar, and his appetising food has won the approval of CAMRA's food writer, Susan Nowak. Breakfast is not included in the room rate, and costs £4 per person. Children are welcome to stay (at half price) and pets may be accommodated (check when booking).

🛏 Five double, five twin-bedded and three family rooms
£ Room rate £
🍺 Brakspear Bitter; Goose Eye Bitter; Taylor Golden Best, Landlord; Worth Alesman; guest beers
🍽 Meals and snacks lunchtime and evening, Monday to Saturday
CC accepted

—— HEBDEN BRIDGE ——

White Lion Hotel
Bridge Gate, Hebden Bridge HX7 8EX
☎ *(01422) 842197;* FAX *(01422) 846619*
Directions: Hebden Bridge is on the A646 between Halifax and Burnley

Standing on the bank of Hebden water, with a garden overlooking the weir at the centre of Hebden Bridge. Dating back to the mid-17th century and originally a coaching inn, the interior has been opened out in sympathetic fashion offering a mix of styles and areas to appeal to its varied clientele. The pub itself has a wheelchair WC and two guest rooms on the ground floor are suitable for guests with disabilities. Some bedrooms are in the main building, and some in the converted coach house in the grounds; all have en-suite facilities (some with bath and shower, others just a shower) and the usual amenities of TV and tea/coffee making equipment. The pub enjoys a good reputation locally for its meals. It serves an extensive menu with additional blackboard daily 'specials'; light meals and snacks are available at all times between noon-9pm, except Sunday. The White Lion is centrally located for visitors to Calderdale and Brontë country, with easy access to the M62 and M65 motorways. Local attractions include the NT's nature trail at Hardcastle Crags and the Broadland Clough Nature Reserve at Cragg Vale, run by the Yorkshire Naturalists Trust.

- ⇥ Five double, two twin-bedded and three family rooms
- £ £ – ££ according to facilities (single occupancy ££)
- 🍺 Boddingtons Bitter; Castle Eden Ale; Flowers Original; Taylor Landlord; always one Whitbread guest beer, plus another
- 🍴 Snacks and meals daily, lunchtime and evening
- CC accepted

—— HOLMFIRTH ——

Old Bridge Hotel
Market Walk, Holmfirth, Huddersfield HD7 1DA
☎ *(01484) 681212;* FAX *(01484) 687978*
Directions: off the A6106/A635 in the town centre

Holmfirth was a sleepy little place that kept its charms to itself, until TV's *Last of the Summer Wine* told the world just how delightful this part of the country really is – Sid's Café is just 50 yards down the road from the hotel. An area of outstanding natural beauty, it is not surprising that tourists now flock here as a base for exploring the region. Those who choose the Old Bridge will not be disappointed. Privately owned and run, it was converted from a gentleman's residence, parts of which date back to the early 18th century. It provides a pleasant setting and excellent service in comfortable surroundings. Meals can be taken either in the spacious oak-beamed lounge bar or the restaurant. The guest rooms – all en-suite – are furnished and equipped to a high standard, with all the usual amenities, including 24-hour room service. Children are welcome to stay, indeed, the telephones incorporate a baby listening device so parents can relax in the bar without worries. The hotel offers secure private parking for residents. Special weekend mini breaks are available, and escorted walks can be arranged. Pets can be accommodated.

- ⇥ Seven singles, eleven double and two twin-bedded rooms
- £ ££
- 🍺 Black Sheep Best Bitter; Taylor Best Bitter, Landlord; Tetley Mild, Bitter; guest beers
- 🍴 Snacks and meals daily, from 7.30am-9.30pm
- CC not accepted

—— HUDDERSFIELD ——

Huddersfield Hotel
Kirkgate, Huddersfield HD1 1QT
☎ *(01484) 51211;* FAX *(01484) 435262*
Directions: just off the Huddersfield ring road

This hotel is a far cry from the traditional country inn which most of us seek out. However, it is very convenient for visitors to Huddersfield, particularly for the university and New Theatre, and does serve a decent pint of real ale. It is an attractive building which has won the *Yorkshire in Bloom* competition as well as awards for its hospitality and service. It also has the advantage of offering meals at all times of day, up until 11pm in the restaurant and even later in the brasserie. A nightclub attached to the hotel is open until 3am. All the guest rooms have en-suite facilities, with either bath or shower, plus colour TV with three free movie channels, trouser press, hairdryer and hospitality tray. The hotel has a secure car park. Pets can be accommodated.

ᕬ 12 single, 30 double, four family rooms
£ **£££**
ᐧ Bass Worthington Bitter, Draught Bass; Stones Best Bitter; Wadworth 6X; Whitbread Castle Eden Ale
▮ᐧ Snacks and meals daily until midnight
CC accepted

—— OUTWOOD ——

Kirklands Hotel
605 Leeds Road, Outwood, Wakefield WF1 2LU
☎ *(01924) 826666;* FAX *(01924) 826682*
Directions: on the A61, between Leeds and Wakefield, near jct 41 of the M1

With its ecclesiastical-sounding name, and situated next to the church, it is easy to understand that the Kirklands was originally built as a vicarage, although it would be hard to tell now. Having recently undergone a complete refurbishment, this attractive pub, tied to the small independent Old Mill Brewery, now offers a very pleasant venue for locals and visitors alike. It features three large rooms grouped around a central bar with restaurant seating for 60 people – the meals here are very reasonably priced, but good quality, based on fresh produce. The six en-suite guest rooms are comfortably furnished and can accommodate families – children are also welcome in the public areas of the hotel until early evening. The rooms are equipped with TV, telephone, trouser press and tea/coffee making equipment. With easy access to the M1, the hotel is convenient for those visiting Leeds or Wakefield, and is popular for business and social functions.

ᕬ Three single, three double/twin-bedded rooms
£ **££** (**££££** single room)
ᐧ Old Mill Mild, Nellie Dene, Bitter, seasonal beers
▮ᐧ Snacks and meals daily, lunchtime and evening (except Sunday evening)
CC accepted

—— TODMORDEN ——

Staff of Life

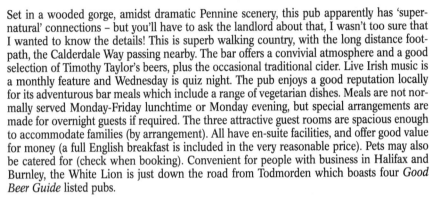

550 Burnley Road, Knotts, Todmorden OL14 8JF
☎ *(01706) 812929;* FAX *(01706) 813773*
Directions: one and a half miles from Todmorden, on the A646, Halifax-Burnley road

Set in a wooded gorge, amidst dramatic Pennine scenery, this pub apparently has 'super-natural' connections – but you'll have to ask the landlord about that, I wasn't too sure that I wanted to know the details! This is superb walking country, with the long distance foot-path, the Calderdale Way passing nearby. The bar offers a convivial atmosphere and a good selection of Timothy Taylor's beers, plus the occasional traditional cider. Live Irish music is a monthly feature and Wednesday is quiz night. The pub enjoys a good reputation locally for its adventurous bar meals which include a range of vegetarian dishes. Meals are not nor-mally served Monday-Friday lunchtime or Monday evening, but special arrangements are made for overnight guests if required. The three attractive guest rooms are spacious enough to accommodate families (by arrangement). All have en-suite facilities, and offer good value for money (a full English breakfast is included in the very reasonable price). Pets may also be catered for (check when booking). Convenient for people with business in Halifax and Burnley, the White Lion is just down the road from Todmorden which boasts four *Good Beer Guide* listed pubs.

🛏 Two double, one twin-bedded room
£ £
🍺 Robinson's Best Bitter; Taylor Golden Best, Best Bitter, Landlord; guest beers
🍽 Snacks and meals daily, lunchtime and evening (see above)
CC accepted

TRY ALSO:

Haworth Old Hall
Sun Street, Haworth BD22 8BP
☎ *(01535) 642709*

Characterful 17th-century inn in Brontë country. Two en-suite rooms. B&B £

Red Lion
Sheffield Road, Jackson Bridge, Holmfirth HD7 7HS
☎ *(01484) 683499*

Reputedly haunted, this pub is convenient for the Peak District and the Yorkshire Dales National Parks. Three en-suite rooms, three with shared facilities. B&B £ (££ single en-suite)

Plough Inn
45 Warmfield Lane, Warmfield, Wakefield
☎ *(01924) 892007*

Two reasonably priced en-suite rooms in a semi-rural area of Wakefield. B&B

Kirklands Hotel, Wakefield, W.Yorks.

BRITISH INSTITUTE *of* INNKEEPING
MEMBER
SETTING *professional* STANDARDS

All lovers of good pubs should keep an eye out for outlets bearing the British Institute of Innkeeping logo and membership plaques, as its aims are to promote high standards of professionalism in licensed retailing and to provide the skills, training and nationally recognised qualifications to help members run some of the best pubs in the country.

WALES

—— ELAN VALLEY ——

Elan Valley Hotel
Elan Valley, near Rhayader, Powys LD6 5HN
☎/FAX *(01597) 810448*
Directions: from Ryadader, follow the B4518 in the direction of the reservoirs for 2.5 miles

Built as a fishing lodge for the Victorian gentry, this family-run hotel is a short walk from the Elan Valley reservoirs, dubbed the Welsh Lakeland. The scenery around here is breathtaking and attracts not only walkers, cyclists and (naturally) anglers, but also painters, photographers and poets. The peaceful surroundings enable visitors to catch a glimpse of the wildlife that abounds – pole cats and otters on the ground, red kites and buzzards in the air. The hotel offers a very relaxed and comfortable atmosphere in all its public rooms, which include two bars, a restaurant and a tea room. The owners say that 'dominoes, darts, an occasional quiz and good conversation provide the entertainment, whilst substantial home-cooked bar meals and well-kept Welsh ales provide the sustenance'. What more could one ask for? The overnight accommodation, rated three-crown status by the Welsh Tourist Board, is in 11 guest rooms, all but one of which has en-suite facilities. There is a choice of a full, cooked breakfast or the continental option. Children are welcome and pets can be accommodated.

- ⇥ Six double, five twin-bedded rooms
- £ £ – ££ (supplement for single occupancy)
- 🍺 Hancock's HB; guest beers
- 🍴 Snacks and meals daily, lunchtime and evening
- **CC** accepted

Cain Valley Hotel
Llanfyllin, Powys

—— GLASBURY-ON-WYE ——

Harp Inn
Glasbury-on-Wye, via Hereford HR3 5NR
☎ *(01497) 847373*
Directions: on the B4350, south of Hay-on-Wye

The Harp is only just in Wales, and in fact I was about to list it under Herefordshire when I noticed it won an award a few years ago as *Welsh Village Pub of the Year*, so that settled it. On the banks of the River Wye, four miles upstream from Hay, now famous for its second-hand bookshops and the annual Sunday Times Literary Festival, the Harp was built in the 18th century as a cider house, and is now a family-run free house. Glasbury, which lies under the shadow of a ruined Norman castle, is just north-west of the Black Mountains which attract pony trekkers of all abilities. Canoeing is another popular pursuit here and the area has great appeal for artists and craftworkers; indeed the village has a thriving craft centre open to the public. Nearby Brecon (12 miles) draws large crowds to its International Jazz Festival which takes place annually in August. This friendly pub offers visitors good value bar meals and accommodation. Two rooms have en-suite shower and WC, the other two rooms have private but separate facilities. TV and tea/coffee making equipment are provided in the rooms which are strictly for non-smokers. Children are welcome.

🛏 Two double, two twin-bedded rooms
£ £
🍺 Boddingtons Bitter; Brains SA; Robinson's Best Bitter; guest beers
🍽 Snacks and meals daily, lunchtime and evening
CC accepted

—— HOWEY ——

Drovers Arms
Howey, Llandrindod Wells LD1 5PT
☎ *(01597) 822508;* FAX *(01597) 822711*
Directions: off the A483, one and a half miles south of Llandrindod Wells

This Victorian red-brick pub was built over a 13th-century cellar, so it is obviously not the first inn to have stood at this site on the old drovers' route. Owners, Janet and David Day maintain the pub well, keeping its paintwork and furnishings fresh, so visitors can enjoy its pleasant character and friendly atmosphere to the full. The bedrooms are comfortable and well equipped, with TV, hospitality tray, hair dryers and trouser press/iron. One of the rooms has its own bathroom. The Drovers also has an attractive patio garden with seating for summer days. The owners do all the cooking themselves, producing an interesting and varied menu using only the best local produce. The bar stocks a house beer brewed by the small independent Wood Brewery in Shropshire. Howey is a picturesque little village with a pretty bridge over a stream, where the old mill has been turned into an art gallery. The spa town of Llandrindod Wells is popular with tourists; keen cyclists can visit the National Cycle Museum there before taking off on one of the many local routes. The Brecon Beacons and Radnor Forest are both easily accessible, and for bird lovers, the Red Kite Feeding Station near Rhayader makes an interesting trip. Children are welcome.

🛏 One double, one twin-bedded room
£ £
🍺 Beer range varies – mostly from Welsh breweries
🍽 Snacks and meals daily, lunchtime (except Tuesday) and evening
CC accepted

—— KNUCKLAS ——

Castle Inn

Knucklas, near Knighton, Powys LD7 1PW
☎ *(01547) 528150*
Directions: on the B4355, two miles from Knighton

Situated alongside Offa's Dyke, and close to Glyndwr Way and the Jack Mytton Way, three of the most popular walkers' routes in these parts, the Castle is naturally much frequented by ramblers. It opens at 8am to serve breakfast to non-residents. The landlord, Peter May is himself a keen walker and will readily suggest a number of circular walks to get you back to the inn in time for one of their delicious home-cooked dinners. Family-run, the pub comprises a characterful main bar furnished with old settles and featuring exposed beams, stone walls and a large inglenook. The dining room, which seats 20, is popular with families (children are welcome to stay overnight). There is also a function room. The accommodation is in a converted coach house offering five en-suite rooms. A full English (sorry, Welsh) breakfast is provided. Being close to the English border, this area is steeped in history and it is worth hopping over to Shropshire to explore Ludlow, Clun or Shrewsbury from where you can take a trip on the mid-Wales railway line which runs through some beautiful scenery, stopping at Knucklas on its way to Swansea. Pets can be accommodated.

ᵴ Two double, three twin-bedded rooms
£ £
🍺 Draught Bass; Worthington Bitter; guest beer
🍴 Snacks and meals daily, lunchtime and evening
CC not accepted

—— LLANDRINDOD WELLS ——

Llanerch Inn

Llanerch Lane, Llandrindod Wells, Powys LD1 6BG
☎ *(01597) 822086;* FAX *(01597) 824618*
Directions: in town centre, near the Police Station

Llandrindod Wells is at the heart of the old county of Radnor, and is now the county town of Powys, ideally situated for discovering the delightful countryside of Mid Wales. The inn is at the edge of the town with a large garden and orchard at the front and views of the Cambrian foothills to the rear. Dating back to the 16th-century the inn was established before the town, which developed as a spa resort in the 19th century – it now hosts a popular Victorian Festival for a week in August, when the townspeople dress up and the streets are alive with musicians and entertainers. The Llanerch hosts a number of events at the same time, including a beer festival with a choice of a dozen real ales to be sampled straight from the cask. The inn has been well preserved, retaining many original features, including a Jacobean staircase and a huge inglenook in the friendly bar. An extensive menu, with additional daily specials, is served both in the bar and the restaurant. Outdoors there is a boules pitch and a children's play area. The guest rooms were refurbished in 1997 and all but one converted to en-suite accommodation and represent good value. A two-night, half-board break is available at special rates.

ᵴ Two single, five double, three twin-bedded and two family rooms
£ £ (single room ££)
🍺 Hancock's HB and always two guest beers
🍴 Snacks and meals daily, lunchtime and evening
CC accepted

—— LLANFYLLIN ——

Cain Valley Hotel
High Street, Llanfyllin, Powys SY22 5AQ
☎ *(01691) 648366;* FAX *(01691) 648307*
Directions: off the A490 from Welshpool

The smartly painted, black and white exterior of this family-run hotel is indicative of the quality and standard to be found inside, as recognised by CAMRA over the last 20-odd years when it has regularly featured in the *Good Beer Guide*. A former coaching inn of great character, this Grade II listed building boasts many period features, including heavily beamed bars and a magnificent Jacobean staircase. The public bar has been refurbished, using old oak posts which have added even more to its charm. This is where the locals choose to congregate over a game of darts or dominoes. The plush, wood-panelled lounge is used for casual dining and there is also a stylish restaurant. The 13 guest rooms are all very comfortably furnished and have en-suite facilities, TV and courtesy tray. The little country town of Llanfyllin stands amidst some stunning scenery, with the Berwyn Mountains, Bala Lake and the spectacular Llanrhaeadr Waterfall all within easy reach. The coast and Mount Snowdon are both within an hour's drive. Children are welcome (three-13 year olds are charged at half price). Pets can be accommodated.

ᕼ One single, six double, three twin-bedded and three family rooms
£ ££ (£££ single room)
◖ Ansells Bitter; Draught Bass; Worthington Bitter; guest beers
⦿ Snacks and meals daily, lunchtime and evening
CC accepted

—— LLANIDLOES ——

Mount Inn
China Street, Llanidloes, Powys SY18 6AB
☎/FAX *(01686) 412247*

The cobbled stone floor of this inn is a listed feature as it is believed to have originally been part of the motte and bailey castle that once stood here. Dating back to the 14th century and formerly serving the coaching trade, this excellent many-roomed inn offers two basic bars, a plush lounge and a games room with TV, pool table and dartboard. One of the bars features a stove and old settles, while good quality meals are served in the lounge which opens on to a patio with lovely views. The large garden has play equipment for children who are welcome to stay at the inn. The guest rooms all have en-suite showers, TV and tea/coffee making facilities. Llanidloes has grown up around the 13th-century church and now incorporates a variety of architectural styles, from the 16th-century market hall through to the Victorian period and later. The Severn runs through the town and affords pleasant riverside walks, or for a longer hike you can follow the Glendower Way. There are opportunities for bikers of all kinds – practise your motorcycling skills on the nearby Enduro Course or ride quad bikes through the forest. The road to Machynlleth offers a challenge to mountain bikers. As well as a car park, the inn offers storage for cycles and motorbikes.

ᕼ One double, one twin-bedded and one family room
£ ££
◖ Draught Bass; Worthington Dark, Bitter, guest beer (occasionally)
⦿ Snacks and meals daily, lunchtime and evening
CC not accepted

—— LLANWRTYD WELLS ——

Neuadd Arms Hotel
The Square, Llanwrtyd Wells, Powys LD5 4RB
☎ *(01591) 610236*
Directions: on the A483, Builth Wells–Llandovery road

Llanwrtyd Wells may be the smallest town in Britain, but it certainly has big ideas about attracting visitors – its programme of events from the local tourist office includes something for almost every month of the year, from a Saturnalia Festival in January and a Man versus Horse marathon in June, through to the World Bog Snorkling championships in August and (last but not least) a beer festival in November. Gordon Green, the owner of the Neuadd Arms organises many of these events and indeed, the pub plays host to several of them. Gordon also arranges real ale rambles and guided walking and mountain bike holidays for his guests. I can't imagine he ever has time to pull a pint. His hotel, which is in part Georgian but extended in the 19th-century, has a characterful bar and lounge, both warmed by log fires in winter. Good food can be enjoyed in the bar or the restaurant which overlooks the square and surrounding hills. The guest rooms are spacious and comfortable; 15 have en-suite bath or shower, the others have washbasins; most have a TV. There is also a TV lounge and a games room where children are welcome. Once they are in bed, you can keep a check on them with the baby listening service at reception. Pets can be accommodated.

- ⍩ Six single, five double, eight twin-bedded and one family room
- £ ££ (not en-suite £)
- ⌾ Felinfoel Double Dragon; Hancock's HB; guest beer
- ⍩ Snacks and meals daily, lunchtime and evening

CC accepted

—— MONTGOMERY ——

Dragon Hotel
Montgomery, Powys SY15 6PA
☎ *(01686) 668359;* FAX *(01686) 668287*
Directions: in the town centre, off the B4385

This striking hotel, at the centre of a small town on Offa's Dyke, has an interesting history and boasts a number of unusual features; some of the beams and stonework in the bar and lounge are said to have been taken from Montgomery Castle after it was destroyed by Oliver Cromwell. Ideal for families, there is a residents' lounge which is set apart from the public bar and plush lounge. The weekly changed guest beer usually comes from an independent brewery. Added attractions are the regular live jazz sessions on Wednesday evenings and the indoor swimming-pool which is open all year to guests. Pleasantly decorated and comfortable throughout, this 17th-century hotel has 20 attractive bedrooms, all with en-suite bathrooms, TV, telephone and tea/coffee making facilities. In the same room children are charged at £5 for the bed, plus breakfast. High standards are maintained in the kitchen, which means that lunchtime bookings are often needed for the restaurant. Leisure pursuits in the locality include tennis, bowls and quad biking. Powis Castle is a popular local tourist destination. Pets can be catered for by prior arrangement.

- ⍩ Two single, nine double, five twin-bedded and four family rooms
- £ £££ (single ££££)
- ⌾ Flowers IPA; Wood Special; guest beer
- ⍩ Snacks and meals daily, lunchtime and evening

CC accepted

—— NEWTOWN ——

Bell Hotel

30 Commercial Street, Newtown, Powys SY16 2DE
☎ *(01686) 625540;* FAX *(01686) 626727*
Directions: on the B4568

The Bell has a most unusual mission – aside from the expected one of providing good hospitality – it is the Welsh 'Houston', the HQ for *Project Dragonfire*, the Space Mission which aims to send a rocket into space for the purpose of furthering the scientific education of the children of Wales. The project (which is more serious than it may sound) is the brainchild of the landlord, Peter (Berty) Burt, who has only been at the pub a year or so, but has already captured the interest of many local people. Berty is a space fanatic and the hotel is littered with space memorabilia including his earlier prototype rockets. However, space exploration is not Berty's only concern, he has managed to persuade the local Six Bells Brewery to supply their beers to him without the usual fish finings or other chemical additives, making them truly vegetarian products. This edge-of-town hotel attracts a wide ranging clientele and offers live music at weekends and special theme nights in its cellar restaurant. Meals can also be taken in the bar. The 18 guest rooms all offer en-suite accommodation, and a cooked breakfast is provided.

↩ Seven single, seven double, one twin-bedded and three family rooms
£ £ - ££
🍺 Six Bells Big Nev's, Cloud Nine; Tetley Bitter; guest beer
🍽 Snacks and meals daily, lunchtime and evening
CC accepted

—— NEW RADNOR ——

Eagle Hotel

Broad Street, New Radnor, Powys LD8 2SN
☎ *(01544) 350208;* FAX *(01544) 350401*
Directions: a quarter of a mile off the A44, four miles inside the Welsh border

I received more recommendations for the Eagle Hotel than any other pub for this edition of the guide, and the praise was unanimous – not for the beer (though that is good too), or the accommodation (said to be comfortable), but for the range of local outdoor activities that go on, and for the wealth of information, advice and contacts for leisure-seekers that the friendly owner, Angela Hoy has at her fingertips. Walking, cycling, bird-watching, pony-trekking, canoeing, climbing and caving can all be enjoyed here. Special two-day breaks are offered by the hotel, which can accommodate groups of up to 16 people. Set in a picturesque village, surrounded by unspoilt countryside, the Eagle, somewhat altered since its days as a coaching inn, now offers two bars – one is a cosy lounge, a coffee shop and a restaurant. The breakfast room opens at 8am for non-residents and stays open all day for snacks, including teas with home-made cakes. An award-winning menu caters for vegetarians, vegans and others with special dietary needs. There is a pretty, partially-covered terrace which is used for barbecues. All but two of the guest rooms have en-suite facilities; the family room sleeps four people. Pets can be accommodated.

↩ Two double, three twin-bedded and one family room
£ £ (££ single occupancy of en-suite room)
🍺 Draught Bass; Hook Norton Best Bitter; guest beer
🍽 Snacks and meals served daily, 8am-11pm
CC accepted

—— PENGENFFORDD ——

Castle Inn

Pengenffordd, near Talgarth, Powys LD3 0EP
☎/FAX *(01874) 711353*
Directions: on the A479, four miles south of Talgarth

The Castle Inn takes its name from the ancient hill fort of Castell Dinas (the highest such site in Wales) which stands behind the pub. At over 1,000 feet above sea level, this one-time farm-cum-drovers' inn, is situated at the heart of the Black Mountains, in the Brecon Beacons National Park. As at the Eagle in New Radnor, advice about the many outdoor pursuits, such as pony trekking, caving and mountain biking, is freely given. There are five main bedrooms, built in the last few years in an extension to the main building, and some rooms may be suitable for guests with disabilities. They are all pleasantly furnished, predominantly with pine; two rooms have en-suite facilities, the others have washbasins and they all have colour TV and a hospitality tray. Additionally, the pub offers bunkhouse accommodation in a converted barn where 20 people can stay overnight in two large rooms, one with eight beds, the other with twelve. There is also a field for campers who can share the showers and toilet facilities in the bunkhouse. If you want a rest from the active leisure pursuits on offer here, and fancy something a little more cultural, you can take a trip to the fortified manor, Tretower Court (10 miles).

🛏 One single, two double, two twin-bedded rooms, one family room
£ £ (single en-suite ££)
🍺 SP Sporting Ales Grand Prix; Wadworth 6X; guest beer
🍽 Snacks and meals daily, lunchtime and evening
CC accepted

—— TALYBONT-ON-USK ——

Star Inn

Talybont-on-Usk, Brecon LD3 7YX
☎ *(01874) 676635*
Directions: half a mile off the A40, between Abergavenny and Brecon

In a delightful setting beside the River Usk and the Brecon-Monmouth Canal, this old inn was renovated in 1995 following a flood, but with care taken to retain its traditional feel. The main bar boasts a splendid open fireplace. Although very rural, the Star has a lively, cosmopolitan atmosphere, due in part perhaps to the live music sessions held every Wednesday evening. In winter, additional entertainment is offered in the form of a Monday night quiz. The home-made bar meals are very popular and represent good value, as does the accommodation in the two en-suite guest rooms which are both spacious enough to include an extra bed, so children are welcome. Lovers of real ale make a bee-line for the pub, as the beer range is constantly changing, and up to 12 beers are on tap in summer; traditional cider is also stocked. Summer is a good time, too, to come and enjoy the lovely garden, and take advantage of the pub's situation in the Brecon Beacons National Park with all the outdoor pursuits that the area has to offer. The Taff Trail passes nearby. Pets can be accommodated at the inn by prior arrangement.

🛏 One double, one twin-bedded room
£ £
🍺 Beer range varies
🍽 Snacks and meals daily, lunchtime and evening
CC accepted

—— WELSHPOOL ——

Royal Oak Hotel
The Cross, Welshpool, Montgomeryshire SY21 7DG
☎ *(01938) 552217;* FAX *(01938) 556652*
Directions: off the A483 Oswestry road

Once the manor house of the Earls of Powis, this 350-year-old hotel has been run by the same family for over 60 years. It has been extensively renovated and upgraded, but still considers itself to be very much a local hotel, catering for the surrounding community. Now boasting 24 en-suite guest rooms of a high standard it also provides a very pleasant base for visitors to the area. Special weekend rates for half board are available. Two bars, the Oak and Ostler offer real ales and good food, whilst the Acorn café bar and restaurant serve light meals all day. The hotel has facilities for business and social functions, and children are welcome to stay. At the town centre, the pub has secure overnight parking. Welshpool, an historic border town in the delightful upper Severn Valley is dominated by Powis castle (two miles from the hotel). Other tourist attractions in the vicinity include the Llanfair Caereinion light railway, popular with children and steam enthusiasts alike, the Montgomery Canal, Offa's Dyke and the Powysland Museum.

ᕼ Seven single, 17 double/twin-bedded rooms
£ **£££** (**££££** single room)
⌻ Worthington Bitter; guest beers
⦿ Snacks and meals daily, at all times
CC accepted

TRY ALSO:

Bear Hotel
Crickhowell NP8 1BW
☎ *(01873) 810408*

This ancient inn has won awards for its food and bar. Twenty-eight rooms. B&B **££££**

George Hotel
George Street, Brecon LD3 7LD
☎ *(01874) 623421*

17th-century inn, just off the Struet. Good variety of meals and guest beers. Eight rooms. B&B **££**

Bell Hotel
Glangrwyney, Crickhowell NP8 1EH
☎ *(01873) 810247*

Old inn at the foot of the Black Mountains. Four rooms. B&B **££** (**£** sharing twin-bedded room)

WALES (NORTH)

—— ABERGELE ——

Bull Hotel

Chapel Street, Abergele LL22 7AW
☎ *(01745) 832115*
Directions: in the town centre, on the Llanrwst road

One of the oldest buildings in town, the Bull is popular with local CAMRA members for its beer quality and good atmosphere, a fact that well compensates for the simplicity of its guest rooms. All the five bedrooms share bathroom facilities, although each has a washbasin. They are simply furnished, but comfortable nonetheless, and guests can make their own hot drinks. The breakfasts are hearty. The pub itself has a spacious, but homely lounge and a smaller public bar, although you may need to brush up on your Welsh if you wish to join in the conversation. Meals may be taken in the bar or restaurant (where children are welcome); on Tuesday meals are available to residents only, by arrangement. The Bull is said to be haunted and the story is interesting enough for the pub to have featured in a BBC 2 series on the subject, *Myths and Legends*. This is one of the few pubs in the guide to offer beers from the family-owned Lees Brewery in Manchester, including their seasonal ales. Abergele is a pleasant market town, and Bodelwyddan Castle nearby is worth a visit.

🛏   One single, one double, one twin-bedded and two family rooms
£   £
🍺   Lees GB Mild, Bitter, seasonal beers
🍴   Snacks and meals, lunchtime and evening Wednesday-Monday (see above)
CC   not accepted

TRY ALSO:

White Horse

Capel Garmon, near Betwys-y-Coed LL26 0RW
☎ *(01690) 710271*

Quaint old pub in a tiny village perched on the mountainside in Snowdonia National Park. Seven en-suite rooms. B&B ££

——— BEAUMARIS ———

Olde Bull's Head

Castle Street, Beaumaris, Anglesey LL58 8AP
☎ *(01248) 810329; FAX (01248) 811294*
Directions: follow the A545 from the Britannia road bridge to Beaumaris in the town centre

The Olde Bull's Head is a famous hostelry, frequently listed in guide books, including CAMRA's own *Good Beer Guide*. If the rooms are outside your budget, then it is worth a detour just to call in for a beer. The historic Grade II listed building dates back to the latter half of the 15th century, although most of what you see today was built in the early 17th century. Former guests include Cromwell's General Mytton when he laid seige to Beaumaris Castle; Dr Johnson and Charles Dickens were presumably more welcome visitors (indeed the names of Dickens' characters have been used for the guest rooms). The present owners took over in 1987 and have invested heavily in upgrading the facilities. Their latest project has been to convert the stables into a modern brasserie where informal meals with a Mediterranean twist offer a cheaper option to the more elaborate menu served in the restaurant which has a good reputation and prices to match (closed Sunday). There are two huge bars, the main one featuring oak beams and antique weaponry. The 15 bedrooms are of a high standard; all have en-suite bathrooms and are individually furnished with period pieces. Some of these rooms, too, feature exposed timbers and one has a four-poster bed. Children are welcome, and guests are offered a choice of a cooked or continental breakfast. Luxury short breaks are available.

⇥ One single, seven double, six twin-bedded rooms
£ **££££**
🍺 Draught Bass; Worthington Bitter; guest beer
🍽 Snacks and meals daily, lunchtime and evening
CC accepted

——— BETWYS-Y-COED ———

Glan Aber Hotel

Holyhead Road, Betws-y-Coed LL24 0AB
☎ *(01690) 710325; FAX: (01690) 710700*
Directions: on the A5 at the village centre

Betws-y-Coed is a picturesque village at the heart of the Snowdonia National Park, and convenient for the North Wales coast. The stone-built Glan Aber Hotel is very popular with tourists who come particularly for 'active' holidays – walking, climbing, angling and golf. Accordingly, the owners thoughtfully provide a drying room for guests' outdoor clothes. Indeed, the hotel is very well equipped throughout, with the usual bar, lounge and restaurant being supplemented by a games room, a health suite with sauna and solarium, a meeting room and a comfortable residents' lounge. The main rooms are very attractively decorated in traditional style, while the two en-suite guest rooms are slightly more modern, and again well equipped. They each have Sky TV, hairdryer, trouser press, telephone and tea/coffee making facilities. Children staying in the family rooms are charged a reduced rate. A cooked breakfast is provided and a wide range of meals is served, in the bar or restaurant, and these, too, are of a high standard. Pets can be catered for.

⇥ Five single, eight double, nine twin-bedded and three family rooms
£ **£ – ££**
🍺 Dyffryn Clwyd Four Thumbs; Morland Old Speckled Hen; Tetley Dark Mild, Bitter
🍽 Snacks and meals daily, lunchtime and evening
CC accepted

—— BETWS-YN-RHOS ——

Wheatsheaf Inn

Betws-yn-Rhos, Abergele, Conwy LL22 8AW
☎ *(01492) 680218;* FAX *(01492) 680666*
Directions: on the B5381 St Asaph-Conway road

The Wheatsheaf is well-placed for visitors wishing to tour some of the most beautiful and historic sites of North Wales, including Conwy's medieval castle, the Bodnant Gardens, the Welsh Mountain Zoo at Colwyn Bay and the well preserved Victorian town of Llandudno. Originally built as an ale house to serve the local population in the 13th century, it was expanded in the 17th-century to serve the coaching trade and has since been extended again to the rear, giving a split-level interior. It retains a pleasant bar at the front, featuring stone pillars and oak beams, and the original hayloft ladder. There is also a cosy lounge, where children are welcome and a restaurant (good food is served in both areas). The pub itself has a wheelchair WC, but the guest rooms are not adapted to the needs of disabled visitors. Three rooms have en-suite shower and WC, whilst the family room, which sleeps four, has the use of an adjoining bathroom (children are charged reduced rates). They all have TV and tea/coffee making facilities. The pub has a garden and large car park. Betws-yn-Rhos is a pretty village, boasting a twin-towered church; it lies between the coast and the mountains.

⌺ One single, two double and one family room
£ £ (££ single room)
🍺 Banks's Mild; Marston's Bitter, Pedigree; Taylor Landlord; guest beer (occasionally)
🍽 Snacks and meals daily, lunchtime and evening
CC accepted

—— BRYNFORD ——

Glan yr Afon Inn

Milwr, Brynford, near Holywell, Flintshire CH8 8HE
☎ *(01352) 710052*
Directions: Milwr is signed from the A5026

This friendly inn is a traditional Welsh longhouse which dates back to the 13th century, where the multi-roomed layout has been preserved. The inn has a good local reputation for its food which is home produced using fresh ingredients. Meals are served in the dining room which is for non-smokers, or in the bar. The guest accommodation is a very recent addition, completed just before this guide went to press. Happily some of the rooms have been designed to accommodate guests with disabilities. All the rooms have en-suite facilities. Children are welcome. A cooked breakfast is provided and the rates are reduced considerably for weekend visitors. Outside, the garden has a play area for children and offers panoramic views over the Dee valley. Pets can be catered for by arrangement. Nearby is the Llyn y Mawn, another *Good Beer Guide* listed pub which hosts the Ales of Wales beer festival annually in February or March.

⌺ Seven double rooms
£ ££
🍺 Courage Directors; Ruddles Best Bitter; Webster's Yorkshire Bitter;
guest beers (occasionally)
🍽 Snacks and meals daily, lunchtime and evening
CC accepted

—— CAERNARFON ——

Black Boy Inn
Northgate Street, Caernarfon, Gwynedd LL55 1RW
☎ *(01286) 673604;* FAX *(01280) 674130*
Directions: near the castle

This ancient inn stands within the walls of the historic castle, which was built by Edward 1 when he conquered Wales in the late 13th century. The pub itself dates from the mid-16th century and is welcoming to all (even the English!). A *Good Beer Guide* regular, offering a wide selection of guest beers, it has retained much of its original character. The public bar and small lounge are both warmed by open fires, while the beamed restaurant features an inglenook. Meals can also be served in the bar. The overnight accommodation is not luxurious, but some of the rooms are characterful with exposed timbers. With a cooked breakfast included, it represents good value. All but four of the bedrooms have en-suite facilities, and they each have direct dial telephone, tea/coffee making equipment and TV. There is also a comfortable residents' lounge with TV. Children are welcome and pets can be accommodated. There is however, limited parking at the pub. Caernarfon is a good base for exploring the lovely north Wales coastline with its sandy beaches, and the Isle of Anglesey.

- Two single, four double, four twin-bedded and two family rooms
- £ £
- Everards Tiger; Morland Old Speckled Hen; guest beers
- Snacks and meals daily, lunchtime and evening
- CC accepted

—— CAPEL CURIG ——

Bryn Tyrch Hotel
Capel Curig, Betws-y-Coed, Gwynedd LL24 0EL
☎ *(01690) 720223;* FAX *(01690) 720338*
Directions: on the A5 to Bangor, five miles from Betws-y-Coed

The Bryn Tyrch has a well established reputation for catering for small groups, students on field trips, management training groups and walking and climbing clubs – special rates are available for group bookings. Packed lunches can be provided and, at the end of the day, guests can tuck into hearty meals with a very healthy bias – vegetarian and vegan meals are the speciality here, but meat eaters are also catered for. All the food is prepared on the premises and ice cream comes from a local supplier. The hotel is open all day for food and speciality teas and coffees are served. The hotel has a spacious main bar with a good, friendly atmosphere and views of the Snowdon Horseshoe. There is also a small public bar where darts and pool can be played; the dining room is a no-smoking area, but meals can also be taken in the bar. There are many local attractions for non-climbers in the vicinity: the Swallow Falls, Ffestiniog Railway, Bodnant Gardens and the remarkable village of Portmeirion are all within 20 miles. Ten of the hotel's 15 bedrooms have private bathrooms; they all have a TV and the usual amenities. A choice of cooked or continental breakfast is provided. Children are welcome and pets can be accommodated.

- Five double, ten twin-bedded and one family room
- £ £(single occupancy of en-suite room ££)
- Castle Eden Ale; Flowers IPA; Marston's Pedigree; Wadworth 6X; guest beer (on occasion)
- Snacks and meals daily, at all times
- CC accepted

Cobdens Hotel & Brasserie

Capel Curig, Betws-y-Coed, Gwynedd LL24 0EE
☎ *(01690) 720243;* FAX *(01690) 720354*
Directions: on the A5, four miles north of Betws-y-Coed

The Goodall family, owners of Cobdens, define a brasserie as 'a place that serves food with beer'. So that's what you get here, very much in the Belgian style – a small team in the kitchen preparing dishes based on local produce and shunning 'fast food', accompanied by a choice of real ales. In the same vein, the hotel aims for 'no starchiness, no frills...just warm hospitality'. The informal atmosphere of this family-run establishment is much appreciated by visitors who come to climb, walk or just soak up the natural beauty and relaxing atmosphere of the Snowdonia National Park. The hotel stands at the foot of Moel Siabod, and Plas-y-Brenin, the national mountain centre, is nearby. The hotel's climbers' bar has a natural rock face as a feature; there is also a lounge and the restaurant doubles as a meeting room. All 16 bedrooms have en-suite bathrooms and drying facilities are available for guests. The hotel has its own garden, and children are made very welcome: those under 14 are charged £12.50 per night, under-twos are free. 'Well groomed, house trained, sociable' dogs can also be accommodated.

- ⊨ Four single, five double, five twin-bedded and two family rooms
- £ ££
- ⬛ Ind Coope ABC Best Bitter; Morland Old Speckled Hen; Tetley Bitter; guest beer (occasionally)
- ⦿ Snacks and meals daily, lunchtime and evening
- **CC** accepted

—— CLYNNOG FAWR ——

Coach Inn

Clynnog Fawr, Caernarfon, Gwynedd LL54 5PB
☎ *(01286) 660212;* FAX *(01286) 660785*
Directions: on the A499 coast road between Caernarfon and Pwellheli

The Coach Inn is becoming increasingly popular for all kinds of events from hot air ballooning and kite festivals to motor rallies and folk music, so if you book in there, you're likely to get some extra entertainment, in addition to that which is normally provided by the way of skittle evenings and quiz nights in winter or the family disco in summer (Mondays and Fridays). The Inn bills itself as very much a family venue; there is a family room in the pub and the gardens are a haven for geese and ducks (duck food can be bought at the bar if children wish to feed them). The accommodation is fairly basic (only two rooms have en-suite facilities), but that does make it more accessible to family budgets. A continental-style buffet breakfast is provided, or a cooked breakfast is available (£3 supplement). Pets can be accommodated. Situated at the edge of the Snowdonia National Park and overlooking the sea, the pub gets particularly busy in summer. Dating back to the 17th century, the building is Grade II listed as being of special architectural and historical interest. Open fires, exposed stone walls and timbers add to its appeal. Meals can be taken in the bar or restaurant.

- ⊨ Two double, three twin-bedded and three family rooms
- £ £
- ⬛ Marston's Bitter, Pedigree; guest beers
- ⦿ Snacks and meals daily, lunchtime and evening
- **CC** accepted

—— GWYTHERIN ——

Lion Inn

Gwytherin, near Abergele, Conwy LL22 8UU
☎/FAX *(01745) 860244*
Directions: four miles off A548 Abergele–Llanrwst road

The black and white exterior of this cosy old inn is typical of the north Welsh borders. The original inn, reputed to be over 300 years old, would have been quite small, but it has been extended at various times over the years, incorporating a mix of old and new styles. The older features include exposed stone around the welcoming open fireplaces, and timber beams. A wide range of snacks is available in the cosy lounge and full meals are served in the restaurant. There are five comfortable bedrooms, rated three-crown status by the tourist board. All but one of the rooms have en-suite bathrooms; TV and tea/coffee-making facilities are standard. Off the beaten track, the Lion is the only remaining pub in a village that once supported three hostelries. Presumably not so many pilgrims go there these days to visit the resting place of St Winifred of Holywell. Set among some of the most beautiful scenery in North Wales, the Lion is within easy reach of the Snowdonia National Park (seven miles), Betws-y-Coed (eight miles) and the coast (around 13 miles). Children are welcome and pets can be accommodated at the inn which is normally closed on Mondays, except in high season.

- ⊨ One single, two doubles, one twin-bedded and one family room
- £ £
- ◨ Marston's Bitter, Pedigree; Tetley Bitter; guest beer (occasionally)
- ◉ Snacks and meals daily, lunchtime and evening
- CC accepted

—— LLANELIAN-YN-RHOS ——

White Lion

Llanelian-yn-Rhos, Colwyn Bay, Conwy LL29 8YA
☎ *(01492) 515807;* FAX *(01492) 512368*
Directions: off the B5383, signed from A55 at Old Colwyn

It is said that ale has been served on the site of the White Lion since the 8th century! The present pub, then, is a mere youngster; the oldest part of the building dates back to the late 16th century. This lovely old inn has been well preserved, particularly the bar, which has a slate floor and a beamed ceiling. There is also a tiny snug and a lounge. The guest bedrooms have been converted from a first floor barn and nicely decorated; all three have private bathrooms and TV. A true family-run free house, the pub's beer range changes frequently and landlord, Jack Cole makes sure Welsh ales are often featured. An extensive menu is supplemented by daily specials, and all the meals come well presented in either the lounge or dining area. Llanelian lies just inland from the seaside resort of Colwyn Bay, popular for its three-mile stretch of golden beaches. Children (who are welcome at the White Lion) will also enjoy nearby Dinosaur World and the Welsh Mountain Zoo, set above the town. Adults may possibly prefer a visit to the pretty fishing port of Rhos-on-Sea which has some elegant shops and good facilities for water sports.

- ⊨ Two double, one twin-bedded room
- £ £
- ◨ Burtonwood Top Hat; Marston's Bitter, Pedigree; guest beers
- ◉ Snacks and meals daily, lunchtime and evening
- CC accepted

—— LLANFACHRAETH ——

Holland Hotel

Llanfachraeth, Holyhead, Anglesey LL65 4UH
☎ *(01407) 740252;* FAX *(01407) 741344*
Directions: take the A5025 (Camaes) turn off the A5, the Holland is two miles further on

Our second entry for the Isle of Anglesey is a traditional Welsh village inn. A friendly atmosphere can be enjoyed in its several pleasant little rooms which are served from a central bar, stocking the Manchester brewer, JW Lees beers as well as traditional cider, which is quite unusual for these parts. One of the rooms serves as a restaurant, offering a range of good quality meals, including a vegetarian choice. A good cooked breakfast is served and the same high standards are to be found in the four en-suite guest rooms which can accommodate families. Children will enjoy the safe sandy beaches around here, and the area is also popular for coastal walks and fishing (sea, game and coarse anglers are all well provided for). The village is close to Holyhead where the Irish ferries sail from, and it is possible to go for a day trip on the exciting, high speed catamarans that are now in operation. The hotel can cater for pets by arrangement.

- ⇔ One double, two twin-bedded and one family room
- £ ££
- ◨ Lees GB Mild, Bitter, Moonraker (summer); guest beers (occasionally)
- ⦿ Snacks and meals daily, lunchtime and evening
- CC accepted

—— LLANGOLLEN ——

Wynnstay Arms Hotel

Bridge Street, Llangollen, Denbighshire LL20 8PF
☎ *(01978) 860710*

This 16th-century pub stands on the old London–Holyhead coaching road; the former stable yard now forms a spacious enclosed garden, overlooking the river, and has a grassy area. Inside, the pub has a traditional wood-panelled bar – warmed by an open log fire, a snug, a lounge, and a restaurant, although meals can be taken in the bar. The menu, offering home-cooked dishes, caters for children who are welcome to stay overnight. The three guest rooms are all en-suite. The River Dee offers amenities for angling and canoeing, and the pub provides a convenient base for visitors to the area. Llangollen itself, at the heart of the mountains, is famous for its little steam railway and the delightful canal that passes through; it also has a ruined medieval castle. The room rate does not include breakfast, which is available for a supplement.

- ⇔ Two double, one twin-bedded room
- £ Room rate £
- ◨ Greene King Abbot; Ind Coope Burton Ale; Morland Old Speckled Hen; guest beers
- ⦿ Snacks and meals daily, lunchtime and evening
- CC not accepted

—— MENAI BRIDGE ——

Liverpool Arms Hotel

St Georges Pier, Menai Bridge, Anglesey LL59 5EY
☎ *(01248) 712453;* FAX *(01248) 71335*

The Liverpool Arms was built over 150 years ago to serve the ferry trade and has retained its original atmosphere and nautical theme, by its display of pictures and artefacts. Still popular with today's sailing fraternity, it also attracts students, who appreciate its small bars with plenty of nooks and crannies for conversation. There is also a conservatory. The food here wins hearty local approval. Specialising in seafood and game, when available, the meals are all freshly prepared in the hotel's own kitchens, and are served in the bar or restaurant. Evening meals finish relatively early (8.30pm) and there is a limited evening service on Sunday, between 7 and 8pm. The overnight accommodation is also of a high standard. The twelve en-suite rooms are situated in an annex (the Fisherman's Loft). Children are welcome. A full cooked breakfast or a lighter continental breakfast is provided as required, served between 7.30 and 8.45am.

⨝ Twelve double rooms
£ £ – ££
🍺 Draught Bass; Greenalls Bitter, Original; guest beers
🍽 Snacks and meals daily, lunchtime and evening
CC accepted

Victoria Hotel

Telford Bridge, Menai Bridge, Anglesey LL59 5DR
☎ *(01248) 712309;* FAX*: (01248) 716774*
Directions: follow signs for Menai Bridge Town, the hotel is near the Suspension Bridge

Our second entry in this town is equally as popular as the Liverpool Arms and has a similar three crown tourist board rating. This substantial, family-run hotel, just yards from the suspension bridge affords panoramic views of the Menai Straits and Snowdonia. Ideally situated for exploring the Isle of Anglesey, it is also convenient for many of the other attractions of North Wales, such as Caernarfon and other local castles, the Sea Zoo, beaches and slate mines open to the public. The hotel has two comfortable bars and a TV lounge. Meals are served in the restaurant or bars. The conservatory and garden look out on to the Straits. Slightly larger than the Liverpool Arms, the Victoria is licensed to conduct weddings. Most of the guest rooms offer en-suite facilities and good views; some are suitable for guests with disabilities. There are special offers available for weekend and longer breaks. Children are welcome (charged at £8 each per night) and pets can be accommodated.

⨝ 15 double/twin-bedded, three family rooms
£ £
🍺 Draught Bass; guest beers
🍽 Snacks and meals daily, lunchtime and evening
CC accepted

—— NORTHOP ——

Soughton Hall & Stables Bar
Soughton Hall, Northop, Mold, Flintshire CH7 6AB
☎ *(01352) 840577;* FAX *(01352) 840382*
Directions: the hall is signed off the A5119

They must at one time have kept an awful lot of horses at Soughton Hall, since the stables have been converted into a spacious bar, specialising in real ale, and a restaurant. This unusual development in the grounds of the former stately home (now a small country house hotel), has been carried out with great care to take full advantage of the original character of the building. The bar has a heavily beamed ceiling, wood panelling and rustic furniture, while upstairs the haylofts have been opened up to provide a characterful restaurant, with bare brick walls and high beamed ceilings. Diners can select their food from a large display in the open kitchen area and watch the meal being prepared if they wish. A blackboard, bistro-style menu here, where the emphasis is on fresh fish and meat, provides an informal alternative to the upmarket restaurant in the hall itself, which is where the luxurious guest rooms are located. The large rooms are decorated and furnished in period style to a high standard; all are en-suite and enjoy views over the surrounding parkland. Children are welcome. Soughton Hall is close to the River Dee and within easy reach of Chester.

- 14 double rooms
- £ ££££
- Dyffryn Clwyd Four Thumbs; Goff's Jouster; Hanby Drawwel; Morland Old Speckled Hen; many guest beers
- Snacks and meals daily, lunchtime and evening
- CC accepted

—— ST ASAPH ——

Kentigern Arms
High Street, St Asaph, Denbighshire LL17 0RG
☎ *(01745) 584157*
Directions: off the A55 North Wales Expressway

Just down the hill from the smallest cathedral in Britain, this traditional local welcomes travellers just as it has done for the last 300 years. Grade II listed, this former coaching inn has a central bar serving a lounge with a large hearth. Meals can be taken here or in the dining room. It enjoys a good local following, but is also well placed for visitors to this part of Wales. It is just two miles from Bodelwyddan Castle, where the National Portrait Gallery's 19th-century works are displayed in Williams Hall, a restored Victorian country house in the castle grounds. Visitors can also enjoy the gardens and woodland walk, and the tea room. It is only a little further (six miles) to the seaside resort of Rhyl and many other coastal towns are accessible via the A55. The overnight accommodation at the pub is not luxurious, but represents good value in en-suite rooms, with a cooked breakfast provided. Children are welcome.

- One double, three family rooms
- £ £
- Bateman Mild; Marston's Bitter, Pedigree
- Snacks and meals daily, lunchtime and evening
- CC not accepted

WALES (SOUTH)

—— ABERGAVENNY ——

Lamb & Flag Country Hotel

Brecon Road, Abergavenny, Gwent NP7 7EW
☎ *(01873) 857611;* FAX *(01873) 859206*
Directions: on the A40, two miles north of Abergavenny

Nestling under the Sugar Loaf Mountain, this small country hotel, a rare Brains Brewery house so far east, is fairly new. The welcome and service are excellent here, and although our reporter found the rooms a tad on the pricey side, this is compensated by the two restaurants which serve good value meals. There is also a lounge bar and garden with children's play area. The guest bedrooms are very comfortable; all but one has en-suite facilities. A choice of cooked or continental-style breakfast is provided, and children are welcome to stay. Abergavenny is a pleasant market town which makes an ideal base for a holiday in the Black Mountains and the Brecon Beacons, situated as it is on the eastern edge of the National Park. In the immediate vicinity, you can visit the town's museum in the grounds of the medieval castle, and also White Castle, one of the so-called 'Three Castles of Gwent'.

🛏 Three double, two twin-bedded rooms
£ £££
🍺 Brains Bitter, SA; guest beer (occasionally)
🍽 Snacks lunchtime, meals daily, lunchtime and evening
CC accepted

—— BAGLAN BAY ——

Baglan Bay Hotel

42 Church Road, Baglan, Port Talbot,,
West Glamorgan SA12 8ST
☎ *(01639) 813228;* FAX *(01639) 814289*
Directions: leave the M4 at jct 41, follow the A48, signed Briton Ferry, take Port Talbot turn from first roundabout, then first left and left again

Port Talbot would not feature on most people's tourist route, but if you have business in the area, then you could do worse than to check in at this comfortable hotel, which is well away from the centre, and you are guaranteed a decent pint of ale. This spacious former country house stands in two acres of secluded gardens which include a play area for children, tables and chairs for summer drinking, and a large car park. The hotel's public bar and lounge are open all day and lunchtime meals and snacks are available. The restaurant opens for evening meals and Sunday lunches. The ten guest rooms all have en-suite bathrooms and TV, telephone and tea/coffee making facilities. Special rates are available for weekends and long stays. Pets can be accommodated.

🛏 Three single, two double, four twin-bedded and one family room
£ £ (£££ single room)
🍺 Courage Best Bitter; guest beer
🍽 Snacks and meals daily, lunchtime and evening

—— CLYTHA ——

Clytha Arms
Clytha, near Abergavenny, Monmouthshire NP7 9BW
☎/FAX *(01873) 840206*
Directions: off the B4598, on the old Raglan–Abergavenny road

Susan Nowak, author of CAMRA's *Good Pub Food* is ecstatic about the breakfasts at the Clytha Arms. The selection here is much more than your average eggs 'n bacon – you may be offered Manx kippers, smoked sewin or leek and laver bread rissoles, from an extensive breakfast menu, which also offers a vegetarian option. The no-smoking restaurant, too, has an excellent reputation for its adventurous (but not cheap) menu, and you generally need to book. Meals and snacks can also be taken in either of the bars of this pub, which was converted from a dower house. It has been refurbished and all three bedrooms given an individual style. By far the largest (and thus most expensive) of the three en-suite rooms has a four-poster bed, plus chairs and a sofa. Each room has tea/coffee making equipment and a TV. Children are welcome to stay (the garden has a safe play area). Pets can be accommodated by arrangement. The pub won CAMRA's South and Mid Wales *Pub of the Year* award in 1995. Note that no meals are served on Sunday night (when the rooms are not available for letting), or Monday. The pub is three miles from Raglan, with its 15th-century castle, and six miles from the market town of Abergavenny.

- ⊨ Two double, one twin-bedded room
- £ ££ (supplement for single occupancy)
- ⬧ Banks's Mild; Draught Bass; Hook Norton Best Bitter; guest beers
- ⦿ Snacks and meals Tuesday-Saturday, lunchtime and evening, plus Sunday lunch
- CC accepted

—— GILFACH ——

Capel
Park Place, Gilfach, Bargoed, Mid Glamorgan CF81 8LW
☎/FAX *(01443) 830272*
Directions: on the A469, 17 miles north of Cardiff

Lying at the northern end of the Rhymney Valley, this traditional valleys pub offers a friendly and warm welcome to all visitors. For tourists there is much to see and do within a few minutes' drive from the pub, including Caerphilly Castle, one of the largest in Europe, and the fascinating Welsh Folk Museum at Llancaiach Fawr, which features reconstructed buildings and streets, giving a living history of the country. Within half an hour you can reach Cardiff Castle and the Big Pit (working pit museum) at Blaenavon. The Cwmcarn Scenic Drive is also accessible. The guest accommodation is fairly basic, but inexpensive. The two bedrooms share a bathroom. Meals can be provided for residents at any reasonable time, so you are not restricted to the sessions shown below. A cooked breakfast is provided. Children are welcome.

- ⊨ One twin-bedded, one family room
- £ £
- ⬧ Courage Best Bitter; Brains SA; John Smith's Bitter; guest beer
- ⦿ Snacks and meals daily, lunchtime and evening
- CC not accepted

—— LLANDOGO ——

Sloop Inn

Llandogo, near Monmouth, Gwent NP5 4TW
☎ *(01594) 530291;* FAX *(01594) 530935*
Directions: on the A466 between Monmouth and Chepstow

Boasting fine views of the Wye Valley, a designated area of outstanding natural beauty, the Sloop Inn offers excellent accommodation at very reasonable prices. Llandogo is surrounded by hills and forests, and walks along the River Wye will delight anyone with an interest in wildlife. The inn is also within easy reach of Tintern Abbey (two miles), Monmouth and Chepstow. Dating back to the 18th century, it takes its name from the barges that used to carry trade between Bristol and Llandogo. The large traditional bar, featuring some huge exposed timbers, is warmed by a log fire in winter, while the lounge at the rear has the best view and this is where meals, including breakfast, are served. The guest rooms have been designed with care to feature dormer windows, built-in wardrobes and co-ordinated furnishings. They all have either a bath or shower en-suite, plus the usual facilities of a TV and tea/coffee making equipment. For a touch of luxury, book yourself into the four-poster suite which has French windows opening on to a private balcony with clear river views. Children are welcome and pets are catered for by arrangement.

🛏 Three double, one twin-bedded room
£ **£ – ££**
🍺 Buckley's Rev. James; Freeminer Bitter; guest beer (summer and Bank Holidays)
🍴 Snacks and meals daily, lunchtime and evening
CC accepted

—— LLANVIHANGEL CRUCORNEY ——

Skirrid Mountain Inn

Llanvihangel Crucorney, Abergavenny,
Monmouthshire NP7 8DH
☎ *(01873) 890258*
Directions: signed off the A465, Hereford road, four and a half miles north of Abergavenny

The Skirrid is recorded as the oldest public house in Wales, having stood on its site below the Skirrid Mountain for the best part of nine centuries. Its long history has produced some amazing tales, not least because of its connections with the 'Hanging' Judge Jeffries. You can read about some of them while you sup your pint of Ushers by the vast open fireplace in the flagstoned, heavily beamed bar, before retiring to one of the charming en-suite guest rooms with four-poster beds. But first, enjoy a meal in the atmospheric dining room, where the panelling is said to come from a warship of Raleigh's time, and award-winning food is served. You are always assured of a warm welcome at this most characterful of inns which is very poplar with the local community and walkers. Skirrid forms part of the Black Mountain range and is much appreciated by horse-riders and cyclists as well as hikers. The pub makes good use of its beautiful setting where the garden, too, has won awards. Children are welcome to stay overnight and pets can be catered or.

🛏 Two double rooms
£ **££**
🍺 Ushers Best Bitter, Founders, seasonal beers
🍴 Snacks and meals daily, lunchtime and evening
CC not accepted

—— MERTHYR TYDFIL ——

Tregenna Hotel
Park Terrace, Merthyr Tydfil CF47 8RF
☎ *(01685) 723627;* FAX *(01685) 721951*
Directions: The hotel is off the A4102, which is a turn off the A470, Swansea to Cardiff road

The Tregenna is a pleasant, family-run hotel built on the site of a Roman fort (AD 75), and just five minutes from the Brecon Beacons National Park. Apart from offering a good guest ale list, it also stocks a traditional cider and serves very good food which ranges from Welsh favourites to more exotic dishes, served in the bar and restaurant. The acclaimed home-made puddings are the responsibility of the landlady, Kathleen. All the guest rooms have en-suite bathrooms and are furnished and equipped to a high standard of comfort; some feature four-poster beds, and all have TV, trouser press, direct dial telephone and tea/coffee making facil-ities. Some rooms are adapted to the needs of guests with disabilities. Pets can be accom-modated. The hotel is very popular with tourists and is convenient for the Brecon Mountain Railway, the narrow gauge steam railway which runs through the National Park during the summer. Another local attraction is Cyfarthfa Castle Museum, an 1830s 'Gothic' ironmas-ter's house with an eclectic collection of artefacts. As well as the hotel accommodation, the owners offer self-catering holiday cottages and bed and breakfast accommodation at Penrhadw Farm, deep in the National Park. Details available on request.

- ⊨ Four single, seven double, seven twin-bedded and six family rooms
- £ ££ (£££ single room)
- ◧ Draught Bass; Brains SA; Worthington Best Bitter; Wye Valley Bitter; guest beers
- ◉ Snacks and meals daily, lunchtime and evening
- CC accepted

—— PANTYGELLI ——

Olde Crown Inn
Old Hereford Road, Pantygelli, Abergavenny, Monmouthshire NP7 7HR
☎/FAX *(01873) 853314*
Directions: two miles from Abergavenny, the village is signed from the A465 to Hereford at Llanfihangel Crucorney

The Olde Crown is a 15th-century former coaching inn; the only pub in what is barely more than a hamlet. It stands at the gateway to the Black Mountains in the heart of the Brecon Beacons National Park, and provides an ideal base for walkers and ramblers, with its com-fortable, good quality rooms ensuring a good night's rest after a tiring day. The rooms share bathroom facilities. Children are welcome to stay and a cooked breakfast is provided. The Crown has an open-plan layout, but the restaurant area is well divided from the main bar. Friendly informality is the key here and an extensive menu is complemented by a specials board. There is also a colourful patio affording terrific views of the Holy Mountain. Pets can be accommodated.

- ⊨ Four single, one family room
- £ £
- ◧ Draught Bass; Felinfoel Double Dragon; Hancock's HB; guest beers
- ◉ Snacks and meals daily, lunchtime and evening (except Sunday evening)
- CC accepted

—— PONTYPRIDD ——

Market Tavern
Market Street, Pontypridd CF37 2ST
☎ *(01443) 485331;* FAX *(01443) 402806*
Directions: in the town centre

Good pub accommodation is not always easy to find in town centres; what makes the Market Tavern even more of a rarity is that it can also cater for overnight guests with disabilities. Within five minutes' walk of the railway station, it is convenient for both the business guest and tourist. A thriving establishment with a bustling atmosphere, it attracts a diverse clientele to three drinking areas. Meals can be taken in the bar or the restaurant at the rear, which doubles as a function room. The cellar bar hosts live music at the weekend. There is plenty to see and do in this area of South Wales; children (who are welcome to stay at the pub) might enjoy a visit to the Rhondda Heritage Park in nearby Trehafod, where visitors can experience what it was like to actually go underground in a working colliery. All of the pub's 11 bedrooms have en-suite bathrooms, and guests are offered a choice of a cooked or continental breakfast included in the very reasonable prices.

⓫ Four singles, three double, three twin-bedded and one family room
£ £
🍺 Courage Directors; Hancock's HB; Worthington Bitter; guest beer (occasionally)
🍽 Snacks and meals daily lunchtime, and evening (except Monday and Saturday evenings)
CC accepted

—— SHIRENEWTON ——

Tredegar Arms
The Square, Shirenewton, Chepstow, Monmouthshire NP6 6RQ
☎ *(01291)641274*

Situated on the square at the village centre, the Tredegar Arms has a large, comfortable bar, offering a good range of real ales, with a games area, and a smaller lounge. Open fires, exposed beams, dried flowers and much bric-a-brac characterise this warm friendly pub – I'm told the gents' loo has interesting features too – but it is not for me to discover what they are! The restaurant enjoys a good reputation locally and the diners often spill into the lounge. The pub has just two guest rooms which are both en-suite and suitable for adults only. A cooked breakfast is provided. The pub has its own garden and the village is surrounded by countryside, so is good for walking and horse-riding. There is also a local golf course and tennis club. The Wye Valley, Tintern Abbey, Monmouth and Chepstow are all within easy reach and there is good access to Cardiff and Bristol.

⓫ One double, one twin-bedded room
£ £ (single occupancy ££)
🍺 Draught Bass; Fuller's London Pride; Hancock's HB; Hook Norton Best Bitter; RCH Pitchfork; guest beers
🍽 Snacks and meals daily, lunchtime and evening
CC not accepted

—— USK ——

New Court Hotel
62 Maryport Street, Usk, Gwent NP5 1BQ
☎ *(01291) 673848*

The New Court would not normally be considered for entry in a CAMRA guide because it has just been taken over by new owners and CAMRA members usually like to wait a year to make sure the ale is of a consistently high standard before putting a pub forward in such circumstances. However, I am making an exception in this case as the owners are undertaking a good deal of refurbishment and part of the work is to adapt a ground-floor bedroom to the needs of guests with disabilities. As so few pubs can accommodate their particular requirements, it seemed important to include this one, but you will need to check when booking that the work has been completed and (all) the rooms are ready for guests. At the time of writing, only one of the rooms is en-suite, but this may change, too. I'd welcome any feedback from guests. Children are welcome to stay and pets can also be accommodated. This small hotel offers five real ales and a varied restaurant menu of home-cooked food which includes daily specials and a cooked breakfast. Freshly cut sandwiches are always available. There is a garden with a play area for children.

- ⋈ One single, two double, two twin-bedded and one family room
- £ £
- 🍴 Snacks and meals daily, lunchtime and evening
- 🍺 Ushers Best Bitter, Founders, seasonal beers; John Smith's Bitter
- **CC** not accepted

TRY ALSO:

Somerset Arms
Victoria Street, Abergavenny, Gwent NP7 5DT
☎ *(01873) 85458*

Just one en-suite room which is suitable for children, in a family-run free house. B&B £

King Arthur Hotel
Reynoldston, Gower, Swansea, Glamorgan SA3 1AD
☎ *(01792) 391099; fax (01792) 390775*

Six en-suite rooms where children are welcome. B&B ££

WALES (WEST)

—— JAMESTON ——

Tudor Lodge

Jameston, near Tenby, Pembrokeshire SA70 7SS
☎ *(01834) 871978*
Directions: on the A478, Tenby–Pembroke road

This is a good spot for holidaymakers, at the edge of the Pembrokeshire Coastal National Park and near the seaside resort of Tenby. The NT's Colby Woodland Garden, Carew Castle and the Great Wedlock Dinosaur Experience (popular with families) are all within easy reach. The Tudor Lodge itself is a country manor house, at the edge of the village, dating from the 17th century, and set in attractive gardens with a play area for children. Families are made very welcome at this friendly inn, which is frequented by tourists and locals alike. The pub has an interesting internal layout, combining original features such as a stone bread oven, with modern amenities. The *à la carte* restaurant offers a children's choice, or you can choose from a comprehensive menu in the bar; vegetarians are catered for. Food is not available at lunchtime on weedkays in the winter. A traditional cider is occasionally stocked. The five rooms all have en-suite bathrooms; one room is suitable for families. A cooked breakfast is provided.

⨅ Three double, one twin-bedded and one family room
£ £
⬛ Worthington Bitter; guest beer
🍴 Snacks and meals lunchtime (daily in summer; weekends in winter), and evening (daily)
CC accepted

—— LLANARTHNEY ——

Golden Grove Arms

Llanarthney, Carmarthen SA32 8JU
☎ *(01558) 668551;* FAX *(01558) 668851*
Directions: on the B4300, midway between Llandeilo and Carmarthen

Situated between the country town of Carmarthen and delightful Llandeilo, in the beautiful Towy (or Tywi) Valley, this roadside pub enjoys panoramic views of the Black Mountains and offers easy access to the coastal resorts of West Wales. The historic castles of Dryslwyn, Dinefwr and Carreg Cennen could be included on your touring itinerary. Once a coaching inn, and now a family-run free house, the Golden Grove stocks mainly Welsh ales. It enjoys a good reputation for its home-cooked meals, which are based on local produce, including Welsh lamb, and salmon and sewin from the River Tywi which flows through the valley. Meals can be taken in either the bar or restaurant. Families are made very welcome here and the large garden has a play area. All eight guest rooms have en-suite bathrooms, as well as tea/coffee making facilities and TV. The very reasonably priced accommodation includes a cooked breakfast. Pets may be catered for by prior arrangement.

⨅ One single, two doubles, two twin-bedded and three family rooms
£ £ (single £)
⬛ Buckley's Best Bitter, Rev. James; Tomos Watkin Whoosh; guest beer (occasionally)
🍴 Snacks and meals daily, lunchtime and evening
CC accepted

—— LLANDOVERY ——

Castle Hotel

Llandovery, Dyfed SA20 0AW
☎ *(01550) 720343;* FAX *(01550) 720673*
Directions: on the A40

If you stay at the Castle Hotel, particularly if you choose the room with the four-poster, you will be following in heroic footsteps. Lord Nelson stayed here in 1802 and his bed is still in use today. Modern guests, however benefit from such facilities as en-suite bathrooms, direct dial telephone and a TV in the room. Children are welcome to stay. The Castle stands at the heart of this small, but attractive market town which is home to Llandovery College, founded in 1847 to support the Welsh language and culture, which numbers the Prince of Wales amongst its patrons. The town is also known for its annual ballooning festival and town crier's competition. A short drive from the hotel will take you to Bethlehem, whose post office is very popular around Christmas time, the ancient Roman Dolaucothi Gold Mines – now owned by the NT and open to the public, and many other places of tourist interest. Meals at the Castle can be taken either in the friendly bar or the restaurant. A cooked breakfast is provided. Pets can be accommodated.

- ⊨ Seven single, seven double and seven twin-bedded rooms
- £ ££ – £££ according to the room
- ⛁ Draught Bass; Tomos Watkin OSB, Worthington Bitter; guest beers
- ⦿ Snacks and meals, lunchtime and evening Monday-Saturday
  (Sunday only by prior arrangement)

—— LLANELLI ——

Thomas Arms

Thomas Street, Llanelli, Carmarthenshire SA15 3JF
☎ *(01554) 772043*
Directions: on the A476

A small but elegant hotel whose comfortable main bar, the haunt of fanatical rugby union devotees, serves as the brewery tap for Buckley's (now owned by Brains Brewery) and offers the full range of Buckley's beers. There is a quieter Cocktail Bar with an adjoining restaurant, where the main features are the engraved glass panels, one depicting the local RU team – the 'Scarlets' – and one saluting the town's miners. The food served is of consistently good quality. The guest rooms are furnished and decorated to a high standard, and all ten have en-suite bathrooms, trouser press, hairdryer, TV, direct dial telephone and tea/coffee making facilities. The bridal suite boasts a four-poster bed. The hotel caters well for the business community, with self-contained conference facilities. Children are welcome to stay overnight. Llanelli is a large coastal town with a sandy beach, and three *Good Beer Guide* listed pubs. It is proud of its connections with Dylan Thomas, after whom the hotel was named. Nearby Bryncaerau Castle is worth a visit for its museum and art gallery. The hotel has its own car park, which is necessary as there is no local station.

- ⊨ Ten double rooms
- £ £££
- ⛁ Crown Buckley CPA, Buckley's Dark Mild, Best Bitter, SBB, Rev. James Original
- ⦿ Snacks and meals daily, lunchtime and evening
- CC accepted

Waun Wyllt Inn

Horeb Road, Horeb, Five Roads, Llanelli, Carmarthenshire SA15 5AQ
☎ *(01269) 860209*
Directions: on the B4309, three miles from Llanelli on the road to Carmarthen; take right turn at village of Five Roads, pub is 800 yards further on

The Waun Wyllt is a very popular country inn, set in its own grounds, which include a caravan site and a pleasant garden with swings for children. The spacious lounge bar boasts exposed stone walls and beams, hung with horse brasses and mining and farming artefacts. A house beer is brewed specially for the pub and an occasional traditional cider is also stocked. Good bar meals include a choice for children and vegetarians. There is also a restaurant (booking is advisable at weekends). The comfortable guest rooms are all en-suite and are equipped with tea/coffee making facilities and TV. Some rooms may be suitable for visitors with disabilities. Horeb is a tiny hamlet, not far from Llanelli and a 15 minute drive from Pembrey Country Park which has a seven-mile stretch of sandy beaches, ideal for families (children can be accommodated at the pub). The Celtic Trail cycle track passes close to the inn, which offers storage for bikes, as well as ample car parking. The pub stays open all day in summer and offers a warm welcome to all.

⌘ Five double/twin-bedded rooms
£ £
⛃ Felinfoel Double Dragon, plus two or three guest beers
⧫ Snacks and meals daily, lunchtime and evening
CC accepted

—— RHANDIRMWYN ——

Royal Oak

Rhandirmwyn, Llandovery SA20 0NY
☎ *(01550) 760201; FAX (01550) 760332*
Directions: take the A40 from Llandovery and follow signs to Llyn Brianne Dam, the pub is seven miles further on

This large, stone-built, village inn was once Earl Cawdor's hunting lodge; these days its visitors tend to pursue gentler outdoor interests. Right on the doorstep is the RSPB Dinas Bird Reserve (habitat of the red kite). Indeed, this whole delightful valley is a protected area and walkers can ramble in the Cambrian mountains or around the spectacular Llyn Brianne Dam. Other, less energetic places of tourist interest include the Roman Gold Mines (NT) and several arts and craft centres in the vicinity. Impressive views can be enjoyed from the hotel's dining room, which opens on to the garden, and from the three main bedrooms. These have en-suite bathrooms (the two singles share amenities), and all have colour TV and tea/coffee making facilities. Popular with locals and visitors alike, this family-run establishment is decorated in very traditional style; the bar has exposed brick walls and beamed ceilings, while the dining area has plush velvet seating. Pets can be accommodated.

⌘ Two singles, one double, one twin-bedded and one family room
£ ££ (single £)
⛃ Ind Coope Burton Ale; Tomos Watkin Bitter, plus three guest beers
⧫ Snacks and meals daily, lunchtime and evening
CC accepted

—— TREGARON ——

Talbot Hotel

Tregaron, Ceredigion SY25 6JZ
☎/FAX *(01974) 298208*
Directions: in the town's main square

The Talbot is the principal hotel in one of the smallest and most remote towns in Wales. This family-run establishment makes an ideal base for exploring the Cambrian Mountains. There are good amenities locally for mountain biking, bird-watching, fishing and simply just walking. A little further away, Aberystwyth offers more cultural pursuits, with its arts centre and theatre, but also the tourist sites of the Silver Lead Mine and the Devils Bridge Falls and narrow gauge railway. Originally established as a drovers' inn in the 13th century, but rebuilt in the 1870s, this friendly hotel is full of olde-worlde charm and character, enhanced by exposed stone walls and beams, period furniture and open log fires. Enjoy the warm atmosphere and the banter of the local customers in the bar, or take a meal in the restaurant. Weekend breaks of two nights, including dinner, are available at special rates (except during Bank Holidays). Only a limited number of the guest rooms (four) have their own en-suite bathrooms, but they all have washbasins, TV and tea/coffee making facilities. Children are welcome to stay and pets can be accommodated.

- ⊨ Three single, four double, six twin-bedded and one family room
- £ £ (££ en-suite)
- ◙ Boddingtons Bitter; Flannery's Celtic Ale; Marstons Pedigree
- ◉ Snacks and meals daily, lunchtime and evening
- CC accepted

TRY ALSO:

Red Lion

6 Llandeilo Road, Landybie, Ammanford SA18 3JA
☎ *(01269) 851202*

Homely pub with good, freshly prepared food on a limited menu. One en-suite family room. B&B £

SCOTLAND

THE BORDERS & LOTHIAN

Allanton Inn

Allanton by Duns, Borders TD11 3JZ
☎ *(01890) 818260;* FAX *(01361) 882014*
Directions: on the B6437, one mile south of Chirnside (off A6105)

Set in picturesque surroundings, this busy country village inn lies near the rivers Whiteadder and Blackadder (where fishing can be arranged by the landlord). It is popular walking country and also handy for the historic town of Berwick-upon-Tweed, and other tourist sites, including Holy Island and stately homes, such as Floors Castle, Manderston and Paxton House. A former coaching inn – it still has the hitching rings for horses outside – this free house, with a stone-flagged, functional, yet comfortable bar, offers three real ales in winter (always including a Scottish brew), plus another two in summer, along with a traditional perry. There is also a restaurant which is highly recommended and has won awards for its haggis. The pub has a children's certificate, which in Scotland means that children are allowed in any part sanctioned by the landlord, until 8pm. The guest accommodation for families is in a suite of two bedrooms with a separate shower and WC. Children are charged £5 per night in their parents' room (or half the adult price if occupying a separate room). The other bedrooms have recently been updated to give en-suite accommodation which is furnished to a high standard. Pets can be catered for.

🛏 Two double, one twin-bedded room, one family suite
£ ££ (£££ single occupancy)
🍺 Beer range varies
🍽 Snacks and meals daily, lunchtime and evening
CC accepted

—— AUCHENCRAW ——

Craw Inn
Auchencraw, Eyemouth, Borders TD14 5LS
☎/FAX *(01890) 761253*
Directions: on the B6438, signed from the A1 at Reston

The Craw Inn has a murky past – apparently witches used to be hanged in the garden! Nowadays its reputation hangs on the warm hospitality offered to visitors and locals alike. Dating back to the late 17th-century, this little country pub is at the heart of the rural community it serves in a tiny hamlet not far from the Berwickshire coast. The cosy, beamed bar is decorated with equestrian trophies, warmed by a log fire and free from electronic machines and juke boxes. There are dining areas for smokers and non-smokers and a small snug is used as a family room. Children are welcome to stay and guests with disabilities can also be catered for. The five guest rooms are attractively decorated in country style and all offer en-suite facilities. There is a good choice at breakfast, from a simple continental style, to the full cooked option, including Loch Fyne kippers if required. The beer range varies, but always two real ales are stocked along with a traditional cider. The pub has its own garden, and ornithologists can pursue their hobby at nearby St Abbs. Pets can be accommodated by arrangement.

- ⊨ One single, three double and one family room
- £ ££
- ⊈ Beer range varies
- ⦿ Snacks and meals daily, lunchtime and evening
- CC accepted

—— BALERNO ——

Grey Horse
20 Main Street, Balerno, Lothian EH14 7EH
☎ *(0131) 449 3092*
Directions: off the A70

Both the guest accommodation and the restaurant are fairly new additions at the Grey Horse. The previous owners bought the house next door to the pub and converted the upstairs into guest rooms and the ground floor into a restaurant. The restaurant is open Wednesday to Saturday evenings until after Easter when it is open every night (except Monday) for the summer season. The guest rooms have recently been redecorated and each have TV and tea/coffee making facilities. The bathroom is shared between the three rooms. The price is very reasonable, considering a full cooked breakfast provided. This 200-year-old traditional, stone-built pub stands on the pedestrianised shopping street at the centre of the village. It has an unspoilt public bar and a small, but comfortable lounge where bar snacks and meals are served at lunchtime, and in the evening by request. The pub has its own garden and stands at the foot of the Pentland Hills, near the start of several major footpaths. The Water of Leith nearby is also popular with walkers. There is a good, frequent bus service into the centre of Edinburgh – the journey takes around half an hour.

- ⊨ One double, two twin-bedded rooms
- £ £
- ⊈ Belhaven 80/-, IPA; guest beer
- ⦿ Snacks and meals daily lunchtime, evenings on request
- CC not accepted

—— CLOVENFORDS ——

Clovenfords Hotel

1 Vine Street, Clovenfords, near Galashiels, Borders TD1 3LU
☎ *(01896) 850203;* FAX *(01896) 850596*
Directions: on the A72, west of Galashiels

An unusual statue (made apparently of papier mache) of Sir Walter Scott stands in front of this hotel. Along with fellow poet, William Wordsworth, Sir Walter was a regular visitor to Clovenfords. This 18th-century coaching inn has a busy public bar where one wall is adorned with rugby shirts. The guest beer here is often a Scottish brew, and traditional Addlestones cider is stocked. There is also a comfortable lounge and a bistro-style restaurant where meals are available at all times from noon until last food orders at 8.45pm. Children are welcome – highchairs are provided and there is a children's menu; the garden has a play area. The five guest rooms all offer en-suite accommodation and a cooked breakfast is provided. There are good sporting facilities around here for fishing, shooting, golf and of course, walking. The hotel is convenient for Galashiels, Melrose and all the Border towns. Pets can be accommodated.

🛏 Two double, two twin-bedded, and one family room
£ ££
🍺 Caledonian 80/-; Marston's Pedigree; guest beer (two in summer)
🍴 Snacks and meals daily, noon-9pm
CC accepted

—— DENHOLM ——

Fox & Hounds Inn

Main Street, Denholm, Borders TD9 8NU
☎ *(01450) 870247;* FAX *(01450) 870500*
Directions: on the A698, midway between Hawick (A7) and Jedburgh (A68)

The cosy, beamed bar at the Fox and Hounds is open to residents at any (reasonable) time and it offers a good selection of (mainly Scottish) real ales. There is also a games room, restaurant and residents' lounge. Summer Sunday barbecues are held in the courtyard, and folk musicians also play regularly on Sundays. The comfortable guest accommodation is in the cottage adjoining the pub; families are made welcome. Good, home-cooked food is served at all mealtimes, including a large 'Border' breakfast (given full marks by a reader visiting the pub via our last edition). If you want a bit of variety, go across the picturesque village green to the Auld Cross Keys Inn which has won an award for the *Best High Teas* in the Borders. Fishing, golf, riding and shooting can all be taken up locally, and the inn is within easy reach of the major sites in this area. Pets can be accommodated.

🛏 One single, one double, one family room
£ £
🍺 Belhaven 80/-; Black Sheep Best Bitter; Moulin Braveheart; guest beers
🍴 Snacks and meals daily, lunchtime and evening

——— EDINBURGH ———

Bruntsfield Hotel

69 Bruntsfield Place, Edinburgh, Lothian EH10 4HH
☎ *(0131) 229 1393; FAX (0131) 229 5634*
Directions: on the main road between Tollcross and Morningside

The Kings Bar at the Bruntsfield Hotel is where you'll find the real ale. A wood-panelled cellar bar, it is a lively meeting place for students who are favoured with reduced prices on Wednesday evenings (the rest of us can take advantage of a 'happy hour' 5-7 every evening). This comfortable bar enjoys a warm, friendly atmosphere and hosts a regular Sunday evening quiz. Unusually for Scotland, the bar stocks a traditional cider. The hotel is a town house, overlooking the historic Bruntsfield Links, within walking distance of many of Edinburgh's main attractions, including the Castle and the new National Museum of Scotland. Good food is served at all times in both the bar and restaurant. The hotel offers four-star accommodation in 50 en-suite guest rooms which cater well for families and have facilities for guests with disabilities. Pets can also be accommodated. The prices given below are for the room only – the rates vary considerably according to season. Guests pay a supplement for breakfast according to their requirements – £6.95 for the continental style or £8.95 for a full cooked version.

🛏 15 single, 23 double, ten twin-bedded and two family rooms
£ Room rate £££ – ££££ (single from ££££)
🍺 Caledonian Deuchar's IPA, 80/-
🍴 Snacks and meals daily at all times
CC accepted

Lovat Hotel

5 Inverleith Terrace, Edinburgh, Lothian EH3 5NS
☎ *(0131) 556 2745; FAX (0131) 557 0433*

The Lovat is very convenient for visitors to the world renowned Royal Botanic Gardens and the Water of Leith Walkway. The hotel has a functional lounge bar serving a couple of real ales, plus the occasional guest beer and traditional cider. The food service is restricted to breakfast and snacks. However, finding a decent restaurant should be no problem for visitors to the capital. This small, family-run hotel is not grand (rated two-star by the Scottish Tourist Board), but is well situated, being on a frequent bus route to Edinburgh's main Princes Street, less than a mile away. For drivers, the quiet residential area around the hotel is free from parking restrictions. The guest rooms are comfortable with en-suite shower and WC, cable TV, radio, direct dial telephone and tea/coffee making equipment. A full (Scottish) breakfast is provided and CAMRA members benefit from a 15% reduction in the room rates and can take advantage of brewery trips arranged by the hotel. Pets can be accommodated.

🛏 Two single, two double, three-twin-bedded and one family room
£ ££
🍺 Caledonian Deuchar's IPA, 80/-; guest beer (occasionally)
🍴 Snacks daily, lunchtime and evening
CC accepted

—— GIFFORD ——

Goblin Ha' Hotel
Main Street, Gifford, Haddington, East Lothian EH41 4QH
☎ *(01620) 810244;* FAX *(01620) 810718*
Directions: follow East Lothian Hillfoot Trail

This substantial hotel stands in the centre of the village. It comprises a functional public bar, which is enhanced by an oak-panelled counter, and a lounge/cocktail bar with a comfortable seating area. There is also a conservatory which looks out over the extensive garden where there is a play area for children. Families are made very welcome here and the pub has a children's certificate which allows them to go into any area the landlord permits until 8pm. The bar stocks a good range of (mainly English) beers, as well as a traditional cider in summer. The seven guest rooms all offer en-suite accommodation and a cooked breakfast is provided. Pets can be catered for by arrangement.

⊨ Two single, two double and three twin-bedded rooms
£ ££
🍺 Hop Back Summer Lightning; Marston's Pedigree; Taylor Landlord; guest beers
🍽 Snacks lunchtime, meals daily, lunchtime and evening
CC accepted

Tweedale Arms Hotel
High Street, Gifford, East Lothian EH41 4QU
☎ *(01620) 810240;* FAX *(01620) 810488*
Directions: on the B63355 (off the A1 at Tranent)

A notable feature of Gifford village is its 300-year-old avenue of lime trees. The whitewashed Tweedale Arms benefits from a pleasant outlook across the village greens through the limes, to gates of Yester House, the former home of the Marquesses of Tweeddale. This most attractive little village lies at the foot of the Lammermuir Hills, with easy access to Edinburgh and the coast and the many historic castles, stately homes and other sites in the area. An added bonus for golfers: there are some 17 golf courses (including Muirfield) within striking distance! Gifford itself has a nine-hole course. The hotel's public bar, which boasts a large collection of miniatures, draws a loyal local following, and has a games room attached. The plush lounge bar is popular for meals, which can also be taken in the restaurant. There are 16 en-suite bedrooms, some of which are suitable for guests with disabilities. They all have TV, direct dial telephone, trouser press and tea/coffee making equipment. Children are welcome (under-fives sharing their parents room are only charged for meals). Pets can also be catered for.

⊨ Three single, five double, six twin-bedded and two family rooms
£ ££ (££££ single room)
🍺 Broughton Greenmantle, plus monthly guest beers
🍽 Snacks and meals daily, lunchtime and evening
CC accepted

—— INNERLEITHEN ——

Traquair Arms Hotel

Traquair Road, Innerleithen, Borders EH44 6PD
☎ *(01896) 830229;* FAX *(01896) 830260*
Directions: on the B709, near the A72 jct, six miles south of Peebles

The Traquair Arms is one of the few pubs to sell on draught the ale produced by the nearby Traquair Brewery. Traquair House, the oldest inhabited house in Scotland, is home to the brewery which dates from the 18th century and was pressed back into use by the late 20th Laird of Traquair, Peter Maxwell Stuart, when he discovered it in a wing of the house in 1965. Tours of the brewery can be arranged (telephone 01896 831370), but you can't go in by the main gates – these remain firmly shut until a Stuart is safely back on the throne! The inn itself is an elegant, family-run hotel with comfortable, spacious bedrooms offering en-suite bathrooms and all the usual facilities. Good food – on an imaginative, home-cooked menu, based on local produce – is served in either the plush lounge, warmed by a log fire, or in the adjacent dining room, or, if weather permits, in the charming secluded garden. Visitors can enjoy a round of golf, horse-riding or fishing on the Tweed nearby; the NT's water-powered Printing Works is open to the public and the town of Innerleithen (which was depicted by Sir Walter Scott in his *Waverley* novels as St Ronan's Well) is popular for its cashmeres and tweeds.

⋈ Three single, four double, two twin-bedded, one family room
£ ££ – £££
🍺 Broughton Greenmantle Ale; Traquair Bear Ale
🍴 Snacks and meals daily, noon–9pm
CC accepted

—— LAUDER ——

Eagle Hotel

1 Market Place, Lauder, Borders TD2 6SR
☎ *(01578) 722225;* FAX *(01578) 722426*
Directions: on the A68

This rambling village hotel was built in the 18th century to serve the coaching trade, but has been thoroughly modified to cater for modern visitors' needs. The stone wall surrounding the fireplace remains an attractive feature in the comfortable lounge, whilst in the more functional public bar, look out for the interesting mirror-backed gantry. The Eagle offers a good range of real ales, with at least one guest cask a week, plus an occasional traditional cider. The bar menu offers options for children as well as vegetarians. Children are welcome to stay overnight – as well as the family room, two other rooms can accommodate an additional child's bed. Under-fives stay free, up to 15-year-olds are charged £10 per night. The single room is the only one which does not have an en-suite bathroom. The room prices include a full cooked breakfast. The old Lauder Fort (Thirlstane Castle) is well worth a visit, and the pub is convenient for the Border abbeys – Melrose, Jedburgh and Kelso are all within 15 miles. Edinburgh centre is a 40-minute drive.

⋈ One single, one double, one twin-bedded and one family room
£ £
🍺 Boddingtons Bitter; Caledonian Deuchars IPA, 80/-; Greene King IPA; Marston's Pedigree; guest beer
🍴 Snacks and meals daily, lunchtime and evening
CC not accepted

—— LEADBURN ——

Leadburn Inn

Leadburn, near West Linton, Lothian EH46 7BE
☎ *(01968) 672952*
Directions: three miles south of Penicuik at the A701/A793/A6094 jct

This pub has a most unusual restaurant – a converted railway carriage – and the menu served therein is excellent. The Leadburn, which its owners describe as a 'typical rural hostelry', is in fact, very food-oriented. As the restaurant is only open in the evenings, a varied menu is also available all day (10am-midnight) in the comfortable lounge. This room is linked by a sunny conservatory to the more down-to-earth, slate-floored public bar which boasts two pot-bellied stoves and a picture window offering stunning views of the Pentland Hills. All the countryside around here is spectacular, yet the pub is just 13 miles outside Edinburgh. The renowned Edinburgh Crystal factory, just three miles from the inn, is a popular venue for tourists. There are six guest bedrooms, all en-suite, with TV and tea/coffee making facilities. The inn has ample car parking. Pets can be accommodated.

🛏 Four doubles, two family rooms
£ ££
🍺 Caledonian Deuchars IPA, 80/-; guest beers
🍴 Snacks and meals daily, all day

—— MELROSE ——

Burts Hotel

Market Square, Melrose, Borders TD6 9PN
☎ *(01896) 822285;* FAX *(01896) 822870*
Directions: in the town centre, one mile off the A68, three miles east of Galashiels, via the A6091

The Hendersons describe their hotel as a 'quintessentially Borders inn with modern Borders atmosphere'; in other words, a good mix of the traditional with all the up-to-date amenities demanded by today's guests. This elegant, 18th-century listed, four-star hotel stands on the picturesque market square of one of Scotland's oldest burghs, overlooked by the Eildon Hills. There are good facilities for fishing and other sporting activities, and those whose pursuits are more cultural can visit nearby Abbotsford, former home of Sir Walter Scott, as well as many other stately homes and castles. Renowned for its cuisine, Burts has a stylish restaurant, or you can choose to eat in the warmly decorated bar which has a comfortable seating area for non-smokers. There is a residents' lounge on the first floor, and snooker and billiards tables are available. The hotel has its own garden. The 20 guest rooms are very well appointed and comfortably furnished to a high standard; all have private bathrooms. Children are welcome as overnight guests and pets can be accommodated.

🛏 Six singles, 14 double rooms
£ £££ (single ££££)
🍺 Draught Bass; Belhaven Sandy Hunter's Ale, 80/-; guest beer (occasionally)
🍴 Snacks and meals daily, lunchtime and evening
CC accepted

MOUNTBENGER

Gordon Arms Hotel

Mountbenger, Yarrow Valley, Selkirk, Borders TD7 5LE
☎ *(01750) 82232*
Directions: At the A708/B709 crossroads

Dating from 1828 and situated on an isolated crossroads, this warm, friendly hotel has always had a reputation as a meeting place: originally for drovers and traders, later it appealed to local writers Sir Walter Scott and James Hogg (the Ettrick Shepherd). It is also very popular with ramblers on the nearby Southern Upland Way and others keen on outdoor pursuits (there is good fishing locally). Alongside the hotel accommodation, there is a bunkhouse (a converted hayloft), providing a cheaper alternative for groups (around £5 per person per night) – with a large heated drying room available. The pub itself has two spacious bars, a dining room and a residents' lounge. Children are welcome in both the lounge and dining room. Its beers are served using air pressure a common dispense method north of the border. The six guest rooms share bathroom facilities, but all have washbasins, teamakers and electric blankets. Well-behaved pets can be accommodated. The hotel is closed on Monday and Tuesdays in winter.

🛏 Three double, two twin-bedded and one family room
£ ££
🍺 Broughton Greenmantle Ale; guest beer
🍴 Snacks and meals daily, lunchtime and evening (see text)
CC accepted

NORTH BERWICK

Nether Abbey Hotel

20 Dirleton Avenue, North Berwick, East Lothian EH39 4BQ
☎ *(01620) 892802;* FAX *(01620) 895298*
Directions: on the A198 towards Edinburgh

This part of the East Lothian coast is a magnet for birdwatchers, with winter being the best season for the enthusiast. The rocky shoreline offers ample opportunities, and boat trips can be arranged to the islands in the Firth of Forth. There are also many other local attractions for lovers of the great outdoors, including the John Muir Country Park and the Yellowcraig Nature Trail. The Nether Abbey makes a good centre for touring this region. A Victorian villa, situated on the main road, this family-run hotel has a spacious, extended main bar and dining area. The restaurant specialises in local game and seafood. Twelve of the 16 guest rooms have en-suite facilities. They are individually designed and decorated, and provided with TV and tea/coffee making equipment. Pets can be catered for. There is a good choice of four real ales which changes frequently, and a beer festival is staged every February. The hotel garden features a petanque (boules) court. Pets can be accommodated.

🛏 Two single, six double, five twin-bedded and three family rooms
£ ££
🍺 Beer range varies
🍴 Snacks and meals daily, lunchtime and evening
CC accepted

—— PEEBLES ——

Green Tree Hotel

41 Eastgate, Peebles, Borders EH45 8AD
☎/FAX *(01721) 720582*
Directions: on the A72 at east end of town

Leaded windows are an interesting feature of this busy town-centre hotel. They grace the front bar which is popular with locals. There is also a comfortable lounge at the rear with a relaxed atmosphere where children are welcome. Both bars are warmed by open fires and meals can be taken here or in the restaurant which has recently been refurbished. An imaginative range of dishes is all prepared on the premises. The pub is a rare outlet for the beers from the independent Orkney Brewery, and it also stocks an occasional traditional cider. The eight guest rooms all have en-suite bathrooms and a full cooked breakfast is provided. There are opportunities in the area for all sorts of outdoor pursuits, including golf, fishing, and walking. The pub has its own car park and there is quick and easy access to both Edinburgh and Glasgow.

⋈ Two single, two double, three twin-bedded and one family room
£ ££
🍺 Caledonian 80/-; Orkney Raven Ale; guest beer
🍽 Snacks and meals daily, lunchtime and evening
CC accepted

Tontine Hotel

High Street, Peebles, Borders EH45 8AJ
☎ *(01721) 720892;* FAX *(01721) 729732*
Directions: in the town centre

This plush, tweedy Borders hotel retains the formality that is not found in many local inns. But if you still prefer to be addressed as 'Sir' and 'Madam' then you will be comfortable here. A marble-topped counter is a feature of the cosy, wood-panelled bar whose walls are adorned with pictures of game birds – the Tweeddale Shooting Club meets here regularly. There is also a well-appointed lounge where children are welcome. Meals are served in both these areas but the Adam Room Restaurant is increasingly favoured by diners. Recently sympathetically refurbished, in keeping with its 19th-century origins, the hotel has 36 en-suite rooms, including some that are particularly characterful. All offer radio, TV, telephone and tea/coffee making facilities. Families are welcome and cots, highchairs and a baby listening service are available. Prices for the rooms (which include breakfast) vary according to the season. Pets can be accommodated.

⋈ Five single, 16 double, 14 twin-bedded and one family room
£ ££
🍺 Broughton Greenmantle Ale
🍽 Lunchtime snacks, snacks and meals every evening
CC accepted

—— PENICUIK ——

Craigiebield House Hotel
50 Bog Road, Penicuik, Lothian EH26 9BZ
☎ *(01968) 672557;* FAX *(01968) 679854*
Directions: between the A701 and A766, west of the town centre

This fine red sandstone building can be picked out by its impressive gables. Built as a private house in 1872, it stands alone in its own grounds. The architectural interest is continued inside, where the beautiful panelled dining room, with its open fireplace, is particularly noteworthy. There is also a small comfortable lounge bar, where suppers are served, decorated with golfing prints and local scenes. The bar always has two guest beers on tap which are frequently changed. The guest rooms share bathroom facilities, but they are all spacious and comfortable. Children are welcome to stay. A cooked breakfast is provided. For non-drivers, Edinburgh is easily accessible by bus (25-minute ride), and is probably preferable to trying to find a parking space in the capital. What's more if you don't have to drive back to the hotel, you can freely sample some of the splendid traditional bars in the city. Closer to the hotel (five minutes away) you can visit Rosslyn chapel. This historic 15th-century church is said to be one of the loveliest in Scotland.

➡ One double, three twin-bedded rooms
£ ££
🍺 Caledonian Deuchars IPA; guest beers
🍴 Snacks lunchtime, meals daily, lunchtime and evening
CC accepted

—— ST MARY'S LOCH ——

Tibbie Shiel's Inn
St Mary's Loch, Selkirk, Borders TD7 5LH
☎ *(01750) 42231*
Directions: by the A708, midway between Moffat and Selkirk

The unusual name of this inn derives from Isabella (Tibbie) Shiels who moved in the 1820s to what was then St Mary's cottage on Lord Napier's estate, where her husband worked as a mole catcher. After his death, with six children to support, she turned the cottage into an inn, often accommodating up to 35 guests, many of whom had to sleep on the floor. She had many famous visitors, including Sir Walter Scott and Robert Louis Stevenson. Guests are no longer required to make do with the floor, as the inn now has five comfortable en-suite bedrooms in an extension. The inn has a children's certificate and serves wonderful food, but its spartan origins have not been completely forgotten – the gents' toilet is still outside and the pub itself has retained its original character, with low ceilings and thick walls adding to the atmosphere. In a remote setting in the Yarrow Valley between St Mary's Loch and the Loch of Lowes, with good facilities for sailing, fishing and walking, it makes an excellent centre for holidaymakers.

➡ Two double, one twin-bedded and two family rooms
£ £
🍺 Belhaven 80/-; Broughton Greenmantle Ale
🍴 Snacks lunchtime, meals daily lunchtime and evening
CC accepted

—— SOUTH QUEENSFERRY ——

Hawes Inn

7 Newhalls Road, South Queensferry, Lothian EH30 9TA
☎ *(0131) 331 1990;* FAX *(0131) 319 1120*
Directions: on the promenade by the river

The Hawes Inn and its location by the shore, inspired Robert Louis Stevenson to write his dramatic tale, *Kidnapped*. Stevenson was a frequent visitor to the inn and his affection for the area is clear in his writings. This former coaching inn, standing in the shadow of the great Forth rail bridge, also featured in one of Sir Walter Scott's works, *The Antiquary*. He called it 'a very decent sort of place' and so it remains. There is a small characterful bar with a family room attached, and a larger, comfortable lounge where bar meals are served, as an alternative to the traditional Scottish restaurant. Original wood panelling has been retained throughout the public rooms. The conference suite, named after Stevenson (naturally) hosts business and social functions. The pub has an extensive, attractive garden with a play area for children, offering glorious views across the Firth of Forth. None of the eight bedrooms is en-suite, but they are very attractively furnished, one with a four-poster bed; all rooms have tea/coffee making equipment, TV and direct dial telephone. Children under 12 sharing a room with parents are only charged for meals (small portions are available on request). The hotel is just 10 miles from Edinburgh city centre and convenient for the airport (five miles) and Dalmeny railway station (one mile).

🛏 One single, five double and two twin-bedded rooms
£ ££
🍺 Caledonian Deuchars IPA, 80/-; Ind Coope Burton Ale; guest beer (occasionally)
🍴 Snacks and meals daily, from noon-10pm
CC accepted

—— SWINTON ——

Wheatsheaf Hotel

Main Street, Swinton, Duns, Borders TD11 3JJ
☎ *(01890) 860257;* FAX *(01890) 860688*
Directions: on the A6112 between Duns and Coldstream

This characterful country inn, overlooking the village green is run with a personal touch by chef, Alan Reid and his family. It has retained its multi-roomed layout: the small, dimly-lit snug bar commemorates local hero Jim Clark, while the well-appointed lounge is decorated with prints of rural life. The extensive, good quality menu which specialises in seafood and game is served here and in the bright, modern, wood-panelled conservatory. The attractive guest rooms are all individually styled. Four of them have en-suite facilities. Children are welcome and pets can also be accommodated (but are not allowed in the hotel's public areas). The Wheatsheaf is 12 miles from Berwick-upon-Tweed and makes an ideal base for exploring the lovely Borders countryside and superb coastline.

🛏 Four double, two twin-bedded rooms
£ ££ – ££
🍺 Caledonian 80/-; guest beers
🍴 Snacks and meals lunchtime and evening Tuesday-Sunday (not Sunday evening in winter)
CC accepted

—— TOWN YETHOLM ——

Plough Hotel

High Street, Town Yetholm, near Kelso, Borders TD5 8RF
☎ *(01573) 420215*

I don't quite know why Yetholm is properly called Town Yetholm, since it really is a village, and a very rural one at that. Surrounded by lovely countryside, the hotel stands at the end of two long distance footpaths, the Pennine Way Walk and St Cuthbert's Walk. Country pursuits, such as clay pigeon shooting, salmon fishing on the River Tweed and shooting are all available, and there are good golf courses in the vicinity. The hotel, which serves its friendly local community well, has a public bar that has been sympathetically modernised, with wood panelling featured around the fireplace. There is a games room for fans of pool and video machines and a small, nicely decorated dining room which is strictly for non-smokers (meals can also be taken in the bar if preferred). Children are catered for on the menu, which offers daily specials; a limited range is served at lunchtime and a more extensive choice in the evening. The guest rooms are not en-suite but represent good value, with a cooked breakfast provided. The hotel can cater for small parties of up to twelve, and pets can be accommodated.

🛏 Two single, two twin-bedded and one family room
£ £
🍺 Caledonian 80/-; Morland Old Speckled Hen; guest beer
🍴 Meals daily, lunchtime and evening
CC accepted

TRY ALSO:

Royal Ettrick Hotel

13 Ettrick Road, Edinburgh EH10 5BJ
Tel (0131) 228 6413; FAX (0131) 229 7330

This hotel has recently changed hands and reports have been mixed. Feedback from readers would be appreciated. In a residential area of Edinburgh, but easily accessible from the centre, it has 13 en-suite rooms. B&B £££

CENTRAL SCOTLAND, FIFE & TAYSIDE

—— ABERDOUR ——

Aberdour Hotel
38 High Street, Aberdour, Fife KY3 0SW
☎ *(01383) 860325;* FAX *(01383) 860808*
Directions: Aberdour is on the A921

The Aberdour has grown and developed over the years, but still offers a warm Scottish welcome. The hotel cellar is probably the oldest part of the building, reputed to be 400 years old. The present hotel was built as a coaching inn in the 17th century, but has recently been upgraded to provide all the modern comforts required by today's travellers. One of the most recent developments is the conversion of the old courtyard stables into superior bedrooms. The hotel now has 16 guest rooms, all en-suite, with TV, direct dial telephones and tea/coffee making equipment. Children sharing their parent's room are accommodated free of charge. Two ground-floor rooms are suitable for guests with disabilities. A full Scottish breakfast is provided. Other meals, on a traditional menu, are served in the characterful restaurant which features stone and wood-panelled walls and beamed ceilings, or in the lounge bar. Aberdour is a picturesque coastal village over the Firth of Forth from Edinburgh, which can be reached within 30 minutes by road or rail. Pets can be accommodated.

🛏 Six double, six twin-bedded and four family rooms
£ ££
🍺 Fuller's London Pride; Marston's Pedigree; Taylor Landlord; guest beers
🍽 Snacks daily, lunchtime and evening; lunches Saturday-Sunday; evening meals daily
CC accepted

The Hawes Inn,
Edinburgh

Cedar Inn

20 Shore Road, Aberdour, Fife KY3 0TR
☎ *(01383) 860310;* FAX *(01383) 860004*
Directions: Aberdour lies on the A921

The Cedar is convenient for travellers reliant on public transport. It is a two minute walk from the railway station (which has won awards for its floral displays, so is worth a visit anyway!), with a frequent service to Edinburgh's Waverley Station. The village also benefits from regular bus services. The inn is right by the shore where the beaches are safe and clean, and there is a golf course within five minutes' walk. Aberdour Castle, which was built around 1200, is worth a visit for the attractive gardens and the unusual 16th-century dovecote, and the village boasts some interesting shops. The Cedar is a family-run hotel where the public bar offers an ever-changing range of six real ales, as well as a good choice of malt whiskies. This bar caters for fans of pool and Sky TV, whilst the adjacent snug bar, bearing a nautical theme, is more intimate. There are also two open-plan lounges and a popular restaurant where the menu is supplemented by a daily specials board. This part of the coast enjoys a good climate, so the patio is often used by diners. Four of the guest rooms are en-suite and all have TV and tea/coffee making facilities. Pets can be accommodated.

➤ Three single, two double, one twin-bedded and one family room
£ £ (££ single en-suite)
🍺 Beer range varies
🍴 Snacks and meals daily, lunchtime and evening (Monday for residents only)
CC accepted

—— BRIDGE OF ALLAN ——

Queens Hotel

24 Henderson Street, Bridge of Allan, Stirling, Central FK9 4HP
☎ *(01786) 833268;* FAX *(01786) 832065*
Directions: one mile south of the M9, jct 11

Pubs and hotels which have their own breweries always act as a magnet to CAMRA folk; this one has even more appeal as it has special offers on accommodation for members of the Campaign. The five-barrel microbrewery was set up at the hotel in 1997. It can be viewed from the cask-only bar downstairs, but it also has its own visitor centre and tours are available on request. A second bar also serves a good selection of real ales, plus an occasional traditional cider. The hotel's restaurant specialises in Mexican food. All in all, quite an unusual establishment. Most of the guest rooms have en-suite bathrooms and several can accommodate families. Pets can also be catered for. Bridge of Allan is picturesque village which gained popularity in Victorian times as a spa. Centrally situated for visitors with business interests in the area, and for tourists, the village lies in the shadow of the Wallace Monument and Stirling Castle, which William Wallace recaptured from the English in 1297. The castle is open to the public all year. The Queens is also handy for visits to the Bannockburn Battle site and the popular Trossachs.

➤ Five double, five twin-bedded and four family rooms
£ £ (single occupancy ££)
🍺 Alloa Arrol's 80/-; Bridge of Allan Stirling IPA, Bitter, Brig; Ind Coope Burton Ale; Tetley Bitter; guest beers
🍴 Snacks and meals daily, lunchtime and evening
CC accepted

— DOLLAR —

Strathallan Hotel

6 Chapel Place, Dollar, Central FK14 7DW
☎ *(01259) 742205;* FAX *(01259) 743720*
Directions: on the A91, off the M9; the hotel is signed from the High Street

In a quiet corner of Dollar, overlooked by Castle Campbell and the Ochil Hills, this hotel is an ideal choice for parents visiting offspring at the nearby Dollar Academy, or simply as a base for tourists exploring the southern Highlands of Scotland. There are good facilities for golf (Gleneagles is ten miles away), clay pigeon shooting and many other activities locally. The Strath, as it is affectionately known, underwent a major refurbishment a few years ago and then a change of ownership. Since then, it has built up a good reputation for its range of real ales which are changed frequently, and often features the beers of Harviestoun Brewery, based in Dollar (tours available by arrangement, telephone 01259 742141). The town currently boasts three *Good Beer Guide* listed pubs. One of the four guest rooms has an en-suite bathroom, and all have TV and tea/coffee making equipment. Pets can be catered for by prior arrangement. Snacks and meals are available in the cosy bar, whilst breakfast and evening meals are served in the Bistro restaurant. The menu is based on freshly cooked meals, with daily specials. The Burns Suite can cater for functions for up to 90 guests. There is also a pool room and garden.

- ⊨ Four doubles
- £ £ (single occupancy ££)
- ⦿ Fuller's London Price; Harviestoun 70/-, 80/-; Taylor Landlord; guest beers
- ⦿ Snacks and meals daily, lunchtime and evening
- CC accepted

— DRYMEN —

Winnock Hotel

The Square, Drymen, Loch Lomond, Central G63 0BL
☎ *(01360) 660245;* FAX *(01360) 660267*
Directions: in the village centre

Calling all amateur sleuths! Bored with just watching re-runs of *Inspector Morse* on the telly? Why not book in for a 'Murder Mystery' weekend at the Winnock. These popular overnight packages are held most weekends (except in August). They start with dinner and the 'murder' entertainment in the evening, then all is revealed the following morning after breakfast. The Winnock is an 18th-century hotel, just a short distance from Loch Lomond in the centre of Drymen village. It is very well appointed and offers good quality accommodation and food. All its 49 bedrooms have en-suite facilities and the usual modern amenities. As a change from the hotel restaurant, make a point of visiting the Clachan, also in the Square, which claims to be the oldest pub in Scotland, and serves excellent traditional Scottish fare, alongside more exotic dishes. Like many bars north of the border, the Winnock keeps long hours – it is open from 11am (noon on Sundays) until midnight, and even later on Friday and Saturday, so there's plenty of time to sample the good range of real ales on offer. Meals, too, are available at all times. Families are made very welcome.

- ⊨ Five single, 27 double, 10 twin-bedded and six family rooms
- £ £££ (single ££££)
- ⦿ Broughton Merlin's Ale; Maclay 80/-; Tetley Bitter; guest beers
- ⦿ Snacks and meals daily, noon-9.30pm
- CC accepted

—— DUNBLANE ——

Stirling Arms Hotel
Stirling Road, Dunblane, Central FK15 9EP
☎ *(01786) 822156;* FAX *(01786) 825300*
Directions: Dunblane is signed from the A9/M9 jct 11; the hotel is off the Perth Road dual carriageway (B8033)

Dating back to the 17th century, the Stirling Arms started life as a coaching inn and has, in its time, been host to many famous guests, including Robert Burns and the officers of Bonnie Prince Charlie. It stands by the River Allan in an attractive town of narrow winding streets set around a medieval square. The Cathedral and Bishops Palace, at the other end of the main street, are well worth a visit. Also nearby is the so-called Stevenson's Cave, where Robert Louis Stevenson is said to have written some of his novels. The Stirling Arms has been extensively refurbished and its bars, elegant oak-panelled dining room, serving an award-winning menu, guest rooms and conference facilities all meet a very high standard, as does the service. Four of the seven bedrooms have en-suite bathrooms, and all have TV, direct dial telephone and hospitality tray. Children are welcome; a cot is available for £5, under-twelves are charged £12 per night. A choice of continental or full cooked breakfast is provided. Pets can be catered for by arrangement. The hotel has its own car park.

⊨ One double, five twin-bedded and one family room
£ £ (en-suite ££; single occupancy £££)
🍺 Draught Bass; Caledonian Deuchars IPA; guest beer (occasionally)
🍽 Snacks and meals daily, lunchtime and evening
CC accepted

—— GLENDEVON ——

Tormaukin Hotel
Glendevon, by Dollar, Perthshire, Central FK14 7JY
☎ *(01259) 781252;* FAX *(01259) 781526*
Directions: on the A823, between Kinross on the M90 and Auchterarder on the A9

Surrounded by the Ochil Hills, the Tormaukin, formerly a Drovers' inn, enjoys an idyllic rural setting. Dating back to the 18th century, the pub has been sympathetically refurbished to retain its original charm. The exposed stone walls around the fireplaces and the beamed ceilings add warmth and character. Bar lunches and suppers are served in the cosy lounge and the oak-beamed Glendevon Room where families are welcome. There is also a larger restaurant offering a similar imaginative menu of traditional Scottish and international cuisine, with an extensive wine list. The hotel has built up a very good reputation locally for its meals. The Tormaukin has ten en-suite bedrooms which are attractively furnished and individually styled. All have direct dial telephones and modern amenities. Four rooms on the ground floor may be suitable for guests with disabilities. Pets can be catered for by arrangement. The hotel is very popular in summer months, particularly with golfers, as there are several challenging courses in the vicinity which have the added bonus of beautiful surroundings. In winter, special two and three-night breaks are offered for dinner, bed and breakfast.

⊨ One single, two double, six twin-bedded and one family room
£ £££ (££££ single room)
🍺 Harviestoun Waverley 70/-, seasonal beers; Ind Coope Burton Ale; guest beer (on occasion)
🍽 Snacks and meals daily, lunchtime and evening (Sunday noon-9.30pm)
CC accepted

—— KINNESSWOOD ——

Lomond Country Inn

Main Street, Kinnesswood, Kinross, Tayside KY13 7HN
☎ *(01592) 840253;* FAX *(01592) 840693*
Directions: on the A911, 10 minutes from the M90 (jct 5 northbound, jct 7 southbound)

This family-run inn lies on the slopes of the Lomond Hills in Kinnesswood village. It boasts magnificent views over Loch Leven which has a boat service running in summer to Loch Leven Castle, where Mary Queen of Scots was imprisoned for a year. This is just one of the many tourist attractions in the area, which offers all kinds of facilities for sports and leisure, from golf and fishing, to more unusual pursuits – Scotland's leading gliding school is five minutes' drive from the hotel. Vane Farm RSPB Nature Reserve is a favourite with visiting families, while Edinburgh and Perth can both be reached in half an hour by car. The inn's policy is to offer warm, informal hospitality. It has pleasant public areas, with open log fires in winter. Food ranges from simple bar meals to an award-winning restaurant menu where you can splash out on lobster or smoked salmon, or opt for the less lavish, but equally good, traditional Scottish fare from the fixed price menu. All meals are based on fresh local produce. The guest rooms have a private bath or shower, TV, coffee/tea makers and direct dial telephones. Four rooms are in the pub itself, while a further eight have been added in an extension. Some rooms are suitable for guests with disabilities.

ᕬ Two single, four double, two twin-bedded and four family rooms
£ ££ (£££ single room)
🍺 Greene King Abbot; Jennings Bitter; Marston's Pedigree
🍽 Snacks and meals daily, lunchtime and evening
CC accepted

WHAT CAMRA DOES FOR BEER AND WHAT YOU CAN DO!

Thousands of pubs are being closed or ruined.
The Campaign for Real Ale campaigns
• locally to save individual pubs
• nationally on planning, licensing and tax laws
• with official bodies to extend 'listing' to historic pubs
• to encourage people to use their local pub

The grip of the multi-nationals and nationals is tightening
CAMRA campaigns against monopoly and national brands
• CAMRA promotes the independent brewers and publicises the many interesting new companies entering the market
• in 1997 CAMRA saved the vital guest beer law, threatened with abolition
• CAMRA acts as a vigorous consumer voice in Westminster, Whitehall and Brussels.

CAMRA is a non-profit making body run by an elected panel of volunteers. Add your voice and help safeguard your beer and your pub!

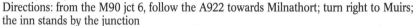

—— KINROSS ——

Muirs Inn

49 Muirs, Kinross, Tayside KY13 7AU

☎/FAX (01577) 862270

Directions: from the M90 jct 6, follow the A922 towards Milnathort; turn right to Muirs; the inn stands by the junction

Like so many rural pubs, the original purpose of this building was agricultural and the history of its development into today's hostelry is fascinating. Built two centuries ago as a single storey crofter's farmhouse, it also provided lodging and a workshop for the local blacksmith. This part of the inn is now the public bar, while the adjacent byre became the lounge, which houses an original still from a nearby (defunct) distillery. A second floor for accommodation, and the stables, were later additions, and the latter has now become the restaurant. The property first became an hotel around the turn of the century, catering both for local people and travellers, as is still the case today. The characterful guest rooms all have en-suite bath or shower and the usual amenities of TV, trouser press and hospitality tray. Children (over 12s only) are welcome. The beer range is impressive – up to eight draught ales are available at any one time, with an emphasis on Scottish brews. It hosts both a beer festival and a malt whisky festival. The food is prepared by award-winning staff, combining traditional local fare with more exotic dishes.

⇥ Five double rooms
£ ££ (single occupancy £££)
🍺 Belhaven 80/-; Orkney Dark Island; six guest beers
🍽 Snacks and meals daily, lunchtime and evening
CC accepted

—— KIRKMICHAEL ——

Aldchlappie Hotel

Kirkmichael, by Bridge of Calley, Tayside PH10 7NS

☎ (01250) 881224; FAX (01250) 881373

Directions: on the A924, midway between Bridge of Calley and Pitlochry

The tiny brewery which opened at the hotel in 1996 is a contender for the title of smallest brewery in Britain. Initially started as an experiment, the beers were well received and the brewery has become an established feature. The beer 'names' commemorate important historic events. This small Highland hotel caters mostly for walkers and skiers, but all kinds of other outdoor pursuits are available and can be arranged by hotel staff. There are for instance, no less than eight golf courses within a 30-minute radius of the hotel. The Alchlappie again, has agricultural origins as a farm or drovers inn, and is not far short of 400 years old. It offers comfortable public areas, where little extra touches make your visit more pleasant, such as fresh flowers, log fires and books and magazines to curl up with at the end of a busy day. There is a choice here between the hotel's five en-suite bedrooms and three self-catering apartments in a separate building. All the accommodation is comfortably furnished and equipped to a high standard and pets can be accommodated. The hotel has a lounge and a public bar, and a dining room where all the meals are home cooked. There is also a family room and a garden.

⇥ Two double, three family rooms
£ £
🍺 Beer range varies
🍽 Snacks and meals daily, lunchtime and evening
CC accepted

—— LEVEN ——

Hawkshill Hotel
Hawkslaw Street, Leven, Fife KY8 4LS
☎/FAX *(01333) 426056*
Directions: on the A915 between Kirkcaldy and East Neuk

I'm beginning to get the feeling that no-one in Scotland does anything but play golf! It's true that St Andrews, the home of the sport is just up the road from Leven, but even so, can there really be enough golfers for the 28 courses that are dotted within a 15-mile radius of this hotel? If (dare I say it?) golf doesn't happen to be your thing, then there are plenty of other amusements to be had in this coastal town. Children will enjoy the beach and the leisure centre with its swimming-pool and flume, whilst Letham Glen Park offers a variety of activities during the summer and the Silverburn Estate includes an animal sanctuary, a children's farm and landscaped gardens. Fans of *Robinson Crusoe* can visit the birthplace of his real-life original, Alexander Selkirk, at nearby Lower Largo. The Hawkshill itself lays on entertainment most weekends and hosts a mini beer festival in July. This comfortable, family-run hotel has a lounge with an open fireplace and a cosy, intimate dining room; excellent meals are served in both areas. High teas are served on Sunday 5-7pm, in place of an evening meal. The guest rooms all have en-suite facilities, plus tea/coffee making equipment. Pets can be catered for by arrangement.

- ⇥ One single, two double, one family room
- £ £
- 🍺 Alloa Arrol's 80/-; Ind Coope Burton Ale; Morland Old Speckled Hen; Tetley Bitter; guest beers
- 🍽 Snacks and meals daily, lunchtime and evening (see text)
- **CC** accepted

—— LUNDIN LINKS ——

Old Manor Hotel
Lundin Links, Fife KY8 6AJ
☎ *(01333) 320368;* FAX *(01333) 820911*
Directions: off the A915, between Leven and Elie

The Old Manor is a four-star hotel in an enviable setting, on the edge of the delightful Lundin Links village, overlooking Largo Bay and (guess what?) two championship golf courses. The Old Manor successfully combines the expectations of guests in an upmarket country hotel with a more informal relaxed atmosphere in the Coachman's bistro, where I am reliably informed, the real ales are kept in perfect condition and the food is good and reasonably priced. If you desire more elegant surroundings, dine in the Aithernie Restaurant where an imaginative menu is based on fresh local produce, game and fish. The adjacent cocktail bar provides an impressive selection of digestifs in the way of single malts, cognacs and armagnacs to enjoy after your meal. The spacious guest rooms are stylishly decorated with comfortable sitting areas, and cater for every need, with hospitality tray, trouser press, direct dial telephone, etc. All the rooms are en-suite and some can accommodate guests with disabilities. Children are welcome. Pets can be catered for by arrangement.

- ⇥ One single, ten double, ten twin-bedded and two family rooms
- £ ££££
- 🍺 Beer range varies
- 🍽 Snacks and meals daily, lunchtime and evening
- **CC** accepted

—— MONTROSE ——

George Hotel

22 George Street, Montrose, Central DD10 8EW
☎ *(01674) 675050;* FAX *(01674) 671153*
Directions: on the A92 between Arbroath and Stonehaven

An imposing building, occupying a corner site at the town centre, the George is a family-owned hotel whose restaurant enjoys a good reputation locally. Prepared under the direction of the head chef, the extensive menu is frequently changed. A varied selection of bar meals is also served in the warm, intimate lounge, where the choice of real ales comes from a rotated list. The hotel's guest rooms have recently been refurbished to a high standard. All en-suite, they offer satellite TV, direct dial telephone and hospitality tray. Guests are offered the choice of a cooked breakfast or a continental option. Montrose is bounded on three sides by water – its famous 'Basin' is a tidal lagoon of 2,000 acres affording sanctuary to many species of seabird. The town is sheltered by some of the loveliest glens in Scotland and this stretch of the coast offers golden beaches and impressive sand dunes. Another attraction for visitors is the nearby Letham Grange, with its golf links, parkland and water hazards. In winter, arrangements for skiing and curling can be made at the hotel. Pets can be catered for by arrangement.

- 13 single, eight double, three twin-bedded and one family room
- £ ££ (££££ single room)
- Beer range varies
- Snacks and meals daily, lunchtime and evening
- CC accepted

—— MOULIN ——

Moulin Hotel

11–13 Kirkmichael Road, Moulin, Pitlochry, Central PH16 5EW
☎ *(01796) 472196;* FAX *(01796) 474098*
Directions: three-quarters of a mile from Pitlochry on the Braemar road (A924)

The oldest part of this hotel, which the owners refer to as the 'Original Moulin Inn', dates back to the late 17th century. It houses a small bar area and an adjacent eating area, both with log fires, and a bar billiards table. The newer part of the building, with most of the guest accommodation, was added a hundred years ago, and has been refurbished throughout. The newest addition, though, is in the stables, where a brewhouse was set up in the summer of 1995, primarily to brew for the hotel, but now also supplying around six other outlets. Meals and snacks are served at all times at the inn, while the hotel restaurant, which overlooks the garden and the Moulin burn, opens for lunch, high tea and evening meals. The en-suite bedrooms are individually styled, but all are comfortably furnished and equipped to a high standard. Pets can be catered for and winter breaks are available at reduced rates. The village is an ancient settlement, borne out in the churchyard which houses some Crusaders' graves and standing stones. It is very convenient for Pitlochry, where the popular Festival Theatre stages five different plays a week between May and October.

- Nine double, five twin-bedded and four family rooms
- £ £ (single occupancy £££)
- Moulin Light, Ale of Atholl, Braveheart, Old Remedial
- Snacks and meals daily, noon–9.30pm
- CC accepted

—— ST ANDREWS ——

Russell Hotel

26 The Scores, St Andrews, Fife KY16 9AS
☎ *(01334) 473447;* FAX *(01334) 478279*
Directions: off the A91, near the Royal and Ancient

You could almost tee off from your bedroom here, as the Royal and Ancient Old Course is only two minutes from the hotel. The Russell is a small, friendly place, run by the de Vries family who are themselves keen golfers and will organise tailor-made packages for visitors. If you are a golfing widow(er), St Andrews offers plenty of other attractions, including a good selection of shops, and historical sights, such as the ruins of the castle and the cathedral. The pub attracts the more mature students from Scotland's oldest university (two minutes away). There are ten nicely decorated en-suite bedrooms (some have views over St Andrews Bay) and they all have satellite TV, shaver points, direct dial telephones and hospitality tray. The comfortable Victorian Bar has a relaxed atmosphere, while the 'Malt Shop' corner offers an extensive range of whiskies, including some rare finds. The supper room serves a good range of meals, with the emphasis on local game, beef and seafood. Lunches are also available in the bar.

- ⇔ Nine double/twin-bedded rooms, one family room
- £ £££
- 🍺 Boddingtons Best Bitter; Broughton Greenmantle Ale; McEwan 80/-; guest beer (occasionally)
- 🍽 Snacks and meals daily, lunchtime and evening
- CC accepted

—— STIRLING ——

Portcullis

Castle Wynd, Stirling, Central FK8 1EG
☎ *(01786) 472290;* FAX *(01786) 446103*
Directions: next to the castle

The Portcullis has a history as unusual as its name. It was built in 1787 as a fee-paying school for the upper classes, but now serves as a high class (three star) hotel. It stands right next to Stirling Castle, a favourite residence with the Scottish royal family (James II was born there), and many local people still feel that Stirling should be the capital of Scotland. This historic town with its medieval streets, bears witness to Scotland's turbulent past. The battles of Bannockburn and Stirling Bridge, along with other events from the history of the area are presented at the Landmark Visitor Centre on Castle Hill. The hotel is a good base for touring the country, with Glasgow and Edinburgh almost equidistant. The Portcullis has a homely lounge bar where meals are served and four en-suite guest rooms, most of which offer superb views over the town. A cooked breakfast is provided and children are welcome. Pets can be accommodated by arrangement.

- ⇔ One single, one double, two twin-bedded rooms
- £ £££ (££££ single room)
- 🍺 Orkney Dark Island; guest beer
- 🍽 Snacks and meals daily, lunchtime and evening
- CC accepted

——— STRATHTUMMEL ———

Loch Tummel Inn
Strathtummel, by Pitlochry, Central PH16 5RP
☎/FAX *(01882) 634272*
Directions: on the B8019

This charming inn has a homely feel in the truest sense of the word. It is also the owners' home and its stylish decor could easily grace the pages of a glossy 'Homes' magazine. A former coaching inn, overlooking Loch Tummel on the 'road to the isles', it is set amongst some spectacular scenery, a few miles from the famous 'Queen's View'. Guests at the inn can take advantage of free fishing on the loch, and there are many other opportunities for outdoor pursuits, such as waymarked walkers' routes through the nearby hills and forests; golf courses and wildlife parks to visit and, for culture, the Pitlochry Festival Theatre. The inn's restaurant is in a converted hayloft, which again benefits from super views, and serves good home-cooked meals, with salmon smoked at the inn a speciality. The former stables have been turned into the bar which stocks the draught and bottled products of the nearby Moulin Brewery and where meals are also available. Two of the guest rooms have private bathrooms, the rest have washbasins, and they all have tea/coffee making facilities and electric blankets for when winter really takes a hold. The best bedroom even has a peat fireplace in the bathroom! A full Scottish breakfast is served. Pets can be accommodated by prior arrangement.

- ⊨ One single, two double, one twin-bedded; three family rooms
- £ ££ (£££ single occupancy of double room)
- 🍺 Moulin Braveheart
- 🍽 Snacks and meals daily, lunchtime and evening
- CC accepted

TRY ALSO:

City Hotel
18 Bridge Street, Dunfermline, Fife KY12 8DA
☎ *(01383) 722538;* FAX *(01383) 623665*

Welcoming, town-centre Maclays hotel. Some of the rooms are en-suite. B&B ££

Chance Inn
Main Street, Inverkeilor, Angus DD11 5RN
☎ *(01241) 830308*

Good value bed and breakfast a lively pub, noted for its good food. Three rooms. B&B £

DUMFRIES & GALLOWAY

—— BLADNOCH ——

Bladnoch Inn
Bladnoch, Newton Stewart DG8 9AB
☎/ғᴀx *(01988) 402200*
Directions: on the A714, six miles south of Newton Stewart

The beer range at the Bladnoch Inn changes frequently, but it is one of the few pubs that regularly features the beers from Galloway's only brewery, Sulwath. Based at Gillfoot Farm in Southerness, this tiny brewery was set up in 1995. If whisky is more your tipple, the Bladnoch Distillery which stands opposite the pub, has recently been reopened. The traditional stone built pub enjoys a good local following, particularly with farmers and anglers, and you are bound to find a friendly welcome here. Its bar is warmed by an open fire and it has a children's certificate. Snacks are served in the bar, whilst the restaurant offers an *à la carte* menu which caters for vegetarians, plus a good wine list. The pub stands on the River Bladnoch and salmon and trout fishing can be arranged right there, as well as on lochs in the area. The pub also organises golfing and shooting breaks, and the Galloway Hills offer unspoilt countryside favoured by walkers. The four guest rooms share bathroom facilities, but all have vanity units alongside the usual amenities. Pets can be accommodated.

- ⊨ Four double rooms
- £ £
- 🍺 Beer range varies
- 🍽 Snacks and meals daily, lunchtime and evening
- CC accepted

—— CANONBIE ——

Riverside Inn
Canonbie DG14 0UX
☎ *(0138 73) 71512*
Directions: off the A7, 14 miles north of M6 jct 44

Just over the border from England, the pretty village of Canonbie, now bypassed by the A7, is a peaceful spot for a first night in Scotland. Our recommendation is the charming Riverside Inn (the river in question being the Esk), which offers comfortable accommodation in prettily furnished rooms. There is a quiet residents' lounge, but my choice would be the friendly bar, with its open fire and comfortable seating. Susan and Robert Phillips pay attention to the little details that make visitors want to return: fresh fruit in the guest rooms, and electric blankets on the beds. All the bedrooms have private bath or shower, colour TV and hospitality tray. Although there are no family rooms as such, children are welcome and guests with disabilities can be catered for. Pets can also be accommodated by arrangement. There is a good quality, imaginative menu which often features game and other seasonal foods. Special two-day winter breaks are available, and there is a five per cent discount for stays of a week.

- ⊨ Four double, three twin-bedded room
- £ £££ (££££ single occupancy)
- 🍺 Caledonian Deuchars IPA; Yates Bitter; guest beer (occasionally)
- 🍽 Snacks and meals daily, lunchtime and evening
- CC accepted

—— GLENLUCE ——

Kelvin House Hotel

53 Main Street, Glenluce DG8 0PP
☎/FAX *(01581) 300303*
Directions: signed off the A75, ten miles from Stranraer

Glenluce enjoys a mild climate, thanks to the Gulf Stream, which also partly accounts for the many botanical gardens open to the public locally, including Logan, Ardwell and the famous Threave Gardens a little further away. This is a very diverse region for landscape, ranging from beaches and clifftops, to hills and forests, so there are ample opportunities for walking tours, cycling and pony trekking in an area with very little traffic to spoil the tranquillity. There are four 18-hole golf courses nearby and guests at the Kelvin House Hotel can obtain discounts at the local county course. Glenluce is a small town, now bypassed by the main Stranraer road, and this unpretentious hotel, built in 1770, is situated on the main street. There are six spacious guest rooms (four with en-suite facilities), with TV, tea/coffee making facilities and individually controlled central heating. The hotel has two bars and a restaurant where the chefs, Christine and Ian Holmes (who are also the owners) are members of the Scottish Chefs Association and provide good food based on fresh local produce. The hotel has a children's certificate and two of the double bedrooms can be adapted for families. Pets can be accommodated.

🛏 Four double, two twin-bedded rooms
£ ££
🍺 Orkney Red Macgregor plus two guest beers usually changed weekly
🍽 Snacks and meals daily, lunchtime and evening
CC accepted

—— ISLE OF WHITHORN ——

Steam Packet Inn

Harbour Row, Isle of Whithorn DG8 8LL
☎ *(01988) 500334*

Three of the guest bedrooms at the Steam Packet overlook the harbour of this popular sailing centre. Situated right on the quayside, of this busy little fishing port, the inn benefits from whatever seafood the day's catch brings in to put on the menu, which also features fresh game when available. Evening meals are served in the main restaurant upstairs, where booking is advised, but there is also a lower dining room which has a no-smoking area, and one of the two bars is sometimes pressed into service as an overflow eating area. A good range of bar snacks is available, too. This quaint inn, which boasts an unusual stone-clad bar, has a conservatory and a garden. Children are allowed in all parts of the establishment except the bar itself; there are reductions for children staying overnight. All the guest rooms have en-suite facilities; dogs can be accommodated. The village, which clusters around the bay, claims to be the spot where St Ninian landed before going on to Whithorn to found his church, thus bringing Christianity to Scotland. The Whithorn Dig can be visited to find out more about St Ninian and the history of this area, which is still relatively unspoiled – a haven for ornithologists and ramblers. The famous Logan Botanic Gardens are less than an hour's drive.

🛏 Three double, one twin-bedded and one family room
£ £
🍺 Theakston XB; guest beer
🍽 Snacks and meals daily, lunchtime and evening
CC accepted

—— KIPPFORD ——

Anchor Hotel
Kippford, Dalbeattie DG5 4LN
☎ *(01556) 620205*
Directions: at the southern end of the village

This attractive white-washed village pub stands opposite a busy yachting marina, and, naturally, is popular with yachtsmen. The Seafarers Bar, with its original fixtures and open fire, has a great atmosphere and attracts local and visiting mariners alike. There is also a lounge bar where good food, imaginatively produced from fresh ingredients, can be enjoyed in large portions (children's menu available). The pub has a children's certificate and, with full tummies, children can make use of the family room where the amusements include a pool table and TV. All of the well-appointed guest rooms have private bathrooms (apart from the single room), as well as Sky TV and tea/coffee making facilities. Ask for a room with a view – some overlook the marina and the Urr estuary. Additional bed and breakfast accommodation is available in a furnished house behind the hotel, which can also be let as a self-catering unit for a family or couples. It has its own garden, which is safe for children, with a barbecue. Two minutes away is a pebbly beach, or take the ten-minute walk to the village of Rockcliffe where there is a sandy alternative.

- ⊨ One single, three double, two twin-bedded and one family room
- £ ££ (single room, not en-suite £)
- ▄ Theakston Best Bitter; two guest beers
- ▮● Snacks and meals daily, lunchtime and evening
- CC accepted

—— KIRKCUDBRIGHT ——

Selkirk Arms Hotel
High Street, Kirkcudbright DG6 4JG
☎ *(01557) 330402;* FAX *(01557) 331639*
Directions: off the A75, between Stranraer and Castle Douglas

A four-star rating from the Scottish Tourist Board indicates the standard (and prices) to be expected at this charming hotel, where Burns reputedly wrote *Selkirk Grace* in 1794. Although it is obviously upmarket, the hotel nonetheless offers warm hospitality in a comfortable environment. Real ale, including a brew from the little local Sulwath Brewery, is on tap in the plush lounge, but will be brought through to the public bar on request. Food is available in the bar or in the award-winning 'Taste of Scotland' accredited restaurant which draws customers from near and far. The hotel has a children's certificate and the Burns Room offers good facilities for business or social functions. The 17 en-suite guest rooms are furnished and equipped to a high standard, to ensure a relaxing stay. All the rooms have TV, direct dial telephone, etc. Pets can be accommodated. Kircudbright is a quaint harbour town, situated on a rugged coastline which boasts some fine beaches, backed by heather-clad hills inland. An arts centre, museum, castle and marina can all be visited in the town itself, while the surrounding area offers many other facilities including pony-trekking, golf, bowling, tennis and hill walking.

- ⊨ Four single, six double, five twin-bedded and two family rooms
- £ £££ (££££ single room)
- ▄ Draught Bass; Sulwath Criffel; guest beers
- ▮● Snacks lunchtime, meals daily, lunchtime and evening
- CC accepted

—— MOFFAT ——

Balmoral Hotel

High Street, Moffat DG10 9DL
☎ *(01683) 220288;* FAX *(01683) 220451*
Directions: take the A701 off the A74

The Balmoral was built in the 18th century as a coaching inn, and has survived to become a popular family-run hotel. Among the attractions for visitors are the 18-hole golf course, and the lovely surrounding countryside, offering plenty of opportunities for walks and trout fishing. Glasgow, Edinburgh, Carlisle and Dumfries are all within an hour's drive of the hotel. Moffat stands in the picturesque Annan Valley – Burns Country (it is said that he used to drink at the Balmoral). This elegant town was once a spa, and its broad main street, where the Balmoral is to be found, is its most notable feature. The hotel has been upgraded since the first edition of this guide, and now all of its 14 rooms offer en-suite facilities, plus the usual amenities of TV and hospitality tray. Reasonably priced home-cooked food is served in both the olde-worlde style bar and the restaurant. The regular beers are usually complemented by up to three guest ales, plus Stowfords cider. Pets can be accommodated. The hotel has a secure car park.

🛏 Two single, six double, four twin-bedded and two family rooms
£ £
🍺 Broughton Greenmantle Ale; Caledonian 60/-; guest beers
🍴 Snacks and meals daily, lunchtime and evening
CC not accepted

—— NEWTON STEWART ——

Creebridge House Hotel

Minnigaff, Newton Stewart D98 6NP
☎ *(01671) 402121;* FAX *(01671) 403258*
Directions: off the A75 Stranraer-Dumfries road

Set in spacious grounds, this fine old country house was built in 1760 as the residence of the Earl of Galloway. Hardly a typical Scottish pub, it boasts a beamed cellar and delightful public rooms, including the homely Bridges Bar and elegant lounge. The kitchen is run personally by chef-cum-proprietor, Chris Walker, preparing award-winning food for the Garden Restaurant and the less formal Bridges Brasserie, based on the finest fresh local produce. The hotel bedrooms are all furnished to a high standard, offering en-suite accommodation with satellite TV, direct dial telephone and hospitality tray. There is a luxury suite, and some rooms with views over the hotel's delightful gardens and woodland. The Creebridge is well equipped for an active holiday – mountain bikes are available for guests to take advantage of the signposted routes through the forest, and golf can be arranged on one of the many courses nearby (you can tee off 400 yards from the hotel) – it is even less far to walk to the nearest salmon fishing stretch. The closest beach is 10 miles away and a slightly longer drive will take you to the famous gardens of Threave or Logan.

🛏 Two single, six double, eight twin-bedded and three family rooms
£ ££££
🍺 Black Sheep Best Bitter; Orkney Dark Island; Taylor Landlord;
   guest beer (occasionally)
🍴 Snacks and meals daily, lunchtime and evening
CC accepted

—— STRANRAER ——

George Hotel
George Street, Stranraer DG9 7RJ
☎ *(01776) 702487;* FAX *(01776) 702488*
Directions: in the town centre

Protected by the Mull of Galloway, this part of Scotland benefits from the mildest climate in the country, and Galloway boasts some of the most varied scenery in the whole of Britain. Stranraer, the major port for Irish ferries in Scotland, stands at the head of Loch Ryan (famed for its oysters). The George Hotel, within walking distance from the Harbour station, is a former coaching inn, built in the 1730s. The Miller family, who have owned it for the last 16 years, have taken care to renovate and update the hotel sympathetically. A single bar serves two lounges and the restaurant. Food is available all day. There is also a family room. The plentiful guest rooms range in size from smallish double rooms, to spacious rooms for families; none is specifically adapted to the needs of guests with disabilities, but some are large enough to accommodate a wheelchair. All have en-suite facilities. Pets can be accommodated.

🛏 Two single, six double, 18 twin-bedded and two family rooms
£ ££
🍺 Maclay Wallace IPA; Theakston Best Bitter; guest beer (occasionally)
🍴 Snacks and meals daily, at all times
CC accepted

TRY ALSO:

Solway Lodge Hotel
Annan Road, Gretna DG16 5DN
☎ *(01461) 338266;* FAX *(01461) 337791*

The majority of rooms here are motel-style, adjoining the hotel which is family run and has a friendly bar and restaurant. Ten en-suite rooms. B&B ££ (single occupancy £££)

FIFE: SEE CENTRAL SCOTLAND, FIFE & TAYSIDE

GRAMPIAN & THE HIGHLANDS

⸺ ABERDEEN ⸺

Atholl Hotel
54 Kings Gate, Aberdeen, Grampian AB15 4YN
☎ *(01224) 323505;* FAX *(01224) 321555*
Directions: off Anderson Drive at the junction of Forest Road

This impressive hotel, built from the sparkling granite for which the city is renowned, makes a distinctive landmark in Aberdeen's leafy West End. Although it has its own car park, the Atholl is equally convenient for public transport, with the railway station just a short taxi ride away – or ten minutes on the regular No. 23 bus service. It is also close to the city centre, and just five miles south of the airport. The traditional lounge bar is divided into an 'East' and 'West' end, and is decorated with scenes of Grampian landmarks. It draws a loyal local, predominantly middle-aged, clientele, and is popular for its good value bar food. The hotel is a member of the 'Taste of Scotland' campaign and offers traditional meals in the restaurant. All the guest rooms are en-suite, mostly with bath and shower (the single rooms just have a shower). They are all well equipped with TV, radio, telephone, trouser press and tea/coffee making facilities. The rates here are inclusive of breakfast and a morning paper. Children are well catered for; they are not allowed to remain in the bar after 8pm, but are welcome in the restaurant after that time, and can be accommodated overnight.

🛏 Six single, 18 double, ll family rooms
£ £££ (££££ single room or single occupancy of double room)
🍺 Two out of three regular beers: Courage Directors; Fuller's London Pride; Taylor Landlord, plus a guest beer
🍽 Snacks and meals daily, lunchtime and evening
CC accepted

Brentwood Hotel
101 Crown Street, Aberdeen, Grampian AB1 6HH
☎ *(01224) 595440;* FAX *(01224) 571593*
Directions: in the city centre, 300 yards from Union Street

The Brentwood is a smart, modern hotel where you'll find a traditional Scottish welcome. Carriages is the name given to its recently refurbished bar and brasserie, which, although generally busy, is nonetheless friendly and relaxed. Well-kept traditional ales (up to ten at any one time) are offered alongside specialist bottled continental beers. The excellent menu caters for a wide range of tastes, including vegetarians; there is also a children's menu. Like the public rooms, the guest rooms are modern and well equipped with TV, direct dial telephone and hospitality tray. All 64 rooms have en-suite facilities and there are two executive suites available. The bed and breakfast rates are considerably reduced at the weekend. Very centrally situated, the Brentwood is within walking distance of Aberdeen's theatres, cinemas and other nightlife, as well as being convenient for shoppers and business visitors.

🛏 17 single, 40 double, three twin-bedded, three family rooms and two suites
£ £££ (££££ single); weekends: £ (££ single)
🍺 Boddingtons Bitter; Caledonian Deuchars IPA; Castle Eden Ale, Courage Directors; Flowers Original; five guest beers
🍽 Meals daily, lunchtime (except Sunday) and evening
CC accepted

Palm Court Hotel

81 Seafield Road, Aberdeen, Grampian AB15 7YU
☎ *(01224) 310351;* FAX *(01224) 312707*
Directions: Seafield Road lies off the main Anderson Drive

Unfortunately, none of our recommendations in Aberdeen are suitable for those on a limited budget, although here again, you get a much better deal at the weekend. The Palm Court is another classy establishment (four-star rated by the Scottish Tourist Board) in a secluded position in the West End. Some of the public rooms are very grand, their high ceilings adding real style to what has been an excellent recent renovation. The beautiful conservatory (the real 'palm court') now houses the restaurant, serving meals based on fresh local produce prepared by award-winning chefs on a weekly changed menu. Nevertheless, the Palm Court does attract a friendly bunch of locals who come for the Scottish real ales and the big screen TV for major sporting events. This family-owned hotel also offers facilities for business and social functions. In keeping with the high standards of the rest of the establishment, the en-suite guest rooms are comfortably furnished and well appointed with Sky TV, direct dial telephone, trouser press, etc. Some rooms are suitable for guests with disabilities. Pets can be accommodated by arrangement. Just a mile from the hotel is Hazelhead Park which features a maze, two public golf courses, gardens and woodland walks, while both Drum Castle and Crathes Castle are within 12 miles.

🛏 Three single, 19 double, one twin-bedded and one family room
£ ££££
🍺 Caledonian 80/-; Tomintoul Stag plus a guest beer from Belhaven
🍴 Snacks and meals daily lunchtime and evening
CC accepted

—— ELGIN ——

Sunninghill Hotel

Hay Street, Elgin IV30 1NH
☎ *(01343) 547799;* FAX *(01343) 547872*
Directions: 200 yards from the railway station

Family-run, this solid stone hotel stands within easy walking distance of the station and town centre. It has a garden and a large car park. The historic cathedral city of Elgin makes an ideal base for touring the sunny Moray coast, and the Spey Valley. You can follow the Whisky Trail and visit distilleries open to the public such as Glenfiddich. The hotel's twelve guest rooms all have en-suite facilities and modern furnishings. They also have TV, radio alarm, hairdryer, direct dial telephone and hospitality tray. Most of the rooms are in the hotel's main building, but four are in a chalet annexe. Being on the ground floor, they may be suitable for visitors with disabilities, but are they have not been specifically adapted to their needs. Pets can be accommodated. Meals can be taken in the quiet, traditionally furnished bar or in the restaurant. A small function room is available for meetings.

🛏 Three singles, one double, five twin-bedded and three family rooms
£ ££ (single ££)
🍺 Ind Coope Burton Ale, plus up to four guest beers
🍴 Snacks and meals daily, lunchtime and evening
CC accepted

—— FINDHORN ——

Crown & Anchor
Findhorn IV36 0YF
☎/FAX *(01309) 690243*
Directions: off the A96, three miles from Forres

The Crown & Anchor was built in 1739 when Findhorn was a busy port and a staging post on the journey from Edinburgh to Inverness. These days its customers are more likely to be naturalists or watersports enthusiasts who come to enjoy picturesque Findhorn Bay, or visitors to the RAF's Kinloss airbase nearby. The Burrells run the pub as a free house and the range of real ales is complemented by a fair selection of bottled stouts and a bewildering array of whiskies. On the Whisky Trail, there is a Malt Whisky Visitor Centre at the pub which also provides a showcase for local crafts. The pub comprises two beamed bars: the public, replete with old prints and a cosy fireplace, is popular for traditional games, while the comfortable lounge has an area set aside for families. Children are made most welcome here (they are allowed in the bar until 9pm), and there is an enclosed garden for all to enjoy. Coffee and reasonably priced, home-cooked meals on a varied menu, including fresh seafood, are served throughout the day. All bar one of the pleasantly appointed bedrooms have en-suite bathrooms.

- ⊨ Four double, two twin-bedded and two family rooms
- £ ££
- ◖ Draught Bass; Orkney Dark Island; four guest beers
- ◉ Snacks and meals daily, at all times in summer and weekends in winter (winter weekdays, lunchtime and evening)
- CC accepted for accommodation

—— FOCHABERS ——

Gordon Arms Hotel
80 High Street, Fochabers IV32 7DH
☎ *(01343) 820508;* FAX *(01343) 820300*
Directions: Fochabers is on the A96, roughly midway between Aberdeen and Inverness

Many of the guests at the Gordon Arms come for the fishing – the River Spey being renowned for its salmon. Hotel staff help make arrangements for anglers and will give information about all kinds of other attractions, such as the nearby Whisky Trail, the many golf courses in the area and facilities for surfing and sailing at Findhorn. This 200-year-old hotel has two bars; the real ale is on tap in the public, favoured by the locals, but can be brought through to the lounge or dining room on request. The food here is highly recommended, using fresh local ingredients on a menu with a Highlands bias, featuring venison, lamb, game in season, Aberdeenshire beef and of course, local salmon. The en-suite guest rooms offer all the usual amenities including TV, hospitality tray, direct dial telephone and trouser press. Some rooms may be suitable for guests with disabilities. There is also a comfortable residents' lounge, which is sometimes used for business meetings. The hotel has a garden with a petanque (boules) pitch. Pets can be accommodated.

- ⊨ One single, four double, eight twin-bedded and one family room
- £ ££ – £££
- ◖ Caledonian Deuchars IPA; guest beers
- ◉ Snacks and meals daily lunchtime and evening
- CC accepted

—— FORRES ——

Carisbrooke Hotel

Drumduan Road, Forres, Moray IV36 0QT
☎ *(01309) 672582;* FAX *(01309) 672123*
Directions: half a mile off the A96 at the east end of the village

This is news to me, but apparently the district of Moray claims to be the 'Riviera of the North'. I imagine this is due to its mild and relatively warm climate, protected as it is from the wind by its surrounding hills. Certainly, it has enough attractions to compete with the Riviera, and as in France, the Forres town council make a point of beautifying their environment and has been consistently successful in the annual *Britain in Bloom* competition – visitors should not miss the stunning floral displays in Grant Park. Forres has its own golf course and visitors can join in the 'Moray for Golf' scheme which provides for one or two rounds on each of ten courses in the area. The Spey acts as a magnet to salmon fishers, as well as being the route of the Whisky Trail, since over 50 percent of the country's distilleries lie alongside the river' taking advantage of its unpolluted water. The Carisbrooke is a family-owned hotel, with two cosy, friendly bars – one has a games area, the other has a quieter atmosphere. Popular with locals and visitors alike, the pub has a garden where regular barbecues are held in summer. All the guest rooms offer en-suite accommodation, complete with satellite TV, direct dial telephones and tea/coffee making facilities. Children are welcome to stay.

- ⇆ 13 double rooms
- £ ££
- 🍺 Belhaven St Andrew's Ale; Boddingtons Bitter; Broughton Greenmantle Ale; Marston's Pedigree; Orkney Raven; Tomintoul Stage; guest beer
- 🍽 Snacks and meals daily, lunchtime and evening
- CC accepted

—— GAIRLOCH ——

Old Inn

Gairloch IV21 2BD
☎ *(01445) 712006;* FAX *(01445) 712445*
Directions: on the A832, at southern end of village, near the harbour

The Old Inn is popular with locals, but is busy all year round, too, with visitors who come to enjoy its beautiful Highland setting amidst lochs and mountains. Hill-walking, golf, swimming and boating are all possible locally, and children enjoy the lovely sandy beaches. The famous sub tropical gardens at Inverewe (seven miles) make a good day trip. The 14 guest rooms are all very comfortable and well appointed, with en-suite bath or shower, TV, telephone and tea/coffee making facilities. Two rooms on the ground floor may be suitable for guests with mobility problems, but they are not specially adapted for the disabled. Pets can be catered for. The food served in the bar and the dining room, is highly recommended. Meals are available at any time during opening hours in the high season. Its range of beers also makes the Old Inn a CAMRA favourite, with up to 12 real ales on tap in summer, and six in winter, predominantly from Scottish brewers.

- ⇆ One single, five double, five twin-bedded and three family rooms
- £ ££ – £££
- 🍺 Up to twelve real ales, changing regularly
- 🍽 Snacks and meals daily, lunchtime and evening (all day April-October)
- CC accepted

—— GLENCOE ——

Clachaig Inn
Glencoe, Ballachulish, Argyll PA39 4HX
☎ *(01855) 811252;* FAX *(01855) 811679*
Directions: just off the A82, on the old Glencoe road (behind NT Visitor Centre)

The Clachaig won CAMRA's coveted Scottish region *Pub of the Year* award in 1994, so you can be assured that the beers (some served by air pressure) are definitely up to scratch. Open all year (despite its isolated setting), it is a very popular local – not least because of its regular live music performances, but its overnight trade comes mainly from walkers and climbers. It runs courses and hosts lectures on mountain sports and safety. Apart from the guest rooms at the inn itself, there are also self-catering chalets to let on a weekly basis. The pub is around 300 years old, but has been well modernised to provide a high standard of accommodation; all but three of the guest rooms have en-suite bath or shower. Pets are accepted. There are two bars and a lounge with good mountain views; the big public bar is known as the Boots Bar where you can come straight in off the hills for a refreshing pint without worrying about getting changed and cleaned up first. The dining room serves good home-cooked meals to satisfy climbers' appetites. The inn enjoys not only a spectacular, but also an historic, setting, at the heart of Glencoe, site of the infamous massacre of the MacDonald clan in 1692.

⊨ Two singles, eight doubles, five twin-bedded and four family rooms
£ £ - ££
🍺 Beer range varies, usually Arrol's 80/- and Heather Fraoch Heather Ale, plus four guest beers
🍴 Snacks and meals daily, noon-9pm
CC accepted

—— INVERGARRY ——

Invergarry Hotel
Invergarry PH35 4HJ
☎ *(01809) 501206;* FAX *(01809) 501400*
Directions: on the A87, near the A82 jct

The Invergarry holds the only full on-licence in this tiny Highland village and serves a wide range of malt whiskies alongside real ales from Scottish independent breweries. The Victorian inn has been substantially modernised, but in a very traditional style: the public rooms feature William Morris wallpapers and dark wood furnishings. The fare is very traditional, too. Guests can choose porridge and kippers at breakfast time; evening meals in the dining room are mainly based around venison, salmon and other local specialities. There is also a self-service restaurant open throughout the day from Easter to October which offers more standard pub fare. The nine bedrooms are comfortably furnished; each has a private bathroom (some also have a shower), plus TV, hospitality tray, hairdryer and direct dial telephone. In addition, the hotel has a drying room for guests' use. Just seven miles from Loch Ness, it provides a good touring base and is popular with walkers and skiers. The hotel holds a children's certificate – youngsters are expected to leave the bar by 8pm.

⊨ One single, five double, two twin-bedded and one family room
£ ££
🍺 Isle of Skye Red Cuillin; guest beer (summer)
🍴 Snacks and meals daily, lunchtime and evening
CC accepted

—— ISLE OF SKYE ——

Sligachan Hotel

Sligachan, Isle of Skye IV47 6SW
☎ *(01478) 650204*
Directions: on the main A850 at the junction with the A863

Our only entry on this beautiful island stands at the head of a sea loch in the heart of the Cuillin Hills. The hills are a favourite with walkers and climbers, and so is this friendly, family-run hotel which dates from the 19th century. Very family oriented, it operates a creche in summer, and has a children's playroom, a garden and a children's certificate. The pub has a games room for adults to play in and hosts live entertainment some weekends in the summer months. It also stages a beer festival in April in October. The regular range in Seuma's Bar is already quite extensive, featuring ales from the island's own brewery alongside a changing list of guests – there's always seven beers on tap. Whisky lovers can choose from an impressive selection of some 70 single malts! The hotel serves good food, either in the bar or restaurant, and a full Scottish breakfast is provided. All but one of the guest rooms offers en-suite facilities. Pets can be accommodated by arrangement. Skye is very tourist-oriented these days, as needs must, but it is still easy to get away from the crowds and explore the wild coastline and rugged country-side. The hotel offers special winter breaks to tempt you out of season.

- ⋈   Four single, six double, ten twin-bedded and two family rooms
- £   £ – ££
- 🍺   Isle of Skye Young Pretender, Red Cullin, Black Cullin, Avalanche; guest beers
- 🍴   Snacks and meals daily, lunchtime and evening
- CC   accepted

—— KIRKTOWN ——

Glenisla Hotel

Kirkton of Glenisla, by Alyth, Grampian PH11 8PH
☎ *(01575) 582223;* FAX *(01575) 582203*
Directions: follow the A926 to Alyth (between Perth and Forfar), bypass Alyth and follow signs to Glenisla (12 miles) via the B954

Glenisla is a picturesque mountain valley, just 17 miles long, and 780 feet above sea level. The hotel stands a third of a way up the glen and has served travellers and local people for over 300 years. The inn has recently been renovated and refurbished with great flair and now offers warm, friendly hospitality. The simply furnished bar, with its heavily beamed ceiling, contrasts with the stylish, but comfortable drawing room, supplied with plentiful books and magazines, and elegant dining room. There is also a function hall, a games room and a large garden for guests to enjoy. The attractively furnished guest rooms each have their own individual char-acter, and all have en-suite bath or shower. Children are welcome to stay. The hotel specialis-es in good, fresh local produce, simply prepared. Meals are served in both the restaurant and the bar which offers real ales from the little independent Inveralmond Brewery (set up in Perth in 1997), and a good choice of malts. Places to visit include Glamis Castle, Balmoral and Dunkeld Cathedral. Perth and Dundee are both within an hour's drive of the hotel.

- ⋈   Six double/twin-bedded rooms
- £   ££ (£££ single occupancy)
- 🍺   Inveralmond Independence, Ossian, Lia Faill; guest beer (occasionally)
- 🍴   Snacks lunchtime; meals daily, lunchtime and evening
- CC   accepted

—— KIRKWALL ——

Albert Hotel
Mounthoolie Lane, Kirkwall, Orkney KW15 1JZ
☎ *(01856) 87600;* FAX *(01856) 875397*
Directions: 300 yards from the ferry terminal

The Bothy Bar at the Albert Hotel has two particularly noteworthy features, the first is its massive open fireplace and the second is the bar itself, which was renovated from blackened, seawormed wood taken from a Spanish galleon which sank in the bay just outside the town. The Bothy is the bar where the locals gather to sup the real ales produced by the island's own brewery; there is a second bar, plus a restaurant, the Stables. The hotel has quite a reputation for the quality of its food which comes in generous portions, and features locally caught seafood – the scallops are particularly recommended by our CAMRA members up there. The extensive menu is served both in the bar and restaurant. This friendly establishment caters for business and social functions, with conference and banqueting rooms available. The guest rooms are on the small side with modern furniture and amenities, equipped to the Scottish Tourist board's three-star standard. Children are welcome and pets can be accommodated by arrangement. Set in the heart of the old town, the Albert is convenient for the ferry terminal. Orkney's attractions include facilities for deep sea diving, birdwatching, angling and just exploring the island on foot, by bus or bicycle.

╼ Ten single, five double, three twin-bedded and two family rooms
£ £££
🍺 Orkney Raven, Dark Island
🍴 Snacks and meals daily, lunchtime and evening
CC accepted

—— MACDUFF ——

Knowes Hotel
78 Market Street, Macduff, Grampian AB44 1LL
☎ *(01261) 832229*
Directions: on the north coast, midway between Elgin and Fraserburgh

This family-run hotel at the centre of Macduff, boasts panoramic views over the Moray Firth. Its bar is quite small, indeed you may have to get in early if you are to beat the locals to the comfy chairs! Good quality bar food is available and the restaurant offers an extensive menu of over fifty main courses! The Knowes has six en-suite guest rooms which welcome families and some are suitable for guests with disabilities. Children may like to visit the aquarium in Macduff itself, whilst in nearby Banff (one mile), Duff House is the home of the Scottish National Portrait Gallery. The Royal Duff Golf course is also there, but you only have to step out of the hotel to be on the greens at the Tarlair golf course. Fishing, too, can be enjoyed practically on the hotel's doorstep.

╼ Three single, two double, one twin-bedded room
£ £ (££ single room)
🍺 Draught Bass; guest beer
🍴 Snacks and meals daily, lunchtime and evening
CC accepted

—— MARYCULTER ——

Old Mill Inn
South Deeside Road, Maryculter, Aberdeen AB12 5FX
☎ *(01224) 733212;* FAX *(01224) 732884*
Directions: on the B9077

At this delightful, family-run country inn by the River Dee, the owners aim to ensure the pub serves as a traditional local as well as offering comfortable, good value accommodation to visitors. Conveniently situated, just five miles from Aberdeen and the coast, it is a mile from the beauty spot of Storybook Glen. Rated three-star standard by the Scottish Tourist Board, the seven guest rooms all have en-suite bathrooms and the usual modern comforts. A full Scottish breakfast is provided and good quality main meals on an innovative menu, based on fresh local produce, are available at reasonable prices.

- 🛏 One single, five doubles, one family room
- £ ££ (single £££)
- 🍺 Draught Bass; Whitbread Fuggles Imperial IPA; guest beer (summer)
- 🍴 Snacks and meals daily, lunchtime and evening
- CC accepted

—— METHLICK ——

Gight House Hotel
Sunnybrae, Methlick, Grampian AB41 7BP
☎ *(01651) 806389;* FAX *(01651) 806577*
Directions: off the B9170

The Gight House, built as a manse on the outskirts of the village of Methlick, is now a small, friendly family-run hotel. This is a peaceful rural area, and the pub's relaxed atmosphere is much appreciated by the local farming community, as well as visitors who come for the fishing, shooting and golf in the vicinity. The NT's Fyvie Castle, Haddo House and Pitmedden Gardens are all within easy reach, and the hotel is well situated for the coastal route and the marked Highlands and Whisky Trails. Golf, fishing, clay pigeon shooting and pony trekking can all be enjoyed locally. Families are made very welcome here; the garden has an adventure play area, a putting green and a petanque pitch. Children's choices are available on an extensive menu, which is based on good quality local produce. Meals can be taken by the fire in the lounge bar or in either of the pleasant twin conservatories (where you could also, if you wished, get married!) which overlook the garden. The guest rooms are all well furnished and decorated to a high standard. Each has a private shower and WC, TV and hospitality tray. Children are charged at a reduced rate for accommodation. A cooked breakfast is provided.

- 🛏 Two doubles, one twin-bedded room
- £ £
- 🍺 Beer range varies
- 🍴 Snacks and meals daily, lunchtime and evening
- CC accepted

—— OLDMELDRUM ——

Redgarth

Kirk Brae, Oldmeldrum, Grampian AB51 0DJ
☎ *(01651) 872353*
Directions: off the A947, Aberdeen–Banff road

The three en-suite bedrooms at the Redgarth are all decorated in lovely fresh colours, with furnishings and fittings of a very high standard. This quality is reflected throughout the pub, as might be expected in a hostelry which is owned by a one-time CAMRA national *Pub of the Year* award-winner. The traditional bar offers well-kept real ales (some served by gravity), which can also be enjoyed in the garden in summer months. Both the bar and garden offer panoramic views of Bennachie and the surrounding countryside. Home-cooked meals, using only fresh produce, feature on a regularly changed menu, and there's always a vegetarian choice. Meals can be taken either in the lounge bar or the restaurant where overnight guests benefit from a discount on food, and there is also a discount on accommodation for stays of three nights or more. Oldmeldrum itself is a medieval market town, within easy reach of Aberdeen and the airport at Dyce. Not far from the hotel you can join the marked Castle Trail for an interesting car tour of the area. Guests are expected to uphold the no-smoking rule in the bedrooms, which have independent access. The accommodation is not suitable for children.

 Two double, one single room
£ **£ – ££**
 Beer range varies on three handpumps, most ales are changed after two days
 Snacks and meals daily, lunchtime and evening
CC accepted

—— STROMNESS ——

Stromness Hotel,

Victoria Street, Stromness, Orkney KW16 3AA
☎ *(01865) 850298;* FAX *(01865) 850610*
Directions: on the pier head

Our second entry for the island of Orkney stands in an enviable position, overlooking Scapa Flow and the harbour. The situation is put to good advantage at the hotel – by siting the Hamnavoe Lounge Bar on the first floor drinkers can enjoy a splendid view. In winter you may prefer the Flattie Bar, with its warm atmosphere and welcoming open fire. There is a cocktail bar for residents which offers a selection of over a hundred malt whiskies, including Highland Park, produced on the island. Informal meals can be taken in the bars, or diners can opt for the Valhalla Restaurant to partake of the menu which specialises in Highland produce. Recently refurbished throughout, the hotel offers a high standard of accommodation in its en-suite guest rooms including direct dial telephones, TV and tea/coffee making facilities. Children are accommodated at reduced rates, and pets can be catered for. There is a lift to all floors and private parking is provided. The hotel has a charming Victorian garden. Scapa Flow is renowned for its wrecks and in summer the Stromness is a popular choice for divers. In winter it becomes more of a local, with price promotions on the beer to tempt in the townspeople. A beer festival is held in September.

 Five single, 12 double, 17 twin-bedded and eight family rooms
£ **£££**
 Orkney Red MacGregor, Dark Island; guest beers
 Snacks and meals daily, lunchtime and evening
CC accepted

TRY ALSO:

Ferryhill House Hotel
169 Bonaccord Street, Aberdeen, Grampian AB1 2UA
☎ *(01224) 590867*

Standing in its own grounds, this city-centre hotel has ample parking. Eight rooms.
B&B £££

LOTHIAN: SEE THE BORDERS & LOTHIAN

BRITISH INSTITUTE *of* INNKEEPING
MEMBER
SETTING *professional* STANDARDS

All lovers of good pubs should keep an eye out for outlets bearing the British Institute of Innkeeping logo and membership plaques, as its aims are to promote high standards of professionalism in licensed retailing and to provide the skills, training and nationally recognised qualifications to help members run some of the best pubs in the country.

STRATHCLYDE

—— AYR ——

Chestnuts Hotel

52 Racecourse Road, Ayr KA7 2UZ
☎ *(01292) 264393*
Directions: on the A719, half a mile south of the town centre

The history of the Chestnuts, before it became established as an hotel in the 1970s, is fascinating. Built towards the end of the last century, it was owned in the 1890s by Captain Hunter-Blair, a Gordon Highlander, and it is said that the ghost which now haunts the hotel kitchen is that of one of his children. The house was first converted into a hotel in 1937 and was frequented during the Second World War by Jewish servicemen stationed locally. Ten years after the end of the war, it was bought by the Hebrew Society of Ayr who used part of the hotel as a synagogue. Now this elegant building (which has changed hands since our last edition) houses a comfortable lounge bar with a notable vaulted ceiling. Meals are served here and in the attractive restaurant. There is also a function room – called the Wedgwood Room because of its classic blue decor. The hotel has a children's certificate. All but one of the comfortable guest rooms have en-suite bathroom, plus TV, radio, direct dial telephone and a baby listening service – there is no designated family room, children are welcome to stay. Ayr is an important resort on the Clyde coast and has much to offer visitors, including Bellisle Park with two golf courses, and the Burns Heritage Trail.

- ⊨ Eight single, five double rooms
- £ **££ (£££** single room)
- ◗ Tetley Bitter, plus two weekly changed guest beers
- ◉ Snacks and meals daily, lunchtime and evening
- **CC** accepted

Old Racecourse Hotel

2 Victoria Park, Ayr KA7 2TP
☎/FAX *(01292) 262873*
Directions: on the A719, south of the centre

Ayr lies at the heart of Burns country – Scotland's favourite poet was born in 1759 in a thatched cottage at Alloway, two miles south of the centre. A museum adjoins the cottage and fans can also pay homage at the Burns memorial nearby. Ten miles further south at Kirkoswald, the home of Souter Johnnie has also been made into a museum. In the cottage garden a restored ale-house features stone figures of Johnnie and other characters immortalised in Burns' *Tam O'Shanter*. The Ayrshire coast is famed for its golf courses; Royal Troon and Prestwick are two of the best in the country. The Old Racecourse is an ideal base for golfers, tourists or anyone with business in Ayr. This warm, friendly hotel has an open, airy lounge bar where an unusual pot still-shaped fireplace is a central feature. The bar serves a good range of regularly changing guest beers. Bar meals are available, and there is a restaurant. Eight of the traditionally styled bedrooms have en-suite facilities and some are suitable for guests with disabilities. A good choice is on offer here for breakfast – a full Scottish version or the lighter continental option.

- ⊨ Three single, four double, two twin-bedded and three family rooms
- £ **££**
- ◗ Beer range varies
- ◉ Snacks and meals daily, lunchtime and evening
- **CC** accepted

—— BALLOCH ——

Balloch Hotel
Balloch Road, Balloch G83 8LQ
☎ *(01389) 752579;* FAX *(01389) 755604*

The landlord at the Balloch has won a clutch of glittering prizes, particularly for his cellar-manship, including joint national winner in 1996 of Allied Domecq's *Master Cellarcraft* award, as well as CAMRA's West of Scotland *Pub of the Year* award 1997, so you can be sure of a great pint! The beer is in fact only on tap in the lounge bar, but will be brought through to the public on request. Good quality meals are available at all times in both the bars, which, like many pubs in Scotland, keep late hours. The bars are open from 11am until midnight, and 1am on Friday and Saturday. The regular beer is complemented by three others, regularly changed, from the Allied Domecq/Carlsberg-Tetley list. This attractive hotel has a pleasant location by the source of the River Leven at the southern end of Loch Lomond, the largest freshwater lake in Britain. Some of the guest rooms benefit from views over the Loch, and all offer en-suite accommodation, rated three-star status by the Scottish Tourist Board. Pets are allowed into the guest rooms, but not in the public areas of the hotel.

- ⊨ Five single, five double, one twin-bedded and three family rooms
- £ ££ (£££ single room)
- 🍺 Ind Coope Burton Ale; guest beers
- 🍽 Snacks and meals daily, lunchtime and evening
- CC accepted

—— BRODICK ——

Ormidale Hotel
Knowe Road, Brodick, Isle of Arran KA27 8BY
☎ *(01770) 302293;* FAX *(01770) 302098*
Directions: take road opposite Brodick Golf Club, then first left after the church

Enjoying a splendid setting in ten acres of woodland, with lovely views over Goat Fell, this imposing Victorian sandstone building is just half a mile from both the centre of Brodick and the beach. Very popular in the holiday season, the hotel has nine guest rooms, and although none are en-suite, they represent good value for money. They all have TV and tea/coffee making facilities. Pets can be accommodated. Children are made very welcome here – the extensive beer garden includes a play area. Plenty of entertainment is laid on during the summer, including discos, folk evenings and quizzes. The hotel has a reputation for its home-cooked meals served in the bar, which extends into a large conservatory. The beers are supplied by the little independent Houston Brewery, just over on the mainland. The bar stays open throughout the year, but rooms are only available Easter-September. The island is a great place for active holidays, particularly golf; there are also facilities for pony trekking, fishing, and of course rambling.

- ⊨ Four single, two double, two twin-bedded and one family room
- £ £
- 🍺 Houston Killellan, Barochan; guest beer (occasionally)
- 🍽 Snacks and meals daily, lunchtime and evening
- CC accepted

—— CASTLECARY ——

Castlecary House Hotel

Main Street, Castlecary Village, Cumbernauld, near Glasgow G68 0HD
☎ *(01324) 840233;* FAX *(01324) 841608*
Directions: off the A80

The accommodation at the Castlecary is very stylish. All but five of the 55 rooms are built as individual 'cottages' set around the main hotel building, each with independent access. The cottages are rated 'standard', 'club' and 'executive' and are priced according to the facilities; rates are slightly reduced at the weekend. Children are welcome (0-12 years old are accommodated free and a cot can be provided; an additional bed costs £10 per night). Spacious, and attractively furnished, the cottages all have private bath or shower (one boasts a jacuzzi), direct dial telephone, TV, trouser press and tea making facilities. Some rooms may be suitable for guests with disabilities. Pets can be catered for. In addition, there are four single rooms (not en-suite) and a twin-bedded room in the main hotel which has three attractive bar areas, with much wood panelling in evidence in the decor. Most of the real ales (and traditional cider) are served in the Castle lounge. Light meals are served in all the bars, and there is a highly recommended dining room which serves good food, including high tea on Sunday (4–7pm). Castlecary in the Forth Valley stands on the site of one of the major forts on the Roman Antonine Wall, midway between Glasgow and Stirling, close to the M80.

⊨ Four single, 51 double/twin-bedded rooms
£ £ – ££
🍺 Draught Bass; Belhaven 70/-, 80/-, St Andrew's Ale; Caledonian Deuchars IPA, 80/-; guest beers
🍽 Snacks and meals daily, lunchtime and evening
CC accepted

—— COYLTON ——

Finlayson Arms Hotel

Hillhead, Coylton, Ayr KA6 6JT
☎/FAX *(01292) 570298*
Directions: on the A70, three miles east of Ayr

This attractive whitewashed hotel stands near the coast in an area known as a 'golfer's paradise'. Arrangements can be made by the hotel for you to play locally, whatever your level. If golf is not your favoured pastime, then salmon or sea fishing and hill walking are available locally and the racecourse at Ayr is easily accessible. For Burns fans, there are several literary pilgrimages to be made: his cottage at Alloway, the Batchelor's Club at Tarbolton and Poosie Nancy's Inn, noted for its association with *The Jolly Beggars*, lie nearby on the Burns Heritage Trail and are all within six miles of the hotel. This privately owned, two-star hotel has a public bar and a comfortable lounge with an open fire. Bar snacks are available and there is a reasonably priced dining room, serving traditional home cooking. The house ale is supplied by Broughton. All the guest rooms have en-suite shower, TV, telephone and tea/coffee maker. The hotel can accommodate guests with disabilities. Children are welcome to stay and pets can be catered for.

⊨ Nine twin bedded rooms
£ £
🍺 Broughton Greenmantle
🍽 Snacks and meals daily, lunchtime and evening
CC accepted

—— GOUROCK ——

Spinnaker Hotel
121 Albert Rad, Gourock PA19 1BU
☎ *(01475) 633107*
Directions: on the A770

The Spinnaker, situated on the main coastal road from Greenock, is a small family-run hotel. It benefits from spectacular views over the River Clyde to Kilcreggan, Dunoon and beyond. There are good local leisure facilities here, including the Waterfront Leisure complex and the McLean Museum and Art Gallery, all in Greenock (three miles). Gourock itself has a yacht club, and a park with sports facilities and a woodland walk. Eight miles away, the Finlaystone Estate is worth a visit for its gardens and Celtic art exhibition; Finlaystone house itself has connections with Robert Burns and John Knox. The hotel comprises an alcove bar and adjacent restaurant, plus an upstairs bar which is open at busy times, and can be hired for functions. Bar snacks and coffee are available all day. The guest accommodation, including a cooked breakfast, is good value. Six of the rooms have en-suite facilities, some may be suitable for guests with disabilities. Children are welcome.

🛏 Four single, one double, two twin-bedded and two family rooms
£ £
🍺 Belhaven 80/-; Houston Killellan, Barochan; guest beer
🍴 Snacks and meals daily, lunchtime and evening
CC accepted

—— INVERKIP ——

Inverkip Hotel
Main Street, Inverkip PA16 0AS
☎ *(01475) 521478;* FAX *(01475) 522065*
Directions: off the A78, near Kip Marina

Inverkip is a small, unspoilt village, with conservation status, on the Clyde coast, midway between Greenock and Largs. The hotel, in the centre of the village, is a former coaching inn. As well as offering hospitality to tourists and business visitors, it is a true village local, where the regulars encourage community spirit by organising outings, etc. Real ale, from Scottish breweries, is served in the welcoming lounge bar; if it gets crowded, take refuge in the two alcoves opposite which offer additional seating. There is a second bar and the recently added Inverkip Room for functions. An extensive menu of freshly prepared meals is served, with half portions often available for children, and a good vegetarian choice. All but one of the comfortable guest rooms has a private bathroom, and they all have TV and tea/coffee making equipment. Guests can make use of the water sports facilities at the excellent Kip Marina, just a stone's throw from the hotel.

🛏 One single, two double, one twin-bedded and one family room
£ ££
🍺 Caledonian 80/-; Houston Barochan; Orkney Dark Island; guest beer (occasionally)
🍴 Snacks and meals daily, lunchtime and evening
CC accepted

—— LOCH ECK ——

Coylet Hotel
Loch Eck, Argyll PA23 8SG
☎/FAX *(01369) 840426*
Directions: on the A815, nine miles north of Dunoon

This charming, family-run inn stands right on the shore of Lock Eck, and has been popular with holidaymakers for many years. A former coaching inn, it dates back to the 17th century. One of its attractions is the cosy bar where visitors can gather round an open log fire to discuss the day's catch after a fishing expedition, or just rest after exploring the surrounding hills and the spectacular Argyll Forest Park. Good bar food is based on fresh local produce and includes home-cooked daily specials. Children are welcome in the dining area and can be accommodated overnight. The guest rooms, which share bathroom facilities, are small, but comfortably appointed. A cooked breakfast is provided. Film buffs may recognise this as the setting for the film *The Blue Boy.* Boats can be hired and fishing permits obtained at the inn.

⊨ One single, two double, one twin-bedded room
£ £
🍺 Caledonian Deuchars IPA; McEwan 80/-; weekly guest beer
🍽 Snacks and meals daily, lunchtime and evening
CC accepted

—— UPLAWMOOR ——

Uplawmoor Hotel
Neilston road, Uplawmoor, Glasgow G78 4AF
☎ *(01505) 850565;* FAX *(01505) 850689*
Directions: just off the A736, Barrhead-Irvine road

This smart, privately owned hotel was built in the 18th century as a coaching inn, ten miles from Glasgow, and convenient nowadays for both Prestwick and Glasgow airports. Uplawmoor is a tranquil village, tucked away in the Renfrewshire hills, so is an ideal spot for people with business in Glasgow, but who would rather stay outside the city; there is ample parking. For tourists, the area offers the fine Burrell Collection, good golf courses, and access to Ayrshire's Burns Country. Paisley with its shops and old Abbey is just six miles away. The hotel has a comfortable lounge bar and a large airy cocktail bar where the central fireplace boasts an impressive copper canopy. The restaurant has been converted from an old barn and offers a cosy, cottagey atmosphere. Bar meals are also served in the lounge. The hotel's garden leads into the village park. The guest rooms are of a good standard (three star rated by the Scottish Tourist Board), with private bathrooms, TV, telephone and hospitality tray. Children are welcome; the family room can accommodate up to five people.

⊨ One single, nine double, three twin-bedded and one family room
£ ££
🍺 Draught Bass; Orkney Dark Island
🍽 Snacks and meals daily, lunchtime and evening
CC accepted

TAYSIDE: SEE CENTRAL SCOTLAND, FIFE & TAYSIDE

What CAMRA does for you

• All CAMRA members receive our monthly newspaper, What's Brewing. It gives hard news from the world of beer and pubs – advance notice of festivals and events as well as information about new beers and breweries.
• We sell a wide range of books, including local guides – you'll find a list of national titles at the end of this book. Ring the CAMRA HQ telephone number to enquire about local publications.
• CAMRA branches run beer festivals, brewery trips, pub visits and other social activities.

Members of CAMRA are ordinary drinkers motivated solely by a love of good beer – they are all ages, both sexes, and from all walks of life.

Join today

You're welcome to get involved.
CAMRA has been called 'Europe's most successful consumer organisation' – but we still need your help.
CAMRA is run locally and nationally by elected, unpaid volunteers.
CAMRA is a not-for-profit body and is completely independent of any commercial interest.
CAMRA relies totally on people like you for funds and support.
Help us stand up for the rights and choice of ordinary drinkers.

You will find a subscription form at the end of this book. It's only £14 for a single subscription and there are discounts for young people, over 65 and joint subscriptions.

OFFSHORE BRITAIN

CHANNEL ISLANDS

── GUERNSEY ──

Captains Hotel

La Fosse, St Martins, Guernsey GY4 6EF
☎ *(01481) 38990;* FAX *(01481) 39312*
Directions: take the main road through St Martins and turn right at the supermarket; the hotel is two minutes' drive

Completely refurbished in the last few years, the Captains Hotel has a spacious bar (serving the island's own real ale from an impressive beer engine), a dining room and a secluded south facing garden. It boasts an excellent reputation for its cuisine, with fresh locally caught fish a speciality. The Bistro restaurant is open every evening in season, whilst the Upper Deck is a new addition, opened in 1998, to serve pizzas and pasta. The hotel enjoys a thriving local trade, as well as offering nine guest rooms to visitors. All en-suite, the rooms all have TV, radio and tea/coffee making facilities. Pets can be accommodated and bed and breakfast is cheaper in winter than in summer. Guernsey, of course, is a perennially popular holiday destination, and this hotel is situated in the wooded lanes of rural St Martins, a very pretty area, ideal for cycling and walking. It is just a few minutes' on foot to the south coast and the sandy bays of Cobo, Vazon and L' Ancresse. Moulin Huet Bay, with its well-known pottery is worth a visit. The bustling capital, St Peter Port, is accessible by car or a 15-minute bus ride (service direct to the hotel).

🛏 One single, three double, four twin-bedded and one family room
£ ££
🍺 Guernsey Sunbeam
🍽 Snacks and meals daily, lunchtime and evening
CC accepted

Chandlers Hotel

Braye Road, Vale, Guernsey
☎ *(01481) 44280;* FAX *(01481) 411671*

Chandlers is a family-run hotel situated in the north of the island, close to l'Ancresse beach and St Sampsons harbour. There are good local shopping facilities and a choice of restaurants in the vicinity, plus a golf course nearby. The hotel's cosy lounge contrasts with the lively public bar, favoured by the locals. The real ale is supplied by Randalls Brewery on the island. The function room upstairs hosts frequent live music and the newly-built skittle alley is a popular feature. The pub offers other traditional games, such as shove-ha'penny. A good value bar menu features Thai cuisine and imaginative 'specials'. The guest rooms, which are rated two-star by the island's tourist board, are all en-suite and have TV and tea/coffee making facilities. Children are welcome and pets can be accommodated. A full English breakfast is served in the separate breakfast room. The rates are reduced in winter. The hotel has a garden.

🛏 One single, five double, eight twin-bedded and one family room
£ ££ (£ low season)
🍺 Randalls Patois Ale
🍽 Snacks and meals daily, lunchtime and evening
CC accepted

Hotel Fleur du Jardin

Kings Mills, Castel, Guernsey GY5 7JT
☎ *(01481) 57996;* FAX *(01481) 56834*
Directions: in Kings Mills village

This stone-built country house hotel, dating from the 15th century, is just one of the lovely old buildings in the pretty village of Kings Mills. Roughly a mile inland from some of the island's best beaches in Vazon Bay, the village is on a bus route, or you may prefer to get around on a hired bicycle. The Fleur has been well modernised in sympathy with its original farmhouse character. It features has some unusually shaped rooms, thick granite walls, exposed beams and low ceilings (mind your head in the bar). The 17 guest rooms are all en-suite and attractively decorated and furnished. They all have direct dial telephone, TV, hairdryer and hospitality tray. Local people favour the lounge bar for meals, but there is also a characterful, award-winning restaurant, specialising in fresh fish and seafood on a changing menu of seasonal specials. The hotel has very well-tended sheltered gardens, ideal for summer meals, with a play area and a solar heated swimming pool exclusively for the use of residents. It is popular with families who are made very welcome. A full English breakfast is served. The bed and breakfast rates are reduced in winter.

- Three double, ten twin-bedded and four family rooms
- £ ££ – £££ (according to season)
- Guernsey Sunbeam, seasonal beers
- Snacks and meals daily, lunchtime and evening
- **CC** accepted

—— JERSEY ——

Anne Port Bay Hotel

Gorey, Jersey JE3 6DT
☎ *(01534) 852058;* FAX *(01534) 857887*
Directions: on the first bay north of Gorey on the east coast

BRITISH INSTITUTE *of* INNKEEPING
MEMBER
SETTING *professional* STANDARDS

Owned and run by a local family, the Caveys, this hotel stands in a peaceful spot on an unspoilt bay on the east coast of the island. It overlooks France and trips there, or to the other Channel Isles, can be arranged in season. The homely atmosphere makes it popular with locals and visitors alike. The hotel has a lounge bar, a residents' sitting room and a dining room (evening meals are available to residents only). The beers are served direct from the cask. All 14 guest rooms have en-suite shower and WC, TV, radio and tea/coffee making facilities. They are simply furnished but do represent good value for the island. Children aged three–11 sharing a parent's room are charged half price; over twelves are charged the adult price. Very reasonable half board rates are also available (bed, breakfast and evening meal). Car and cycle hire can be arranged locally. Within easy reach are the 13th-century Mont Orgueil Castle, Gorey Harbour and the Jersey Potteries. The Royal Jersey Golf Course is also nearby and the beach, which is sandy and safe for bathing, is only a couple of minutes' walk. There is a frequent bus service to Gorey and the island's capital, St Helier.

- Two single, 12 double rooms
- £ £ (single room ££ in high season)
- Draught Bass; Marston's Pedigree
- Snacks daily, lunchtime; evening meals for residents
- **CC** accepted

ISLE OF MAN

—— SULBY ——

Sulby Glen Hotel
Sulby Crossroads, Sulby IM7 2HR
☎/FAX *(01624) 897240*
Directions: on the Sulby straight of the TT course

At the entrance to Sulby Glen, this hotel benefits from uninterrupted views of the valley and mountains and has good opportunities for fishing. Other attractions include the nearby Curraghs Wildlife Park and the golf course at Ramsey (three miles), which also has good shopping facilities. The hotel stands right on the fastest stretch of the famous TT course and, during the race fortnight, it puts up a large beer tent and entertains the crowds with live music nightly. A typical Manx pub, where a friendly welcome is assured, its public and guest rooms are simply furnished. The main bar features displays of TT memorabilia and offers pool and darts, while the residents' lounge has a TV. Lunch and evening meals are served in the dining room, while snacks and hot drinks are available at any time. The choice on the breakfast menu includes Manx kippers. Three of the eleven rooms have en-suite facilities and all have a TV and hospitality tray. Children are welcome to stay, although there are no special amenities for them. The 'Sulby Giant', who grew to be eight feet two inches tall, was born in the house next door to the hotel. Inclusive holidays by sea or air can be arranged by the hotel. Contact the owner, Mrs Rosemary Sayle for details.

🛏 Two single, three double, and six twin bedded rooms
£ £
🍺 Bushy's Bitter; Highgate Mild; Okells Bitter; two guest beers
🍴 Snacks and meals daily, lunchtime and evening
CC accepted

MAPS

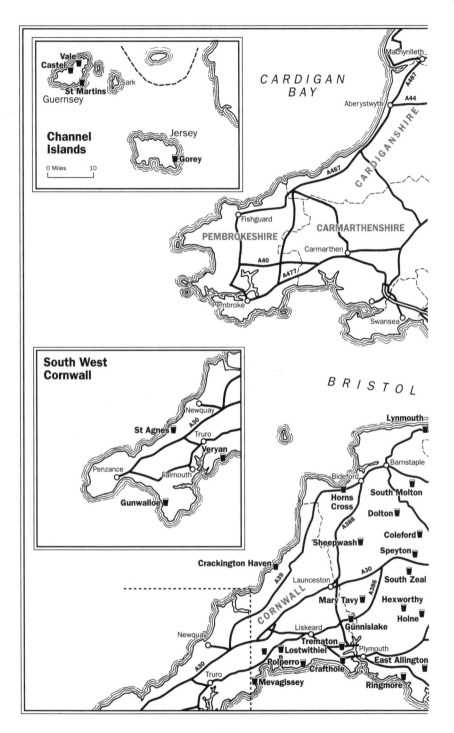

Channel Islands

Vale
Castel
St Martins
Guernsey
Sark
Jersey
Gorey

0 Miles 10

CARDIGAN BAY

Machynlleth
A487
A44
Aberystwyth
CARDIGANSHIRE
A487
Fishguard
PEMBROKESHIRE
CARMARTHENSHIRE
Carmarthen
A40
A471
Pembroke
Swansea

South West Cornwall

Newquay
St Agnes
A30
Truro
Veryan
Penzance
Falmouth
Gunwalloe

BRISTOL

Lynmouth
Barnstaple
Bideford
South Molton
Horns Cross
Dolton
Coleford
Sheepwash
Speyton
Crackington Haven
A39
Launceston
A30
South Zeal
A386
Mary Tavy
Hexworthy
Holne
Gunnislake
Liskeard
Newquay
CORNWALL
Trematon
Lostwithiel
Plymouth
Polperro
Crafthole
East Allington
A30
Truro
Mevagissey
Ringmore

304

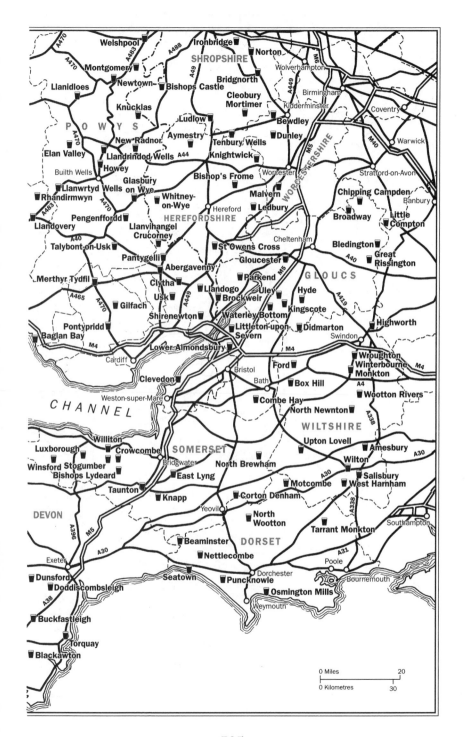

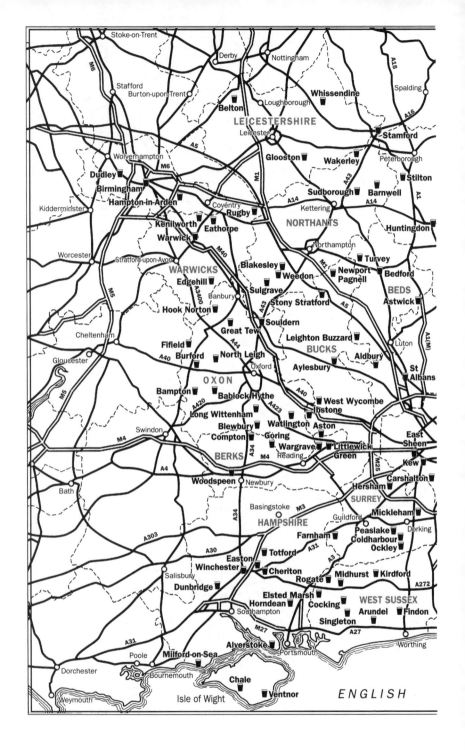

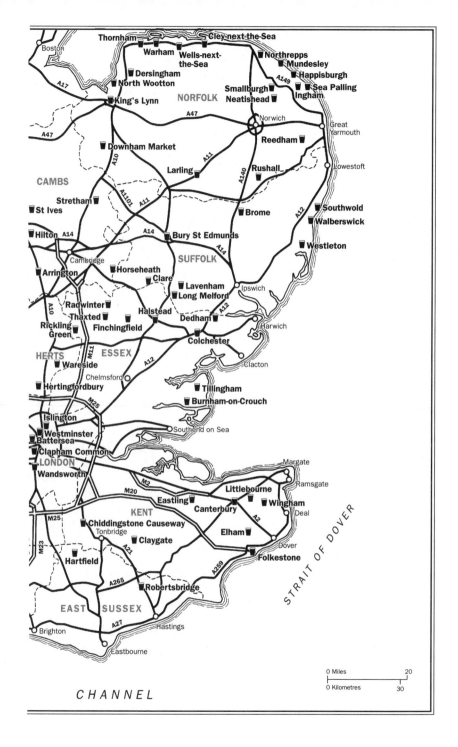

Boston
Thornham
Cley-next-the-Sea
Warham
Wells-next-the-Sea
Northrepps
Mundesley
Dersingham
Happisburgh
North Wootton
Sea Palling
Smallburgh
Ingham
Neatishead
King's Lynn
NORFOLK
A17
A149
A47
Norwich
Great Yarmouth
A47
Reedham
Downham Market
Lowestoft
A10
A11
Larling
Rushall
CAMBS
A140
Stretham
St Ives
A1101
A11
Brome
Southwold
Walberswick
Hilton
A14
A14
Bury St Edmunds
Westleton
Cambridge
SUFFOLK
A14
Horseheath
Arrington
Clare
Lavenham
Ipswich
Radwinter
Long Melford
A12
A10
Thaxted
Halstead
A12
Rickling Green
Finchingfield
Dedham
Harwich
Colchester
HERTS
ESSEX
M11
Wareside
Clacton
A12
Chelmsford
Hertingfordbury
Tillingham
M25
Burnham-on-Crouch
Islington
Westminster
Battersea
Clapham Common
Southend on Sea
LONDON
Wandsworth
Margate
M2
Ramsgate
M20
Littlebourne
Eastling
Wingham
Canterbury
Deal
KENT
A2
M25
Chiddingstone Causeway
Elham
M23
Tonbridge
Claygate
A21
Dover
Hartfield
Folkestone
A259
A265
STRAIT OF DOVER
Robertsbridge
EAST SUSSEX
A27
Brighton
Hastings
Eastbourne

CHANNEL

0 Miles 20
0 Kilometres 30

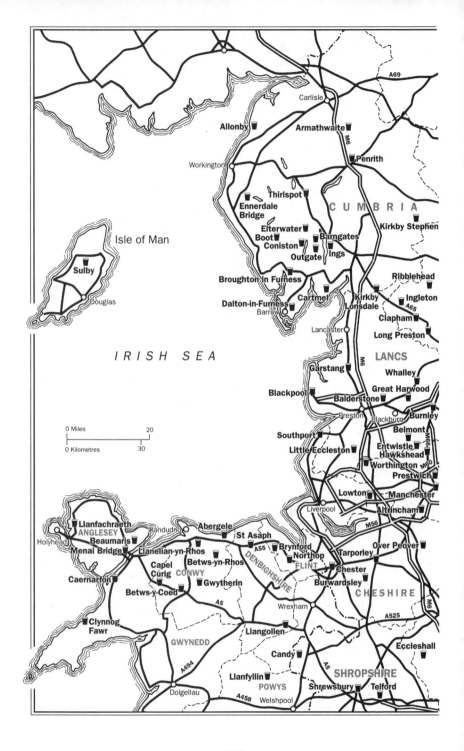

Isle of Man

Sulby

Douglas

I R I S H   S E A

0 Miles 20
0 Kilometres 30

Carlisle
A69
Allonby
Armathwaite
M6
Penrith
Workington
Thirlspot
Ennerdale Bridge
C U M B R I A
Elterwater
Kirkby Stephen
Boot
Barngates
Coniston
Outgate
Ings
Ribblehead
Broughton in Furness
Ingleton
A65
Dalton-in-Furness
Cartmel
Kirkby Lonsdale
Clapham
Barrow
Lancaster
Long Preston
LANCS
Garstang
Whalley
Blackpool
Great Harwood
Balderstone
Preston
Blackburn
Burnley
Southport
Belmont
Little Eccleston
Entwistle
Hawkshead
Worthington
M60
Prestwich
M66
Lowton
Manchester
Liverpool
Altrincham
M56
Llanfachraeth
ANGLESEY
Llandudno
Abergele
St Asaph
Over Peover
Beaumaris
Llanelian-yn-Rhos
A55
Brynford
Menai Bridge
Betws-yn-Rhos
Northop
Tarporley
Holyhead
Capel Curig
DENBIGHSHIRE
FLINT
Chester
Caernarfon
CONWY
Gwytherin
Burwardsley
CHESHIRE
Betws-y-Coed
A5
M6
Wrexham
Clynnog Fawr
Llangollen
A525
Eccleshall
GWYNEDD
Candy
A494
Llanfyllin
Shrewsbury
Telford
Dolgellau
POWYS
SHROPSHIRE
A5
A458
Welshpool

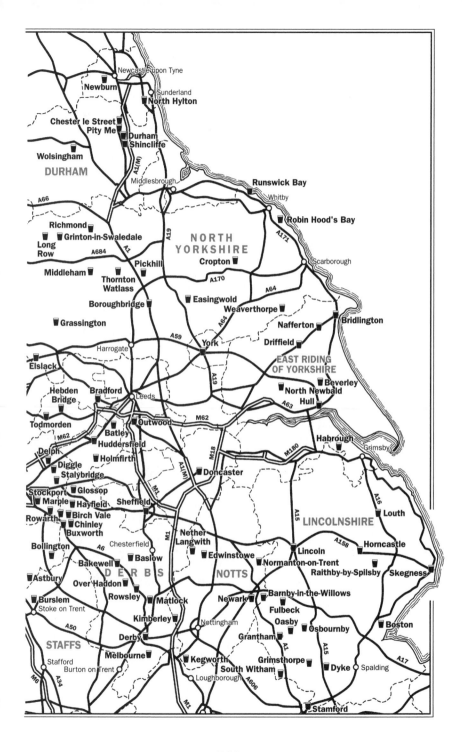

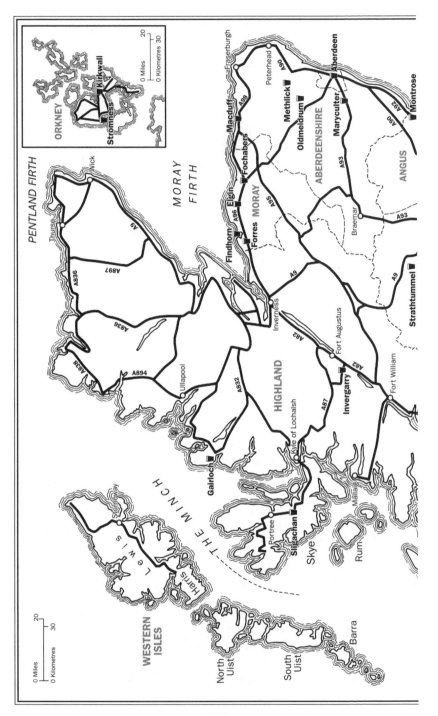

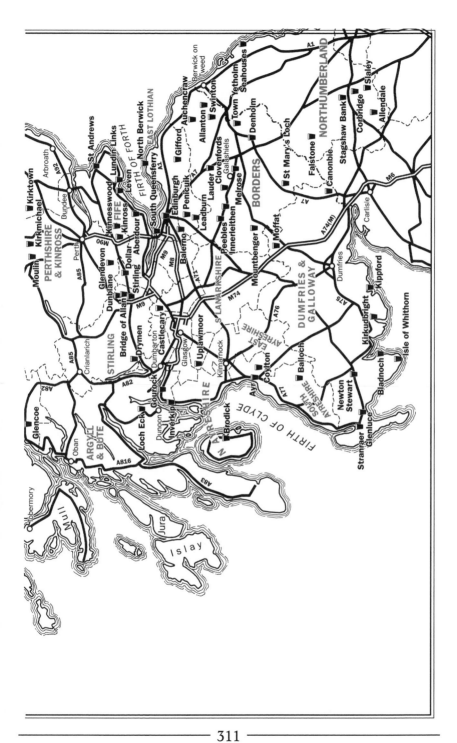

JOIN CAMRA

If you like good beer and good pubs you could be helping to fight to preserve, protect and promote them. CAMRA was set up in the early seventies to fight against the mass destruction of a part of Britain's heritage. The giant brewers are still pushing through takeovers, mergers and closures of their smaller regional rivals. They are still trying to impose national brands of beer and lager on their customers whether they like it or not, and they are still closing down town and village pubs or converting them into grotesque 'theme' pubs.

CAMRA wants to see genuine free competition in the brewing industry, fair prices, and, above all, a top quality product brewed by local breweries in accordance with local tastes, and served in pubs that maintain the best features of a tradition that goes back centuries.

As a CAMRA member you will be able to enjoy generous discounts on CAMRA products and receive the highly rated monthly newspaper What's Brewing. You will be given the CAMRA members' handbook and be able to join in local social events and brewery trips.

To join, complete the form below and, if you wish, arrange for direct debit payments by filling in the form overleaf and returning it to CAMRA. To pay by credit card, contact the membership secretary on (01727) 867201.

I/We wish to join the Campaign for Real Ale and agree to abide by the Rules.

Name(s) ……………………………………………………………………

…………………………………………………………………………………

Address ……………………………………………………………………

………………………………………………………Postcode………………

Signature ………………………………………Date…………………

I/We enclose the remittance for:

Single:	£14	Joint	£17	(at same address)
OAP Single	£8	OAP Joint	£11	(at same address)
Unemployed/Disabled	£8			
Under 26	£8	date of birth:		

For Life and Overseas rates please contact CAMRA HQ
(tel: 01727 867201
Send you remittance (payable to CAMRA) to:
The Membership Secretary, CAMRA, 230 Hatfield Road, St Albans, Herts., AL1 4LW

Instruction to your Bank or Building Society to pay by Direct Debit

Please fill in the whole form using a ball point pen and send it to:

Campaign for Real Ale Ltd,
230 Hatfield Road,
St. Albans,
Herts
AL1 4LW

Originator's Identification Number

| 9 | 2 | 6 | 1 | 2 | 9 |

Reference Number

| | | | | | | | | | | | | | | | | |

Name of Account Holder(s)

_____

FOR CAMRA OFFICIAL USE ONLY
This is not part of the instruction to your Bank or Building Society

Membership Number

Name

Postcode

Bank/Building Society account number

| | | | | | | |

Branch Sort Code

| | | | | |

Instructions to your Bank or Building Society
Please pay CAMRA Direct Debits from the account detailed on this instruction subject to the safeguards assured by the Direct Debit Guarantee. I understand that this instruction may remain with CAMRA and, if so, will be passed electronically to my Bank/Building Society

Name and full postal address of your Bank or Building Society

To The Manager   Bank/Building Society

Address

Postcode

Signature(s)

Date

Banks and Building Societies may not accept Direct Debit instructions for some types of account

- - - ✂ -

This guarantee should be detached and retained by the Payer.

The Direct Debit Guarantee

■ This Guarantee is offered by all Banks and Building Societies that take part in the Direct Debit Scheme. The efficiency and security of the Scheme is monited and protected by your own Bank or Building Society.

■ If the amounts to be paid or the payment dates change CAMRA will notify you 10 working days in advance of your account being debited or as otherwise agreed.

■ If an error is made by CAMRA or your Bank or Building Society, you are guaranteed a full and immediate refund from your branch of the amount paid.

■ You can cancel a Direct Debit at any time by writing to your Bank or Building Society. Please also send a copy of your letter to us.

CAMRA BOOKS

The CAMRA Books range of guides helps you search out the best in beer (and cider) and brew it at home too!

BUYING IN THE UK

All our books are available through bookshops in the UK. If you can't find a book, simply order it from your bookshop using the ISBN number, title and author details given below. CAMRA members should refer to their regular monthly newspaper *What's Brewing* for the latest details and member special offers. CAMRA books are also available by mail-order (postage free) from: CAMRA Books, 230 Hatfield Road, St Albans, Herts, AL1 4LW. Cheques made payable to CAMRA Ltd. Telephone your credit card order on 01727 867201.

BUYING OUTSIDE THE UK

CAMRA books are also sold in many book and beer outlets in the USA and other English-speaking countries. If you have trouble locating a particular book, use the details below to order by mail or fax (+44 1727 867670).

Carriage of £3.00 per book (Europe) and £6.00 per book (US, Australia, New Zealand and other overseas) is charged.

UK BOOKSELLERS

Call CAMRA Books for distribution details and book list. CAMRA Books are listed on all major CD-ROM book lists and on our Internet site: http://www.camra.org.uk

OVERSEAS BOOKSELLERS

Call or fax CAMRA Books for details of local distributors. Distributors are required for some English language territories. Rights enquiries (for non-English language editions) should be addressed to the managing editor.

CAMRA GUIDES

Painstakingly researched and checked, these guides are the leaders in their field, bringing you to the door of pubs which serve real ale and more...

GOOD PUB FOOD 5TH EDITION

by Susan Nowak
448 pages approx   Price: £9.99

The pubs in these pages serve food as original and exciting as anything available in far more expensive restaurants. And, as well as the exotic and unusual, you will find landlords and landladies serving simple, nourishing pub fare such as a genuine ploughman's lunch or a steak and kidney pudding.

You'll discover cooking from a new wave of young chefs who would prefer to run a pub than a restaurant. Many pubs are producing the traditional dishes of their regions, building smokeries, keeping cattle and goats, growing vegetables and herbs, creating vibrant, modern cuisine from fresh ingredients. Recipes from some of them are dotted about this guide so you can try them at home.

Award-winning food and beer writer Susan Nowak, who has travelled the country to complete this fifth edition of the guide, says that 'eating out' started in British inns and taverns and this guide is a contribution to an appreciation of all that is best in British food...and real cask conditioned ale.

Use the following code to order this book from your bookshop: ISBN 1-85249-151-5

HERITAGE PUBS OF GREAT BRITAIN

by Mark Bolton and James Belsey
144 pages hard back   Price: £16.99

It is still possible to enjoy real ale in sight of great craftsmanship and skill. What finer legacy for today's drinkers? Feast your eyes and toast the architects and builders from times past. This full colour collectible is a photographic record of some of the finest pub interiors in Britain. Many of the pubs included have been chosen from CAMRA's national inventory of pub interiors which should be saved at all costs. As a collector's item. As such it is presented on heavy, gloss-art paper in a sleeved hard back format. Delve deep into the history of the British pub through the interiors which must never be lost, each one unique, stunning to the eye, and yet a place to gather for ordinary citizens. The pub interiors have been photographed by architectural specialist Mark Bolton and described in words by pub expert James Belsey.

Use the following code to order this book from your bookshop: ISBN 1-85249-146-9

PUBS FOR FAMILIES

by David Perrott
308 pages   Price: £8.99
Traditional pubs with CAMRA-approved ale and a warm welcome for the kids! Nothing could be better. But where to find such a hospitable hostel on home patch, let alone when out and about or on holiday? This guide is the adult answer to your eating and drinking requirements, with facilities for your children too! Invaluable national coverage with easy to use symbols so that you know what facilities are available and regional maps so you'll know how to get there. Get the best of both worlds.
Use the following code to order this book from your bookshop: ISBN 1-85249-141-8

50 GREAT PUB CRAWLS

by Barrie Pepper
256 pages   Price: £9.99
Visit the beer trails of the UK, from town centre walks, to hikes and bikes and a crawl on a train on which the pubs are even situated on your side of the track!
Barrie Pepper, with contributions and recommendations from CAMRA branches, has compiled a 'must do' list of pub crawls, with easy to use colour maps to guide you, notes on architecture, history and brewing tradition to entertain you. All you have to do is to move your legs and arms! A great way to discover the pubs of Britain. Use it well and we'll make it the first of a series.
Use the following code to order this book from your bookshop: ISBN 1-85249-142-6

GOOD BEER GUIDES

These are comprehensive guides researched by professional beer writers and CAMRA enthusiasts. Use these guides to find the best beer on your travels or to plan your itinerary for the finest drinking. Travel and accommodation information, plus maps, help you on your way and there's plenty to read about the history of brewing, the beer styles and the local cuisine to back up the entries for bars and beverages.

GOOD BEER GUIDE TO BELGIUM, HOLLAND AND LUXEMBOURG

by Tim Webb
286 pages   Price: £9.99
Discover the stunning range and variety of beers available in the Low Countries, our even nearer neighbours via Le Tunnel. There are such revered styles as Trappist Ales, fruit beers, wheat beers and the lambic and

gueuze specialities made by the centuries-old method of spontaneous fermentation.

Channel-hopping Tim Webb's latest edition – the third – of the guide offers even more bars in which an incredible array of beers can be enjoyed. If you are going on holiday to this region then you'll find details of travel, accommodation, food, beer museums, brewery visits and festivals, as well as guides to the cafés, beer shops and warehouses you can visit. There are maps, tasting notes, beer style guide and a beers index to complete the most comprehensive companion to drinking with your Belgian and Dutch hosts.

Use the following code to order this book from your bookshop: ISBN 1-85249-139-6

GOOD BEER GUIDE TO NORTHERN FRANCE
by Arthur Taylor
256 pages   Price: £7.99

Discover the excitement of the bars and cafes, the tranquillity of the village breweries which hold the secrets of generations of traditional brewing. Join the many festivals and cultural events such as the beer-refreshed second-hand market in Lille and the presentation of the Christmas ales. Find out where the best beer meets the best mussels and chips. Cuisine a la bière and more! Arthur Taylor is a leading authority on French beer and a member of Les Amis de la Bière, who have co-operated in the research for this book.

Use the following code to order this book from your bookshop: ISBN 1-85249-140-X

GOOD BOTTLED BEER GUIDE
by Jeff Evans
128 pages   Price: £9.99

When early nights and unfriendly traffic conspire to keep you at home, there's no risk these days of missing out on drinking a fine real ale. Britain's off-licences and supermarkets now stock bottle-conditioned ales – real ale in a bottle. The book describes the ingredients and history behind Britain's traditional bottled beer, and conjures up the tastes and smells.

Bottle-conditioned beers, such as Shepherd Neame Spitfire and Marstons Oyster Stout, contain yeast and continue to mature in the bottle for a fuller, fresher taste, just as real ales mature in the cask at the pub. Discover the seasonal Christmas ales, Millennium Ale, porters and stouts. Find out who brews the supermarket own-brands and check the many varieties of hops and malts in the pale ales, milds and barley wines.

Use the following code to order this book from your bookshop: ISBN 1-85249-147-7

GOOD BEER GUIDE

edited by Roger Protz

500 pages approx   Price: £10.99   Produced annually in October

Fancy a pint? Let CAMRA's Good Beer Guide lead the way. Revised each year to include around 5,000 great pubs serving excellent ale – country pubs, town pubs and pubs by the sea.

The guide includes information about meals, accommodation, family rooms, no-smoking areas and much more.

Fully and freshly researched by members of the Campaign for Real Ale, real enthusiasts who use the pubs week in, week out. No payment is ever taken for inclusion. The guide has location maps for each county and you can read full details of all Britain's breweries (big and small) and the ales they produce, including tasting notes.

CAMRA's Good Beer Guide is still Britain's best value pub guide – a must for anyone who loves beer and pubs.

CELLARMANSHIP

by Ivor Clissold

144 pages   Price: £6.99

This book explains every aspect of running a good cellar and serving a great pint of real ale which does both pub and brewer proud. It's a must have book for all professionals in the drinks trade, for all those studying at college to join it, and for all those who need to tap a cask of real ale for a party.

The CAMRA Guide to Cellarmanship is the only manual dealing with the care of all cask beers. It draws together information previously only known within certain breweries, and adds valuable experience from hundreds of cellar and technical staff.

Farmers, hop growers, maltsters, brewers and drayers all play their part to produce and deliver our great British drink but too often it falls at the last fence: indifferent cellar and bar management – especially in the face of an unknown guest beer – can turn a treat into a tragedy.

Use the following code to order this book from your bookshop: ISBN 1-85249-126-4

BREW YOUR OWN

Learn the basics of brewing real ales at home from the experts. And then move on to more ambitious recipes which imitate well-loved ales from the UK and Europe.

BREW YOUR OWN REAL ALE AT HOME
by Graham Wheeler and Roger Protz
194 pages   Price: £8.99
This book is a treasure chest for all real ale fans and home brew enthusiasts. It contains recipes which allow you to replicate some famous cask-conditioned beers at home or to customise brews to your own particular taste. The authors have examined the ingredients and brewing styles of well-known ales and have gleaned important information from brewers, with and without their co-operation. Computer-aided guesswork and an expert palate have filled in the gaps where the brewers would reveal no more.

As well as the recipes, the brewing process is explained along with the equipment required, all of which allows you to brew beer using wholly natural ingredients. Detailed recipes and instructions are given along with tasting notes for each ale. Conversion details are given so that the measurements can be used world-wide.

Use the following code to order this book from your bookshop: ISBN 1-85249-138-8

BREW CLASSIC EUROPEAN BEERS AT HOME
by Graham Wheeler and Roger Protz
196 pages   Price: £8.99
Keen home brewers can now recreate some of the world's classic beers. In your own home you can brew superb pale ales, milds, porters, stouts, Pilsners, Alt, Kolsch, Trappist, wheat beers, sour beers, even the astonishing fruit lambics of Belgium... and many more.

Graham Wheeler and his computer have teamed up with Roger Protz and his unrivalled knowledge of brewing and beer styles. Use the detailed recipes and information about ingredients to imitate the cream of international beers. Discover the role played by ingredients, yeasts and brewing equipment and procedure in these well-known drinks. Measurements are given in UK, US and European units, emphasising the truly international scope of the beer styles within.

Use the following code to order this book from your bookshop: ISBN 1-85249-117-5

HOME BREWING

by Graham Wheeler
240 pages   Price: £8.99
Recently redesigned to make it even easier to use, this is the classic first book for all home-brewers. While being truly comprehensive, Home Brewing also manages to be a practical guide which can be followed step by step as you try your first brews. Plenty of recipes for beginners and hints and tips from the world's most revered home brewer.
Use the following code to order this book from your bookshop: ISBN 1-85249-137-X

OTHER BOOKS

CAMRA QUIZ BOOK

by Jeff Evans
128 pages   Price: £3.99
Fun and games for beer fans, and their relations. Use this book to quiz your mates on real ale and CAMRA history. Great for fund-raising quiz events and for catching up on the campaign.
Use the following code to order this book from your bookshop: ISBN 1-85249-127-2

KEGBUSTER CARTOON BOOK

by Bill Tidy
72 pages, including colour cartoons   Price: £4.99
A classic, hilarious, collection of cartoons from well-known funny man and cartoonist extraordinaire Bill Tidy. The perfect gift for the beer lover in your life!
Use the following code to order this book from your bookshop: ISBN 1-1-85249-134-5

BREWERY BREAKS

by Ted Bruning
64 pages   Price: £3.99
A handy pocket guide to brewery visitor centres and museums. Keep this in the car on your travels and you'll never be far from the living history of brewing. An ideal reference for CAMRA members, and others, wishing to organise a trip to one of Britain's best known breweries or a tasting at a local microbrewery.
Use the following code to order this book from your bookshop: ISBN 1-1-85249-132-9

CORRECTIONS AND AMENDMENTS

Every year sees many of the country's pubs change hands. A new licensee can bring improvements or disaster to even the finest establishments. While most details were checked shortly before going to press, errors will inevitably occur and changes come thick and fast.

If you come upon listed pubs which have been ruined or if you find an undiscovered gem on your travels, let me know and I will investigate for the next edition.

Complete the forms printed here or write to: Jill Adam, *Room at the Inn*, CAMRA Books, 230 Hatfield Road, St Albans, Herts AL1 4LW.

Thank you for your help.

ROOM AT THE INN

County _____

Town or village _____

Name of pub _____

Address _____

Location (A or B road) _____

Tel no. _____ Name of licensee _____

Description of pub (including bars, food, family room and any special facilities)

_____

_____

_____

_____

Beers _____

_____

Rooms _____

_____

_____

Reasons for inclusion in/deletion from the guide

_____

_____

_____

Your name and address _____

_____

_____

Postcode _____

Send to: Jill Adam, CAMRA, 230 Hatfield Road, St Albans, Herts, AL1 4LW

ROOM AT THE INN

County _____

Town or village_____

Name of pub_____

Address _____

Location (A or B road) _____

Tel no. _____Name of licensee_____

Description of pub (including bars, food, family room and any special facilities)

_____

_____

_____

_____

_____

Beers_____

_____

Rooms _____

_____

Reasons for inclusion in/deletion from the guide

_____

_____

_____

Your name and address _____

_____

_____

Postcode _____

Send to: Jill Adam, CAMRA, 230 Hatfield Road, St Albans, Herts, AL1 4LW